Being Relational

LAW AND
SOCIETY

Law and Society Series
W. Wesley Pue, General Editor

The Law and Society Series explores law as a socially embedded phenomenon. It is premised on the understanding that the conventional division of law from society creates false dichotomies in thinking, scholarship, educational practice, and social life. Books in the series treat law and society as mutually constitutive and seek to bridge scholarship emerging from interdisciplinary engagement of law with disciplines such as politics, social theory, history, political economy, and gender studies.

A list of titles in the series appears at the end of the book.

Edited by Jocelyn Downie
and Jennifer J. Llewellyn

Being Relational
Reflections on Relational Theory
and Health Law

UBCPress · Vancouver · Toronto

21 20 19 18 17 16 15 14 13 12   5 4 3 2 1

Printed in Canada on FSC-certified ancient-forest-free paper (100 percent post-consumer recycled) that is processed chlorine- and acid-free.

Library and Archives Canada Cataloguing in Publication

Being relational : reflections on relational theory and health law / edited by Jocelyn Downie and Jennifer J. Llewellyn.

(Law and society, 1496-4953)
Includes bibliographical references and index.
Also issued in electronic format.
ISBN 978-0-7748-2188-9 (cloth); 978-0-7748-2189-6 (pbk.)

 1. Medical laws and legislation. 2. Medical policy–Social aspects. 3. Interpersonal relations. I. Downie, Jocelyn, 1962- II. Llewellyn, Jennifer J., 1972- III. Series: Law and society series (Vancouver, B.C.)

K3601.B44 2011   344.041   C2011-906184-8

Canadä

UBC Press gratefully acknowledges the financial support for our publishing program of the Government of Canada (through the Canada Book Fund), the Canada Council for the Arts, and the British Columbia Arts Council.

This book has been published with the help of a grant from the Canadian Federation for the Humanities and Social Sciences, through the Aid to Scholarly Publications Program, using funds provided by the Social Sciences and Humanities Research Council of Canada.

UBC Press
The University of British Columbia
2029 West Mall
Vancouver, BC V6T 1Z2
www.ubcpress.ca

Contents

For our sons
Sam, Nick, Owen, and Elliott

The House

Because we lived our several lives
Caught up within the spells of love,
Because we always had to run
Through the enormous yards of day
To do all that we hoped to do,
We did not hear, beneath our lives,
The old walls falling out of true,
Foundations shifting in the dark.
When seedlings blossomed in the eaves,
When branches scratched upon the door
And rain came splashing through the halls,
We made our minor, brief repairs,
And sang upon the crumbling stairs
And danced upon the sodden floors.
For years we lived at peace, until
The rooms themselves began to blend
With time, and empty one by one,
At which we knew, with muted hearts,
That nothing further could be done,
And so rose up, and went away,
Inheritors of breath and love,
Bound to that final black estate
No child can mend or trade away.

Mary Oliver

Acknowledgments

First and foremost, we owe an enormous debt of gratitude to the authors in this collection. They entered into this endeavour with enthusiasm and curiosity and persevered through it with a commitment to rigorous intellectual engagement and unfailing mutual support.

Two anonymous reviewers provided us with challenging and constructive comments on all of the chapters. We, and all of the authors, are grateful for their insights, suggestions, and enthusiastic support for the project. Shawna Gray and Chrystal Gray provided exceptional administrative support from the organization of our group meetings through the production of the book and all steps in between. Victoria Apold also provided valuable assistance with the production of the manuscript. Brad Abernethy provided incisive, thoughtful, and highly effective editorial assistance. Blake Brown willingly and skilfully edited various iterations of the project proposal and introduction. Randy Schmidt and Anna Eberhard Friedlander were enthusiastic supporters of the book at UBC Press and helpful shepherds through the publication process. We are grateful to all of these individuals for their dedication, hard work, and constant good humour in the face of looming deadlines.

We are also grateful to the Canadian Institute for Health Research (CIHR) (particularly the Institutes of Gender and Health, the CIHR Ethics Initiative, the Institute of Health Services and Policy Research, and the Knowledge Synthesis and Exchange Branch), the Nova Scotia Restorative Justice Community University Research Alliance (funded by the Social Sciences and Humanities Research Council), and the Aid to Scholarly Publication for their generous support of various aspects of the generation and production of this book.

Finally, we would like to thank the women who, through our relationships with them, have shaped and inspired us – our mothers, sisters, mentors, colleagues, and friends. With and because of you, we have come to understand what it is to be relational.

A Note on the Cover Art

The image on the cover of this book is *Kaleidescope XXX: Tree Grate, 53rd and 7th,* by Paula Nadelstern. In addition to being beautiful, this image of a quilt metaphorically expresses this volume's core messages. First, the historical practice of quilting is representative of the process of writing this book. Traditionally, quilting was a process of collaborative work among women (often multiple generations of women). A single "product" constituted of many pieces resulted from the labours of a group of individuals. A quilting bee was a safe place for women to discuss their lives, their ideas, and their views on the world around them. It served as an important site for raising consciousness. The process of producing *Being Relational* was a modern interpretation of the quilting bee. The authors came together twice for two two-day intensive workshops on all of the chapters and engaged with each other in between the meetings on the ideas and drafts of the chapters, shaping each other in the process.

Second, quilts are much like the substance of this book. A quilt is a single object made up of many distinct parts. Yet the discrete elements become part of a whole when seen in relation to the other elements. The pieces used to construct a quilt were often brought from the homes of the women involved in making the quilt. An old sheet, a child's nightgown, a man's jacket were not discarded but, rather, brought together to make a new object with a new purpose – meaningful in its connection to its prior context and useful in its new form. The chapters of *Being Relational* are like pieces of a quilt. They were brought to the table by the individual authors and reflect the intellectual homes from which they were drawn. They are discrete and can be viewed one chapter at a time, but they are best understood in relation with one another and in the context of the whole.

Being Relational

Introduction

Jennifer J. Llewellyn and Jocelyn Downie

Inception

This collection was initially motivated by two selfish desires shared by its editors. First, we wanted to create a book that we wished we had on our shelves for our use and inspiration. Although we had both benefited greatly from the previous works of the leading relational theorists, we were increasingly frustrated by the patchwork nature of the scholarship in this area.[1] It generally focused on the development of single concepts in isolation and thus could not bring to the surface those insights only accessible through attention to the interplay of the various relational concepts. We were also frustrated by the fact that while relational theory was gaining prominence within the fields of philosophy, women's and gender studies, and bioethics, it had yet to make substantial inroads into many areas of law and policy.[2] This has meant that a powerful new theoretical framework has not been being sufficiently challenged or revised in light of attempts at application nor used to its fullest transformative potential. We sought to address these frustrations through this collection by generating an integrated synthesis of previous work from leading relational scholars while, at the same time, expanding and developing this work through consideration of its implications for one area of law and policy.

Our second desire was to literally bring together leading scholars in relational theory. The prior limitation of discussions to individual concepts, and largely within, instead of across, disciplines, had hampered the emergence of a connected research community. Paradoxically, there was no broad network of relational theory scholars. While relational autonomy scholars are certainly known to one another,[3] those scholars working on relational justice, identity, equality, conscience, and so on seem to have much less direct interaction. This relative isolation has limited the opportunities for the richest possible development of relational theory. We sought to assist with the development of this scholarly community by bringing relational theorists together for reflection upon the interplay and connections among relational concepts as well as consideration and exploration of their implications and applications. Confident that there were others out there who shared our frustrations and desires, we decided to build a collection defined relationally in both substance and process.

Substance

We designed this book to have two integrated and interconnected parts. For the first part, we asked leading scholars in relational theory to synthesize their prior work and then to expand upon and otherwise develop it. The volume thereby contributes to the advancement of scholarship in the field of relational theory – in particular, relational conceptions of autonomy, judgment, equality, justice, identity, memory, and conscience. For the second part, we asked leading scholars in health law and policy to reflect upon the implications of the concepts discussed in the first part for specific areas of health law and policy: the allocation of scarce resources, reproduction, Aboriginal health, mental health, and non-human animal experimentation. The volume thereby serves as a crucible in which to test the difference that relational concepts and relational theory might make in a particular field of application. It also illustrates the transformative potential of bringing relational theory to law and policy more generally. With this approach, new issues surface, and old issues are approached in new ways. The very table of contents in this book demonstrates these effects since it is not organized around traditional health law and policy topics such as consent, confidentiality, regulation of health professionals, and negligence. Instead, it is organized largely around groups that find their health needs deeply affected by social structures that, for example, constrain their autonomy and fail to treat them equally.

Readers will also note the interplay both within and among the chapters. As noted, chapters in the first half of the volume begin with the explanations and elaborations of key concepts, while the chapters in the second half begin with the application and implications of these concepts. From these different starting points, however, each chapter engages with both theory and practice and concept and application. The "concept chapters" go on to explain, develop, and refine the concepts in light of their applications and implications in the world. Likewise, the "application chapters" consciously consider how insights from practice shape and develop our conceptual understanding.

This interplay of theory and practice and concept and application within the volume is not merely the product of editorial and authorial choice but, rather, is a direct consequence of the nature of relational theory itself. Attention to the significance of relationships even at a theoretical, conceptual level necessarily demands attention to the contexts and specifics of

relationships and the parties in them. A relational approach must be con-
textually grounded and able to reveal interconnections. The result is "concept
chapters" that are concerned with, and affected by, their implications in
the world and "application chapters" that reflect upon and develop relational
concepts through a consideration of their applications.

Process
The interplay of theory and practice and the interconnection between the
various concepts and applications was made possible by the process through
which this volume emerged. We undertook an intense collaboration that
self-consciously created space for discussion, debate, and exploration of
relational theory, its implications for key philosophical, ethical, and legal
concepts, and, finally, the illumination and testing of the difference it makes.
As much as possible, the process reflected the very relational insights that
are the subject of this volume. Twice we brought all of the authors together
for two days of conversation. The team "workshopped" drafts of the chapters
on the core concepts at its first meeting and the chapters exploring these
core concepts in light of their application to selected topics in health law
and policy at its second meeting. The authors revised their individual chapters in light of both sets of discussions. The revised chapters were then sent
to subsets of fellow contributors and the editors for further comment, and
the authors revised their chapters one last time in light of this feedback.
This process ensured a much deeper level of engagement and effect (among
both the ideas and the participants).

Throughout the volume, the reader will notice the discussions and interactions between the authors. The interplay and influence among them is
both implicit and explicit in the various chapters and within and between
the two parts of the volume. For example, Sue Campbell develops her theoretical account of relational memory in the context of current attempts to
make reparation for Native residential school abuses. In doing so, she draws
upon Jennifer Llewellyn's development of restorative justice as a relational
theory of justice. Llewellyn's theory of justice in turn relies upon Christine
Koggel's work on relational equality. Maneesha Deckha's chapter pushes
the boundaries of both relational conceptions of justice and equality, among
others, as she considers the use of non-human animals in medical research.
The interplay between relational autonomy and judgment developed in
Jennifer Nedelsky's chapter is central to Sheila Wildeman's consideration of
capacity assessments in mental health. Their discussions of autonomy interact with Susan Sherwin's chapter in which she develops her relational conception of autonomy in the context of global threats. The global perspective
invited by relational theory is also explored in Christine Koggel's chapter
on relational equality. Sherwin's work is central to Constance MacIntosh's

chapter on Aboriginal health. MacIntosh's chapter also attends to the health implications for Aboriginal people and communities of Campbell's relational construction of memory and collective history and Françoise Baylis' conception of relational identity. Dianne Pothier's chapter also explores the implications of relational conceptions of identity as articulated and developed in Baylis' chapter. Baylis' chapter is closely related to Carolyn McLeod's relational account of conscience, which Jocelyn Downie works with in her chapter on reproduction. Downie's chapter also considers the procedural implications of Llewellyn's relational theory of justice. Thus, it can be seen that, as a result of this intensely interpersonal process, the volume is not simply a collection of isolated individual pieces. Rather, as is appropriate for a book on relational theory, it is a set of chapters constituted through their relationships to the others and to the whole as much as they are individual pieces that contribute to the whole.

Foundations (Relational Theory and a Relational Conception of the Self)

As its title suggests, this volume focuses on relational theory. For those readers unfamiliar with this theory, a brief description is in order. Relational theory, as it is understood and articulated within the pages of this volume, is focused on relationality – the fact of relationship (an intentionally singular statement). Through this lens, it is said that we can see the ways in which being in relationship is integral to self-understanding and to interactions with others at individual, collective, and even institutional levels. The central question in each case is not so much "what is X in relationship to or with?" but, rather, "what is the effect of being in relation?"

A relational conception of the self serves as the common foundation upon which the authors in this volume build. The claim that human selves are relational is more than an empirical claim about the way in which human beings live. It is true that humans enter into and live in a range of relationships with others that influence and shape the course of their lives directly or through socialization.[4] The claim that the human self is relational in its nature is, however, a more fundamental one. The relational conception of the self with which we are concerned recognizes not only that we live in relationships with others but also that relationship and connection with others is essential to the existence of the self. The human self in this view is constituted *in and through* relationship with others. We define ourselves *in* relationship to others and *through* relationship with others.[5] In this view, relationships play a constitutive role because of the "*inherently* social nature of human beings."[6]

A number of authors have wrestled with the challenge of how to describe and explain the relational conception of the self. Jennifer Nedelsky explains:

We come into being in a social context that is literally constitutive of us. Some of our most essential characteristics, such as our capacity for language and the conceptual framework through which we see the world, are not made by us, but given to us (or developed in us) through our interaction with others.[7]

Catriona Mackenzie and Natalie Stoljar explain that this conception of the self proceeds from the understanding "that persons are socially embedded and that agents' identities are formed within the context of social relationships and shaped by a complex of intersecting social determinants, such as race, class, gender and ethnicity."[8] Annette Baier uses the idea of "second persons" to denote the formative and fundamental role that others necessarily play in the creation of the self. She claims: "A person, perhaps, is best seen as one who was long enough dependent upon other persons to acquire the essential arts of personhood. Persons essentially are *second* persons, who grow up with other persons ... Persons come after and before other persons."[9] Lorraine Code, in turn, suggests that "uniqueness, creativity, and moral accountability grow out of interdependence and continually turn back to it for affirmation and continuation."[10] Through these similar, but distinct, descriptions, each of these authors sheds some light on, and provides content for, the claim that the self is relational.

It is important to note here that, while relational theory names the significance of relationship in the constitution of the self, it does not posit a self wholly determined by these relationships. A relational conception of the self seeks to recognize the intrinsically relational nature of the self without denying the significance of the individual and the agency of the self. This balancing is reflected in the image of the relational self as constituted in and through relationships. Our choice of *in and through* rather than *by* is intended to reflect the presence of an individual self with agency who is able to reflect and choose but who cannot do so alone.[11] As Nedelsky recognizes, "[the] problem, of course, is how to combine the claim of the constitutiveness of social relations with the value of self-determination."[12] Code argues that this

requires a delicate balancing act, at once placing an appropriate emphasis on connectedness and caring, acknowledging the separateness of human subjects even in their interdependence, and taking into account the fact that there are no unmediated relationships. Like the subjects who make them, relationships are located, and mediated by the structures of their location.[13]

Christine Koggel, in turn, states that a "relational conception of the self suggests that we come to know ourselves and others only in a network of interactive relationships and that this shapes and is necessary for exercising self-determining capacities."[14] Each of the authors in this book take this brief description further as they articulate how they understand and seek to work with relational theory and its foundational relational conception of the self.

Relative Positions (Feminism, Liberalism, and Communitarianism)

A volume such as this one must situate itself relative not only to its foundations but also to other relevant theoretical approaches. In this case, the relevant approaches are feminism, liberalism, and communitarianism.

Feminism

The version of relational theory found in this book owes a significant debt to the insights offered by various feminist theories and approaches. In particular, it owes much to the insights offered by the ethic of care, care feminism, and relational feminism.[15] Through her influential work, Carol Gilligan has brought attention to the significance of relationships for human selves and their moral reasoning. Relational theory, as considered in this volume, shares this view of the significance and centrality of relationships. However, while it has taken inspiration from feminist scholarship, it is not committed, as some take the ethic of care to be, to the affirmation of certain models or types of relationship or activities as inherently valuable. Rather, it affirms the significance of the fact of relationships and signals the importance of attending to their nature and to what is required of them to ensure well-being and flourishing. The focus, then, is not on particular relationships or types of relationships as might be supposed on some versions of care feminism (for example, mother/child, same sex, opposite sex, marital, or sibling as models of relationship). Rather, the focus is on the dynamics or characteristics of relationship that need to be supported and encouraged in order to foster human flourishing. Susan Sherwin, in her work, offers a helpful clarification as she explains that the focus of metaphysical and moral attention should not be solely on interpersonal relationships but also on the full range of influential relationships, personal and public, in which we exist and are constituted as human selves.[16]

In addition, the relational theory found in this volume can be described as feminist in its commitments and orientation. The authors in this volume share the feminist commitment to recognizing oppression (particularly, but not exclusively, of women) and seeking its end. The theory is more than simply instructive about the fact of relationality since it is also interested in the implications of this insight for understanding and responding to oppression. The relational theory in this collection is thus feminist in its evaluative and transformative ambitions.

Liberalism

When discussing the position of the work in this volume relative to liberalism, one participant in the process suggested that we were trying to describe "the dance with liberalism." Carrying this metaphor forward, it can be said that the authors in this volume differ in terms of what they see to be the nature of the dance, who is in the lead, or, for some, whether liberals are on the dance floor at all. For some, relational theory seeks the reform or revision of traditionally liberal concepts, goals, and ideals. Others deny that such concepts, ideals, or goals are inherently liberal and, thus, maintain that relational theory's interest in them does not require a relationship with liberalism. Still others claim that liberalism is entirely irrelevant to their project. However, whatever their position with respect to liberalism, there is a shared recognition among the authors that relational theory poses a challenge to the picture of the self traditionally identified with liberalism.

The relational theory found in this volume rejects the individualism of the traditionally liberal self, although in doing so it does not lose individuality.[17] As Diana Tietjens Meyers describes it,

> [t]he view of the self that has dominated contemporary Anglo-American moral and political philosophy is that of homo-economicus – the free and rational chooser and actor whose desires are ranked in a coherent order and whose aim is to maximize desire, satisfaction. This conception of the self isolates the individual from personal relationships and larger social forces.[18]

Marilyn Friedman identifies abstract individualism as underlying the traditional liberal conception of the self as it "considers individual human beings as social atoms, abstracted from their social contexts, and disregards the role of social relationships and human community in constituting the very identity and nature of individual human beings."[19] Koggel suggests, though, that it "is not that liberals deny the relationality of selves, but that they do not take these aspects to be relevant to an account of what it is to be a person or to treat people with equal concern and respect."[20] In response to such individualistic accounts of the self, the authors in this book assert the importance and centrality of relationship. In doing so, they need not reject independence in favour of dependence or seek some middle ground. Rather, their starting point facilitates a revision of dependence, independence, and interdependence and an approach with which to evaluate and consider these relationships and their implications.

Communitarianism

The authors in this volume also differ in terms of whether and how they relate their relational theory to communitarianism. Again, for some, their relational theory stands independent of other theories, and it does not need to engage in such comparisons in order to define itself. For others, their relational theory is informed by the contemporary debate between communitarians and liberals. Others recognize that their relational theory shares a common commitment to the social self that is constituted in relationships with others. However, as Linda Barclay argues, the communitarian claim

> that the self is constitutively social incorporates the claim that the self is socially determined, for it certainly suggests that the self's aims and aspirations are determined by the communities of which one is a part. However, the constitutively social self is also meant to capture the idea that the *content* of the self's ends are social, in the sense that they represent not just my ends but also our shared ends.[21]

Thus, despite the commitment to the importance of relationships shared by relational theory and communitarianism, all of the authors would differentiate their relational theory and communitarianism insofar as the latter takes relationships of attachment and the communities in which we exist as not only influencing and affecting self identity but also as being determinative of self. This perspective is reflected in the communitarian claim that the self "discovers" its ends.[22] The account of the relational self that is found within these pages does not go so far. It affirms the significance and centrality of relationship but is not solely dependent upon existing communities and attachments for identity. It is able to reflect upon the nature of existing communities and exercise agency within these relationships. Where communitarians emphasize unchosen relationships as the focal point for the self, the authors in this volume recognize the significance of both voluntary and involuntary relationships. They are not then committed to preserving or replicating existing relationships as some communitarian theory risks. Instead, they are focused on the recognition of the significance of relationship in the process of making and remaking the self.

Conclusion

Out of this intensely relational process, built upon a relational conception of the self, through the shared commitment to feminist values and objectives and the shared rejection of the traditional liberal and communitarian conceptions of the self, and despite the different positions taken with respect to the dance with liberalism and communitarianism, the chapters in this book offer up the first coordinated reflection on a set of core concepts as seen through a relational lens and as applied to a set of practical areas of concern (specifically in the area of health law and policy). Our selfish desires for such a volume have been met, and we hope that readers with the same or even different needs and wants will all find something of interest and use between these covers.

Notes

1 For example (and it must be emphasized that these are but some examples from among many theorists), Susan Sherwin, Jennifer Nedelsky, Christine Koggel, Lorraine Code, and Diana Tietjens Meyers.

2 This is, of course, not to suggest that relational theory was absent in law and policy. See, for example, Jennifer Nedelsky, "Property in Potential Life? A Relational Approach to Choosing Legal Categories" (1993) 6 Can. J.L. & Jur. 343; Jennifer Nedelsky, "Reconceiving Rights as Relationship" (1993) 1 Rev. Const. Stud. 1; Martha Minow and Mary Lyndon Shanley, "Relational Rights and Responsibilities: Revisioning the Family in Liberal Political Theory and Law" (1996) 11:1 Hypatia 4; Susan Brison, "Relational Autonomy and Freedom of Expression" in Catriona Mackenzie and Natalie Stoljar, eds., *Relational Autonomy: Feminist Perspectives on Autonomy, Agency and the Social Self* (Oxford: Oxford University Press, 2000) 280; Robert Leckey, *Contextual Subjects: Family, State, and Relational Theory* (Toronto: University of Toronto Press, 2008); Jennifer J. Llewellyn, "Dealing with the Legacy of Native Residential School Abuse: Litigation, ADR, and Restorative Justice" (2002) 52 U.T.L.J. 253; Jennifer J. Llewellyn, "A Healthy Conception of Rights? – Thinking Relationally about Rights in a Health Care Context" in Jocelyn Downie and Elaine Gibson, eds., *Health Law at the Supreme Court of Canada* (Toronto: Irwin Law, 2007) 57; and Jocelyn Downie and Jennifer J. Llewellyn, "Relational Theory and Health Law and Policy" (2008) Health L.J. (Special Edition) 193.

3 Coming together, for example, at the Conference on Feminist Perspectives on Agency and Autonomy held at the Australian National University in June 1996.

4 This is similar to what Catriona MacKenzie and Natalie Stoljar refer to as the claim that selves are "causally relational." This is juxtaposed with constitutively or intrinsically relational conceptions of the self, which reflect the metaphysical claim that we take to underlie relational theory. See Catriona Mackenzie and Natalie Stoljar, "Introduction: Autonomy Revisited" in Mackenzie and Stoljar, *supra* note 2 at 22.

5 Caroline Whitbeck, "A Different Reality: Feminist Ontology" in Ann Garry and Marilyn Pearsall, eds., *Women, Knowledge, and Reality: Explorations in Feminist Philosophy* (Boston: Unwin Hyman, 1989) 68; Jennifer Llewellyn, "Justice for South Africa: Restorative Justice and the Truth and Reconciliation Commission" in Christine M. Koggel, ed., *Moral Issues in Global Perspective* (Peterborough, ON: Broadview Press, 1999) 96; Jennifer Llewellyn and Robert Howse, *Restorative Justice: A Conceptual Framework* (Ottawa: Law Commission of Canada, 1998) at 1-107.

6 Jennifer Nedelsky, "Reconceiving Autonomy: Sources, Thoughts and Possibilities" (1989) 7 Yale J.L. & Feminism 7 at 8.

7 *Ibid.* at 8.

8 Mackenzie and Stoljar, *supra* note 2 at 4.

9 Annette Baier, *Postures of Mind: Essays on Mind and Morals* (Minneapolis: University of Minnesota Press, 1985) at 84-85 [emphasis in original].

10 Lorraine Code, *What Can She Know? Feminist Theory and the Construction of Knowledge* (Ithaca, NY: Cornell University Press, 1991) at 82.

11 Jennifer Llewellyn and Robert Howse, "Institutions for Restorative Justice: The South African Truth and Reconciliation Commission" (1999) 49 U.T.L.J. 355; Llewellyn and Howse, *supra* note 5; Caroline Whitbeck, "A Different Reality: Feminist Ontology" in Ann Garry and Marilyn Pearsall, eds., *Women, Knowledge, and Reality: Explorations in Feminist Philosophy* (Boston: Unwin Hyman, 1989) 51 at 68.

12 Nedelsky, *supra* note 6 at 9.

13 Code, *supra* note 10 at 93-94.

14 Christine M. Koggel, *Perspectives on Equality: Constructing a Relational Theory* (New York: Rowman and Littlefield, 1998) at 128.

15 For example, Carol Gilligan, *In a Different Voice: Psycological Theory and Women's Development* (Cambridge, MA: Harvard University Press, 1982); Virginia Held, *Justice and Care: Essential Readings in Feminist Ethics* (Boulder, CO: Westview Press, 1995).

16 Susan Sherwin, "A Relational Approach to Autonomy in Health Care" in Susan Sherwin, ed., *The Politics of Women's Health* (Philadelphia: Temple University Press, 1998) 13 at 19. See also Susan Sherwin, *No Longer Patient: Feminist Ethics and Health Care* (Philadelphia: Temple University Press, 1992).

17 Lorraine Code offers this helpful distinction and maintains that it is possible. Code, *supra* note 10 at 82.

18 Diana Tietjens Meyers, "Introduction" in Diana Tietjens Meyers, ed., *Feminists Rethink the Self* (Boulder, CO: Westview Press, 1997) 1 at 2.

19 Marilyn Friedman, "Feminist and Modern Friendship: Dislocating the Community" in Cass R. Sunstein, ed., *Feminism and Political Theory* (Chicago: University of Chicago Press, 1990) 143 at 143.

20 Koggel, *supra* note 14 at 128.

21 Linda Barclay, "Autonomy and the Social Self" in Mackenzie and Stoljar, *supra* note 2, 52 at 61.

22 See Michael Sandel, *Liberalism and the Limits of Justice* (Cambridge: Cambridge University Press, 1982). For a similar expression of the significance of community to the self, see Alasdair MacIntyre, *After Virtue: A Study of Moral Theory* (Notre Dame, IN: University of Notre Dame Press, 1982).

Part 1
Relational Theory

1
Relational Autonomy and Global Threats
Susan Sherwin

I have been developing and deploying the concept of relational autonomy for a number of years, and I continue to struggle to unpack its multiple dimensions.[1] In using the term "relational autonomy," I mean to invoke the socially and politically situated positions in which persons live and from which they may exercise (or seek to exercise) control over aspects of their lives that are important to them. I use this concept to make visible the ways in which specific details of agents' embodied identity, and the social practices that shape their experiences, may affect the degree of autonomy available to them.

In this chapter, I explore a new direction in my understanding of relational autonomy, but in order to do so I find it necessary to first review some key elements of my own earlier and current work. I will begin by summarizing my previous work on relational autonomy, and, then, I shall outline some key elements of my current project in which I am proposing a new approach to ethics writ large that attempts to deal with serious global threats such as climate change and ethnic hatreds. After presenting this brief personal intellectual history, I shall explain how I now see relational autonomy functioning with respect to the types of global moral issues that now occupy me, and I shall sketch out some of the ways that I hope to deploy the concept of relational autonomy in this project.

Where I Have Been: Relational Autonomy
I first started using the term "relational autonomy" in the context of the 1992-98 Social Sciences and Humanities Research Council of Canada (SSHRC) interdisciplinary research project on feminist health care ethics that led to the publication of *The Politics of Women's Health*.[2] In the early stages of that project, I toyed with abandoning the concept of autonomy altogether in light of its problematic central role within the masculinist, individualist world view of mainstream philosophy, law, and political theory. I noted that

the term "autonomy" is often used to invoke an ideal of human independence and self-interested rationality – an ideal that conjures up the metaphor of "rugged individualism."[3]

I found myself very sympathetic to feminist critiques of this model of autonomy and the associated ideal of total independence – that is, freedom from dependence on specific others. Clearly, complete independence is impossible and undesirable. As social beings, we are all deeply interdependent. Indeed, I shared Margaret Urban Walker's view that a principal task of ethics is to sort out responsibilities for addressing the multiple ways in which people are dependent on others.[4] Equating autonomy with independence tends to obscure the many ways in which all humans depend on one another, and it prevents us from undertaking the important work of determining responsibilities for the complex set of tasks associated with interdependent care. It can also devalue persons with visible sorts of needs for assistance by others, such as needs associated with being very young, very old, or disabled in some way.

In addition, I was disturbed by the ways that the moral ideal of autonomy was used in political debates to generate a tension with feminist ideals of social justice.[5] Specifically, those on the political right often invoke "autonomy" (or "freedom") to object to government actions aimed at reducing injustice through social programs by describing the required coercive taxation as improperly intruding on realms that belong within the autonomous control of individuals.[6] At best, autonomy often appears to be a goal that is primarily of interest to – and accessible by – those with privilege and power; they have far more opportunities than most people to choose among an array of options for many dimensions of their lives. Typically, people who lack social and economic power have a far smaller range of options regarding many aspects of their lives than their more advantaged compatriots. They are more likely to be occupied with meeting material needs and have less chance to engage with abstract ideals.

Indeed, autonomy discussions tend to mask the workings of privilege and power by making invisible the ways in which the efforts of others are generally part of the background conditions that enable "autonomous choices" on the part of the most advantaged, such as by creating and maintaining infrastructure that supports their personal projects. For example, most applicants know the importance of appearing for job interviews clean and well groomed, and they take pride in their exercise of autonomy in presenting a professional appearance. Few give any thought to the difficulties faced by homeless people who must show up wearing the clothes in which they sleep. In such ways, use of the language of "autonomy" encourages the well-off to imagine that their successes are simply a product of their own determination and good sense, while effectively hiding or trivializing many of the barriers to autonomous action that face those who are disadvantaged.

Of particular concern to me were the serious difficulties that arise by virtue of the ways in which the ideal of autonomy functions in the field of bioethics. Within bioethics, autonomy is generally used to set a standard of self-determination through rational deliberation that is thought to be achieved by setting adequate procedures of informed consent. As such, it is typically used in a generic way, as if the basic requirements for informed consent (information, competence, and voluntariness) will guarantee autonomy in similar ways for all patients or research subjects. This usage ignores important differences among patients and subjects and renders invisible dimensions of their lives that limit their degrees of control. All of these features remain troublesome in the various ways in which the concept of autonomy is often deployed in non-feminist discussions.

Although I was tempted to abandon the concept entirely, a transformative trip to Argentina dissuaded me from this step. At the second meeting of the International Association of Bioethics, which was held in Buenos Aires in 1990, I had the good fortune to meet with several South American feminist bioethicists. They told me how valuable they found the ideal of autonomy to be in the context of their own work. In particular, they found it to be a rhetorically powerful tool in their efforts to promote women's rights to control their medical and reproductive care within a system that grants enormous authority to doctors and male partners and generally pays little heed to the needs or desires of women. The Western bioethics literature generally speaks of the contest between autonomy and paternalism, in which decision-making authority belongs either to the patient or to the physician, but both are expected to act in accordance with their own understanding of the best interests of the patient. In a society that is quite blatantly patriarchal, the alternative to patient autonomy is often not paternalism but, rather, some other value such as the interest of a woman's husband, church, or state in her reproductive life.[7] Under such conditions, appeal to the widely accepted ideal of autonomy provides feminist health activists with an important moral concept that allows them to secure greater power for women to determine the course of their health care and, especially, their reproductive lives. Ironically, it seemed that it was my own privilege and relative social power that was encouraging me to think it desirable to abandon the aspirational and moral clout of appeals to autonomy. I took very seriously the fact that women with far less opportunity to make important decisions in their own lives than me still saw value in the ideal of autonomy.

As a result of this experience, I reoriented my approach to autonomy in the 1990s and sought to develop a relational understanding of the concept, building on work that other feminist theorists were doing in the area of relational theory.[8] I sought a way to retain the value of appeals to autonomy as a way of reducing oppression without accepting its baggage as a concept that sustains the ideals of individualism. This was the first time that I adopted the language of relational theory, although I believe that the approach that I had been developing in my earlier writings also represents a relational approach. For example, in my book *No Longer Patient*, I proposed a relational conception of personhood to address the moral debates regarding abortion.[9] I also challenged the simplistic dyad in which most bioethics discussions positioned paternalism as the only alternative to patient autonomy. I reflected on what people really seek under the label "autonomy" and what might be practically possible in the social, political, and economic world of real life, specifically within medical contexts. I argued that we must be more attentive to the circumstances in which decisions are made. I also challenged the reigning conception of persons as ideally independent of outside influences, emerging into society as already fully formed, and I proposed, instead, a view of persons as essentially social beings, created through intense and continual interactions with others. Their values and deliberations are, by necessity, pursued within a social environment that is always larger than an individual in isolation. Throughout, I stressed the importance of attending to the ways in which socially salient characteristics such as gender, race, and class tend to shape people's experiences with the health care system.

My own thinking on the concept of relational autonomy in the 1990s and subsequent years was greatly advanced by the work of other feminist theorists working with relational conceptions, especially Jennifer Nedelsky,[10] Christine Koggel,[11] and the authors in the collection edited by Catriona Mackenzie and Natalie Stoljar.[12] Unlike other theorists who have focused on the political uses of autonomy, my own interest was in the context of health ethics, which resulted in some differences in emphasis and interpretation. I sought to explore how a concept of relational autonomy might help to make sense of puzzles involving health practices and policies rather than questions of citizenship. I was now more explicit in my rejection of the stripped-down liberal theory conception of persons as abstract, politically interchangeable beings working under a Rawlsian veil of ignorance,[13] and in favour of a view of them as embodied agents, situated in a particular social, economic, and historical time and place, whose identities are formed through personal and political (impersonal) relationships. I sought to understand autonomy in a way that made sense of how the various socially salient features of persons' identity such as gender, race, age, disability, sexuality, or class (and various combinations of these categories) are likely to affect their social position and range of opportunities for making choices. Specifically, I sought to make central ways in which systemic patterns of oppression affect people's experiences with respect to health matters and health care.

In writing the chapter on relational autonomy for *The Politics of Women's Health*,[14] I drew heavily on Diana Meyers' work regarding the notion of autonomy as involving a set of skills that need to be learned and practised.[15] A person cannot simply assert autonomy; she needs to learn how to make important decisions in ways that respect her own values and convictions. Adopting an oppression theory of feminism, I concluded that oppression is a major barrier to developing the skills necessary for exercising autonomy.[16] I argued that those who are socialized to roles associated with oppression (by virtue of gender, race, or other features) are generally disadvantaged in their ability to act autonomously since they often do not have the opportunity to develop the necessary skills. In fact, they are often deliberately thwarted in the development of these important skills.

Finally, I introduced a distinction between the concepts of agency and autonomy in order to make sense of the puzzling fact that people frequently choose options that are, in some sense, contrary to their overall well-being. Specifically, I sought to highlight the fact that it is common for circumstances to be such that members of oppressed groups are better off (at least in the short term) in pursuing options that are, in a deep sense, contrary to their broader interests. I had in mind various options that are frequently chosen even though they are contrary to the interests of an oppressed group to which the agents belong. For example, in a highly homophobic community or workplace, gay people frequently choose to keep their sexuality secret and may even participate in anti-gay conversations and activities. Indeed, oppression, especially gender oppression, is often structured to reward members of oppressed groups who choose options that are part of larger practices that are, overall, supportive of the ongoing oppression of the groups in question. In addition, those who choose options that challenge patterns of oppression are often punished.

Following Marilyn Frye, I noted that this phenomenon of actively supporting activities that reinforce one's own oppression is a hallmark of being oppressed in that it reflects the classic double bind where, no matter which option one chooses, there are negative consequences for the agent.[17] When in a double bind, a person can certainly display agency – she can make an informed and rational *choice* – but it does not seem right to call her choice autonomous when the structure does not offer her any option that fully reflects her deepest values and interests. It is not unusual for oppressed people to have no option that is practically available to them that would not reinforce their oppression in some manner or other. For example, a refugee woman who immigrates on visas assigned to her husband may have no good option if he becomes abusive – she can remain in a violent relationship or leave it and risk deportation.

Throughout the 1990s, I focused on the use of the concept of relational autonomy in the context of health practices and policies, either in therapeutic or research settings. As such, I was heavily influenced by the literature concerning personal control over decision making that involved interventions in the lives of particular patients or subjects. I engaged with a well-developed bioethics literature in which the most serious threats to autonomy are thought to be a failure on the part of the clinician or researcher to provide adequate information or a lack of competence on the part of the patient or the subject. I sought to make clear that health care providers or researchers may also fail to get adequate autonomous consent when the options available fail to meet important interests of the person making the choice. I was particularly concerned with circumstances in which the reasonable options available to individuals required their active collaboration in practices that support the continuing oppression of members of their social group(s) – and, by extension, themselves. In such cases, autonomy cannot be achieved merely by providing the patient or research subject with better education or more time to deliberate without pressure. To truly support the autonomy of oppressed patients and research subjects, what is often required is serious change in the social circumstances in which the choice is being made.

I cited examples such as the frequent use of cosmetic surgery and reproductive technology by women. When women are primarily valued in terms of physical appearance or reproductive capacity (as they are in most societies), each woman is encouraged to choose these kinds of medical interventions to promote her own security (and that of her dependents) by increasing her personal worth through such practices. In doing so, each woman contributes to the further normalization of the practice in question and thereby puts pressure on other women to participate in these sorts of activities. In such ways, each woman ends up reinforcing the problematic social pattern of improperly judging the worth of women by their instrumental value. Of course, there are many reasons why a woman might choose to engage in such activities other than mere compliance with oppressive norms. Indeed, the many ways in which women find their personal lives enriched by acting in accordance with these sorts of norms (even while actively opposing gender oppression) are constitutive of modern gender oppression. The difficulty is that as long as women are valued instrumentally for their "feminine" attributes, they are not equal members of society. So, while women, as individuals, are likely to find rewards when they choose to act in accordance with these oppressive norms and to risk punishment and personal loss if they choose to resist them, each act of compliance also reinforces the norms and further entrenches women's oppression. Such is the nature of the double bind.

I used the term "agency" to capture the sort of circumstances where a person reasonably chooses an option that is the most attractive or reasonable for her under the prevailing conditions but is incompatible with the overall interests of the groups to which that person belongs and, hence, is in some sense incompatible with her own interests. Since the background social conditions make such behaviour reasonable for individuals, even as it makes it disastrous for the groups, we must acknowledge that the choices they make are pragmatically "rational," and so it is appropriate to describe their behaviour as an expression of agency.

I reserved the term "autonomy" to refer to actions that are consistent with a person's broader interests, values and commitments, including the well-being of her group (based on gender, race, class, sexual orientation, age, ethnicity, and so on). To be autonomous, an action must not only reflect a reasonable calculation of the benefits and costs at issue given the existing background conditions, but it must also not work against the promotion of projects and values that are important for the agent (including reducing the impact of oppression on one's group). Often, oppressed people fail to act with full autonomy because the options that are meaningfully available to them do not include a choice that is compatible with their deepest values and needs or because the rewards and punishments for choosing an action that reinforces oppression outweighs the personal benefits of choosing one that would help to undermine oppression. In such cases, increasing autonomy requires making changes to the background conditions, not (only) the agent.

Thus, to promote autonomy in realms such as cosmetic surgery or assisted reproduction, we need to do more than help to educate women or demand that health care providers use more careful procedures for ensuring fully voluntary informed consent. We need to develop and pursue policies and programs that will make available (and attractive) options that will help agents reduce, rather than reinforce, patterns of oppression and enable them to identify options that are compatible with their deepest values and needs. Often, this goal will require actions by agents other than the patient or the health care provider. For instance, it may require legal or political changes as has occurred in many nations with respect to the use of certain types of reproductive technologies. In Canada, after many years of study and political lobbying, the government excluded certain reproductive practices (primarily the commodification of gametes, embryos, and surrogacy) through the *Assisted Human Reproduction Act* in 2004,[18] and thereby removed these options entirely from the array of (legal) choices available to those seeking assistance with infertility.[19]

In my early work on relational autonomy, I emphasized the ways in which social and political patterns interfere with the range of meaningful options available to members of oppressed groups and with their ability to take the risks associated with changing well-entrenched practices. I invoked the concept of relational autonomy to shed light on the need to promote empowering background conditions and to support the development of necessary skills in order to enhance the autonomy of members of oppressed groups. In my current research, I find myself looking at ways in which oppression does not constitute the only barrier to the effective deployment of autonomy in complex social circumstances. I find that I need to better understand how agency often takes the place of autonomy in a wider range of cases. I believe that it is common for agents of all levels of social and political status to be complicit with practices that are, ultimately, contrary to their own deepest values and interests. Moreover, it is not unusual that agents will fail to notice or object to the lack of real autonomy in important circumstances even when oppression is not evident. To explain this search for an extension of the earlier work on relational autonomy, I must now spend some time describing the sorts of problems that now occupy me.

Where I Am Now: Towards a New Ethic for Global Threats

In the last few years, my research has had a wider scope than health ethics. I have not been directly engaged in discussions of relational autonomy but have reoriented my research to the ambitious and immodest project of trying to reinvent ethics to save the world. As I shall explain in the fourth part of this chapter, I think that these two projects ultimately come together and that relational autonomy will play a key role in the new ethics I am developing, but first I shall outline my ideas regarding a new approach to ethics.

The first published version of this project appears in an article entitled "Whither Bioethics? How Feminism Can Help Re-orient Bioethics."[20] In this article, I argue that the ethical theories and practices promoted by Western analytical philosophers and bioethicists are not adequate to deal with a wide range of problems that I consider to be major global threats to continued human and other animal life on this planet.[21] The list of threats is long and diverse, including environmental degradation (climate change, loss of habitat for many species, limited clean water supplies, and the pollution of air, water, and soil); the ongoing build-up and wide dispersion of nuclear, chemical, biological, and conventional weapons; the ever-growing gap between rich and poor; unrelenting (and, in some cases, worsening) ethnic and religious hatreds; and the development of new infectious diseases (HIV, SARS, H1N1) along with the return of old ones in new, more robust forms (tuberculosis).

I claim that the moral theories and systems that we have developed in the West are simply not up to identifying and providing guidance with respect to the complex interconnections of responsibilities that must be assumed if we are to avoid impending catastrophes (or deal appropriately with many already present disasters).[22] I have identified some key difficulties. One is that ethics has largely been developed to deal with one layer of moral duty at a time. Most of Western thought has gone into determining the moral obligations of individuals towards other individuals, which generates a variety of rules: tell the truth, avoid cruelty, respect property, keep your promises, be compassionate, and so on. I speculate that this orientation may be a product of the origin of moral systems in an era in which the principal problems had to do with relations between and among particular humans. Whether we believe that ethics originates in religious law (originally prescribed to tribal cultures), that it is a product of our evolution as a social species that lives in groups, or that it is the outcome of rational deliberation (as Immanuel Kant would have it), the scope of most systems of ethics that developed in earlier eras focuses on behaviour towards other humans who are relatively close and often relatively similar.[23] This is a worthy target, and I believe that traditional ethics still has a role to play for guiding us in such circumstances. (It is the basis of many of the rules that we have codified into law, such as the prohibitions against murder, assault, theft, and so on.) The types of global threats that concern me now, however, involve far more complex problems, and I do not believe that they can be fully addressed by the tools designed for the moral problems of an earlier age. I claim that we need a new approach to ethics that is capable of discussing the interconnections of moral responsibilities for many different types of agents (that is, agents of many levels of human organization).

To clarify, I am not claiming that all ethicists have been occupied with the actions of individual agents in their relationships with other humans. For example, political theorists concern themselves with the duties of nation-states; business ethicists address the moral obligations of corporations; and bioethicists study the moral responsibilities of health care institutions and systems. Yet, most theorists working in these various areas of collective obligations limit their focus to a single level of human organization (government, corporations, or specialized institutions). I believe that the ethics we need now must operate on multiple levels of human organization simultaneously.

There are additional difficulties with the traditional approaches to ethics from the perspective of feminist relational theory. One is that the leading approaches tend to seek universal, abstract rules that are binding through all specific contexts unless there are rule-defined exceptions. Another difficulty is that the focus is primarily on questions of duty, while, as discussed earlier, various feminist theorists (most notably Margaret Urban Walker[24] and Joan Tronto[25]) have argued that what we really need to do is to sort out matters of responsibilities: who is responsible for doing what and for whom? In combining these two worries, I believe that the scope of ethics should not be limited to a set of injunctions and norms that can be identified in the absence of any contextual details. Rather, ethics should be concerned with the process and substance of determining how we will assign and assume the specific responsibilities associated with the various actual needs that arise within particular social units. We need to find fair mechanisms to ensure that the needs of all persons (and, probably, also of other life forms)[26] can be met without imposing unjust burdens on those members of society who have insufficient power to protect their own rights and promote their own needs. Ethics must attend much more explicitly to matters of responsibility and context.[27]

From this perspective, it is easier to see that there are moral responsibilities to be assigned and assumed by actors at each level of human organization. I mean to capture by the term "level of human organization" any grouping that can demonstrate agency by taking on responsibilities. It includes such categories as individual persons, family groups, governments of all levels, international bodies, corporations, churches, community groups, boards of education, health authorities, and non-governmental organizations (NGOs).

In "Whither Bioethics?" I argue that the tendency of ethicists to focus on a single level of human organization while assuming that other levels remain relatively constant constitutes a structural problem that precludes appropriate ethical analysis and resolution of the large moral issues of our time.[28] The problem is that the reasonable options available to agents at each level of human organization are usually limited by the choices made at other levels. For example, an individual's ability to reduce her use of fossil fuels may depend upon the availability of reliable public transportation and affordable insulation. However, a government's ability to provide the infrastructure for a good public transit system depends also on the willingness of citizens to use such a system. So, too, the ability of individuals to break the cycle of ethnic violence will depend on their access to honest information from their neighbours, media, and leaders regarding the nature of the "enemy." By the same token, a government's ability to engage in peace talks may depend on its ability to maintain credibility and order if it surrenders some "non-negotiable" items as a condition of peace (for example, the border between Israel and Palestine). Moreover, the ability of citizens and governments to institute sustainable practices often depends on the existence of businesses that are willing and able to conform to the terms of environmental responsibility, while the cooperation of the relevant businesses may require that consumers be willing to pay more to purchase environmentally sustainable products.

In multitudes of ways, the actions of individuals and those of the various human organizations in which they participate are framed and constrained by the opportunities that are available within their society, which is a matter determined by other agents of many types. Indeed, even a person's ability to imagine a course of action may depend upon the range of options available within her frame of reference and that is generally shaped by her society. Conscientious individuals, community groups, corporations, or governments who seek to use a responsibility lens and look beyond an explicit set of moral obligations to consider how they should act to help avert impending catastrophe cannot make these calculations in isolation from the decisions of other types of actors. Hence, I argue that it is *because* the actions of individuals and those of the organizations they belong to are deeply intertwined that the moral responsibilities of actors at each level must be determined in relation to the opportunities made available at the other levels. We need to look not only at the choices of various agents but also at the background conditions that structure those choices. The situation involves a distressingly complex array of coordination problems. Sorting out the responsibilities that are properly assigned to each agent – that is, to each level of human organization – in relation to the others constitutes a complex, intimidating task, but one that I believe is essential if we hope to avoid catastrophe.

We must be sensitive to these sorts of interconnections and the ways in which the behaviour of some types of agents limits or opens up opportunities for other agents to act responsibly. In discussing duties, Kant famously said that "ought implies can," meaning that we are only obligated to do what we are able to do.[29] The same is true of responsibilities. Agents' moral responsibilities are limited to actions that are within their power to execute, and they cannot be held responsible to do what is impossible for them to do. They have neither moral obligation nor moral responsibility to do the impossible. Hence, we need an ethics that is sensitive to the complex interactions among these various levels of responsibility and possibility, one that can reflect ways in which responsibilities are dispersed according to the level of human organization that can contribute effectively to a morally informed solution to the large problems facing humanity.

In "Whither Bioethics?" I sketched out some key elements of one version of this sort of new ethics under the working title of "public ethics."[30] I proposed that public ethics be thought of as being analogous to some dimensions of public health – a set of activities that involves responsibilities and cooperation at many levels of human organization. Consider the example of hand washing, an extremely important measure for reducing the spread of infection in hospitals and the community. While the obligation to wash one's hands rests with individuals, their ability to fulfil this obligation requires the provision of readily accessible soap and clean water. In order for a hospital to be able to fulfil its obligation to provide the necessary water, the municipality must ensure a safe water supply regulated by effective provincial or state laws. In the face of natural or human-caused disasters that contaminate or disrupt the public water source, national or international bodies will have to become involved in delivering clean water. In such ways, public health depends on the appropriate actions of players at many levels. One layer of human actors is able to fulfil its responsibilities with respect to reducing the spread of infection only if actors at other levels of human organization take appropriate steps to fulfil the corresponding responsibilities regarding their actions.[31] The situation is very similar in public ethics in the many areas of global threats that concern me. In each type of threat, agents of many sorts must take action, and the options available to each agent are likely to be determined by decisions at other levels of human organization.

There is a further link between public health and public ethics, as it turns out. Although I initially invoked the connection with public health as an analogy for the new type of ethics that I am proposing and have used it as the basis for naming this multi-layered approach "public ethics," I subsequently learned that Madison Powers and Ruth Faden, in their important book *Social Justice: The Moral Foundations of Public Health and Health Policy*, defend a literal conjunction between public health and a type of public ethics (though they do not use the term "public ethics"). Their argument claims that public health is inseparable from ethics and should be grounded in social justice. Indeed, they say that "social justice is the foundational value for public health."[32] In their discussion of public health as an enactment of social justice, they also speak of multiple layers of responsibility belonging to different types of agents:

> Many of the duties entailed by these health rights require positive, collective action and thus fall upon those entities best positioned to achieve collective ends. The most obvious candidates are governments, but social institutions of all sorts, formal and informal, professional and community, can be understood as having collective duties that bear on the right to health.[33]

In other words, in public health, there are many levels of responsibility that are interrelated with responsibilities at other levels, including those of individuals. Public health is, then, both an instance of, and a model for, what I have in mind for the complex, multi-layered responsibilities of public ethics. In both arenas, there are moral responsibilities at every level of human organization regarding how we are to behave, individually and collectively. Ethics must help us learn to see these interconnections and provide guidance on the appropriate kinds of responsibility in complex cases.

The new ethics must provide guidance to agents at all levels of organization to help them to recognize and take up the appropriate responsibilities if we are to avoid worsening climate change, environmental degradation, growing poverty, threats of war or terrorism, a serious pandemic flu, and so on. Most of us in the affluent West, at least, seem to be caught in a system whereby we deeply want to avoid these outcomes and yet we participate in actions and organizations that contribute to making many of these problems worse. While we are not all victims of oppression as I have understood the term, we all seem to be caught in a frightening gap between agency and autonomy. In fact, the affluent may experience this gap particularly strongly with respect to consumption and growth. We live at a rate of energy and resource consumption that is simply not sustainable. Moreover, we cannot justify the massive differences in access to the earth's finite resources that are central to levels of consumption pursued by most members of industrialized countries. Our agency keeps directing us to familiar, problematic practices that are contrary to our deepest interests. We lack the skills and infrastructure options necessary for making choices that give proper weight to the long-term consequences of the practices in which we collectively engage, and we find ourselves continually encouraged to focus on immediate gratification.

"Whither Bioethics?" was written as a kind of call to action, meant to identify a major problem with dominant moral theorizing and to suggest the direction of a solution.[34] It did not attempt to spell out a solution since it is my view that the ethics needed will have to be developed through the collaborative efforts of an interdisciplinary, international collection of scholars, activists, practitioners, and communicators. It requires empirical as well as theoretical knowledge, including expertise in human behaviour, politics, economics, national and international law, religion, and the ability to stimulate moral imagination. Like the topics that it takes on, it requires an understanding of the complexities of human organization and human motivation. I have no illusions about being able to present such a theory by myself. Nonetheless, I think there is a piece of the puzzle to which I can contribute, and it involves returning to the idea of relational autonomy and developing this concept more fully and in a different direction than originally conceived. Hence, the long detour through the framing of a new form of ethics project. I shall now revisit the concept of relational autonomy in the context of a new sort of ethic of multi-layered responsibilities to address several urgent global threats.

Where I Am Trying to Go: Relational Autonomy for Public Ethics

I see the project of developing this new sort of ethics that I seek (public ethics) to be centred on feminist work in relational theory, especially relational autonomy, and in this final, forward-looking section of the chapter I shall attempt to show how I expect it to unfold. Public ethics is relational in that it reflects the feminist insights that persons are, inevitably, connected with other persons and with social institutions. Moreover, it requires the feminist understanding that we are each embodied products of distinct historical, social, and cultural processes and interactions. For each of us, our interests and values are relative to, discovered by, and pursued within social environments that help to shape our identities, characters, and opportunities. These environments operate at the level of intimate personal relationships (family, close friends), community (schools, neighbourhoods, churches), ethnic and language groups, civic structures (municipal, national), as well as professional and amateur interest groups (philosophers, golfers, square dancers, computer hackers), social roles (grandmother, teacher), and purchasers of brand name products (Jeep, Gap, Nike) or non-brand name products (Salvation Army). Even international relations play important roles in structuring our identities as citizens, immigrants, or refugees, as workers and/or consumers, as First World or Third World men or women, as racialized in particular ways, and so forth.

The various groups, or social organizations, that we belong to are also relational in that each is a complex set of relationally constituted persons, formed under specific historical, social, political, and economic circumstances. Each person is, herself, a multi-dimensional organism shaped and determined by a vast array of natural, social, and political forces in addition to personal temperament and choice, and each social group is an even more complex system shaped by a web of social and political structures. Hence, those of us keen to encourage critical reflection and change in problematic behaviours must carefully consider the levels of social organization that we should seek to affect in each case.

To briefly recap, my earlier work on feminist relational autonomy theory stressed that autonomy is not achieved simply by making an informed and uncoerced choice from an existing array of options. An individual cannot always improve her degree of autonomy by improving her understanding of the nature of the decision that she is to make or by reducing internal compulsions and external threats. In most cases, she must also be situated in favourable circumstances. While most autonomy theorists recognize that others have responsibilities to support individuals in their pursuit of autonomy, they tend to focus on the need to remove barriers to free and informed choice that may be confronting particular individuals. Relational autonomy makes all of the familiar demands on others regarding the need to ensure that the agent has an adequate degree of understanding and is free of direct coercion. In addition, it looks critically at the prevailing background conditions and the nature of the available options. It asks that individuals be able to choose from a set of options that includes some that do not undermine their objectives. To make a judgment about the degree of autonomy that may be present in a given context, we must examine the types of options that are on offer and ask questions about how these have arisen and also inquire about potentially constructive options that are not available or accessible. The perspective of relational autonomy requires us to examine the social values and processes that have led to the specific options that seem available and meaningful in choice situations, and it encourages us to seek strategies that will make available alternatives that are more compatible with each agent's ultimate values and needs. This is not to say that adding options can increase autonomy. Additional options can simply add confusion or increase the sense that a particular type of solution is preferable. For example, increasing the range of cell phone models just reinforces the sense that each modern citizen should possess a cell phone. What is needed is access to particular types of choices – those that are empowering and help to reduce oppression.

Feminist relational theory also directs us to pay particular attention to ways in which power arrangements structure options and opportunities. It makes visible the fact that different social groups are affected differently by various practices, and it encourages us to pay particular attention to the ways in which patterns of privilege and disadvantage can be reinforced by prevailing practices and policies. As I noted earlier, feminist relational theory is particularly valuable for helping to explain how it is that members of groups that are systematically disadvantaged by a given practice – as women are, for example, by the normalization of certain forms of cosmetic surgeries – may nonetheless still choose to comply with the very practices in question. In other words, feminist relational theory helps us to understand how it is that as individuals, and as members of collectives, we continue to participate in practices that serve powerful interests but are, ultimately, contrary to our own deepest interests. It can also help us gain insight into how we can learn to identify and pursue practices of collective resistance and empowerment. It can, I believe, help to identify what is morally problematic about current practices and also point towards ways of making the changes needed to avoid impending disasters.

What is different now from my earlier work in relational autonomy is that I no longer see the problem of skewed background conditions supporting actions that are ultimately harmful to the agent as being characteristic only of oppression. I think that even those individuals with privilege and power are caught up in patterns of behaviour that are contrary to their deeper interests. For example, it feels nearly impossible for individuals accustomed to patterns of consumption and waste to fully reorient our behaviours to consume only our fair share of the earth's resources even if we recognize the moral responsibility to do so. Projecting from my own experience, I believe that most of us will only be able to manage such drastic retraining of our habits and thinking if we have appropriate supports (social "scaffolding") in place to help guide and support our decisions to act responsibly.[35]

Moreover, it is now clear to me that we must look at barriers to responsible choices that affect other layers of social organization beyond individual agents. Governments, community groups, NGOs, corporations, religious groups, and so on also face serious constraints on the range of meaningful options that they can pursue. In this sense, they, too, face structural limits to their "autonomy" or ability to act in accordance with their long-term interests. There is a sense in which we can apply the distinction between agency and autonomy to organizations as well as to individuals since organizations often find themselves adopting practices and policies that make sense in light of the existing background conditions (agency) but find themselves unable to act in ways that would make a responsible contribution to the serious moral issues of our time (autonomy). There are a multitude of reasons for this phenomenon, including a competitive environment, bureaucratic regulations that limit initiatives, an uninformed public, and a sense of futility. Whatever the explanation, the phenomenon is quite real.

In other words, if agents of any level of social complexity are to make responsible choices regarding practices that collectively constitute threats to the survival of human and other life forms, they must do so through some sort of collaborative engagement with many sorts of human organizations. Individuals must comply with government policies aimed at sustainable practices and must not punish political leaders for promoting radical changes in individual lifestyles. Corporations must look beyond short-term profit and consider how they can avoid environmental damage and help to restore fragile ecosystems. Community groups must consider ways of educating citizens of all ages about the ways in which the actions of each impact on others. No one level of human organization can be successful in such transformations on its own. Each one's freedom to act in a manner consistent with its responsibilities to avert disaster is deeply intertwined with the choices made by other types of actors. As such, the autonomy of each type of agent is largely shaped in relation to that of others.

The problem of finding ourselves making voluntary, informed choices as agents that are inconsistent with the values that our autonomy would encourage is not limited to those who are oppressed even though in this, as in so many things, the most disadvantaged will be the most seriously and quickly affected by impending disasters. In some ways, power and privilege seem to make things even worse. (Since the largest carbon footprints belong to the wealthy, they are the ones called on to make the most drastic cuts in consumption.) We seek ways of living that will reduce, rather than increase, the global crises that threaten us all, yet, in many cases, the immediate options from which we choose are incompatible with those deeper values. Many of us are accustomed to comfort and convenience and cannot imagine living in accordance with the fraction of our current income that would constitute our personal "fair share" of the planet's resources. Somehow, the choice set must be modified to help us find and pursue practices that will move humanity in more peaceful, sustainable directions, yet it is not clear how such actions will happen and who will take leadership in this endeavour. Most people lack the skills for deliberating about such topics and determining how to modify our lives in effective ways.

My current focus on relational autonomy sees it as a key to understanding what sorts of responsibility attach to each of us who plays a part (actually many parts) in sustaining or challenging the problematic global threats that keep me awake at night. If we understand relational autonomy as applying to institutions as well as to individuals, it can help reveal ways in which both collectives and individuals can be constrained or empowered by the practices in which others engage. It can also help us to see how our own actions (as collectives and individuals) can constrain or empower other agents. As such, increased relational autonomy is a morally desirable ideal for all types of agents who seek to collaborate and coordinate their actions and responsibilities with respect to the important goal of averting global threats. For this task, I turn to work by Iris Marion Young that provides some valuable guidelines for this phase of my project.[36]

Young has introduced a version of social connection theory to explain how many types of responsibilities belonging to different types of agents can be seen and taken up. Her focus is on the social injustice associated with the globalization of markets. She uses the example of sweatshop production of clothing to discuss the responsibilities of the many layers of participants that sustain this particular form of injustice. Social structures are complex sets of "institutional rules and interactive routines ... [and] physical structures ... which are relatively stable over time ... [They] serve as background conditions for individual actions by presenting actors with options; they provide "channels" that both enable action and constrain it."[37] People act under conditions that have been largely shaped by previous actions, and the choices they make will strongly determine the choices that they and others will be able to make in the future, whether they intend these outcomes or not.

Young does not use the language of relational autonomy, but I believe her argument is useful to my efforts to expand the scope of relational autonomy beyond concern about the situation of agents who must act under conditions of oppression. I think I can fairly reinterpret her project in terms of relational autonomy by saying that the scope of anyone's relational autonomy with respect to a global system of injustice (sweatshops) is strongly affected by the actions of others, and their actions will have a significant impact on the relational autonomy of others regarding this system in the future.

In addition, Young provides illumination regarding the ways in which we can think of responsibilities and, ultimately, of autonomy that belongs to collective agents as well as to single individuals. She observes that people participate in social structures as individuals and as members of various kinds of collectives that contribute to the patterns that put "large categories of persons under a systematic threat of domination or deprivation ... at the same time as these processes enable others to dominate or have a wide range of opportunities."[38] She argues that "all the persons who participate by their actions in the ongoing schemes of cooperation that constitute these structures are responsible for them, in the sense that they are part of the process that causes them."[39] All those who are active participants in problematic structures have a role to play in changing the patterns, and this responsibility belongs to them as individual agents and as members of organizations.

It is not only the victims of sweatshop exploitation who are caught up in cycles where the actions that agents choose today structure future choices that may be at odds with the intents and interests of those same actors. For example, most participants in the social structures that sustain sweatshops would prefer not to contribute to the brutal, exploitative conditions that their workers endure. Consumers are looking for affordable garments, and retailers, wholesalers, distributors, managers, and local governments are doing their jobs within a globally competitive environment. Insofar as each actor participates in the practices that maintain this form of production, however, they play a role in sustaining the social structure of sweatshop labour. And this participation means that they (we) have a responsibility to try to eliminate the injustice at the core of the system, but we will only be successful in this endeavour if we are able to work collaboratively at many levels of human agency. Through her extensive discussion of the causes of sweatshop labour and appropriate strategies to eliminate the associated injustice, Young provides an illuminating practical example of how relational autonomy can work in a global context. Thinking through this perspective provides us with positive guidelines for action that can help us discharge our multi-layered responsibilities.

Given the many complex problems before us and the fact that we all participate in most of the social structures that generate or sustain them, we need to determine how an agent (be it a person, business, government, labour union, or other type of agent) is to know where to begin to assume responsibility and seek to change the problematic processes. Young does not offer a definitive solution, but she does briefly sketch a set of four parameters that we can use in thinking about our actions in relation to social injustice.

1 Power: Individuals and organizations should focus on those structural injustices "where they have a greater capacity to influence structural processes."[40]
2 Privilege: Structural injustices tend to produce both victims and beneficiaries who acquire relative privilege by virtue of those structures – those with greater privilege have greater responsibility for change. For example, the greater privilege of the middle class relative to those of lower classes means that middle-class consumers would suffer less from resisting participation in this system than poorer people and so they bear a greater responsibility for resisting this form of social injustice.
3 Interest: Those who are most harmed by social injustice have the greatest interest in ending it – as participants in the social structures that generate injustice, they have a role to play in ending it. They often have particular knowledge and insight as to the workings of the injustice, and they will

need to act collectively if it is to be ended. Other persons or agencies that seek to end a particular form of injustice should consult with its victims in devising policies to end it.

4   Collective ability: It is sometimes the case that "a coincidence of interest, power, and existing organization enables people to act collectively to influence processes more easily regarding one issue of injustice than another."[41] In such cases, it is desirable that they take advantage of their ability to make change at this time.

The set of parameters that Young provides represents an excellent model of how to make actual the new sort of complex, multi-layered ethics of responsibility I am trying to understand. It illustrates ways in which the actions and choices of different actors and different types of agents influence one another and provides guidance for who can and should take responsibility for seeking to make changes in global problems. Young's discussion of responsibility for change regarding sweatshop labour also makes very clear that while there is a role for individuals and for governments to play, these are not the only types of agents with responsibilities for change. There is a limit to what individuals can achieve qua individuals when dealing with well-entrenched social practices. Similarly, there is a limit to what governments can accomplish. Not every social problem can be resolved by appropriate legislation and enforcement. Some types of problems require action by other types of human actors, including community groups, religious organizations, educational bodies, media, and even corporations. The difficulty is that each type of actor must work collaboratively with others at the same and different levels of human organization if it is to develop sufficient scope to act effectively for positive change. An understanding of relational autonomy can help to inform our understanding of the ways in which social, economic, and political patterns enable and constrain the taking up of responsibilities with respect to climate change, violence, extreme poverty, and other major problems by different types of human agents. It helps us to understand what sorts of training can support the development of skills required by each type of organization so that it can determine where its deepest interest lies and to find strategies for working effectively with others to support a morally responsible change in direction.

I see my task now as rethinking my understanding of relational autonomy to make sense of the ways in which social structures constrain some choices and enable others for all individuals (and not just those who are oppressed) as well as for institutions with respect to the global threats before us. While my thoughts to date are largely programmatic, I deeply hope that this way of thinking about ethics and responsibilities will have something quite substantial to say to people regarding their responsibilities to change globally dangerous patterns of behaviour. My more personal hope is that thinking more widely about relational autonomy will allow me to make a modest contribution to this goal.

Notes

I want to thank the other members of this research group for their valuable comments on earlier drafts of this chapter and the ideas I was able to glean from their early drafts throughout the process of this project. I want to especially thank the editors, Jennifer Llewellyn and Jocelyn Downie, and Constance MacIntosh for their particular attention to the penultimate draft.

1   Susan Sherwin, *No Longer Patient* (Philadelphia: Temple University Press, 1992); Feminist Health Care Ethics Research Network, Susan Sherwin, coordinator, *The Politics of Women's Health: Exploring Agency and Autonomy* (Philadelphia: Temple University Press, 1998); Susan Sherwin, "A Relational Approach to Autonomy" in Feminist Health Care Ethics Research Network, *ibid.,* 19; Susan Sherwin, "Feminist Reflections on the Role of Theories in a Global Bioethics" in Rosemarie Tong, Gwen Anderson, and Aida Santos, eds., *Globalizing Feminist Bioethics* (Boulder, CO: Westview Press, 2001) 12; Susan Sherwin, "Normalizing Reproductive Technologies and the Implications for Autonomy" in Tong, Anderson, and Santos, *ibid.,* 96; Susan Sherwin, "The Importance of Ontology for Feminist Policy-Making in the Realm of Reproductive Technology" (2003) 26 Can. J. Phil. 273; Susan Sherwin "Genetic Enhancement, Sports, and Relational Autonomy" (August 2007) 1:2 Sport Ethics & Phil. 171; Susan Sherwin, "Whither Bioethics? How Feminism Can Help Re-orient Bioethics" (2008) 1:1 Int'l J. Feminist Approaches to Bioethics 7; Susan Sherwin, "Relational Existence and Termination: When Embodiment Precludes Agency" in Sue Campbell, Letitia Meynell, and Susan Sherwin, eds., *Agency and Embodiment* (University Park, PA: Penn State Press, 2009) 145; Carolyn McLeod and Susan Sherwin, "Relational Autonomy, Self-Trust, and Health Care for Patients Who Are Oppressed" in Catriona MacKenzie and Natalie Stoljar, eds., *Relational Autonomy: Feminist Perspectives on Autonomy, Agency and the Social Self* (Oxford: Oxford University Press, 2000) 259; Françoise Baylis, Nuala Kenny, and Susan Sherwin, "A Relational Account of Public Health Ethics" (2008) 1:3 Public Health Ethics 196.
2   Feminist Health Care Ethics Research Network, *supra* note 1.
3   These arguments are spelled out in various places, including Sherwin, "Relational Approach," *supra* note 1; McLeod and Sherwin, *supra* note 1; Sherwin, "Feminist Reflections," *supra* note 1; Sherwin, "Normalizing Reproductive Technologies," *supra* note 1; Sherwin, "Importance of Ontology," *supra* note 1; Sherwin, "Genetic Enhancement," *supra* note 1.
4   Margaret Urban Walker, *Moral Understandings: A Feminist Study in Ethics* (New York: Routledge, 1998).
5   Sherwin, "Relational Approach," *supra* note 1.
6   Such commentators tend to equate autonomy with liberty and rather simplistically interpret both terms to mean "doing what one chooses."
7   Of course, in many circumstances the alternative to autonomy is not paternalism but, rather, concern for someone else's interests. Nonetheless, the debate within the bioethics literature has largely presumed that doctors always seek to promote their patients' interests and so they only ignore autonomy when they believe they have a superior understanding of what is best for a patient. Recognition that other people's interests often take precedence over those of a patient's tends to make the case for autonomy even stronger than when it is contrasted with paternalism. In addition, I do not mean to suggest that Western medicine is free of patriarchy – only that it is less blatant than my South American colleagues describe the situation in their countries.
8   Diana Tietjens Meyers, *Self, Society, and Personal Choice* (New York: Columbia University Press, 1989); Jennifer Nedelsky, "Reconceiving Autonomy" (1989) 1:1 Yale J.L. & Feminism 7; Lorraine Code, *What Can She Know? Feminist Theory and the Construction of Knowledge* (Ithaca, NY: Cornell University Press, 1991); Christine Koggel, *Perspectives on Equality: Constructing a Relational Theory* (Lantham, MD: Rowman and Littlefield, 1998).

9   Sherwin, "Relational Approach," *supra* note 1.
10 Nedelsky, *supra* note 8.
11 Koggel, *supra* note 8.
12 Catriona Mackenzie and Natalie Stoljar, eds., *Relational Autonomy: Feminist Perspectives on Autonomy, Agency and the Social Self* (Oxford: Oxford University Press, 2000).
13 As spelled out in John Rawls, *A Theory of Justice* (Cambridge, MA: Harvard University Press, 1971).
14 Sherwin, "Relational Approach," *supra* note 1.
15 Meyers, *supra* note 8.
16 I follow Iris Marion Young in understanding oppression as group-based and identifiable by one or more of its distinctive five "faces": exploitation, powerlessness, marginalization, cultural domination, and violence. Iris Marion Young, *Justice and the Politics of Difference* (Princeton, NJ: Princeton University Press, 1990) at 39-65.
17 Marilyn Frye, *The Politics of Reality: Essays in Feminist Theory* (Freedom, CA: Crossing Press, 1983).
18 *Assisted Human Reproduction Act*, S.C. 2004, c. 2.
19 For example, the legislation prohibits the use of financial incentives for the provision of human gametes or surrogacy services and establishes penalties for professionals who help to facilitate commercial trafficking in these areas.
20 Sherwin, "Whither Bioethics?" *supra* note 1.
21 I believe the same is true of many other systems of ethics, but I am too ignorant to speak authoritatively on other approaches.
22 In stating that Western theories are not up to this task, I do not mean to claim that non-Western approaches fare any better. I am simply expressing the limits of my own expertise regarding the ethics traditions prominent in Western thought.
23 Immanuel Kant, *Groundwork of the Metaphysics of Morals*, translated by Mary J. Gregor, in Mary J. Gregor, ed., *Practical Philosophy* (Cambridge: Cambridge University Press, 1996; originally published 1785) 43.
24 Walker, *supra* note 4.
25 Joan Tronto, *Moral Boundaries: A Political Argument for an Ethics of Care* (New York: Routledge, 1993).
26 See Maneesha Deckha, "Non-human Animals and Human Health: A Relational Approach to the Use of Animals in Medical Research" in this volume.
27 Walker, *supra* note 4.
28 Sherwin, "Whither Bioethics?" *supra* note 1. I do not mean to suggest that the structural problem I am describing belongs only to large moral issues. It is often relevant in more limited domains (as, for example, I discussed with respect to specific health policies in my earlier work). Rather, I focus on large global issues since I believe there is a real urgency to finding new ways to address them.
29 Immanuel Kant, "Religion within the Boundaries of Mere Reason," translated by George di Giovanni, in Immanuel Kant, *Religion and Rational Theology*, translated and edited by Allen W. Wood and George di Giovanni (Cambridge: Cambridge University Press, 1996) 57 at 92, 94, and 105. Compare with Immanuel Kant, "Toward Perpetual Peace," translated by Mary J. Gregor, in Immanuel Kant, *Practical Philosophy*, translated and edited by Mary J. Gregor (Cambridge: Cambridge University Press, 1996) 317 at 338.
30 Sherwin, "Whither Bioethics?" *supra* note 1.
31 A sad and shameful example of this problem occurred in the early summer of 2009 when the spread of the H1N1 virus seemed to hit remote First Nations communities in Canada with particular intensity. The communities were hampered in their efforts to slow the spread of the virus by an absence of clean running water despite years of promises by the federal government to supply this basic necessity. See Aboriginal Nurses Association of Canada, "Aboriginal Nurses Concerned about Impact of H1N1 on First Nations, Métis and Inuit People at High Health Risk" (16 July 2009), http://www.anac.on.ca/Documents/H1N1/PRpercent20H1N1percent20Eng.pdf.
32 Madison Powers and Ruth Faden, *Social Justice: The Moral Foundations of Public Health and Health Policy* (Oxford: Oxford University Press, 2006) at 81.

33   *Ibid.* at 85.
34   Sherwin, "Whither Bioethics?" *supra* note 1.
35   I am grateful to an anonymous reviewer for suggesting this metaphor.
36   Iris Marion Young, "Responsibility and Global Justice: A Social Connection Model" (2006) 23:1 Soc. Philosophy & Pol'y 102.
37   *Ibid.* at 100-11.
38   *Ibid.* at 114.
39   *Ibid.*
40   *Ibid.* at 127.
41   *Ibid.* at 129.

2

The Reciprocal Relation of Judgment and Autonomy: Walking in Another's Shoes and Which Shoes to Walk In

Jennifer Nedelsky

Autonomy and judgment stand in a reciprocal relation to each other. Judgment, to be true judgment, requires autonomy. And the exercise and development of autonomy requires constant judgment. Relational conceptions of both autonomy and judgment assist in understanding the relationship between them and the way each enables freedom within community. The relational approach I take here treats the relevant relationships as existing at several levels: personal, societal, institutional, global, and environmental. Each level affects the others – for example, an individual marriage is shaped by, and can shape in turn, the norms of gender roles, family law and its interpretation, employment practices, the global economy, and global warming.[1]

Autonomy in Judgment

In this chapter, I am building on Hannah Arendt's conception of judgment, which she, in turn, developed from Immanuel Kant's *Critique of Judgment*.[2] Arendt thought that Kant had correctly perceived that the human capacity to make judgments is a distinct cognitive capacity. In taking up Kant's concept, Arendt is defining judgment in a very particular way, which does not simply match up with ordinary usage. People make what might seem like judgments about all kinds of things. However, for Arendt, there is an important distinction between forming an opinion about something and actually exercising the cognitive capacity for judgment. Judgment, in her terms, involves a particular use of the mind, including imagination. People are only "really" judging, or making "true" judgments, when they engage their capacity for the "enlarged mentality," which I discuss later in this chapter. For both Kant and Arendt, judgment, by definition, involves a claim of agreement upon others. In my discussion, I use various terms such as "true" or "genuine" judgment to remind the reader that there are distinctive requirements for judgment in the Arendtian/Kantian sense. These requirements distinguish judgment from other forms of opinion or evaluation. Similarly, I will note Arendt's understanding of the conditions for "valid" judgment as well as her views on the scope of validity.

Of course, here I can only offer a brief introduction to this concept of judgment.[3] As we will see, this distinctive, sometimes counter-intuitive, concept makes two crucial contributions. First, it offers an articulation of the way that human cognitive abilities can be simultaneously autonomous and reliant on communication with others. (Although, as I will argue, this contribution becomes clearer in the context of relational theory.) Second, this understanding of judgment makes the vital contribution of showing how judgments that are genuinely subjective are, nevertheless, *not* merely arbitrary matters of personal preference. In the realms of both science and law, we can see particularly clearly why it is important that the contemporary recognition of the inevitability of subjectivity in judgment should not lead to a collapse into the inevitability of arbitrariness. For Arendt, it was particularly important that the judgments inherent in politics be understood both as inherently subjective *and* as distinguishable from arbitrary preference. In all of these realms, the Kantian/Arendtian conception of judgment allows us to see the possibility of claims of validity for judgments with an inherently subjective dimension.

Let me begin with the claim that judgment requires, or one might say entails, autonomy. For Arendt, the very meaning of the term involves the exercise of autonomous judgment. It is the capacity of each person to make her own judgments that can free one from the power of public opinion and enable her to form judgments and make decisions even when the existing canon of concepts seems unable to capture the nature of a new phenomenon. (Arendt called this latter capacity "thinking without banisters."[4]) It is the autonomous nature of these capacities that make them genuine judgment, and it is this exercise of autonomy that provides the "freeing" quality of true judgment.

As I have discussed in an earlier article, Arendt's approach to judgment generates a puzzle that I believe a relational conception of autonomy solves.[5] Her approach, which draws on Kant, makes the taking of the perspectives of others central to judgment. Judgment in Arendtian/Kantian terms is called for when the issue at hand is neither a truth claim nor a mere subjective preference.[6]

Arendtian/Kantian Judgment

I begin with an introduction to Arendt's theory of judgment drawn from my earlier work.[7] Let me provide an example with which most academics will be familiar. When professors grade papers, I think few of us believe that the statement "this paper deserves an A" is a truth claim. Such a statement is not something we think we can prove or demonstrate in the way we could demonstrate a right answer to a math question, to most questions of spelling, or to questions about the way gravity or centripetal force works. Nevertheless, most professors want to claim that the grade of A means something quite different from "I liked it." "I liked it" is a statement of subjective preference, such as the classic claim "I like vanilla ice cream better than chocolate." It makes no claim on the agreement of anyone. We like to believe that when we grade a paper, other colleagues who know both the field and the institutional context would either give it the same or that we could explain why we graded it that way and thus persuade them to agree that an "A" is the appropriate grade. The claim that an essay is an "A" paper is thus not a truth claim about which we can compel agreement by proof. And it is not merely a statement of subjective preference. It is a statement of judgment that makes claims upon the agreement of others.[8]

The formulation I have just offered follows that of Kant. He identified what I see to be the central problem of judgment: how can a judgment that is genuinely and irreducibly subjective also be valid? What does the claim of validity mean if we do not transmute the subjective into something objective – and thus lose the essence of judgment as distinct from ascertaining a truth that can be demonstrably, and thus compellingly, proven?[9] The language of judgment, as developed by Kant and appropriated by Arendt, offers us an answer. They offer us a conception of judgment as a distinct human faculty that is subjective, but which is not therefore something merely arbitrary.[10] Genuine judgment makes claims of validity – at least for others in the community of judgment.

The focus of Kant's *Critique of Judgment* was aesthetic judgment, our capacity to judge something as beautiful. As I noted earlier, Kant situates judgment between the objective and mere matters of subjective preference. Truth claims can be proven objectively, and thus we can (cognitively) compel the agreement of others. The preference for flavours of ice cream is purely subjective and makes no claim of any kind on others. Aesthetic judgment falls between the two. The very nature of the claim "this picture is beautiful," Kant tells us, distinguishes it from the statement "I like this picture." What is the difference between these two statements? What does it mean to assert beauty rather than express liking? In Kant's terms, to assert beauty is to make a claim of agreement upon other judging subjects. Thus, when we claim that the picture *is* beautiful (instead of just that we like it), we make a subjective judgment that has a quasi-objective quality to it. We are saying that others who bring their judgment to bear on the picture will also find it beautiful, if they are truly, that is autonomously, judging.

As Kant puts it, a "judgment of taste must involve a claim to subjective universality." It is not the act of liking that has this quality but, rather, the actual judgment. And what gives something the quality of judgment is ensuring that one's idiosyncrasies, one's interests, and, for Kant, even one's inclinations are not affecting one's judgment. The judger "must believe that he is justified in requiring a similar liking from everyone because he cannot discover, underlying this liking any private conditions, on which only he might be dependent, so that he must regard it as based on what he can presuppose in everyone else as well." When the judging person is free of any interest or inclination, he "feels completely *free* as regards the liking he accords the object."[11]

Although true judgment entails this freedom, it also demands the agreement of others by the nature of the claim. For Kant, this demand is premised on the underlying commonalities of our cognitive faculties (imagination and understanding, in this case) and the resulting capacity for the communicability of judgments. Indeed, one of the pleasures of beauty (perhaps, for Kant, *the* pleasure) is that although the experience is subjective we can communicate it to others. Now the nature of the claim upon the agreement of others is extremely important. Unlike truth claims, for which our reason compels agreement, one cannot compel another's agreement with one's judgment. One can only persuade. To quote Arendt, "the judging person – as Kant quite beautifully puts it – must 'woo the consent of everyone else in the hope of coming to an agreement with him.'"[12]

In the Kantian framework, as we form our judgment, we imagine trying to persuade others. We test our judgment against what others would say. So to return to the contrast with mere liking or preference, when we say "I like that picture" we have no need to wonder whether others would agree or what it is we would say to them to persuade them of the validity of our assessment. Validity cannot be ascribed to preference. However, when we say the painting is beautiful, we know we are making a judgment, which claims the agreement of others. So we try to imagine what others would say, we enter into an imaginary dialogue with them, and we try to woo their consent.

What enables us to make judgments that are not merely idiosyncratic statements of preference – what puts us in a position to "woo the consent of others" – is our capacity for "enlarged thought." In her lectures on Kant, Arendt introduces Kant's concept of "enlarged thought" through quotes from Kant's letters to a friend.[13] I want to offer a long quote in which we see the links that she is making between these quotes and the core of Kant's theory of judgment. She begins with the following quote:

"You know that I do not approach reasonable objections with the intention merely of refuting them, but that in thinking them over I always weave them into my judgments, and afford them the opportunity of overturning all my most cherished beliefs. I entertain the hope that by thus viewing my judgments impartially from the standpoint of others some third view that will improve upon my previous insight may be obtainable."

[Arendt comments] [Y]ou see that *impartiality* is obtained by taking the viewpoints of others into account; impartiality is not the result of some higher standpoint that would then settle the dispute by being altogether above the melee. In the second letter, Kant makes this even clearer:

"[The mind needs a reasonable amount of relaxations and diversions to maintain its mobility] that it may be enabled to view the object afresh from every side, and so to enlarge its point of view from a microscopic to a general outlook that it adopts in turn every conceivable standpoint, verifying the observations of each by means of all the others."

[Arendt continues] Here the word "impartiality" is not mentioned. In its stead, we find the notion that one can "enlarge" one's own thought so as to take into account the thoughts of others. The "enlargement of the mind" plays a crucial role in the *Critique of Judgment*. It is accomplished by "comparing our judgment with the possible rather than the actual judgments of others, and by putting ourselves in the place of any other man." The faculty that makes this possible is called imagination. When you read the paragraphs in the *Critique of Judgment* and compare them with the letters just quoted, you will see that the former contain no more than the conceptualization of these very personal remarks.[14]

Arendt emphasizes that communication with others, with one's fellow judging subjects, is essential for the capacity for judgment (even though it is the imagination that "make the others present" in the solitary moments of judgment). The core of why Arendt saw Kant's theory of judgment as essentially political is what she saw as its inherent social dimension. For her, Kant's focus on communicability is a focus on the ways in which judgment requires community. She says:

Now communicability obviously implies a community of men who can be addressed and who are listening and can be listened to. To the question, Why are there men rather than man? Kant would have answered: In order that they may talk to one another ... Kant is aware that he disagrees with most thinkers in asserting that thinking, though a solitary business, depends on others to be possible at all.[15]

In her focus on communication with others, Arendt is arguably making a leap outside Kant's framework as she tries to show how Kant's conception of aesthetic judgment is the kind of judgment that is at work in political judg-ment. For my purposes in this chapter, we do not want to get lost in detailed interpretations of Kant. However, the core issue is relevant to my central concern with the autonomy and impartiality of judgment. Although Arendt thought otherwise, a standard interpretation is that in the *Critique of Judgment,* as in the first two critiques, Kant is talking about a transcendental realm, where there are no real conversations among actual people. When we "woo the consent" of others, it is the consent of all others, at all times, in all places – and, thus, necessarily only in the imagination. Judgment is founded in an appeal to common sense, but common sense is shared among all people by virtue of their having the same basic human faculties (understanding and imagination, in particular). This common sense is universal because it is based on the common structure of our minds (understanding, imagination, and the nature of their interaction, in particular). This idea is the basis for his (contro-versial) claim that the nature of beauty is universal.

However, Arendt grounds judgment in an appeal to a common sense that is shared by virtue of sharing an actual community, not by virtue of universally shared cognitive faculties. When we form our judgment in the process of imagining trying to persuade others, it is the perspectives of real others that is involved. I think Arendt's account of how she translates Kantian claims into her own is best seen in her discussion of transcending individual limitations through the perspectives of others. As she explains, "judgment, to be valid, depends on the presence of others. Hence judgment is endowed with a certain specific validity but is never universally valid."[16] Kant, however, states that "a judgment of taste must involve a claim to subjective universality."[17] Arendt accounts for this by saying that when Kant says judgment is valid for "every single judging person," the "emphasis in the sentence is on `judging'; it is not valid for those who do not judge or for those who are not members of the public realm where the objects of judgment appear."[18]

What matters here is that Arendt shares the Kantian objective of seeing the link between the perspectives of others and judgment that is autonomous, that can transcend the inevitable limitations of one person's experience, in-terests, and inclinations. Arendt says that when we take the standpoint of others into account to achieve an enlarged mentality we do not want to know what is actually in their minds, for that would be simply to replace our own idiosyncrasies with theirs. Rather, we should ask how we would judge in their position (or, to draw on the metaphor from the title, how we would judge standing in another's shoes). The reference to the perspectives of others is necessary to make truly free judgment possible. The ability to think in the place of others makes it possible for us to liberate ourselves from the "subjective private conditions" – that is, as Arendt says, from the "idiosyncrasies which naturally determine the outlook of each individual in his privacy and are legitimate as long as they are only privately held opinions, but which ... lack all validity in the public realm. And this enlarged way of thinking, which, as judgment, knows how to transcend its own individual limitations, cannot function in strict isolation or solitude; it needs the presence of others 'in whose place' it must think, whose perspectives it must take into consideration, and without whom it never has the opportunity to operate at all."[19]

The Puzzle of Autonomous Judgment

The puzzle is how can taking the perspectives of others lead to genuinely autonomous judgment. Is there not some kind of contradiction in terms here? Does taking the actual perspectives of others not amount to the sort of "groping about" in the opinions of others that Kant explicitly contrasts with true judgment? The answer lies first with the recognition that the enlarged mentality that one achieves through taking the perspectives of others still requires an exercise of judgment. The second step is to see that the puzzle is driven in part by a failure to see that autonomy itself is relational.[20] In other words, taking the perspectives of others is part of, not a substitute for, judgment.

Let me begin with what the use of the enlarged mentality involves. Arendt, having never written her planned volume on judgment, did not spell out how she envisioned the process of judgment that the enlarged mentality made possible. However, as I see it, there must be a process of judgment in the use of the multiple standpoints that one has taken. In judging with an enlarged mentality, one does not simply amass a large number of different perspectives from which autonomous judgment automatically emerges. As I see it, the process involves an ongoing iteration of comparing one's initial judgment with another perspective, considering whether to revise one's initial judgment, comparing this revised judgment with another perspective, and so on. Sometimes this process will be highly conscious, involving careful deliberation and an assessment of all of the other relevant perspectives. Sometimes one will have recourse to the results of an earlier careful deliberation and use the "outcome" as a reference point without revisiting all of the previous steps in the judgment. Without some such shortcut, we could not engage in all of the ongoing judgments that are part of daily life. Yet whether elaborate and highly conscious or very quick, there is an act of judgment (or many acts of judgment) that is involved in the use of the enlarged mentality. There is thus no simple deference to, or counting up of, the perspectives of others.

Standpoint as Relational

The process of judgment that is called for will depend on the nature of the perspective that one is considering. There are many puzzles about what is entailed in taking the perspective of another and, indeed, the extent to which it is possible. At this point in the chapter, I want to reflect on how we must understand standpoint itself in a relational way: people stand in different relations to their "location."

Arendt says that "to accept what goes on in the minds of those whose 'standpoint' ... is not my own would mean no more than passively to accept their thought, that is, to exchange their prejudices for the prejudices proper to my station." And she parenthetically defines standpoint as "actually, the place where they stand, the conditions they are subject to, which always differ from one individual to the next, from one class or group as compared to another."[21] She cautions as well that "the trick of critical thinking does not consist in an enormously enlarged empathy through which one can know what actually goes on in the minds of others."[22]

Arendt quotes Kant in saying that "'enlarged thought' is the result of first 'abstracting from the limitations which contingently attach to our own judgment,' of disregarding its 'subjective private conditions ... by which so many are limited.'" She follows this statement by presenting the scope of one's enlarged thinking as being shaped by "the realm in which the enlightened individual is able to move from standpoint to standpoint." And she emphasizes the *particular* conditions of the standpoints one has to go through in order to arrive at one's own "general standpoint."[23]

This language can be read to suggest that the project is to imagine how one would judge from the standpoint of another – which is not about "what goes on in the mind" of the other.[24] However, I think (as I have argued in the different context of the role of religiously based argument) that "standpoint" must to some extent take into account what has gone on in the mind of the person whose standpoint one is considering.[25] One need not imagine that one can actually and fully know what goes on in the mind of another (even one whose standpoint seems very close to one's own). Yet there is not simply an objective location on a map of social and economic terrain one can stand in and try out one's judgment.

People stand, as I have said, in different relations to their location, and those relations must be seen as part of the standpoint that one must consider. For example, a person who is poor in a rich country such as Canada may feel that it is her fault that she is poor. Or she may have a carefully developed critique of the distribution of wealth, of the subsidy of corporations, and of the very limited extent to which Canada has a progressive income tax regime. Her standpoint on welfare reform, on corporate tax, and on whom to vote for will depend on the nature of her relation to her "location" as a poor person. Similarly, if she is a racialized person, she may have a critique of systemic racism, or she may have internalized negative stereotypes. I do not think that we can imagine the enlarged mentality doing its work of revealing the limitations of our own perspective and "enlarging" it optimally if we imagine that the people in these examples occupy the same standpoint.

We would need to take all of these perspectives into account, not just imagine what the "location" of poverty or racialized status means in terms of one's standpoint.

Another way of putting this is that how we should relate to the standpoints of others will depend in part on whether the other has exercised judgment in taking her perspective. In the texts that I have worked through carefully, Arendt never says that we should not consider the *judgment* of others (although, as we saw on p. 39, she quotes Kant as saying that we should compare our judgments with the possible, not actual, judgments of others). If we have reason to believe that another person has exercised true judgment, then when we take that judgment into account we are not simply exchanging our prejudices for hers. This does not mean that we should simply grant authority to another's perspective, assume that it requires no further judgment because of the "location" from which it was made (which the crude version of feminist standpoint theory suggests). The way we take another's perspective into account should be shaped both by the kind of judgment that we think she exercised as well as by our own humility about our capacity to understand standpoints that are very different from our own and consciousness of the asymmetries of power that may interfere.

All of this deserves further exploration. However, my point is that people stand in different relations to their location and part of this relation is the kind of reflection and judgment that they have brought to bear on that location. To take their perspective into account, we must attend to this relational component of their standpoint. This does, of course, add to the complications of how many people's standpoints one can actually engage with and how we choose which ones to try to take into account. Recognizing these complexities should add to the humility with which we treat our judgments, recognizing their inherent contingency and incompleteness.

Disclosing Ourselves/Knowing Ourselves

As we judge, and communicate our judgments, we enable ourselves to be known. We disclose ourselves:

> Wherever people judge the things of the world that are common to them, there is more implied in their judgments than these things. By his manner of judging, the person discloses to an extent also himself, what kind of person he is ... Now it is precisely the realm of acting and speaking, that is, the political domain in terms of activities, in which this personal quality comes to the fore in public, in which the "who one is" becomes manifest rather than the qualities and individual talents he may possess.[26]

This statement comes shortly after her comment that

> [w]e all know very well how quickly people recognize each other, and un-
> equivocally they can feel they belong to each other, when they discover a
> kinship in questions of what pleases and displeases. For the viewpoint of
> this common experience, it is as though taste decides not only how the
> world is to look, but who belongs together in it.[27]

I think Arendt is pointing here to the ways in which communicating our
judgments allows others to know us and, in turn, to be better able to take
our perspectives into account. This process is part of how the act of judgment both relies on and helps build a community of judgment.

As we judge, we not only disclose ourselves to others, we come to know
ourselves better. One might say we come to *be* ourselves better or more fully.
One might also say that as we exercise our judgment, we come to stand in
a different relation to our selves. As we free ourselves from our idiosyncrasies
and limitations of experience, we judge not only in a way that can claim
the validity of others but in a way we can say is more truly "ours." Our
idiosyncrasies and limitations distort our judgment. When we "liberate"
ourselves from them by taking the perspectives of others into account in
our judgments, we make judgments that we can stand by – judgments that
are not driven by the quirks of our history, location, or temperament but
that emerge from an (ever increasingly) autonomous process of judging.[28]
The exercise of judgment is an exercise of autonomy – that is what it means
for judgment to be genuine. And, thus, the practice of judgment is a practice
of autonomy. Our capacity for both judgment and autonomy increases as
we engage in the ongoing exercise of judgment, and that is why both autonomy and judgment call forth the language of freedom.

With both judgment and autonomy, we become more fully or truly ourselves in a way that permits us to both connect to, and distinguish, ourselves
from the collectivities of which we are a part. It is here that we come to the
link between the first point – that using the enlarged mentality itself involves
judgment – and the second point – that autonomy understood as relational
shifts the puzzling quality of community-based judgment.

Judgment and Freedom: Judging against Community

Our capacity for judgment allows us not only to (incompletely) transcend
the limitations of our personal experience but also to assess the views of
those around us and come to a judgment that is different from the dominant view. I think it was this dimension of judgment that was crucial to Arendt
in the context of the Holocaust and of the Eichmann trial in particular.[29]
Judgment, thus, has a double edge to it. It requires community. It can only
be exercised because we share a common sense that allows us to take the
perspectives of others. If we did not share a core of common understanding,
we would not be able to understand others enough to take their perspective.

And only when we do so, do we actually exercise judgment. And it is because we do so that we can claim that our judgments have validity for others. We rely on our community of judgment, and we make a claim on it.

At the same time, sometimes we must judge against that community – sometimes in small ways and sometimes in ways that tragically rip us apart from that community.[30] Our capacity for judgment would not really be a capacity for autonomous judgment unless that were possible. We must rely on what are often a variety of "common senses" that are available to us from the different communities to which we belong. For example, we may belong to families, religious communities, professional communities, and national communities that have different "common senses" with respect to basic assumptions about what marriage means, what the proper role of women is, or what equality "really" means. However, in the end, we exercise judgment that distinguishes our own judgment from that of others, from "popular opinion," and from "tradition." The iterative process of comparing our judgments with others does not yield, in the end, a compilation, summary, or counting of the views of others. It yields our unique, autonomous judgment. We can see this in Kant's example of the young poet standing by his judgment of the beauty of his poem against the critiques of experts. We can see it in a young person's insistence on the morality of being a vegetarian, against the wishes of his family, or in a young woman's rejection of the patriarchal dimensions of family structure or religion. It is easy to think of countless examples of individuals' capacities to judge against their communities, even when the result is the pain and disorientation of rejecting, or being rejected by, the communities that have shaped an important part of their common sense and their identity.

The fact that the exercise of judgment requires taking into account the perspectives of others in order not to be limited by one's "location," experience, or history is thus no contradiction to the idea of autonomous judgment. The fact that our capacity for judgment is community based does, however, provide one framework for understanding the profound pain and disorientation of judging against one's community.

Relational Autonomy and Community-Based Judgment: Reframing the Puzzle

We can now see how this response to the "puzzle" of judging with the perspectives of others is connected to the idea of relational autonomy. I think that the puzzle is in part generated by the notion that "relational autonomy" is an oxymoron. In this view, to be autonomous is to be independent of, free from, the influence of relationships. For autonomy itself to require relationship seems a contradiction in terms – just like having autonomous judgment require the perspectives of others seems a contradiction in terms. However, neither idea is a contradiction, and for the same reason. Once one recognizes that it is constructive relationship – not separation or isolation or an impossible independence – that makes autonomy possible, it becomes far less puzzling to see that autonomous judgment is made possible by judging one's own judgments in light of the perspectives of others.

To be true to oneself (as in Kant's story of the young poet) takes more than determination to stand against others. A person first must know that the judgment she is willing to take a stand on is one that she truly wants to call her own. She needs to know that it is not simply the product of habits of thought or preference and that it is not driven by (unacknowledged) self-interest or a narrow partiality that does not reflect the full scope of her values. How can she find this out? By judging her judgments through a process of comparison and reflection on the perspectives of others.

Saying that the core puzzle disappears once one is comfortable with a relational approach to autonomy is not to say that there is nothing difficult about understanding exactly what is entailed in these acts of judging. How exactly is it that one decides that after reflective use of the enlarged mentality one will stand by her judgment against that of her family, religious authority, or nation (as in Nazi Germany)? This question seems to me to be the same question to which a relational conception of autonomy ultimately turns us. After we understand how constructive relations foster autonomy and how our basic framework of perception, values, and even language are inevitably given to us through our relations with others, how do we ever know when a choice or decision we make is actually autonomous? Even after we recognize that there is no such thing as independence, that social construction is an essential dimension of humanness, and that autonomy is essentially relational, there can remain a puzzle about when and why we call our choices, decisions, or preferences autonomous.

Judgment in Autonomy

The Puzzles of Autonomy: The "Solution" of Judgment

It is here that we see the other side of the reciprocal relation between judgment and autonomy: the exercise of autonomy constantly requires judgment. When I think of all the examples that my students and I puzzle over, I have come to see that the exercise of autonomy entails an exercise of judgment – with all of its strengths and limitations. I will explore this link through a set of personal examples.

I became a professor, which was exactly what both my parents wanted me to do. They influenced this career choice in countless ways. And I can see the ways in which at many stages I followed a path that was laid out for me. When I was nineteen, my younger brother saw that path clearly and decided to step off it. He shocked me and my older brother (then in graduate school) by announcing that he did not want to go to university.

Horrified, we asked why. He answered: "You go to college, you go to graduate school. You go to graduate school, you become a professor. I don't want to turn out like you two." He was certainly onto something. In high school, the only choice I saw was which university to go to. In my final year as an undergraduate, the choice was which discipline, which university for graduate school.

However, it also true that many of the choices involved in following that path were difficult, and many were carefully considered. I chose an interdisciplinary graduate program because I thought it would best equip me to understand and take action in the world. I decided to work on issues of private property for my dissertation and followed the advice of one of my advisors to get legal training. I won a post-doctoral fellowship to do so and took law courses in a law faculty whose dean had wanted someone else to get that post-doc and told me that my academic interest in Canadian legal history was a "frill" in the curriculum. I got a "wonderful" first job at Princeton, which I hated. I found the environment paralyzing and published almost nothing. I was denied tenure but was invited as a visitor to the University of Toronto. I loved it there and was offered a tenure-track job. I got pregnant in my first year, and once my baby was born I worked seven days a week and every evening for eighteen months to finally finish my book (which my contract required for me to get tenure).

This story cannot be adequately captured by saying that my parents always wanted me to be a professor. Neither would I want to say that my choices at each stage were fully autonomous. Many of these choices were driven by other choices, having nothing to do with career aspirations. I married a man who got a job in Canada, and getting a post-doc in Canada seemed like a good way for me to build a career there. Getting legal training indeed proved essential to the academic career that I came to have in Canada, but not at all in the way I expected. Each choice was nested in other choices, and some were characterized by careful deliberation and good judgment, while others were driven by motivations that I did not work through very consciously. Somewhere along the way (around when I finally finished my first book), I decided I really was happy doing what I was doing, being an academic at the University of Toronto. I felt very grateful that my irrational hang-ups about publishing had not managed to sabotage a career that was good for me.

I think it is likely that my story is typical in its mix of autonomous decisions, accident, luck, and the shaping of background forces such as family expectations. This mode of life has worked out well for me. I am very well suited to it. So it is not troubling to me that I would not claim that this central part of my life was not clearly an autonomous choice. I now feel able to claim its value for me in quite an autonomous way and feel quite confident in that judgment. However, I also know that there were many steps along the way where I did not exercise much judgment in my choices, and I think those are the steps that do not feel very autonomous.

Oddly, a much less important aspect of my life seems to make clearer the role of judgment in the exercise of autonomy. In my late fifties, I became much more interested in clothes than I had been in a long time. I became interested in wearing skirts, and this interest then raised the issue of shoes. Half-way decent looking, but comfortable, shoes are not too hard to come by if one always wears pants. Shoes for skirts are another matter. Once I started thinking about it, I got interested in high heels. This created in me a mini storm of uncertainty about autonomy and social conditioning. As a feminist coming of age in the 1970s, high heels were anathema. As late as 1994, when I was teaching at the University of Chicago Law School, I shocked (and offended some) students by stating that high heels were the modern equivalent of Chinese foot binding (almost all of those young women were headed to jobs that would require wearing heels). Yet now I wanted some, several pairs actually. And if this were not bad enough, I started getting interested in eye makeup, which I had last used in 1970 when I was twenty years old.

It became clear to me that the constraints of my (chosen) social conditioning as a feminist were as powerful – actually quite a bit more so – than the constraints of the dominant culture's notions of appropriate feminine dress and appearance. For many years, I had not felt free to experiment with such things as high heels or make up. They had seemed a sure path to patriarchal convention. But having recognized the power and unfreedom of these once-chosen constraints, I was not then blind to the obviously socially constructed nature of my desire for high heels. I could not find, or imagine, a fully autonomous stance toward this issue. It seemed at best a choice among social conventions, even if one of them was "counter-cultural" and the other had obvious patriarchal overtones (there was something to my earlier analogy to foot binding).

I think this is just a (relatively) simple and (relatively) unimportant (though it occupied a lot of my time) example of how we are always confronted with choices that are shaped by forces outside our control (although how we make those choices has an impact on the choices available to others, so we are never simply passive in the face of the choices with which we are confronted). All we can do is make a judgment about which choice, in the face of all the multiple constraints, influences, and pressures, is most truly our own. Or we can, at least, be self-conscious when we feel compelled to choose something we would not want to stand by as truly ours.

Marilyn Friedman and Linda Barclay both talk about this puzzle of (relational) autonomy in the midst of pervasive and inevitable social construction.[31] I think the concept of judgment is a helpful addition to those reflections. First, I think it helps to remember that judgment in the Arendtian conception is not about provable truth claims. We can never *prove* that a given choice was autonomous, either to ourselves or to others. So the standard that we are expecting of ourselves in determining whether a choice is autonomous is a standard of good judgment, a standard of what we could persuade judging others about, a standard of validity for one's community of judgment.

Since Arendtian judgment is judgment in relation to a community of judgment, the first question in trying to determine if one is making good judgments is who is the relevant community of judgment. In this small issue of fashion apparel, the issue is the same as in big issues of human rights versus "culture" or "religion."[32] The conflict is often best recast as a question of which community of judgment one turns to and what one does when one feels oneself to be a member of multiple communities, with conflicting "common senses" (as well as how one judges once one recognizes that there is no supervening community of judgment that stands as an Archimedean point above all).

With respect to my fashion problem, the community of judgment that I wanted to judge in relation to was fairly clear: committed feminists of the early twenty-first century. Thus, at a recent event with academics and activists to celebrate the constitution of the Women's Court of Canada and its inaugural decisions in the *Canadian Journal of Women and Law*, I started looking around to see who was wearing high heels. I saw a lot of them – not only on young women but also on women of my generation. I began to wonder if I had just been slow to recognize the constraints of the 1970s for what they were – constraints, feminist taboos, as well as useful challenges to the status quo. I had had an imagined community of feminist judgment for all those years without really checking out what the perspectives of my fellow feminists were. The Women's Court of Canada event was an especially nice testing ground for finally doing some of the work of the enlarged mentality because there were (virtually) only other feminist women there. They were all dressing only for each other.

Perhaps this is an example of getting locked into an earlier judgment and not doing the work of ongoing reassessment. It is odd, for example, that for many years I somehow did not register the fact that I had colleagues who I respected as feminists who wore high heels. If I had consciously framed my view as a judgment that, like all judgments, needs periodic reappraisal, I might not have found my sudden interest in high heels so disorienting (as well as fun).

I think part of my distress about trying to figure out what place there was for autonomous choice in the face of two opposing socially conditioned norms (a 1970s feminist taboo versus a conventional view of feminine attractiveness) was that, despite all my work on relational autonomy and judgment, I still had some kind of fantasy about unconditioned choice. If what we mean by autonomous choices are uninfluenced choices, then, of course, there is no such thing. I now see the question as how to use the concept of judgment to work through the implications of the inevitability of influence, conditioning, and constraint. Our best bet for making autonomous choices is the sort of self-consciousness that I think the enlarged mentality brings. (I think there is a similar argument to be made about the need for judgment in the use of emotions as components of reason and guides to action.)

When I teach judges about the Arendtian theory of judgment, I emphasize that the key to the process is becoming aware of their presuppositions, assumptions, values, and frames of reference. I think that something similar needs to be at work in trying to assess what would constitute an autonomous judgment about which socially conditioned norms one wants to embrace or modify. One can then move beyond the inevitability of conditioning to identify as many of the influences as possible. And one can try to assess the extent to which one *wants* to be influenced by them – knowing that this act of wanting is, of course, also conditioned. So, for example, I recognize that my earlier feminist commitments (constraints) were based on some good judgments. Fashions such as high heels contribute to a kind of subordination of women. They send the message that sexy, alluring women are delicate and slightly debilitated – they cannot run, the terrain on which they can walk safely is limited, they have to sort of pick their way, they are not solidly on the ground, and they are slightly unstable. These are images that I reject and that I want to reject.

I can reflect on the fact that I like the way high heels look because I have been conditioned by advertising and by the practices of those around me. And I know that this sort of conditioning can change. When short skirts were "in," calf-length skirts looked dowdy. I remember the reconditioning it took for me to see them differently. I remember hemming and un-hemming skirts to have them at the "right" length. I think it is a good thing that contemporary fashion admits the full range of skirt lengths. Youth who want to play with extreme minis can, and those who wear full-length skirts for religious reasons do not look out of place.

So I know that my liking for high heels is conditioned and contingent. I also know that I cannot, by an effort of will, make myself think that flat, comfortable shoes look elegant with skirts. The contingency is collectively shaped. I can refuse to go along with it – as I did for well over thirty years. But those thirty years did not enable me to see flat, comfortable shoes with skirts the way I wanted to. I can feel annoyed that I am susceptible to the conditioning of fashion to the extent that it actually shapes what I like. However, while it is useful to recognize the influence of the fashion industry as something that I do not want to encourage, it also now seems to me that imagining that I could be immune to it is naïve. Recognizing the power of collective norms is part of an acknowledgment of our social nature. Consciousness of conditioning and contingency is important. Yet I think it should not be a surprise that consciousness does not simply eliminate conditioning. Knowing the possibility of change opens a path for change, but it does not simply bring it about.

The way I saw high heels *did* change. I used to see them simply as a mark of conformity with patriarchal norms and as a sign of the damage such norms could do (most high heels are hard on the back and the feet). Now I am interested in them. I check to see whether I like this or that particular version of them. And I want them, instead of feeling some range of contempt or pity for those who wear them or ignoring the fact that my feminist colleagues are wearing them. How do I bring judgment to bear on this consciousness of change?

After all, a great deal of feminism is devoted to figuring out ways of transforming social norms. Even if we are conscious about how stereotypes about women still affect us, it does not make us just give in to the inevitability of social conditioning. Why would I now decide that a norm I do not really approve of (high heels) is one I will participate in?

To try to bring judgment to bear, I can try to figure out why at this stage in my life I have started to be interested in these things. If it is a fear of getting old – a desire to hold onto lost youth – then it is not a desire I want to encourage. I experience the desire and wearing the heels as a kind of freedom and playfulness. I have tried to think about why I experience it as freedom. Of course, it is a freedom from previous constraint – a constraint that, of course, importantly freed me from convention. But is this freedom from constraint an illusion? Is it, after all, finally just a succumbing to convention? (Sometimes I have casually expressed it this way: "OK. I give up. I tried to resist for thirty years and could never actually shift how I saw flat shoes. Patriarchy wins.")

I think the sense of freedom is not just an illusion in part because of the dimension of play. I think there are many interesting connections between play and autonomy. Play involves invention, creation, and sometimes disruption. Although it can have rules, it can also bend rules and disregard rules that apply outside the play. My interest in high heels and even makeup feels playful, as opposed to meeting some requirement of conventional femininity. I remember noticing several years ago that the young women I would see on the bus seemed to be playing with makeup. It took all sorts of creative forms. It did not have the look of makeup that one had to wear because one's looks were inadequate without it. That sense of inadequacy and consequent necessity were part of what I remember arguing was wrong with makeup in the 1970s. I think there are still plenty of women who experience makeup in that way. But it looks to me like many of the younger ones do not.

The same can be said for colouring or dyeing hair, which used to be regarded as shameful. A leading commercial in the 1970s claimed that "only your hair dresser knows," which was, of course, desirable because being found out as one who was doing it was embarrassing. Now people dye their hair multiple colours and change the colours all the time. Even law professors can have bright streaks in their hair. No one is pretending they are not doing it (although I have to say that I still experience embarrassment when my dark roots begin to show).

There is a new community of fashion as play rather than as requirement, as expression rather than conformity. I think there is always some tension in this case since there are always norms that one is participating in or confronting. Nevertheless, I think the spirit of play is very different from the norms of female inadequacy that the feminists of the 1970s were critiquing. I think the feeling I have about high heels and makeup participates in this spirit of play rather than in an underlying sense of inadequacy.

Another part of why my reflections make me think the sense of play and freedom is not an illusion is that I do not feel like I am dressing for men. On the contrary, I think it now feels safe to dress this way because I am too old to be a sexual object of interest to most men. Women over fifty have a certain invisibility to men, which brings with it a freedom. However much being attractive was important to me when I was younger, I think it also always felt risky. It could attract trouble and danger in a variety of hard-to-predict ways. This is one idea I tried out with a few women who are about my age to see if it makes sense from their perspective, and they seem to think it does.

Some of the feeling of freedom also comes from finally feeling free of self-imposed constraints of (imagined) feminist taboos – which, as an actual matter of feminist common sense, may have faded away long before I let go of them. I feel much freer to dress according to my mood, my available time, and my level of energy (getting ready in skirts and dress shoes takes me a lot longer than pulling on pants and a sweater).

Finally, there is one other "influence" I am conscious of. I am a bit obsessed with physical comfort. I am physically very sensitive to things such as rough material, tags on shirts, and wool. Not being physically comfortable makes me anxious, and the anticipation of possible discomfort makes me anxious. For example, packing light seems impossible because I have to have the right pillow, I have to be sure I will not be be too hot or too cold, and so on. I recognize these patterns as part of a fear-based obsession (probably passed on to me by my father). It is not something I want to encourage. And, indeed, I think I am slightly less anxious about comfort than I used to be. The idea that shoes might pinch a bit after a few hours (when I can then change) seems to be okay. (I remember a line in *Sex in the City* where Carrie said: "I love these shoes. They pinch my toes, but I love them." When I first heard that line I found it literally incomprehensible. Now I have a pair of shoes like that.) So I see my interest in high heels as arising in part out of a loosening up, a release of fear and anxiety. So far, I feel confident that this loosening up has not been replaced by anxiety about always wearing the "right," or most fashionable, shoes. I have a wide range of footwear, from the most sensible to the fashionable and slightly uncomfortable (no spike heels so far). And I wear them as suits my mood and convenience (although I would not say that I know what accounts for the shifts in "mood" and the long stretches when I lose interest in high heels).

So where does this leave me in terms of whether I think I have made an autonomous judgment or an autonomous decision to which judgment was important? What role did an "enlarged mentality" play? First, I would pose the autonomy question like this: did I make an autonomous decision to take up a fashion convention that I find fun and exciting and that I still disapprove of? (I disapprove in the sense that I think it would be better if everyone thought that optimally comfortable, supportive shoes looked great as dress shoes with both skirts and pants. And it remains worth noting that while cosmetics for men have found their market niche, nothing remotely as impractical as high heels has become a widespread fashion norm for men – especially in the business world where high heels are required for women.)

I would say first that I am not quite certain about the autonomy of my decision. I am not sure that I know or understand all of what motivates this desire. The sense of not knowing was what made me so surprised in the first place. But I think that one cannot be autonomous without exercising judgment about how one engages with the inevitably conditioned preferences, desires, interests, or aspirations that one has. And I think a crucial first step in judgment is to become conscious of one's assumptions and motivations, which is what I have been trying to do.

For example, I emphasized a tuning into my feeling of play, fun, and excitement. It is not clear, however, how this feeling is part of judgment in the Arendtian sense. Where is the enlarged mentality? Judgment always involves self-consciousness, which usually involves a dimension of introspection. It is the next step of comparing what one observes in the introspection that brings in the enlarged mentality. (Actually, I think there are many ways that these different steps can come into play. It can be the reflection on a perspective of someone else that triggers the introspection to see what one's own views are.) So, in my example, as I noted earlier, I compare my sense of play with my earlier observations of young women's apparently playful stance toward makeup and what a big difference I thought that stance made. Playful self-decoration is very different from a felt need to hide inadequacies (thus, for example, I never thought that jewelry fell under the feminist ban I constructed).

I note, however, that in this case, I was using a standpoint that I thought or imagined that I observed. I did not actually talk to these young women to test out my perception. This neglect, in turn, leads to a more general way in which the Arendtian conception of judgment and the enlarged mentality points to a limitation in my introspection as well as limitations in the way that Arendt herself articulates the exercise of judgment.

First, Arendt says virtually nothing about the role of affect in judgment.[33] I think my earlier reflections point to the importance of consciousness about feelings as a dimension of judgment and standpoint as well as the need for the exercise of judgment when one tries to rely on affect – for the purposes of both judgment and autonomy. It is not enough to highlight the importance of emotion in cognition. One needs to think about the distinct forms of judgment that are necessary when we want our emotions to inform our judgment. Knowing when an emotion is a reliable guide is a complex matter that should neither make emotion subordinate to "reason" nor assume that knowing what one is feeling is sufficient ground to act on the feeling.

Second, Arendt says very little about the kind of experience it takes to be able to exercise the enlarged mentality. I think it is important to actually talk to people. Imagination is fine as long as it has a lot of real experience on which to build. And this real experience must be characterized by openness, attentiveness, and receptivity. I think my earlier stance on high heels – disapproval, contempt, and pity – was not marked by these characteristics, which presumably had something to do with my failure to talk to high-heel-wearing feminist friends about my self-imposed stricture.

Reflections on the Conditions of Judgment

It is important to think about all of the necessary components of a flourishing capacity for the enlarged mentality. It is equally important to think about what fosters this capacity and what impedes it. I think it turns out that relations of respect foster it. When one stands in a relation of respect and equality to another person, one is more likely to be attentive to what their actual standpoint is. One is less likely to have the hubris to think one can simply imagine it. I also think that this is a matter of practice – the more work one is willing to put into finding out about another person's perspectives, the more one will develop the appropriate attentiveness and humility.

And what about when the situation is one of inequality of power? There are a variety of complex questions about how this affects the injunction to take others' perspectives into account. While a serious examination of them would require a separate essay, I will note a few issues here. First, there are issues of what one might call temporal context. For example, at the moment that a student is being sexually harassed or abused by a teacher, I do not think the student is under an obligation to take the perspective of the abuser. However, even in this extreme context, it is possible that her judgment about how to best extricate herself from the situation will be improved by her ability to have a sense of how the situation looks from the perspective of the abuser. That is also likely to be the case in her exercise of judgment about how to proceed after the initial encounter. (Of course, if the perspective of the abuser threatens to obliterate her own perspective, it will not enhance autonomous judgment.) These questions touch, in turn, on yet another subject for a separate essay: whether the obligation to take the perspective of another proceeds from a claim of equality and equal respect, from the instrumental requirements that enable good judgment, or from some combination of the two.

I think it is too simple to say that those individuals subject to domination by people with power over them need not take the perspective of those in power. Those who are abusing their power may have no moral claim on their subordinates' attention (though even this position would not be clear if a claim of equal moral worth is part of the basis for taking the perspectives of others). However, good judgment on the part of the oppressed may be crucial to a transformation of the structure of unequal power. And good judgment in such a context is very likely to be aided by taking into account the perspective of the oppressor. This puzzle about what judgment requires in situations of oppressive power relations is just one version of the puzzle of how to determine whose perspectives to take into account (since we cannot, in the Arendtian model, actually take account of everyone's perspective). This area of Arendt's theory of judgment is perhaps in most need of elaboration.[34]

Reflecting on the question of what fosters and what impedes the exercise of the enlarged mentality brought me back to something that has long puzzled me. Why is there such a strong negative connotation to the term "judgmental" if judgment is inevitable and good judgment is a virtue? The answer, I think, is that a judgmental attitude interferes with good judgment. Being judgmental toward others (as in my stance toward women who dress for success) is not a stance of openness and attentiveness. One is not really standing in a relation of equality and respect when one is being judgmental. Of course, this is not an admonition to abandon the responsibility for judgment. It is a recognition that one cannot exercise judgment well when one is being judgmental.

In thinking about my high heels story, one can also see that not only negative emotions such as fear or ambition can interfere with judgment. A commitment to principle (such as mine to feminism) can also take a rigid form that interferes with the openness and responsiveness necessary for taking others' perspectives into account.[35] Similarly, as I just noted, such a commitment can lead to a kind of superiority that also cuts one off from taking the perspectives of others seriously. Finally, something as apparently trivial as embarrassment can also interfere with judgment. This was the case in my difficulties in assessing my new desire for high heels. Feeling embarrassed about this desire, I was reluctant to talk with others about it. I think that this experience turns out to point to another dimension of the humility that the enlarged mentality requires. And it is related to Arendt's point about judgment and disclosure. Not only do we need to be humble about our ability to know another person's standpoint, we also have to be willing to reveal our own standpoint, even when it may not show us in a good light. If we hide from our community of judgment, we freeze our opinions, and we do not subject them to comparison with the perspectives of others. We impoverish ourselves and our community of judgment.

I think this issue of disclosure is, in turn, related to my point about how some forms of commitment to principle can be barriers to judgment (and thus to autonomy). If it becomes too important to maintain an image of ourselves as right thinking and right acting, we may inadvertently close ourselves off from appropriate communities of judgment. We may impede our capacity for judgment and stunt our autonomy.

In sum, part of what we mean by being autonomous in an inevitably conditioned and contingent world is exercising judgment consistently and well. As we exercise judgment about those things we want to do, those values we want to embrace, and those interests we want to pursue, we become more fully autonomous. As we become more experienced in being autonomous, our capacity for judgment increases.

The Responsibility to Judge and the Trivial Nature of the High Heels Dilemma

The arguments above matter in part because judgment is a responsibility. At one level, judgment might be said to be inevitable. We seem to make daily judgments about what to do, whom to be friends with, what newspaper to buy, and what political party to support. The issue is whether these decisions are real judgments, in the Arendtian sense. They might simply be actions in accord with habit, convention, or the unexamined opinions of those around us. Arendt thinks that the failure to exercise real judgment, to engage the enlarged mentality rather than following convention can be tremendously dangerous. In ordinary times, people can get away with it. Their lives may be more impoverished and less autonomous (which is not an argument Arendt explicitly makes), but their failure of judgment may not wreak havoc on the lives of others. Of course, the context that Arendt referred to was Nazi Germany where the collective failure of judgment was catastrophic. As she argues in *Eichman in Jerusalem*, Arendt thinks that understanding that catastrophe also requires judgment. It requires going beyond conventional categories of thought.

Although the circumstances today are very different, I think the world is in equal need of real judgment. Without deep changes in patterns of behaviour, habits of thought, categories of responsibility, and the capacity to see interconnection, life on the planet will deteriorate in its quality, and human life (and that of many other life forms) may not be sustainable. The exercise of judgment allows for the emergence of fresh ways of understanding the world, and it facilitates the capacity to break through habitual, unreflective patterns of thought and behaviour – which is urgently needed for the environment as well as for new forms of resolution to long-standing patterns of injustice.

If the stakes are so high, why choose a "trivial" personal dilemma to exemplify the interconnection of judgment and autonomy? First, my choice echoes a long history of feminists bringing trivial, personal issues into the light of political and philosophical analysis. The question of who does the housework (a still unresolved problem) was an important example from the 1970s. The construction of female sexuality, of what is sexy, what is attractive, and what is an appropriate female professional "look" is not trivial. The issue of what is compulsory attire (which I will return to) is not trivial. Of course, one might still say that my own puzzle about the possibility of autonomous choice of attire is trivial in a way that a sustained critique of high heels and the construction of female sexuality would not be. However, I think that my trivial, personal example helps bring out my core argument that we cannot understand autonomy without understanding how it routinely calls for judgment and how judgment presupposes autonomy. I think the everyday obviousness of the social construction of the choices highlights the impossibility of choice that is free of influence, and this inevitability, then, directs our attention to the need for judgment about influence. It also brings to the fore how even admirable principles can take on a rigidity that undermines both judgment and autonomy.

This last point brings me to my second justification of my choice: the need for humour and humility in good judgment. I have now identified two kinds of failures in the context of judgment: (1) the failure to exercise true judgment and to complacently go along with convention and habits (personal and collective) of thought; and (2) the failure of being judgmental, which forecloses the openness and respect necessary for taking the perspectives of others. In the current state of environmental crisis, I think both are serious dangers. One can hope that there will be a gradual increase in everyone's sense of personal and collective responsibility for the well-being of the planet. The question remains, however, whether there is a way for this urgent matter of shared responsibility – of individual and collective inquiry into how to live in accordance with one's deepest commitments and how to judge those commitments – to be taken up in a way that is not oppressive and that is simultaneously serious, principled, open-minded, good-humoured, and humble. I think it is possible to take the plight of the earth seriously, and our responsibility seriously, without taking ourselves too seriously. I think such a stance may be crucial to getting large numbers of people to share this engagement. Although the example in this chapter is of much less importance, I like to think that my personal dilemma offers a serious engagement with the nature of autonomy, even a serious inquiry into the perspectives and contexts relevant to the puzzle – while revealing a slightly ridiculous story that shows a willingness not to take myself too seriously.

Having raised the issue of the environment, I have to acknowledge an obvious omission from my earlier discussion: the problem of consumption patterns. In my reflections, I did not weigh in the perspectives of those whose priority is the environment – the question of what valuable resources were wasted in the production of high heels and even the question of whether my personal financial resources might have been much better used (this despite the fact that these questions actually troubled me quite a bit as I "found myself" buying high-heeled shoes, along with similar questions about the labour practices involved in producing the shoes). These are perspectives that need to be considered in order to make a good judgment about what is involved in wearing high heels. They do engage the autonomous judgment question of being willing to judge "against one's community," when one's local (professional) community's expectations of consumption and attire are inconsistent with a truly responsible relation to the planet and those (human and other) we share it with. The issue of judging against one's community highlights the need for collective shifts in patterns of consumption – shifts in the common sense about what one should wear, what one should purchase, and what we collectively should be producing.[36] But this question is somewhat different from the one I wanted to focus on, which involves the inevitability of choosing between competing socially constructed norms.

Finally, what is my responsibility to those within my privileged, professional community? As a senior female professor, my attire can send messages about the possibility of non-conformity with conventional norms of female professional attire. What is my responsibility when these norms are actually close to compulsory for young female lawyers and the particular norm of high heels is bad for most women's backs and feet (if worn all day everyday)? Do I reinforce these norms by indulging my own wish to "play" with high heels as I move out of a previously constraining set of norms that forbade such play? A practice that is for me a wider scope of play, self-expression, and experimentation, which I can abandon for months at a time, may be compulsory for others. What kind of responsibility should this impose on my judgment? In practice, I have responded by wearing a wide range of attire, including footwear. I think it would be fair to say that most of the time I dress at the casual end of the spectrum, so that when I wear high heels it looks out of the ordinary and is the sort of thing that colleagues would comment on. I aspire to a more constant mixing up of what I wear, so that there is no predictable norm of my attire. I can hope that what such a style of attire models is not acquiescence to the dominant norm but, rather, the suggestion that there should not *be* a dominant norm (within some very broad range of reasonably modest attire for faculty – this, of course, being a separate subject for debate). Without imagining that any choice of "fashion," or even just clothing, can possibly be other than a choice among social constructions, one can try to foster a norm of (shifting) individual preference and of minimizing what counts as compulsory. It remains an open question for me (a judgment I have not yet worked through) how much scope for "fashion" would be left once one really integrated environmental concerns.[37]

Freedom in and through Community

The freedom of judgment begins with a freeing from internal constraints, limitations, and idiosyncrasies. Arendt uses the word liberation, and these same internal constraints can limit one's autonomy. Without consciousness of how one's perception of choices or values are limited, one's capacity to be one's self is constrained. But there is not simply a fixed self to "uncover" by removing limitations. Who we are develops in part through our increasing exercise of autonomy, which also means our increasing exercise of our capacity for judgment.

Judgment and autonomy are necessary for each other in part because they are both capacities that enable us to be free as social beings. Judgment provides us with an ongoing refraction of our views in light of the perspectives of others. Engaging in the enlarged mentality and communicating our judgments to others connects us to community even as it enables us to stand against it when necessary. It is because we are fundamentally relational beings that we need others to provide us with both the nurture and the touchstones of comparison that enable us to continually become ourselves, to shift and develop our relationship with the different dimensions of our "selves."

There are many kinds of barriers to engaging fully in this process. The one that I want to close by highlighting is fear. Fear takes many forms, and most of them close us off from others. The fear that we might not get it right keeps us from communicating our judgments. This non-disclosure not only deprives our community of our perspectives for the use of others in judgment, but it also deprives us of the possibility of change and development through connection, even in contestation. Even the fear of losing hold of our principled commitments in the face of pressure from the collective can render these commitments rigid and closed to re-evaluation. To really develop an enlarged mentality, it is important to engage seriously with those whose views we reject as well as those whose locations are different from ours. I think fear keeps us from doing both (as well as contempt and superiority).

I think the full engagement with others, which both judgment and autonomy require, takes a kind of courage. And I think we should take heart from a confidence that we are endowed with capacities that allow us to connect in ways that enhance our freedom. In North America, we are all subject to some extent to the idea that community poses a threat to individual freedom. It takes quite a bit of work to reframe this sense so that we see that, while there can be real threats, relating to others is ultimately the source of resistance to these threats. It is the relational and reciprocal nature of judgment and autonomy that enables us to meet, transform, and transcend these threats. We should have the courage to do so.

Notes

1 This idea of reciprocally interacting nested layers of relationships is elaborated in Jennifer Nedelsky, *Law's Relations: A Relational Theory of Self, Autonomy and Law* (Oxford: Oxford University Press, 2011) at c. 1.
2 Immanuel Kant, *Critique of Judgment*, translated by Werner S. Pluhar (Indianapolis, IN: Hackett Publishing, 1987); Hannah Arendt, "Crisis in Culture" in Hannah Arendt, ed., *Between Past and Future* (New York: Meridan Books, 1961) 197; and Hannah Arendt, *Lectures on Kant's Political Philosophy*, edited by Ronald Beiner (Chicago: University of Chicago Press, 1982).
3 I elaborate this argument in Jennifer Nedelsky, "Embodied Diversity: Challenges to Law" (1997) 42 McGill L.J. 91; Jennifer Nedelsky, "Communities of Judgment and Human Rights" (2000) 1 Theoretical Inquiries in Law 245; Jennifer Nedelsky, "Legislative Judgment and the Enlarged Mentality: Taking Religious Perspectives" in Richard Bauman and Tsvi Kahana, eds., *The Least Examined Branch: The Role of Legislatures in the Constitutional State* (Cambridge: Cambridge University Press, 2006) 93; Jennifer Nedelsky, "Law, Judgment, and Relational Autonomy" in Ronald Beiner and Jennifer Nedelsky, eds., *Judgment, Imagination and Politics: Themes from Kant and Arendt* (Lanham, MD: Rowman and Littlefield, 2001) 103. See also the other chapters in this volume.
4 Melvin Hill, ed., *Hannah Arendt: The Recovery of the Public World* (New York: St. Martin's Press, 1979) at 336.
5 See Jennifer Nedelsky, "Judgment, Diversity, and Relational Autonomy" in Nedelsky, *supra* note 1.
6 This is what characterizes "reflective judgment," as distinct from determinate judgment where a principle such as the categorical imperative can determine the outcome of a moral question.
7 This section is taken from Nedelsky, "Judgment, Diversity, and Relational Autonomy," *supra* note 5.
8 We will come later to the idea of a community of judgment, those whose perspectives the judger takes into account and with respect to whom we make claims of validity. Some academic institutions make a great effort to have their entire faculty included in a shared community of judgment about grading norms. Others are willing to accept the idea that the meaning of an A is only shared among sub-sets of like-minded colleagues who agree about the relevant standards. If there were a professor who saw grades as reflecting only her own standards and made no claim of agreement on anyone, her choice of grades would, in Arendtian terms, be a matter of preference or private opinion, not judgment.
9 For the purposes of this chapter, I will largely bracket the question of whether there are any claims that have this sort of truth quality. It seems likely to me that what Kant and Arendt see as the faculty of judgment applies to a much wider range of cognitive activities than either of them thought. Nevertheless, it is helpful to begin with the Kantian analytical distinction

between judgment and truth that can be proven and, thus, compel agreement. The primary source for Kant's theory of judgment is *Critique of Judgment, supra* note 2.

10 Drawing on Aristotle, Martha C. Nussbaum also develops this argument. See Martha C. Nussbaum, *Love's Knowledge: Essays on Law and Literature* (New York: Oxford University Press, 1990).

11 Kant, *supra* note 2 at 54, s. 6.

12 *Ibid.* at s. 19. This is Arendt's translation in Hannah Arendt, "Crisis in Culture" in Hannah Arendt, ed., *Between Past and Future* (New York: Meridan Books, 1961) 197 at 222. Werner Pluhar translates the sentence more prosaically as "[w]e solicit everyone else's assent because we have a basis for it that is common to all."

13 She is speaking here about critical thought: "It is precisely by applying critical standards to one's own thought that one learns the art of critical thought. And this application one cannot learn without publicity, without the testing that arises from contact with other people's thinking. In order to show how it works, I shall read to you two personal passages from letters Kant wrote in the 1770s to Marcus Herz." Hannah Arendt, *Lectures on Kant's Political Philosophy*, edited by Ronald Beiner (Chicago: University of Chicago Press, 1982) at 42. As we see in my discussion earlier, she then moves into a discussion of the *Critique of Judgment, supra* note 2, while continuing to use the language of critical thinking. I think this blurs a distinction she makes in other contexts – critical thinking is not something most people routinely engage in, and it is a mistake to assume that they will when thinking about the optimal structures of government. However, judgment is a capacity everyone has, although it is better educated in some than in others.

14 Arendt, *supra* note 13 at 42-43.

15 *Ibid.* at 42.

16 Arendt, "Crisis in Culture," *supra* note 12 at 221.

17 Kant, *supra* note 2 at 54, s. 6. Kant elaborates: "No one can use reasons or principles to talk us into a judgment on whether some garment, house, or flower is beautiful. We want to submit the object to our own eyes, just as if our likng of it depended on that sensation. And yet, if we then call the object beautiful, we believe we have a universal voice, and lay claim to the agreement of everyone, whereas any private sensation would decide solely for the observer himself and his liking." He then clarifies that "the universal voice is only an idea" (at 60, s. 8, para. 216).

18 Arendt, "Crisis in Culture," *supra* note 12 at 221.

19 *Ibid.* at 220-21.

20 Both the nature of the puzzle and the answer that relational autonomy provides are elaborated in Nedelsky, *supra* note 5.

21 Arendt, *supra* note 13 at 43.

22 *Ibid.*

23 *Ibid.* at 43 and 44. For the importance of this particularity, see Jennifer Nedelsky, "Communities of Judgment" in Nedelsky, *supra* note 1.

24 Arendt, *supra* note 13 at 43.

25 See Jennifer Nedelsky, "Legislative Judgment and the Enlarged Mentality: Taking Religious Perspectives" in Nedelsky, *supra* note 1.

26 Arendt, "Crisis in Culture," *supra* note 12 at 223.

27 *Ibid.*

28 *Ibid.* I would add that one can never completely liberate one's self from the limitations of one's experience.

29 Adolph Eichmann was a Nazi official who was tried, convicted, and sentenced to execution by a specially constituted Israeli court for his role in the genocide of European Jews during the Second World War. Hannah Arendt, reporting for the *New Yorker*, was among the many correspondents who covered this very public trial. Arendt's analysis of the trial was subsequently published in her book, *Eichmann in Jerusalem*. For a discussion of Arendt's theory of judgment in relation to her reports of the Eichmann trial, see Pnina Lahav, "The Eichmann Trial, the Jewish Question, and the American-Jewish Intelligentsia" (1992) 72(3) Boston Univ. L. Rev. 555 at 558-59; Shoshana Felman, "Theatres of Justice: Arendt in Jerusalem, the Eichmann Trial, and the Redefinition of Legal Meaning in the Wake of the Holocaust"

(2000) 1 Theoretical Inquiries in Law 465 at 465, n. 1; Hannah Arendt, *Eichmann in Jerusalem: A Report on the Banality of Evil* (New York: Viking Press, 1963); and Leora Y. Bilsky, "When Actor and Spectator Meet in the Courtroom: Reflections on Hannah Arendt's Concept of Judgment" in R. Beiner and J. Nedelsky, eds., *Judgment, Imagination and Politics: Themes from Kant and Arendt* (Lanham, MD: Rowman and Littlefield, 2001).

30 See Nedelsky, *supra* note 25.

31 Marilyn Friedman, "Autonomy, Social Disruption, and Women" and Linda Barclay, "Autonomy and the Social Self" both in Catriona MacKenzie and Natalic Stoljar, eds., *Relational Autonomy: Feminist Perspectives on Autonomy, Agency, and the Social Self* (New York: Oxford University Press, 2000). I also discuss this puzzle in Nedelsky, *supra* note 1.

32 See Nedelsky, *supra* note 25.

33 See my discussion of affect in Jennifer Nedelsky, "Embodied Diversity: Challenges to Law" in Nedelsky, *supra* note 1.

34 It is worth noting that feminist standpoint theorists, among others, have long argued that the oppressed often learn to take the perspective (learn the language, norms, and assumptions) of the oppressor. They then have the wider perspective because they know both their own and that of those in power, while the latter know only their own. There are also extraordinary stories, such as that of Nelson Mandela while in prison in Apartheid South Africa. His capacity to see the humanity of his jailors not only sustained his own self-respect but claimed respect from them. Nelson Mandela, *Long Walk to Freedom: The Autobiography of Nelson Mandela* (Toronto: Little, Brown and Company, 1995).

35 It seems possible to me that the fact that many young women reject the term feminist may have to do with such rigidity (both real and falsely portrayed in the media).

36 See Nedelsky, *supra* note 25, for the question of shifting common sense.

37 Marge Piercy in *Woman on the Edge of Time* depicted a utopia in which there were frequent "feasts" for which people designed "flimsies," artful creations of disposable attire made of light material (I imagine them being easily biodegradable). Thus, they had individually generated fashion for celebratory occasions, combined with daily practicality and environmental sensibility. Marge Piercy, *Woman on the Edge of Time* (New York: Alfred A. Knopf, 1976).

3
A Relational Approach to Equality: New Developments and Applications
Christine M. Koggel

Introduction to Equality Analysis

The United Nations millennium report, *We the Peoples*, opens its chapter "Freedom from Want" with this description:

> Nearly half the world's population still has to make do on less than $2 per day. Approximately 1.2 billion people – 500 million in South Asia and 300 million in Africa – struggle on less than $1 ... Of a total labour force of some 3 billion, 140 million workers are out of work altogether, and a quarter to a third are underemployed. [The UN millennium report then calls on the international community to] adopt the target of halving the proportion of people living in extreme poverty, so lifting more than 1 billion people out of it, by 2015.[1]

In August 2008, the World Bank redefined extreme poverty from the UN cut-off of US $1 per day to include all those living on US $ 1.25 per day or less. The new definition brought the number living in dire poverty to 1.4 billion – more than 400 million more than under the old definition – thus determining that the UN millennium goal of cutting extreme poverty in half by 2015 will need to lift a lot more people out of poverty than the original target of 1 billion. Moreover, recent events suggest that reaching these targets is very unlikely. A high-level event hosted by the United Nations' secretary-general, Ban Ki-moon, in September 2008 was intended to help re-energize the world's faltering commitment to the millennium development goals. However, the backdrop to organizing this event was the absence of many world leaders at the event and resistance by many countries to increase their aid. Canada, for example, spends 0.28 percent of its gross national income on aid, a ratio that is lower than it was two years ago and puts Canada sixteenth out of the twenty-two donor nations from the Organisation for Economic Co-operation and Development. Following on the heels of this event was the collapse of the global economy, a factor that is increasing the number of people living in poverty. The collapse is also lowering commitments by rich countries to increase aid in a context in which their own citizens are suffering from increased unemployment, failed mortgages, and the collapse of financial institutions and big companies.

The picture of increased poverty is just as dismal when we turn to data showing gaps in income and wealth between the rich and the poor. In *Worlds Apart: Measuring International and Global Inequality*, Branko Milanovic collects data to show that the incomes of the richest 5 percent of people in the world equal those of the poorest 80 percent.[2] In its 2005 annual report, *The State of the World's Human Rights*, Amnesty International makes the following claim: "The fact that so many people live in inhuman conditions, and that the gap between rich and poor is widening between and within countries, directly contradicts the notion that all human beings are born equal in dignity and rights."[3] This last quotation connects inequalities in income and wealth to violations of the equal dignity of all human beings and thereby turns the focus to the moral imperative that motivated equality theory in the liberal tradition in the first place – that all human beings are equal and ought to be treated with dignity and respect.

Although this chapter begins by providing accounts of inequality in terms of low income levels and gaps in wealth, the central argument will be that these data only begin to tell the story about the meaning of equality and the different kinds of inequality. One lesson to be learned from the Amnesty International quotation is that we need to retrieve the basic understanding of what should motivate us to care about removing inequalities in wealth and income – the idea that poverty is a violation of equal dignity and respect. However, retrieving this understanding requires more sophisticated and detailed analyses of equality than that which has been cited thus far in data on inequalities in income and gaps in wealth. Some of this analysis has been done in the past two decades in, for example, the United Nations Development Program's (UNDP) *Human Development Report*, an annual publication that began in the early 1990s and borrows from, and is influenced by, Amartya Sen's capabilities approach, which is examined later in this chapter.

The 2003 *Human Development Report*, for example, links inequalities in wealth and income to other sorts of inequalities: "Many are seeing life expectancy plummet due to HIV/AIDS. Some of the worst performers – often torn by conflict – are seeing school enrolments shrink and access to basic health care fall. And nearly everywhere the environment is deteriorating."[4] The linking of kinds of inequalities, those that come with having low income or gaps in wealth, has been an important development for conceptualizing equality in terms of equal dignity and respect. The idea is that dignity and respect are violated when low income determines that one's life is shortened by not being able to afford medicine or by living in areas with no access to clean water. The description already implies that removing inequalities will involve more than increasing a person's income.

Also evident in contemporary equality analysis are accounts of the people who are more likely to suffer inequalities and what sorts of inequalities they are likely to suffer. The Association for Women's Rights in Development (AWID), for example, draws attention to how the advance of economic globalization has had a disproportionately negative effect on women, including the devaluing and undervaluing of women's work, the disruption of women's access to subsistence resources, the privatization of basic services, the reduction of access to health care and education, the increase in inequalities in income and property ownership, the decrease in women's access to decision making, and the increase in the number of women living in poverty worldwide.[5] As argued by numerous authors in the fields of economics and development, these gender inequalities persist in both Western liberal democracies and Third World countries and are exacerbated when intersecting factors such as race, class, ethnicity, and disability are taken into account.

To summarize the discussion of equality thus far, progress has been made in mainstream accounts that now acknowledge equality analysis to be more complex than citing income levels or gaps in wealth. Progress has also been made in understanding how kinds of inequalities intersect and overlap in ways that generate or perpetuate inequalities for particular others who are members of disadvantaged groups. What is less well understood, however, is what sort of approach is best suited for understanding the full complexity of equality analysis and for addressing the kinds of inequalities that are thereby revealed through this analysis. In this chapter, I take the following steps on the road to defending a relational approach to equality as one that can pinpoint what is still missing in accounts of equality and what is needed to address inequalities.

In the section that follows, I examine what I take to be the main contender for an approach that captures the complexity of equality analysis, namely the capabilities approach. My discussion of the capabilities approach will focus on Sen's version to argue that his approach is important for making the complexity and interconnectedness of kinds of inequalities clear and convincing but that it fails, in the end, to account for the inequalities in power and the role that power plays at the personal, local, institutional, national, and global levels. For this more complex account, we need to move away from an analysis that begins with individuals to an analysis that examines the relationships in which individuals are situated and embedded. By providing a brief sketch of relational theory as feminists have developed it over the past few decades, I argue that relational theory provides this needed analysis of relationships and of the effects of power within them. I then turn to my own work in constructing a relational theory of equality and show its development from an early account that focused on the concept of equality in traditional liberal theory and societies to an approach that is suited to explaining the kinds of inequalities present in the contemporary context of globalization, the global economy, and the greater dependence and interdependence of states and people. I argue that a relational approach to equality can provide a more adequate account of these features of the contemporary global context and of the inequalities that continue to be missed than have mainstream liberal accounts.

In the following sections of the chapter, I illustrate what relational theory offers and why it is effective by exploring two examples that highlight the workings of contemporary global networks of interactive relationships among liberatory social movements: (1) local, national, and international nongovernmental organizations (NGOs) and (2) international financial institutions, agencies, and organizations. These relationships have emerged precisely from that feature of globalization that allows the kind of networking within and across borders that has worked to change the understandings of, and the policies for, removing inequalities. Relational theory is not only able to illustrate these positive features of the interactive and changing nature of relationships in the global context, but it is also able to uncover and challenge relationships of power that perpetuate various kinds of inequalities. As pessimistic as we have reason to be in the current context of the collapse of the global economy, there is reason for optimism and hope in the solidarity and commitment to change that is evident in recent work with titles such as *Blessed Unrest* (by Paul Hawken),[6] *The Geography of Hope* (by Chris Turner),[7] and *New Rights Advocacy* (by Paul J. Nelson and Ellen Dorsey).[8] In the final sections, I work with insights from *New Rights Advocacy* and my own experiences observing and working with a local NGO in Indonesia to illustrate and apply insights from my expanded relational account of equality. I use examples of inequalities in health care throughout the chapter not only because these present clear challenges to equality theory in the liberal tradition but also because they are particularly urgent and vexing in a globalized world. Viewing inequalities through a relational lens and applying the resulting insights, I argue, provides a better understanding of the complex set of inequalities in the global context and more effective ways to address them than has been evident in the literature thus far.

Amartya Sen and the Capabilities Approach

Two features of equality analysis noted in the introduction are worth repeating here. First, an account of equality needs more than statistics on income levels or gaps in wealth. Inequalities in one domain such as income are connected with, and have an impact on, inequalities in other domains such as access to health care, education, paid work, or reproductive choices. It will matter, then, to an analysis of inequalities in income and wealth whether a country has universal health care or access to publicly funded education. In countries without these resources merely increasing the income of those who are poor will not be sufficient for removing inequalities of increased morbidity, disease, infant mortality, or unemployment. The neighborhood in which I live and the schools, hospitals, and services that are available to me can limit what I can do with an increased income to improve health, employment prospects, or daycare options. Second, the fact that inequalities are interconnected calls for a contextual analysis of how these manifest themselves in specific contexts and for specific people. Not only do we need to identify inequalities in wealth and its effects on people, but we also need to identify those who are most harmed and most vulnerable in order to understand how factors such as gender, race, disability, and so on work to create or sustain inequalities of various sorts.

Amartya Sen's decades-long work on answering the question "equality of what?" has made a significant contribution to changing the prevailing and simplified conceptions of equality.[9] This work now finds its way into his version of the capabilities approach, which is an approach that Sen and Martha Nussbaum are credited for launching and then developing in different ways. In brief, the capabilities approach focuses on what people are able to do and to be. The account provides descriptions of how human beings actually function as a base from which to explore the moral question of whether people have the capability of functioning in the ways that matter to them. Notoriously, Sen refuses to go the route of Nussbaum in listing human functions and capabilities.[10] Instead, he discusses capabilities such as the capability to live to an old age, to engage in economic transactions, and to participate in political activities as ones that all human beings have reason to value. His account, thus, is an approach that explores whether people have the freedom to function in ways that matter to their well-being.

In Sen's recent work on the capabilities approach, he turns to an explicit use of the language of freedom to argue for the importance of removing "unfreedoms," such as premature mortality, undernourishment, and ill health, and of enhancing people's freedom to pursue goals and objectives that they have reason to value. Sen thinks income matters, but he argues that poverty is best understood as the deprivation of capabilities: "Policy debates have indeed been distorted by over-emphasis on income poverty and income inequality, to the neglect of deprivations that relate to other variables, such as unemployment, ill health, lack of education, and social exclusion."[11] He uses interpersonal comparisons of cross- and intra-cultural differences to argue that attention needs to be on what people are able to be and to do and not on their incomes alone. According to Sen, data may show that income levels for virtually all Americans are higher than those for people in many parts of the world. Yet they do not tell us about deprivations and inequalities suffered by some Americans that turn out to be worse in terms of what people are able to be and to do than those suffered by people in parts of the world that are taken to be much poorer in terms of levels of income.

In *Development as Freedom,* Sen cites data that show that "even though the per capita income of African Americans in the United States is considerably lower than that of the white population, African Americans are very many times richer in income terms than the people of China or Kerala (even after correcting for cost-of-living differences)."[12] And yet "African Americans have an absolutely lower chance of reaching mature ages than do people of many third world societies, such as China, or Sri Lanka, or parts of India (with different arrangements of health care, education, and community relations)."[13] Measured by income alone, African Americans would seem to be doing well in comparison to people in most parts of the world. Sen argues that we need to expand the informational base to take into account deprivations and various "unfreedoms" that go beyond one's capacity to buy basic goods needed for survival: "The broadening of the informational base from income to the basic capabilities enriches our understanding of inequality and poverty in quite radical ways."[14] On Sen's account, then, comparing the lives and life prospects of African Americans with people in China or Kerala can help to explain why income levels cannot overcome the effects of little or no access to health care for many Americans. Sen's point is that African Americans may have more income than people in poorer countries, but they also have higher rates of early morbidity, disease, and ill health.

The capability approach also fares well in capturing inequalities based on one's membership in a traditionally disadvantaged group. The fact that people live lives and have choices that are shaped and limited by discrimination is open for description and analysis on Sen's account. After describing women's inequalities in Third World countries, for example, Sen concludes: "The extensive reach of women's agency is one of the more neglected areas of development studies, and most urgently in need of correction. Nothing, arguably, is as important today in the political economy of development as an adequate recognition of political, economic and social participation and leadership of women. This is indeed a crucial aspect of 'development as freedom.'"[15] Addressing gender inequalities is important for Sen not only because it limits what women can be and do but also because removing inequalities in health, education, work opportunities, and political participation suffered by women is integrally connected with removing inequalities of various sorts for children, for communities, for countries, and for the global economy.

In summary, Sen's account can be said to capture both of the features of equality analysis mentioned earlier: the interconnectedness of kinds of inequalities and the need for a detailed, contextual account to capture them. Its richness in providing an informational base that demands context-specific attention has implications for theory and for policy: "The respective roles of personal heterogeneities, environmental diversities, variations in social climate, differences in relational perspectives and distributions within the family have to receive the serious attention they deserve for the making of public policy."[16] For Sen, the making of public policy should happen in and through debate and in conjunction with the participation of those who live in, and are affected by, conditions, practices, and values in specific contexts.

Yet I want to argue that Sen's complex, contextual, and integrated account of equality does not go far enough. Its focus is still too exclusively on individuals and on the goal of enhancing their agency so that they can live lives that they have reason to value. It does not delve sufficiently deep to question the actual relationships assumed by, and embedded in, institutions and structures or how these can entrench inequalities that are difficult to understand and to remove. What is missing in Sen, as has been argued by feminists such as myself and Marianne Hill, is an analysis of how the political, economic, and social structures embed norms and institutions that stand in the way of removing some inequalities or of having some people participate in debates about those inequalities. What is needed, therefore, is an account that uncovers, questions, and challenges the existing norms and institutional structures of power at all levels.[17] For this to occur, we need an analysis that captures the effects of personal, social, and institutional relationships on those who do not have the voice or power to contribute to debates, discussion, or decision making about the policies that affect them. What we need, I shall argue, is an account that puts relationships rather than individuals at the centre of the analysis.

Looking ahead to my main argument of what a relational approach to equality can provide, increasing gaps between rich and poor people and countries create and sustain relationships of power that, in turn, make it difficult to challenge or change the neo-liberal policies and global structures that keep those relations in place. These are features and factors that have not been part of the analysis in mainstream political theory or in studies by major international and financial institutions. While Sen's contribution has been critical both for expanding an equality analysis beyond the provision of data on income and wealth and for developing a complex and contextual account of the interconnectedness of kinds of inequalities, these features are also missing in his account.

To close this section and highlight what I take to be missing in equality analysis, it is useful to return to a brief discussion of the *Human Development Report* cited earlier and to contrast this report with Susan Sherwin's account in this volume. The *Human Development Report* describes how life expectancy has plummeted as a result of HIV/AIDS, but it is less explicit in explaining, for example, how this is exacerbated in developing countries when powerful pharmaceutical companies in rich countries control the patents and prices for HIV/AIDS medications. By contrast, Sherwin names the effects of power in her account of autonomy in which she argues that we need to be sensitive to the effects of dependencies and interdependencies emerging from a capitalist global economy. These kinds of social relations, she argues, constrain opportunities at the personal, institutional, and global level to address issues such as global warming, extreme poverty, or public health. As will be evident in the sections that follow, while there is relationality in Sen's account of the interconnectedness of kinds of inequality and of the importance of interpersonal comparisons, a focus on relationships themselves, rather than on the individuals in them, can better explain not only the significance of Sen's contribution but also what continues to be absent in it.

Relational Theory: Background and Summary

As developed by a number of feminists who have worked within, but are critical of, the liberal tradition,[18] relational theory uses as its starting point the fact that human beings exist in relationships and do not come into the world as the independent, fully autonomous, and self-sufficient agents assumed by many traditional liberal theorists.[19] This starting point continues to connect the wide range of recent developments in relational theory, including those in this volume. It is present in Jennifer Llewellyn's account of restorative justice and in Sue Campbell's account of relational remembering, both of which challenge individualism in liberal theory by having us rethink the role of the truth and reconciliation commissions tasked with addressing a history of past injustices. It is also present in Maneesha Deckha's questioning of a humanist paradigm that underlies the use of non-human animals in medical research. These and other authors also work with the central insight that it is often difficult to recognize the very framework that is taken for granted and through which dominant understandings of concepts such as autonomy, justice, or issues in health care or medical research take hold and become entrenched.

This point about a taken-for-granted framework was central in early work on relational theory that made use of, and then departed in significant ways from, Carol Gilligan's *In a Different Voice*. A key insight in Gilligan's text is that an ethic of justice, the dominant approach to moral theory in the liberal tradition, presents but one way of orienting oneself in the world and making moral decisions. While scholars continue to debate whether women are indeed more caring than men, I think this debate misses the real insight that Gilligan herself attempts to clarify in "Letter to Readers, 1993," a preface written for a new edition of *In a Different Voice*: "When I hear my work being cast in terms of whether women and men are really (essentially) different or who is better than whom, I know that I have lost my voice, because these are not my questions. Instead, my questions are about our perceptions of reality and truth: how we know, how we hear, how we see, how we speak. My questions are about voice and relationship."[20]

While feminists such as Fiona Robinson, Joan Tronto, and Virginia Held have focused on care in order to develop an ethic that is meant to rival, supplement, or be compatible with an ethic of justice, others have focused on relationships in order to re-conceptualize traditional liberal concepts.[21] A common goal is to highlight what is missing in individualist accounts of the self and to develop the theory and policy that emerge from the resulting relational approach. A central feature of the relational approach, as it has developed over the years, has been to expand the network of relationships beyond those of dependency on which feminists, and early care ethicists in particular, have tended to focus. As I noted in earlier work on relational theory, "relations of power, oppression, dominance, exploitation, authority, and justice form identities and self-concepts just as much as relations of dependency, benevolence, care, self-sacrifice, and friendship do."[22] On a relational approach, liberal theory's cherished notions of autonomy, justice, or equality are not relinquished, but, instead, they are reinterpreted in and through the network of complex and ever-changing relationships in which each of us is situated.

A relational account of autonomy as sketched by Sherwin, for example, would explain autonomy as a capacity to shape one's life that cannot but emerge through an engagement with particular others in a network of relationships. Moreover, those relationships and the possibilities for changing or expanding them are in turn shaped by social practices and political contexts. In other words, by analyzing the network of relationships in which one is situated we obtain a more coherent and accurate understanding of what can enhance but also hinder an agent's capacity to make choices and determine the course of his or her life than if we understand agents as best able to know and pursue their own interests free from the influence and interference of others. While this specific criticism of the primacy of non-interference (negative rights) does not apply to Sen, it can be said that as broad as his account of inequalities is it does not cover those inequalities that are shaped by relationships (and the institutional norms embedded in them) that one is powerless to exit, challenge, or change. In justifying the range and potential of relational theory, feminists have argued that paying attention to the relationships that people are in draws special attention to the workings of power and to the ways in which factors such as race, gender, disability, and so on are entrenched in norms and institutions that limit one's autonomy or determine the kinds of inequalities that one suffers.

In my early work on the concept of equality, I argued that a focus on relationships challenges the traditional liberal understanding of equality but does not jettison equality as a concept or goal. A relational approach to equality has us examine the details of concrete kinds of relationships and the shaping of them through particular social practices and in specific contexts. With respect to challenging simplified accounts of equality, a relational approach is like Sen's in highlighting the interconnectedness of kinds of inequalities. Unlike Sen, however, a relational approach examines the kinds, levels, and extent of inequalities by understanding them in the context of relationships in which people are without power or situated at the margins of society. An adequate conception of equality needs to connect these basic relational features of a person's life to the analysis of the range of inequalities that thereby emerge for some people – specifically, people who are members of groups or of countries who have been traditionally disadvantaged and who continue to suffer inequalities.

As is the case in Sen's account as well, a relational account holds that narrow and abstract accounts of equality as resources, as well-being, or as opportunity cannot stand alone and be an all encompassing theory of equality. According to Sen, well-being is tied to agency in ways that also connect with accounts of the resources and opportunities that an agent has in the context in which she lives. However, relational theory provides a different description and analysis of these factors than does Sen. A relational approach can show how an account of the opportunities that people in relationships of inequality or oppression actually have is tied to an account of inequalities in resources, well-being, life prospects, and so on. It then moves from here to also show that a person's opportunities are limited by oppressive relationships at the level of both the personal and the institutional in ways that determine the resources one gets, the perceptions of what one deserves or is capable of, and the power that one has to make changes. Yet it is at the level of the institutional structures that are in place that it becomes more difficult to grasp where power has its hold in the taken-for-granted assumptions about "proper" social, political, and economic structures and arrangements. These points about relationships and taken-for-granted assumptions can be illustrated through a discussion of homelessness.

Being homeless in a society that upholds the primacy of individual property rights means that the homeless have no place to satisfy basic bodily needs of washing, cooking, sleeping, or going to the bathroom unless someone with property lets them into their home or there are areas of public or common property that allow these activities. Having no home and no address in turn affect one's ability to do basic things such as apply for jobs, vote, receive welfare checks, go to school, or get a health card. Moreover, in a society in which having property gives you access to resources and to standing as a citizen, perceptions of, and attitudes toward, the homeless are reflected in increasingly popular laws and policies that remove them from the public places where they can be seen, heard, or encountered. By examining relationships between homeless people and the public or law officials who "deal" with them, a relational approach can thereby reveal that those who are homeless have no power or voice to do things such as challenge stereotypes of them, affect policy, or change the conditions under which their inequalities in well-being, life prospects, self-respect, income, opportunity, or participation are even understood, let alone alleviated.

A focus on relationships can also reveal that institutional norms have consequences that rarely get recognized, let alone challenged, when the framework of property rights is taken for granted. The situation for those who are homeless is different from what Sen describes in the data he cites about African Americans having higher rates of early morbidity and infant mortality than many people in developing countries. In the case of homeless people without addresses, income, or access to health care facilities in the United States, studies on the effects of homelessness on health would be difficult to conduct, let alone compile. At least two things can explain this situation: the absence of universal health care in the United States and the lack of sympathy for homeless people who are taken to have brought on their own state of affairs. Even in a country such as Canada with universal health care, getting a health card that legitimates your status as a receiver of health care benefits requires that you have an address.

If we were to open up space for recognizing that the primacy of rights to individual freedom and to property are norms that are not universal but that are assumed and taken for granted in specific countries and cultures, discussions of homelessness could change. Describing the real life situation of homelessness from the perspective of homeless people helps to show the contradiction in holding that property rights enhance freedom when those without property lack freedom in the most basic ways. Moreover, in confronting norms that result in their lack of power to affect change, a space could be opened up for questioning the relationships, or absence of them, that are set up between those with property and those without. Policies for addressing homelessness could move from the too narrow and exclusive goal of finding jobs or homes for them and thereby opening up their "opportunities." Instead, attention could be given to what can be learned about the very structures that continue to allow and even increase the numbers of people who are disenfranchised, marginalized, and powerless in societies committed to achieving equality.

A focus on relationships shows that inequalities cannot be studied in isolation one from the other or reduced to a generalized account that has one kind of inequality addressed (providing more income) or one kind of equality propounded (expanding opportunities). As shown earlier, Sen convincingly makes the case for equality analysis that uses a broad informational base. When it comes to policy implications, however, he turns to a defence of the fundamental value of public participation and discussion as a way to shape policy: "[P]ublic participation in these valuational debates – in explicit or implicit forms – is a crucial part of the exercise of democracy and responsible social choice. In matters of public judgment, there is no escape from the evaluative need for public discussion."[23] Sen defends the importance of having a voice in public debate at the same time as he fails to acknowledge the very institutional norms and structures that bar some from having a say. As is evident in the discussion of homelessness, this lack of recognition reflects a failure to confront and question existing norms and structures that make some voices easy to ignore or hard to hear and understand. This point about the role of norms has been forcefully defended by Gilligan in the case she advances for a different voice, one that has been hard to hear and understand. It is also a point that I incorporate and defend in my relational account of equality, an account that we can begin to assemble by identifying its key features.

In previous work, I have argued that attending to the broad network of relationships in which people are situated allows us to identify several features distinctive to a feminist relational approach. A relational approach (1) is contextual in that it allows us to attend to the details of the lives of those affected by various kinds of unequal and oppressive relationships – relationships that are in turn shaped by particular social practices and political contexts; (2) uncovers the governing norms and practices that sustain various inequalities for those who are powerless and disadvantaged; and (3) reveals the importance of the perspectives of those adversely affected by relationships of power as sources for learning about various kinds of inequalities and the structures that sustain them. The discussion of homelessness illustrates the importance of all three features. With the all too brief sketch of Sen behind us, it can now be said that Sen's account succeeds in capturing the need for a contextual and detailed analysis of equality as outlined in the first feature but that it fails to capture the significance of relationships of power in specific contexts with respect to forms of inequality that emerge from them. In the section that follows, I want to further probe the strength and potential of relational theory by building on the features already outlined and then apply this expanded account to an analysis of equality in the contemporary global context.

Expanding the Scope and Reach of Relational Theory: The Global Context

In an increasingly interdependent world, lives, relationships, and conditions are as affected by global structures and policies as they are by local and national factors. The local, national, and global spheres also intersect in various ways to shape inequalities and to determine people's life prospects in specific contexts and through particular conditions.[24] A focus on the complex network of relationships in the global context can show that the very ways in which inequalities are measured, policies are implemented, and power is enacted are fashioned in and through relationships of power.

These relationships are exemplified at the global level between rich and poor countries, between multinational and transnational corporations and their workers in Third World countries, between international financial institutions and national organizations and movements, and between powerful international NGOs and the local NGOs that rely on them for funding. These relationships are complex in that they can intersect and overlap in ways that reflect their interactive dimensions and their ever-changing dynamics in the global context.

In previous work, I have attempted to develop a relational account applicable to the global context by incorporating two features in addition to the three outlined earlier.[25] First, human beings have bodily needs, and being able to respond in morally appropriate ways to these embodied realities matters to accounts of autonomy and to an analysis of equality. Achieving equality of any sort is restricted when bodily needs are not met or when bodies are unhealthy or susceptible to disease or premature morbidity. These claims are easily illustrated in the example of homelessness where the most basic bodily needs of going to the bathroom, eating, and sleeping are made increasingly difficult in North American cities that reduce the number of public washrooms or implement laws that prevent the homeless from sleeping in public or common areas. Possibilities for enhancing autonomy and for removing inequalities are improved through bodies that are fed, sheltered, safe, healthy, and engaged in meaningful participation in relationships and communities. While it may fit with an account of rights to individual freedom and property to say that equality is satisfied when no laws prevent a person from owning a home, these rights are meaningless for the homeless person confronted with barriers to basic freedoms that people with homes either take for granted or ignore in the case of the homeless. Since a key feature of care ethics is its call for responding to the concrete needs of others, relational theory can only be enriched when an account of the importance of responding to bodily needs is incorporated.

The second feature makes use of the fact that bodies and their needs are increasingly affected by globalization to argue that attention needs to be paid to relationships of power at local, national, and global levels that shape bodies disempowered by the very structures and relationships in which they are embedded. One way to apply this insight to the example of homelessness is to say that the collapse of the global economy has had an effect not only on the numbers of people who are homeless in a particular country but also on the ability of some countries to maintain their once strong commitment to social welfare policies in the face of pressures to decrease the national debt or to accept loans on condition that they dismantle these programs. Expanded in this way, relational theory can highlight the workings of power and its detrimental effects on relationships of all kinds and at all levels, including those in the contemporary global context.

The expanded account of the significance of bodily needs can explain how social processes and political structures that are part of an increasingly interdependent global order determine which bodies are, or become, needy in ways that highlight the responsibilities we have to respond to those needs. While she does not use the word "relational," Iris Marion Young's work on a social connection model fits the kind of account that I am describing and defending. Young's focus is on defending an account of responsibility that is "grounded in the fact that some structural social processes connect people across the world without regard to political boundaries."[26] While she is concerned to draw out responsibilities that demand our attention in the current global context, I am concerned about uncovering and analyzing norms that shape and structure the social processes and global order in ways that determine the kinds of inequalities that people suffer.

An important part of this analysis is to acknowledge that mainstream liberal understandings of equality as having the opportunity to compete in a free market, to have property, and to have one's negative rights of non-interference upheld are expectations and norms that are not universal – they are challenged in non-Western parts of the globe. We need to be able to understand the relationships of power that have allowed liberal assumptions about the virtues of the market and of capitalist structures to dominate conceptions of equality, justice, development, human rights, and globalization itself. We need to pay attention to relationships of power both within and across borders, to how these relationships are created and sustained by inequalities in wealth and income prevalent in the current economic global order, and to why these inequalities entrench a host of other inequalities. To return to the example of inequalities in health care, inequalities in this domain can be created when one lives in a poor country that is forced to remove funding for health care facilities as part of an agreement for repaying loans to an international financial institution or as a condition for receiving aid from a rich country. The resulting increased susceptibility to things such as disease, infant mortality, and low life expectancy in the poor country help to reveal the close connection between the failure to meet bodily needs and the range of inequalities that thereby emerge. Importantly, the example also shows that in addition to naming these factors as inequalities, we need to expose and question global economic structures and policies that can paralyze the ability of poor countries to set their own public policy or to respond to the needs of their own citizens.

One lesson is that features of globalization have succeeded in entrenching relations of power within and across borders, and these have in turn shaped dominant assumptions and expectations that neo-liberal commitments to open markets and to the undermining of economic, social, and cultural rights can succeed in removing inequalities. While these assumptions may be more open to challenge now in the aftermath of the collapse of the global economy, we still need the tools that relational theory gives us for providing the kind of detailed, contextual, and accurate descriptions of the range of inequalities and for uncovering and analyzing relationships of power that create or sustain them. At the same time that it is difficult to conceive how globally dominant norms, structures, and institutions can be changed, insights emerge when the focus is on the interactive aspects of the relationships themselves.

The engagement with concrete others as they set about to satisfy needs, struggle with barriers, advocate for others, or challenge structures and policies holds promise for drawing out the ways in which power and relationships of power can be used in positive ways to enact and implement new policy ideas and initiatives. The promise is in relational theory's ability to highlight the positive potential of new and emerging interactive networks of liberatory social movements and of local, national, and international NGOs and institutions. The final sections that follow attempt to provide this description and analysis by using two examples of relationships in their interactive settings, one from a recent publication called *New Rights Advocacy* and the other from my own research that involved observing and working with a local NGO in Indonesia. When interpreted through the lens of relational theory, these examples show the potential for changing the discourse and the means of communication as well as the theory and policy.

Avenues of Hope and Change

In *New Rights Advocacy: Changing Strategies of Development and Human Rights NGOs*, Paul Nelson and Ellen Dorsey agree with the analysis in the introduction to this chapter, namely that poverty and inequality are not only more acute now than they were a generation ago but that "they are more widely and prominently discussed."[27] The widespread discussion is evident in the formulation of the millennium development goals and its aftermath of sustained global pressure to adopt commitments to alleviating poverty. Rather than comment on the why and how of this growing awareness of poverty and the acknowledgment of the need to alleviate it, Nelson and Dorsey focus instead on the dynamics of the dialogue, the relationships, and the interactions and what is being changed as a result of them.

Nelson and Dorsey point out that the contemporary context presents enormous challenges and frustrations for development agencies as well as human rights activists. While there are flashes of local successes, there is a "worsening global pattern of poverty, deepening inequalities, marginalization and indignity."[28] Yet they also argue that the stated commitments to alleviating poverty have also had positive effects. Nelson and Dorsey uncover local, national, and global relationships that are using this awareness of poverty and stated commitments to alleviating it to pursue new and positive avenues of change. They find hope and promise in the relationships and interactions that have developed between international NGOs and national and local organizations as well as between professionals in the human rights movement and in the policy-oriented development field:

> [W]e have ourselves experienced the movement in the two fields toward an approach to economic and social policy that draws on human rights standards and principles. We are also researchers trained in the social sciences and engaged in research on international development and international affairs, and contemporary theory on international relations, development, human rights, NGOs, and social movements appears unable to capture the changes we have participated in and studied.[29]

Their research supports the claim that the current attention on alleviating inequalities in wealth has pushed the boundaries of each of the two fields of human rights and development. They argue that there is now a pressing need to answer questions about why poverty is not widely recognized as a human rights issue or why human rights to food, health, and housing are not taken seriously in setting and implementing development priorities. Once these questions are asked, it becomes clear that attention moves away from an exclusive focus on negative rights of non-interference and free markets to positive ones of economic, social, and cultural rights. These interactions of various theory and policy people in the global context, they argue, are challenging and changing discourse and policy with respect to both human rights claims and development policy.

While they do not use the language of relational theory to defend their claims about change, their main thesis is that the common goal of addressing poverty has created the kind of *contact* and *interaction* of human rights organizations, development funders, and social movements that has had the effect of challenging and changing theoretical visions as well as disciplinary and professional boundaries. They concentrate on four significant theoretical and applied issues that are changed in and through these various interactions: "[T]he quest for power by NGOs reflected in their strategic choices, the origins and significance of new rights claims, the changing relationship between international NGOs and states, and the challenge to orthodox development theory and practice."[30] Relational theory can explain each of these factors, but, for now, I will concentrate on highlighting how it can explain the first. We will then understand how relational theory takes the four factors as intersecting and interdependent.

Nelson and Dorsey reject the standard analysis of NGOs perpetuating their own organizational identities as "principled, independent political agents advancing values-based agendas" in favour of an integrated analysis of how their use and exercise of political power is always situated in the complex dynamics of their own organization in ways that then shape possibilities for identifying and advancing objectives.[31] In other words, NGOs are not entities that advance values-based agendas in isolation or abstraction from the everyday realities of needing to plan organizational agendas and objectives in and through the process of negotiating and applying for funding on which they depend. What I would like to add to their account is how strategies and objectives are always up for revision in the context of the lived and concrete interactive relationships that are created, utilized, or negotiated in specific contexts and for specific purposes. To keep its power and legitimacy on the world stage, an organization such as Amnesty International, for example, continues to alert the public about harms and rights violations in specific contexts. In the process of doing this in a changing global context, Amnesty International also creates new relationships, strategies, and objectives in its own organization and with states and other NGOs. Nelson and Dorsey argue, for example, that whereas Amnesty International once focused on violations to civil and political rights, it has now expanded its mandate to include violations to social, economic, and cultural rights. This loop of interaction, feedback, learning, and changing in a global network of relations permits an understanding of how new human rights claims emerge, what inequalities get identified as needing to be addressed, and which development projects will work to actually empower the people who are meant to benefit from them.

With respect to this relational account of change, international NGOs may not be innovators as such. Instead, since they have, or have gained, sources of support and legitimacy in the global context, they are, or have become, positioned to give voice to rights claims made by social movements or by local or national NGOs in countries without that power and legitimacy. Giving voice to people, groups, or organizations in specific contexts or advocating for particular rights claims can in turn change relationships between those states and the local or international NGOs to whom they now give audience. And these strengthened relationships between states and NGOs or social movements can in turn increase pressure on economically powerful countries, international financial institutions, and transnational corporations to expand their understanding of human rights and change their market-driven approaches to development policy. It is in these avenues of change, for example, that international NGOs can lobby to challenge policies by rich countries that tie loan payment plans to the removal of state funding for health care and education in poor countries. And it is in these places as well that international NGOs and agencies can help give voice and power to local NGOs in states with corrupt governments or repressive laws and practices.

What is important about the Nelson and Dorsey research is that they have studied these interactions and have provided empirical evidence of some key developments in order to "shed new light on the theory and practice of

NGOs as political actors and as organizations, on the theory and practice of human rights, and on the theory and sometimes embattled practice of promoting economic and social development."[32] The result, they argue, is a new rights advocacy that represents "concrete activity among actors in two fields: the embrace of ESC [economic, social, and cultural] rights among human rights activists; the adoption of human rights-based approaches in the development field; and the formation of new advocacy campaigns, networks, and movements that involve organizations from both fields as well as social movements."[33] On their account, recognizing the need to address the detrimental effects of economic globalization has shaped calculated responses to system changes, changed the role and influence of government actors, powerful countries, and organizations, and increased the power and growth of social movement solidarity across the globe. All of these factors, they argue, have reoriented the theory and the practice of both human rights and development. The second example in the section that follows on the work of a local NGO in Indonesia adds to this account of new rights advocacy possibilities by opening up spaces for the recognition of inequalities at the local level and devising effective policies for alleviating them.

As is the case in the relational approach that I have been advancing, Nelson and Dorsey recognize the fundamental need to uncover and analyze the effects of relations of power: "Understanding the different ways development and human rights practitioners talk and think about power, and the relationships between social movements' power claims and economic and social rights, requires a conceptual framework that recognizes the various forms power takes."[34] They borrow from Michael Barnett and Raymond Duvall to define power as "the production, in and through social relations, of effects that shape the capacities of actors to determine their circumstances and fate."[35] Given the relational account of equality thus far, this definition can be said to obscure the fact that power hides in globally dominant norms and expectations and exerts its influence in unequal ways. People can be in social relations and institutional structures that are omnipresent and taken for granted and yet these same relations and structures leave some of them powerless to determine their circumstances and fate. I would want, therefore, to extend the analysis further than Nelson and Dorsey do by using those features of a relational approach that lay bare the dominant norms and institutional structures that shape the "circumstances and fate" of global, national, local, and group relationships as well as those of individual actors.

I argued earlier in this chapter that political theorists in the liberal tradition tend to assume the virtues of free market mechanisms, neo-liberal policies, and global capitalism and thereby fail to recognize how these very features of the current global order create and sustain relations of power. Elsewhere,

I have made use of insights from feminist post-colonial theory[36] to argue that development organizations and institutions such as the World Bank have been reluctant to confront and discuss the power they wield over people, NGOs, and countries.[37] Their focus, instead, has been on providing accounts of empowerment and advocacy that avoid acknowledging the power over relations that pervade the development policies they endorse.[38] Much of this comes about, I have argued, because of assumptions that poverty and inequality can be erased through minor adjustments made to the workings of open markets, neo-liberal policies, and global capitalism.

The relational theory that I have defended has us pay attention to relationships of power and to the ways in which factors such as race, gender, disability, and so on affect the power one has to articulate and remove inequalities of various sorts. Without an account of the lived and concrete realities of human lives that are learned from engagement and interaction that reduces the influence of power, the possibilities for uncovering dominant norms and taking the perspectives of those in disadvantaged positions seriously are drastically reduced. This point is evident in the example of loan repayment plans, which have capitalist countries and financial institutions assuming that funding for health care and education are barriers to a poor country's ability to expand market opportunities or create jobs. What emerges instead when health care facilities are no longer funded or closed down are increases in disease, early morbidity, and infant mortality. The fact that these inequalities in health have a detrimental impact on market and job opportunities seems obvious to those affected by these policies that are imposed on poor countries by rich countries.

New possibilities for theory and for policy emerge when we shift the focus from independent, isolated individuals to individuals in relationships that need to understand and then respond in morally appropriate ways to the needs of others. The account outlined in this chapter expands relational theory from its roots by refusing to turn the focus back to what happens to individuals once attention is paid to the governing norms, relationships, and perspectives. Instead, it attempts to maintain its focus on relationships and the effects of them on beings whose bodies, physical activities, and bodily movements are shaped by these relationships. Once we settle into examining what relational theory can reveal, we become better learners and knowers as well as better agents for change through engaging and interacting with different others and being changed by these relationships and interactions. In the second and final example, I illuminate these insights by exploring what I learned through my own experience of observing and working with a local NGO in Indonesia in the summer of 2006. This experience highlights the importance of interactive engagement as a way of acquiring better knowledge of lives, relationships, structures, policies, and the global order itself. In this example, the importance of interaction in the ever-changing environments in which people live and to which they are forced to respond becomes clear. Without this knowledge gained from a situated awareness of the needs of others, the risk is high for exacerbating, rather than alleviating, a range of inequalities present in a particular context – whether of income, health, opportunities, well-being, life prospects, and so on – which are all affected by overarching factors of economic interests, structures, and institutions at the national and global level.

Lessons from a Local NGO in Indonesia

The Nelson and Dorsey analysis of "new rights advocacy" reveals what can emerge when relationships between and among various local, national, and global actors are examined. Conceiving of relationships as being interactive and dynamic helps to explain how those who are involved in expanding the understandings of human rights and development make use of the dominant discourse in order to strengthen stated commitments and push the boundaries of what these commitments mean or entail. In the process of using and then subverting the dominant discourse, they can themselves be changed in terms of identifying effective strategies, objectives, and goals. Nelson and Dorsey are less explicit than I want to be about the need to recognize and question globally dominant expectations and entrenched power dynamics that shape the possibilities for interactive engagement. I think that my travels to observe the work of a local NGO in Indonesia can illustrate in a concrete way the importance of confronting norms and stereotypes that frame "how we know, how we hear, how we see, how we speak."[39]

To understand how this potential can be realized involves applying the insights of relational theory sketched thus far. Relational theory pays attention to the relationships of power and oppression by uncovering the norms that keep these structures in place and by taking the perspectives of those in less powerful positions seriously. What can be gained from interacting with, rather than reading about or observing, different others is linked to the features of the expanded relational account – the significance of knowing about bodily needs in a globalized world in which bodies are shaped by the vicissitudes of histories, conditions, and contexts as well as by the overarching factor of economic globalization. This became evident in the most striking way after I arrived in Yogyakarta, Indonesia, in June 2006 just days after a major earthquake in Central Java killed 5,782 people, injured 36,299, damaged 135,000 houses, and left an estimated 1.5 million people homeless.

My research project on "The Ethics of Empowerment" involved working with, and learning from, a local NGO in Yogyakarta called SATUNAMA. I went with an anthropologist, Jan Newberry, whose area of study has been Central Java for the past few decades. We arrived when the staff time and resources of SATUNAMA were devoted to responding to the bodily needs of providing food, shelter, and clothing in communities where relationships with people they worked with and for had already been established. The significance of perspectives for understanding those needs was confirmed through observing the work of SATUNAMA, whose members, in visiting and talking with people in the communities affected by the earthquake, could produce a more informed account of the needs of people they had worked with for years than could international NGOs who delivered supplies that often did not get to the people that needed them.

Observing what SATUNAMA could do for people and communities, which could not be done by national or international bodies, taught me another lesson as well. It was important to confront stereotypes of who has knowledge. State, international agencies, and academics not only know less about specifics of meeting needs than those who engage with the locals on a daily basis, but they may also know less about policies at state and international levels that will be effective for dealing with natural disasters. An example illustrating the importance of local knowledge of people's needs emerged in discussions at SATUNAMA and in the local schools over what to do about the children traumatized by the earthquake and unable to talk about what they saw or trust that it would not happen again. In a way that emphasized the significance of bodies in the world, one effective strategy was to have children play with sand, water, and clay as a way to "open up" their senses and emotions again. This strategy used physicality and embodiment with respect to relating to things in the world and, especially, the things in the world that can harm people in order to encourage children to experience and be in the world again. Discussions revolved around how this sort of strategy was appropriate and effective in a context in which "scientific" explanations were not effective in allowing children to regain their trust and confidence about *being* in the world. As is also the case in Sheila Wildeman's chapter in this volume, this example challenges our assumptions about mental health and the often too easy acceptance of fixes such as institutionalization, individualized psychotherapy, or drugs. None of these "fixes" were discussed as options for dealing with trauma in the aftermath of the earthquake.

An example that illustrates the importance of situated knowledge is that staff working with SATUNAMA and for people in the community were able to engage with the ideas and the discourse used by philosophers, government officials, people at the World Bank, and officials from donor countries. A central insight from the Nelson and Dorsey analysis is that NGOs and social movements need to have this knowledge in order to do the work that they do – work in which meanings shift and strategies are altered in the process of engaging, interacting with, and negotiating the terms of the debate and the policies affecting those for whom they advocate. I have been arguing that we need to take this a few steps further by exposing the norms that are assumed by state and international agencies and by showing that they are hard to dislodge. This fact was evident in the plan that the director of SATUNAMA took to the meetings about the earthquake, which were held in Jakarta and which involved Indonesian government officials and international NGOs. His plan sketched problems with the approach that others were recommending in which the government was to take out new international loans instead of providing aid through debt-forgiveness programs. He knew in a way that they ignored or failed to recognize that the money would increase the country's debt load and that a government that had reneged on its initial promise to provide each family with resources to rebuild their homes was unlikely to get the money to the people suffering in the aftermath of the earthquake. The fact that the director's warnings and advice were not heeded reveals the power that national governments and international agencies have to ignore or thwart the efforts of local NGOs and communities to set their own public policy or to respond to the needs of their own citizens.

These descriptions of my own research confirm the central features and advantages of a relational approach to theory and policy: its attention to detail, its uncovering of norms, its legitimizing of perspectives, its critical analysis of power and of relations of power, and its awareness of what can be achieved in and through embodied engagement with different others who are marginalized and powerless. I am not arguing that academics must travel to places around the world in order to better understand the inequalities experienced by different others. Some of these lessons can be learned through a less resistant engagement with homeless people in our own communities – including an examination of our own reactions and reluctance to encounter them in the streets. Nor am I suggesting that it is easy for academics to extricate themselves from the power dynamics of research, of those who are researched, or of the externally motivated goal of producing research that fits the mandate of funding agencies. The risks of exploiting local communities are as real for academics as they are for state officials or international NGOs. The risk of exploitation is also evident in health policy, where the objectives of those in power who are conducting the research are determined by funding sources or particular agendas, which are in turn determined by big pharmaceutical companies or rich countries interested in maximizing or controlling profits.

I do not have answers to these criticisms of the potential for power to exploit and manipulate, but using key components of relational theory to allow for a critical examination of the very relationships that shape research projects and methodology is a crucial step in the direction of acknowledging power and its significance. Most importantly, the multi-dimensional features of an expanded relational approach can explain that the situated knowledge and expertise of local NGOs is needed – sometimes by way of a corrective to national and international policies and sometimes by way of being able to respond to needs effectively and efficiently when and where they arise. Without this expertise, aid can be misdirected and inequalities can be hard to discern or even be exacerbated.

The relational account that I have sketched in this chapter allows the constant evaluation of relationships of power at all levels and in ways that can uncover the norms and perspectives that shape theory and policy and keep inequalities of particular sorts in place. Each of the two examples that I have provided, from a recent publication that describes the changing discourse and from on-the-ground experiences with a local NGO, apply relational insights to reinterpret and better grasp what is possible by way of understanding and removing inequalities of various sorts.

Conclusion

I began this chapter by describing inequalities of income both within and across borders because this is the backdrop against which equality is typically understood. There is now a global awareness of, and commitment to, the importance of addressing inequalities in income and wealth at the same time as these and other inequalities have grown and become entrenched in the contemporary global context. Growing gaps between the rich and the poor both within and across borders combine with the rising influence and power of economically powerful countries, multinational corporations, international financial institutions, and trade organizations to create, sustain, shape, and entrench the complex set of inequalities described in this chapter. It is fair to say that relationships of interdependency and dependency characterize the global scene and that they are manifested in relationships of power between countries and peoples that are rich and poor, Western and non-Western, First and Third World, North and South. These descriptions and analyses of the global context and of relations of power within it are a needed corrective to mainstream theory that proclaims the virtues of open markets and global capitalism and the promise that these structures can reduce inequalities.

In this chapter, I have outlined features that are distinctive to a relational approach to equality. First is the need to examine the details of concrete kinds of relationships and the shaping of them through particular social practices and in specific contexts, including the global context in which we now live. Second is the importance of revealing the norms, standards, and practices that are in place and to which those who are in relationships of power and oppression need to respond. Third is the argument that the perspectives of those in relationships of oppression are important vantage points for understanding inequalities and what is needed to remove them. As applied to the global context, focusing on relationships highlights the role of perspectives in uncovering norms that reflect dominant beliefs and expectations, ones that are assumed by those in power and challenged by those whose lives and circumstances have been shaped by them in detrimental ways. Globally dominant norms shape "outsider" perspectives on structures of power differently from "insider" perspectives on this same power.

Globally dominant expectations that economic globalization in the form of markets, multinational corporations, and global financial institutions can and will remove inequalities can be said to perpetuate these inequalities if it means that human lives and their needs are shaped and reshaped by these norms and institutional forces. In this context, it is fair to say that people in many locations have lives and needs shaped from the outside by these economic forces and in ways that determine the kinds of inequalities they suffer. A relational approach to equality in the global context can explain how lives and needs are being shaped in complex ways by the multi-dimensional and varied intersections of local, state, civil, and global institutions. Since economic globalization affects differently situated people in diverse ways, detailed accounts of conditions, practices, policies, perspectives, embodied realities, and relationships of power are needed. This is evident in understanding how an earthquake in Central Java, for example, shapes what might need to be done differently when the context is one in which a government cannot be trusted to respond to the needs of its own citizens or when NGOs are not positioned to know in the same way as local NGOs do what is needed by those in areas affected by the earthquake. These are important aspects of an account that attempts to understand and alleviate inequalities.

A framework for conceptualizing equality that assumes or unquestioningly promotes neo-liberal commitments to open markets and to negative rights of non-interference may not reveal the whole story about the kinds of inequalities, including those that may be created by these very structures and policies. We need to pay attention to how the multi-dimensional and varied intersections of state, civil, and global institutions shape and reshape embodied realities when it increases gaps between the rich and poor, when it destroys ways of life that once sustained families and communities, when it pushes people into densely populated urban centres where basic material needs are not being met, when it exploits embodied realities of race, ethnicity, gender, and disability to increase profits, when it exacerbates relations of power with and in countries that have colonial and imperial histories, when it means that health issues such as HIV/AIDS in poor countries are under the control of powerful global drug companies, and when it turns attention from aid intended to alleviate poverty to that which increases militarization in the fight against terrorism. These are only some of the examples opened up for critical evaluation when a relational approach to equality is applied to the global context.

Notes

This volume and this chapter would not have been possible without the good vision and planning of the editors Jocelyn Downie and Jennifer Llewellyn. I am grateful to them and to all of the contributors to this volume for the productive discussion of the ideas, issues, and papers at the two workshops that then facilitated the process of clarifying and revising. I am also grateful to the Social Sciences and Humanities Research Council of Canada for a research grant that allowed me to discover the fine work being done by a local non-governmental organization (NGO) in Indonesia. I hope I have done justice to the lessons and insights learned from SATUNAMA and incorporated in this chapter.

1 United Nations, *We the Peoples: The Role of the United Nations in the Twenty-First Century* (New York: Department of Public Information, 2000) at 19-20.
2 Branko Milanovic, *Worlds Apart: Measuring International and Global Inequality* (Princeton, NJ: Princeton University Press, 2005).
3 Amnesty International, *Report 2005: The State of the World's Human Rights*, Amnesty International Index, Doc. POL 10/001/2005 at 8.
4 United Nations Development Program, *Human Development Report 2003* (New York: Oxford University Press, 2003) at v.
5 Association for Women's Rights in Development, *Achieving Women's Economic and Social Rights: Strategies and Lessons from Experience* (Toronto: Association for Women's Rights in Development, 2006).
6 Paul Hawken, *Blessed Unrest: How the Largest Social Movement in History Is Restoring Grace, Justice, and Beauty to the World* (New York: Penguin, 2007).
7 Chris Turner, *Geography of Hope: A Tour of the World We Need* (Toronto: Random House, 2007).
8 Paul J. Nelson and Ellen Dorsey, *New Rights Advocacy: Changing Strategies of Development and Human Rights NGOs* (Washington, DC: Georgetown University Press, 2008).
9 Amartya Sen, *Inequality Reexamined* (Cambridge, MA: Harvard University Press, 1992).
10 A sample of work discussing the key issues between Sen and Nussbaum can be found in Martha Nussbaum, "Capabilities as Fundamental Entitlements" (2003) 9:2/3 Feminist Econ. 33; Amartya Sen, "Capabilities, Lists and Public Reason" (2004) 10:3 Feminist Econ. 77; Ingrid Robeyns, "Selecting Capabilities for Quality of Life Measurement" (2005) 74 Social Indicators Research 191.
11 Amartya Sen, *Development as Freedom* (New York: Anchor Books, 1999) at 108.
12 *Ibid.* at 21.
13 *Ibid.* at 6.
14 *Ibid.* at 97.
15 *Ibid.* at 203.
16 *Ibid.* at 109.
17 Christine M. Koggel, "Globalization and Women's Paid Work: Expanding Freedom?" (2003) 9:2 Feminist Econ. (Special Issue on the Ideas and Work of Amartya Sen) 163; Marianne Hill, "Development as Empowerment" (2003) 9:2 Feminist Econ. (Special Issue on the Ideas and Work of Amartya Sen) 117.
18 Examples include: Samantha Brennan, "Recent Work in Feminist Ethics" (1999) 109 Ethics 858; Sue Campbell, "Dependence in Client-Therapist Relationships: A Relational Reading of *O'Connor* and *Mills*" in Law Commission of Canada, ed., *Personal Relationships of Dependence and Interdependence in Law* (Vancouver, UBC Press, 2002) 3; Sue Campbell, *Relational Remembering: Rethinking the Memory Wars* (Lanham, MD: Rowman and Littlefield, 2003); Lorraine Code, *What Can She Know: Feminist Theory and the Construction of Knowledge* (Ithaca, NY: Cornell University Press, 1991); Lorraine Code, "How to Think Globally: Stretching the Limits of Imagination" in Uma Narayan and Sandra Harding, eds., *Decentering the Center: Philosophy for a Multicultural, Postcolonial, and Feminist World* (Bloomington, IN: Indiana University Press, 2000) 67; Jennifer Nedelsky, "Reconceiving Autonomy: Sources, Thoughts, and Possibilities" (1989) 1 Yale J. L. & Feminism 7; Jennifer Nedelsky, "Reconceiving Rights as Relationship" (1993) 1:1 Rev. Const. Stud. 1; Susan Sherwin, "A Relational Approach to Autonomy in Health Care" in Feminist Health Care Ethics Research Network, ed., *The Politics of Women's Health: Exploring Agency and Autonomy* (Philadelphia: Temple

University Press, 1998) 19; Catriona Mackenzie and Natalie Stoljar, eds., *Relational Autonomy: Feminist Perspectives on Autonomy, Agency, and the Social Self* (New York: Oxford University Press, 2000); Christine M. Koggel, *Perspectives on Equality: Constructing a Relational Theory* (Lanham, MD: Rowman and Littlefield, 1998); Christine M. Koggel, "Equality Analysis in a Global Context: A Relational Approach" (1993) 28 Can. J. Phil. (Supplementary Volume on Feminist Moral Philosophy) 247.

19 For a fuller discussion of individualism in liberal theory, consult Chapter 2 of Koggel, *Perspectives on Equality, supra* note 18.

20 Carol Gilligan, *In a Different Voice: Psychological Theory and Women's Development* (Cambridge, MA: Harvard University Press, 1993) at xiii.

21 Recent work by each of Fiona Robinson, Joan Tronto, and Virginia Held that expands an ethic of care can be found in (2010) 4:2 Ethics and Social Welfare (Special Issue on Care Ethics: New Theories and Applications).

22 Koggel, *Perspectives on Equality, supra* note 18 at 163.

23 Sen, *supra* note 10 at 110.

24 Koggel, *supra* note 17; Koggel, "Equality Analysis in a Global Context," *supra* note 18; Christine M. Koggel, "Equality Analysis: Local and Global Relations of Power" in Christine M. Koggel, ed., *Moral Issues in Global Perspective: Human Diversity and Equality,* volume 2, 2nd edition (Peterborough: Broadview Press, 2006) 376.

25 Christine M. Koggel, "Agency and Empowerment: Embodied Realities in a Globalized World" in Sue Campbell, Letitia Maynell, and Susan Sherwin, eds., *Agency and Embodiment* (Philadelphia: Pennsylvania State University Press, 2008) 313.

26 Iris Marion Young, "Responsibility and Global Justice: A Social Connection Model" (2006) 23:1 Social Philosophy and Policy 102.

27 Nelson and Dorsey, *supra* note 8 at 3.

28 *Ibid.* at 4.

29 *Ibid.* at 5.

30 *Ibid.* at 6.

31 *Ibid.*

32 *Ibid.* at 9.

33 *Ibid.* at 19.

34 *Ibid.* at 36-37.

35 Michael Barnett and Raymond Duvall, "Power in Global Governance" in Michael Barnett and Raymond Duvall, eds., *Power in Global Governance* (Cambridge: Cambridge University Press, 2005) 1 at 8.

36 Chandra Mohanty, "Women Workers and Capitalist Scripts: Ideologies of Domination, Common Interests, and the Politics of Solidarity" in M.J. Alexander and C. Mohanty, eds., *Feminist Genealogies, Colonial Legacies, Democratic Futures* (New York: Routledge, 1997) 3.

37 Christine M. Koggel, "Empowerment and the Role of Advocacy in a Globalized World" (2007) 1:1 Ethics and Social Welfare 8.

38 Deepa Narayan, *Voices of the Poor: Can Anyone Hear Us?* (Washington, DC: World Bank, 2000); Deepa Narayan, *Voices of the Poor: Crying Out for Change* (Washington, DC: World Bank, 2001); Deepa Narayan, *Voices of the Poor: From Many Lands* (Washington, DC: World Bank, 2002); Deepa Narayan, *Empowerment and Poverty Reduction: A Sourcebook* (Washington, DC: World Bank, 2004); Deepa Narayan, *Measuring Empowerment: Cross-Disciplinary Perspectives* (Washington, DC: World Bank, 2005).

39 Gilligan, *supra* note 20 at xiii.

4
Restorative Justice: Thinking Relationally about Justice
Jennifer J. Llewellyn

During the past decade, restorative justice has garnered significant attention in domestic and international contexts as an alternative approach to responding to crime and other wrongs.[1] Despite the rapid and impressive development of restorative justice practices in a range of contexts, the conceptual underpinning and theory of justice at the core of these practices has received significantly less attention. The restorative justice movement developed largely in response to the failure of existing justice systems and approaches to account for, and address, the needs of offenders, victims, and communities in the wake of wrongdoing.[2] Driven by such concerns, restorative justice developed in practice on the ground well ahead of the theory explaining and supporting it. It is, perhaps, not surprising given the history of its development that restorative justice is sometimes viewed as simply an alternative justice practice – a different way of achieving justice that is more inclusive, participatory, and accessible without questioning the ultimate aim of such processes. This view of restorative justice is not so much wrong as it is limited, in that it fails to fully appreciate the alternative that restorative justice represents as a relational theory of justice.

The significance of relationships figures prominently in restorative justice practice and has been affirmed by its successes.[3] Restorative justice is grounded in a commitment to understanding the fact of relationship and connection as central to the work of justice. Many practitioners and scholars of restorative justice ascribe to Howard Zehr's now well-known claim that, at its core, restorative justice offers a new "lens" on crime and justice – a "paradigm shift."[4] Where the current criminal justice system focuses on law breaking, restorative justice focuses attention on harm to people and their relationships. The nature of the "paradigm" shift underlying restorative justice and appreciation of its scope and implications has not yet, however, been fully explored or articulated. Throughout my previous work, I have argued that restorative justice does indeed require a different lens, but, that, crafted well, this different lens is not limited to a new view of criminal justice.

Rather, it is a wider lens, carved and illuminated by a relational conception of the self and its implications for how we are in the world. Restorative justice is, I suggest then, best understood as a relational theory of justice.[5]

Relational theory should be looked to, I claim, as the starting point to understand the conception of justice at the core of the idea and practice of restorative justice. This starting point explains and makes sense of the centrality of relationships in much of restorative justice practice. Relational theory at once helps underpin and explain restorative justice and at the same time provides a theoretical framework for challenging and critiquing current thinking and practice. This vantage point invites restorative justice advocates and scholars to see the broader implications of this theory of justice. This chapter offers a relational account of justice and suggests it as a conceptual framework for the burgeoning theory and practice of restorative justice. It explores the difference it makes to justice if the fact of relationship, of unavoidable connection to others, and of interdependence is taken as a starting assumption for thinking about and doing justice. It further claims that this is precisely the difference that restorative justice represents at a conceptual level and reflects the practical potential it holds. This chapter thus seeks to both explain and develop restorative justice by rooting it as a relational theory of justice.

A Relational Theory of Justice: The Importance of Equal Respect, Concern, and Dignity

Feminist scholars have challenged the traditional image of the individualistic human self that rests at the core of much of liberal social and political theory.[6] In place of the liberal individualist vision of the self, relational theorists offer a relational account of the self that takes connection over separation as essential to the constitution and maintenance of the self. Connection and relationship with others is seen as essential to understanding the self and to its making and remaking.[7] Relational theory thus suggests a different starting point from which to understand the world. It compels us to take the fact of relationship, of connectedness, as our starting assumption. As such, relationality must inform the ideas, principles and conceptions that shape our interactions and social life. Liberal-inspired assumptions about the nature of the self and its interactions with others and the world have shaped and structured (sometimes explicitly but often implicitly) fundamental social, political, and legal ideas, institutions, and systems, among them, justice.

Justice is our response to the powerful moral intuition that something is wrong and begs response and redress.[8] In its service, we have created processes, institutions, and systems tasked with recognizing and responding to wrong. Prevailing conceptions of justice that underlie and animate contemporary justice systems (at least in the West and increasingly exported throughout the world) are rooted in a particular set of assumptions about selves and ideal social conditions drawn from the liberal tradition. As a result, these theories privilege the protection of individual independence through separation as the animating ideal of justice. This is evident in our criminal justice system with its focus on identifying individuals responsible for wrongdoing who can be blamed and punished (often through isolating mechanisms designed to remove them from society).[9] It is also evident in our civil law system, which conceives of harms as caused by one individual toward another and seeks remedy in a material transfer from one to the other aimed (as much as possible) at a return for the complainant to his or her prior circumstances (without inquiring into the nature of that prior state).[10] Indeed, the very divisions that rest at the core of our justice system between public and private justice and that separate both from questions of social justice reflect an underlying individualistic approach and set of assumptions.

Insights about the relational nature of the self offered by feminist relational theorists suggest a different starting point for thinking about the meaning and nature of justice and what is required for its doing. If justice is to be relevant to life here on earth and not simply the abstract preserve of poets and gods, then it must take account of our relationality. Conceiving of justice then must start from the fact of connection and interdependence. What then are the implications of this relational starting point for justice? What difference does it make if we take relationship as the starting point for thinking about justice?

Justice understood relationally is concerned with the nature of the connections between and among people, groups, communities, and even nations. Justice aims at realizing the conditions of relationship required for well-being and flourishing. It identifies as wrong those acts or circumstances that prevent or harm such conditions. With respect to this relational understanding, the goal of justice – either in response to specific wrongful acts or existing states of injustice – is the establishment of relationships that enable and promote the well-being and flourishing of the parties involved. Justice conceived relationally seeks what I refer to in this chapter as "equality of relationship."

The identification of justice with equality is not unusual. Indeed, Ronald Dworkin has argued that "most theories of justice in the contemporary literature of political philosophy can readily be understood" as "interpretations or conceptions of equality."[11] Dworkin's claim is specifically about theories of political justice or social justice. I have argued elsewhere, though, that both the corrective justice of the civil law system and the retributive justice of the criminal justice system are, at their core, similarly concerned with equality.[12] Through the use of compensatory damages, corrective justice seeks to correct the inequality created through the interference with the sufferer's rights.[13] The conception of justice that some retributivists adhere to is rooted in a commitment to achieving equality between the wrongdoers and victims. Perhaps the most trenchant and persuasive account of retributive justice is that offered by Georg Hegel.[14] John Rawls has referred to this kind of equality as "fundamental."[15] According to Dworkin, this notion of equality entails "[t]he right to equal concern and respect [which] is more abstract than the standard conceptions of equality that distinguish different political theories."[16]

However, while relational justice shares this focus on equality with other theories and conceptions of justice, the equality at which it is aimed is different from that which is rooted in the liberal tradition. Starting from a relational approach, it aims at more than our familiar notions of formal equality or even substantive equality – both of which take the individual as their point of departure. The equality that rests at the core of a relational theory of justice is necessarily *relational* equality.[17] To claim that justice is, at its core, about relational equality is not to say simply that it is concerned with equality of treatment or outcome for individuals (although, to be certain, this would be a desirable result). Relational equality is a more fundamental commitment to the nature of connection (of relationship) between and among parties. Understanding equality in this way makes it easier to see how relational justice is concerned with equality. It is not to reduce matters of justice (and injustice) simply to inequality or equality claims in the sense we understand them in our Western liberal legal tradition.

Relational justice is not concerned, for example, with the equality that some retributive theories of justice seek through a particular set of historical practices (typical of a wide range of societies), which are often known as punishment. Retributive accounts seek equality through an evening of the score between wrongdoer and victims by inflicting harm against the wrongdoer (typically exercised through isolating punishment) in even measure to that done to the victim. By contrast, as will be elaborated further in this chapter, relational justice problematizes the issue of what set of practices can or should be employed toward the goal of restoring equality in the context of the relationships involved. It demands concrete consideration of the needs of each party to realize equality of relationship. A relational theory of justice, then, does not approach equality in individualistic terms. Equality cannot, then, on this account be achieved by ensuring the same treatment or equal measures of benefits or burdens or even identical outcomes for individuals. Rather, equality in relational terms can only be understood and achieved through attention to the relationships in and through which selves exist and is fundamentally concerned with the nature of such relationships.

Justice understood relationally, thus, takes as its aim equality of relationship, not in the sense of sameness but, rather, in the sense of satisfying the basic elements required for well-being and flourishing. These basic elements sometimes become more apparent by their absence. We know from experience that certain types of connection (for example, oppression and violence) or the denial of connection (through isolation, neglect, and abandonment) do not promote or permit well-being and flourishing. Indeed, these models of relationship are often described as self-destructive or as destroying lives (even where physical death is not the result).[18] From this knowledge of what is destructive and harmful, we are able to identify the basic qualities of relationship that are necessary to allow all selves to be well and to flourish. What is required are relationships marked by equal respect, concern, and dignity. These qualities underpin *equality of relationship*. It is notable that these same requirements underpin our ideas of basic or fundamental human rights.

The equality sought by relational justice shares the fundamental commitment to equal respect and concern that animates liberal notions of equality. Unlike the liberal commitment, though, the equality sought by relational justice is not abstract in nature but, rather, as noted above, relies on a relational notion of equality. Some might argue that equality is always relational in the sense that it is a comparative concept, but such comparisons can and often are formal and almost mathematical in character. Equality of relationship, however, requires more than simple comparison at an abstract level. It is concerned with equality as it is realized in the real and lived relationships between people. It is contextual and grounded. Achieving this equality thus requires attention to the particular context, to the parties involved, and to what will be required to ensure respect, concern, and dignity in the relations between and among parties.

Thus, while these elements of equality of relationship – respect, concern, and dignity – resemble liberal descriptions of equality, their intention and implications are different owing to their grounding in a relational approach.[19] For example, one of the founding commitments of liberal theory (and liberal justice in particular) is the Kantian commitment to the dignity of human beings. This inherent dignity is said to flow from our rational nature and requires that respect be paid (as a moral imperative) both to one's self and to others.[20] This grounding commitment is often expressed as a commitment to the "equal moral worth" of persons and as a requirement to treat persons with respect and concern. The formulation of equal respect, concern, and dignity that underpins relational justice does not sound all that different from liberal justice. However, while the terms sound the same, there is, in fact, a significant difference with real implications for justice (what it requires and how it might be achieved).

The formulation of the characteristics of equality of relationship at which relational justice aims – respect, concern, and dignity – must be understood as themselves relational values. From a relational starting point, these values are not rooted in our *rational* nature as autonomous agents, as they are for liberals, but, rather, in our *relational* nature. They detail what we require of one another, and in relation to one another, for our well-being. Indeed, as other authors in this volume help us to see, once revised from a relational point of view, the very notions of equality, autonomy, identity, and judgment require more than individual rationality and, indeed, destabilize rationality as the basis for treatment of and by others.[21]

This relational approach is reflected in the intentional connection and mutually modifying articulation of respect, concern, and dignity as the values and elements of equality of relationship. They inform and give content to one another, distinguishing a relational account from the liberal reference to such values. "Respect" denotes the importance of recognizing, and not violating or interfering with, the rights and needs of others. This respect, however, is not founded upon disinterest or self-interest as it is in many contemporary liberal approaches.[22] It is thus more robust than the notion of respect that undergirds the modern approach to individual rights. It is not the notion of respect as captured by the metaphors of shields or swords often deployed in liberal rights talk. It is not predicated upon separation and protection from others. It is not achieved simply by recognition alone or negatively by non-interference but, rather, by respect rooted in (and understood in the context of) concern for others.[23]

The inclusion of "concern" in the formulation makes clear that knowledge of, and interest in, others and their well-being is to serve as an animating and motivating factor in equality of relationship. This notion reflects insights gained from care feminists and some communitarian critiques of liberal justice that are incorporated into some liberal accounts.[24] They point out that the connections we have and want with others cannot be fully explained or accounted for in individualistic and self-interested terms. We are not only concerned with or for others because it is in our interests as rational agents to be so. For example, we are not simply concerned so that others will have similar concern for us or because it is rational or because it will be to our credit to do so. Rather, we have concern for others because, as relational and connected selves, we cannot respect ourselves or others without such concern and interest. Once we recognize that selves are relational, it becomes clear that to respect them requires some knowledge and concern for their needs and aims and for their position in relation with others. Respect then requires more than non-interference or doing no harm. Our interconnectedness makes clear the importance of concern from and for others.

Finally, the inclusion of dignity as an element of the equality of relationship at which justice aims makes clear that this equality cannot be satisfied through process alone but is substantive in nature. Dignity requires attention to be paid to the needs and interests that give fundamental meaning to those involved in relationships and that their satisfaction be an animating concern for justice. However, once again, dignity conceived of relationally is different than the dignity reflected in liberal justice. Dignity does not refer to the inherent value of the individual qua *rational* agent. Dignity is not something that resides in the individual alone. Rather, it marks the relationship between and among parties. Dignity refers here to the way in which we are connected with others – that such connections must reflect our own value and that of others. It is the commitment that others to whom we are connected cannot be simply a means to an end but must also be accorded value in and of themselves, and this value must be reflected in the nature of our relationship with them. This idea is, perhaps, clearer from the notion of indignity. An indignity is done to someone when they are not being valued or treated as having value. Yet one can only make sense of treating others as having value in the context of relationships or connections between people and not in an abstract or universalist way. This relational nature of dignity is reflected in the way we talk about indignity, as something we do to one another or cause through our treatment and interactions. For example, we speak of "doing an indignity" or "causing an affront to dignity." As we conceive of it, indignity results from degrading, humiliating, or debasing another. Interestingly, while we clearly recognize the relational nature of indignity as brought about through our social interactions and arrangements, we do not similarly conceive of dignity in this relational way. Human dignity viewed through the lens of liberal individualism is more an individual and personal possession or right.

It is important, before proceeding, to clarify the implications of this relational approach. The claim is that justice is relational, not relative. We can and should articulate basic principles and criteria – respect, concern, and dignity – of what justice requires. However, these principles must be made meaningful and lived out in different contexts in which people are in relationships with particular others.

A Relational Theory of Justice: Implications for Liberal Justice

While there are differences as discussed earlier, the similarity in terms and commitments between relational and liberal justice are significant. The similarity makes clear that relational theory does not require abandonment of many of the goals and aspirations that drive liberalism.[25] Indeed, the strength of relational theory is that it is often able to offer a deeper and richer sense of these aspirations and a better means of achieving them than liberalism itself is able to offer, hampered, as it is, by an individualistic perspective.

A relational view of justice is fundamentally concerned with the character and conditions of relationship. Wrongdoing (injustice) is then also understood relationally on this account. Wrongdoing is defined in terms of the harm that results to equality of relationship. Injustice, on a relational justice account, reflects the existence of inequality of relationship between and among individuals, groups, and communities. This approach stands in stark

contrast to the current justice system's understanding of wrong as law breaking. This is not to say that the law is irrelevant on a relational justice account.
But, rather, that a relational conception of justice requires assessment and
evaluation of our laws in terms of their protection or facilitation of relationships that promote well-being and flourishing. According to this approach,
unlawful behaviour warrants response not simply because it flaunts the law
but also because of the harm it is likely to cause to relationships and, thus,
to those involved. A relational approach provides a place from which to
understand and assess the significance of a breach in the law. It might be
discovered, for example, that while the law was broken there was no harm
to relationships in a particular situation or that the law does not relate to,
or adequately reflect, a concern with the quality of relationship at all and
ought to be reformed. It is important at this point to clarify, though, that
this is not meant to suggest that the parties in a process might not find the
act of breaking an established law to be worthy of acknowledgment and
response given the harm that such behaviour might cause if generalized.
Rather, relational processes provide a space for contextualized discussions
about such issues so that it might be determined whether the breach of the
law in a given case actually flags an unjust law. Relational justice thus might
provide social and political spaces in which victims, offenders, and relevant
communities are empowered to explicitly reflect upon and discuss the law
and its effects. In this way, relational justice processes might serve as feedback loops for the law-making process where necessary. In doing so, such
processes can allow for meaningful democratic reflection upon, and participation in, the law-making process, which is sometimes relegated to an uncomfortable "dialogue" between courts and legislatures.[26] Thus, relational
justice is not an account of justice outside of, or hostile to, the law but,
rather, creates an opportunity to consider and deepen the relationship between justice and law.

Understanding wrong in terms of harm to relationships not only casts a
different light on the relationship between justice and law but also challenges
the division of criminal and civil law at work in our legal system. From a
relational perspective, it becomes clear that wrongs cause harm not only to
individual offenders and victims but also to their immediate communities
of care and support and extends further to the broader communities to which
they belong. Such wrongs also have implications for the fabric of society,
constituted as it is by the relationships between its members. A relational
account of justice, thus, reveals the fiction that rests at the heart of the distinction between civil and criminal law – that some conflicts are private in
nature and not of public concern. In contrast, a relational theory of justice
reveals the public nature of all wrongs because of their effect on relationships.
From a relational justice perspective, then, what is relevant is harm to relationships and not whether such harm is labelled a crime or a tort.[27]

Through a relational lens, it becomes clear that the distinction between private and public wrongs is really concerned with the scope of harm and those that are affected. Private wrongs may affect fewer relationships – that is, they may be felt throughout less of the "webs of relationships" in which we are all embedded. Those harms that we deem public are often broader harms involving a greater expanse of the webs of relationships. To offer a different metaphor, the ripple effect caused when one throws a stone into still waters might be helpful in illustrating that from a relational perspective the distinction between public and private wrongs is more concerned with the degree of wrong than with the kind of wrong. Depending on how it is thrown or the weight of the stone (or, indeed, several other contextual factors), a stone thrown into the water will make more or less ripples. The resulting concentric circles will be more or less in number and size depending on these various factors. However, what remains the same is that the stone will cause ripples that will necessarily affect the surrounding water beyond the entry point, even if to different degrees. In this way, the disturbance is never limited simply to the rock and the point of contact but always has a wider effect. A relational lens can recognize that the same is true for the harm caused by wrongdoing. It can have different effects that range from only a narrow set of relationships to those that extend to the broadest level of social relationship. Yet on a relational approach, wrongdoing always affects relationships to some extent.

A relational lens also reveals that injustice may be produced by a specific identifiable act of wrongdoing or it might mark existing relationships or patterns of relationship without any single traceable cause. In regard to a relational theory of justice, both situations prompt a justice response because both entail inequality of relationship – that is, in terms of the basic elements (respect, concern, and dignity) that are crucial for well-being and flourishing. This clarification addresses perhaps one of the most obvious objections to a relational account of justice, namely that relational equality cannot be achieved in response to a particular case in the face of broader social inequalities. A relational conception of justice must be concerned not only with inequality resulting from specific wrongdoing but also with the general state of inequality in social relations. Furthermore, from its focus on relationships, a relational approach to justice is able to identify the connection between the harms to relationships resulting from wrongdoing and social injustice. On a relational account, wrongdoing results in harm to individuals affecting their relationships and causes harm to relationships that affects individuals. Harm is not limited to the direct wrongdoer and victim but, rather, extends through the networks of relationships in which they exist. The act of wrongdoing is often connected to existing inequalities in social relations and, in turn, can contribute to such inequalities. Rather than posing a dilemma for a relational account of justice, however, the recognition of the connection between wrongdoing and social inequality is a potential strength of the theory. A relational theory of justice comprehends and forces attention upon the connections and implications that lie between criminal, civil, and social justice. In doing so, it speaks to one of the most significant weaknesses of our current justice system – its blindness to the role that context, causes, and circumstances play not only in the creation, but also in the resolution, of social conflict and wrongful conduct.

This recognition of the connection to social justice raises another issue for a relational account of justice. It is not clear which concern should be primary, addressing social injustices or addressing injustices resulting from specific wrongful acts. The challenge is to ensure that the right balance between macro- and micro-justice issues is struck so that, for example, social justice questions do not overshadow or drown out the concerns of particular parties affected by a specific wrong. The right balance is, however, more likely to be struck in relational justice-based processes for, as we will discuss in the next section of this chapter, these processes are both inclusive and participatory. A relational approach understands wrongdoing in light of the harm resulting for all those involved and is committed to attending to the discrete wrong as well as its contexts and causes. This means that through restorative processes parties are able to consider the role that existing social inequalities have played in the situation and what steps might be taken to address them. It is, of course, not quite this simple since the resolution of existing social inequalities will often not be within the power of the parties in a restorative justice process. However, the fact that these broader social inequalities cannot be solved solely through processes aimed at addressing individual incidents of wrongdoing does not render such processes irrelevant to the cause of social justice. By placing issues of social injustice on the table in a central way, parties are empowered to consider their significance and seek solutions to these injustices. These solutions might take the form of small steps that are within the grasp of the parties or recommendations and advocacy aimed at the political or legislative processes.

Doing Justice Relationally

Relational theory, thus, has significant implications for our thinking about justice. But it profoundly affects not only our thinking but also our approach to doing justice. Indeed, it requires an adjustment in the very way that we understand the work that justice requires. Taking relationships as the focal point of justice requires a contextual approach. The question of what justice requires, then, cannot be met by standard and formulaic answers but, rather, must take into account what is needed in a particular context to achieve just relationships between and among the parties involved. This is work that, like the relationships it seeks to achieve, is dynamic and fluid. Thus, it may be more appropriate to adjust our justice discourse from talking about justice "done" to "doing justice," which is not to suggest that relational justice is purely procedural in nature. In its idea of equality of relationship, relational justice does have a substantive goal or endstate that it seeks. However, the shift in language is an acknowledgment that relational justice does not identify justice with any one set of practices but, rather, requires the input and participation of those involved to understand the nature of the harm to relationships in order to determine how to respond, and to commit themselves, to their role in the restoration of relationships. Relational justice is, thus, able to take account of the significance and complexity of the interconnected webs of relationships in and through which we exist and come to define and understand both ourselves and what justice requires.

Since a relational theory of justice is grounded and contextual, it requires careful attention to justice processes. A relational theory of justice requires processes that are inclusive and participatory. They must be as inclusive as possible of those individuals affected, including but not limited to the victims, the offenders, their communities of care and support, other relevant communities, and the members of the wider communities affected. Through dialogical processes, these parties are able to understand the harms resulting from the wrong, recognize the significance of broader injustices, and arrive at a plan for addressing the harms with a view to realizing equality of relationship in the future.[28] Through broad inclusion, such processes are able to ensure the appropriate balance between macro- and micro-justice issues and to avoid sacrificing the needs and interests of individual parties. Such processes also have the potential to be democratic in the sense that they strive to ensure that those affected can participate in the processes of decision making about how to do justice in a particular situation. It is, thus, not sufficient for parties to simply be included, they must be given the opportunity to participate in a meaningful way, which includes, but is not limited to, taking part in a process of dialogue about the requirements of justice.[29]

What Is in a Name: Relational Justice as Restorative Justice

As suggested at the outset of this chapter, a relational theory of justice has found expression (although not often full or explicit) in the restorative justice movement as it has developed over the past three-and-a-half decades. As such, restorative justice practice and theoretical accounts of it provide fertile ground to consider the implications and possibilities of a relational approach to justice. Relational theory stands able to provide a basis from which to articulate and explain the foundational commitments and convictions of restorative justice and to assess and develop current theory and practice. Restorative justice is sometimes viewed as a set of alternative practices.

However, when one seeks deeper explanations or justification for these practices or if one probes the underlying insights and intuitions, fundamental questions about the idea of justice and the principles at the core of restorative justice emerge. Restorative justice is, as I suggest, best conceived as a theory of justice that takes relationality as its starting point grounding its commitments and claims in a relational conception of the self.[30] It is important to be clear that this is a claim about how restorative justice should or can ground itself and not a descriptive claim about restorative justice scholarship or literature. Indeed, far too little attention has been paid within restorative justice literature and practice to its underlying theory of justice. Throughout my previous work, I have argued for the importance of developing such a theoretical account of restorative justice and for grounding it in relational theory.

The centrality of relationships has been a hallmark of the development of restorative justice thus far. However, insofar as this commitment is explained or considered, it is often grounded in, and expressed in terms of, a particular set of religious or spiritual convictions. This religious association has sometimes made it difficult to bring such ideas from the periphery as alternative practices and to realize its broader implications for the mainstream justice system. Such a move would require a way of articulating and grounding restorative justice in a secular justice system. Relational theory offers a basis for restorative justice that is accessible to secular audiences. It does so, however, in a way that resonates with the significance given to relationship within many religious and faith traditions.[31] This point is not made to build the case for a relational approach but, rather, to note that the fact of relationality finds recognition in a wide range of sources even while the explanation for this fact differs.[32]

This grounding in relational theory is not only helpful insofar as it assists advocates of restorative justice to extol its virtues to the secular world but also because it provides a basis to assess, challenge, and develop current restorative justice practices and theories, some of which have been unwittingly influenced by a liberal individualist approach. Where such influence is evident, restorative justice advocates nevertheless focus on the relevance of relationships, but they understand their significance through a focus on the individual and insofar as relationships are useful or necessary for, or affect, individuals. Given the pervasiveness of this worldview, it is not surprising that it would find its way into some restorative justice theory and practice. These ideas are even reflected in some of the most familiar expressions of restorative justice, such as when Zehr describes the nature of the new "lens" and what can be seen through it. The lens focuses, for Zehr, on individuals first – on their needs and on their relationships.[33] A relational conception of justice, however, sees the centrality of relationships not as that which is useful for the individual or simply as part of their lived experience but, rather, as essential to the very imagining or understanding of the individual. The idea of relationships that promote well-being and flourishing by meeting the basic need for equality of relationship is meant to capture these ideas that are central to a relational conception of justice. To use Zehr's familiar lens metaphor, restorative justice as a relational theory of justice requires us to see relationships not through an individual lens as one might through a standard single lens reflex camera. This view is limited in terms of what it can see and capture. A relational approach requires a different way of seeing – one that might be better described using the analogy of the way in which human sight works. The process of "seeing" for human beings is different from the way in which cameras capture images.[34] Human "seeing" inherently involves an element of understanding. To gain such understanding, we rely not solely on our two lenses (our eyes working together) but also on our other ways of knowing the world including hearing, smelling, feeling, and tasting. Our brains take on the complex task of relating and integrating all of this input so that we can see. Doing so engages the relationship between the seer and that which is seen. Similarly, a restorative approach cannot proceed from the limited view through an individual lens if it is to see and understand relationally.

Understanding restorative justice as a relational theory of justice also helps to clarify the aim of restorative justice and respond to persistent misunderstandings of the notions of "restore" and "relationship." Consideration of these misconceptions also brings clarity to some important issues for relational theory. The first such misconception is that justice, understood restoratively, is inappropriate for the vast majority of cases where no prior state of equality existed that needs to be restored. This critique is particularly persistent and prolific because of the term "restore." The term "restore" evokes the idea of a return to a prior state. Rooting restorative justice in feminist relational theory helps to explain the sense in which "restoration" of relationships is sought. It is not restoration to some prior existing state but, rather, to the ideal of equality of relationship that justice seeks.

Admittedly, this use of the term "restore" is not what we are used to in common parlance, which might be a reason to reject the nomenclature but not the theory it reflects. The term "restorative justice" has, however, achieved substantial recognition throughout the world. It might cause significant confusion and detract from the real issue of our understanding of justice to change the name now. The interests of understanding and clarity are better served by explaining what restorative justice means and not in arguing over its name.[35] It is helpful then to stipulate the definition of "restore" in the sense that it is used in restorative justice. A relational theory starting point is helpful in these efforts to explain how the word "restore" is used. For restorative justice, equality of relationship as its goal is inherently possible and, indeed, necessary because it is grounded in the nature of the self – it is latent in the very nature of selves as relational beings. If we are relational then realizing equal respect, concern, and dignity, which is essential to our well-being and flourishing, requires connection with others. The latent potential of the equality of relationship at which restorative justice aims helps to see the sense in which "restore" is intended – it is to bring out, or to realize, our full potential and capacities as relational beings. Just as a carpenter who lovingly restores an old piece of furniture may realize from it a potential and beauty that was never fully realized at an earlier time – its restoration is not dependent upon or determined wholly by its previous states. The fact that a table enjoys a better finish or is no longer weakened by a knot or gouge does not make the accomplishment any less a restoration of the piece.

Even absent the word "restore" though, a concern might be expressed with respect to a relational theory of justice if one assumes that the goal is to repair or preserve particular relationships. To exemplify the problem, critics charge that justice so conceived would require a woman who is a victim of violence at the hands of her spouse to "hug and make up" for the sake of preserving her marriage relationship. In this and many other situations, critics rightly point out that there is often no prior state of equality in relationship to return to and, even in cases where such equality once existed, it is foolish and even dangerous to presume that it might be re-created and the relationship maintained. This objection is also interestingly often made with reference to seeking justice in the wake of serious abuses and violations committed in the context of a civil conflict or war. In these situations, the argument is made that such conflicts are generally the result of long-standing inequalities and injustices, and it is hard, if not impossible, to identify a time of justice that might be recouped.[36]

These critics are right. A return to "the good old days" in most cases would not see justice done. The critique is wrongheaded, however, as a critique of restorative justice. Justice, according to a relational theory, is not to be found in the preservation or resurrection of particular relationships. Rather, it takes the fact of relationship and the need to attend to the nature of our connections to one another as the concern of justice. Restorative justice thus is not committed to preserving existing relationships or returning to some prior state, but, rather, requires careful attention to the current conditions and terms of relationship so that they might be altered or changed as needed to find the equality of relationship that justice requires. As a relational theory of justice, restorative justice maintains, then, that the woman and her abuser continue to be connected (by history and perhaps by sharing children and by sharing the same political, social, and/or geographical space), but justice requires that their connection reflect equality of relationship – in terms of respect, concern, and dignity. In practical terms, this may well require physical and emotional separation, not reconciliation or maintenance of the existing relationship. The concern animating the earlier critique of restorative justice is reflective of that which some feminists make of communitarianism or even of care theory – namely, that it is conservative in its unquestioning protection and preservation of existing social relations.[37]

The example of the woman who is the victim of violence at the hands of her spouse raises another common concern about restorative justice that reflects a misconception of relational theory and its implications for justice. Here, it is not the word "restore" that is the cause of the misunderstanding, it is "relationship." The focus on relationships evokes for some the idea of intimate or personal relationships of attachment. Just as restorative justice does not require the preservation or re-instantiation of particular relationships, it also does not take as its focus intimate or personal relationships. The concern of a relational theory of justice is, rather, with connection at, what one might call, a social level – that is, with the basic elements and conditions of relationship required for peaceful and meaningful coexistence and flourishing. This is not to say that justice will never involve the restoration of intimate or personal relationships. Such an outcome is not precluded if it serves to achieve equality of relationship in a particular case, but, it is not the goal of justice on a relational account. Of course, the conditions of relationship with which restorative justice is concerned are not irrelevant to intimate and personal relationships since these elements form the basic building blocks of healthy intimate or personal relationships just as they do for social/political relationships. Personal and political relationships are also connected to one another as the structure of personal relationships collectively construct or influence the public and, at the same time, exist within the structures of public relationships.[38]

A relational theory of justice is not, however, reliant upon, nor primarily concerned with, relationships in the intimate and personal sense. Restorative justice is not intent upon establishing or re-establishing relationships of an intimate or personal character. It recognizes that, at a minimum, human selves will be and must be connected to others through networks of social relationships and is concerned with the justice of these connections. This misconception about the goal of restorative justice is related to another misconception that is often held about relational theory, namely that it idealizes certain models of relationship, particularly caring personal relationships exemplified by care-taking relationships or friendships. This is not the case for relational theory generally nor for restorative justice more specifically. Such relationships may in some instances model or provide insights into the values that mark equality of relationship – respect, concern, and dignity – but not necessarily so. It is thus not helpful or accurate to identify relational theory with idealized models or types of relationships.

Approaching restorative justice as a relational theory of justice also poses a challenge to another prevailing assumption or conception of restorative justice – that it is simply a theory or approach to criminal justice. As the prior discussion of relational justice reveals, it is not a theory relevant only to a narrow set of wrongs labelled criminal or public. Indeed, relational theory forces us to revisit these very divisions and categories. As a relational theory of justice then, restorative justice is a comprehensive theory in the sense that it is not limited in its application to one realm, which runs counter to the common perception of restorative justice as a theory of criminal justice. Even while the applicability of its practices has been recognized far beyond the criminal realm, the general description of restorative justice as being about criminal justice persists. The adherence to this understanding of restorative justice is evident in the use of "restorative practices" as opposed to restorative justice to distinguish applications outside the criminal realm.[39] Conceiving of restorative justice as a relational theory of justice makes such a limit untenable. Restorative justice is concerned with responding to the harms to relationships that flow from wrongdoing or that mark the existing structure of relationships. Restorative justice is thus concerned with criminal, civil, and social injustices. However, challenging this limited conception of restorative justice does not mean that it is boundless. Other restorative justice advocates make claims at the other end of the spectrum – instead of claiming too little for restorative justice they claim too much. This misconception is evident in those within the movement who have begun to advocate an approach that sees restorative justice as a "way of life" or as being appropriate to address all manner of relational ills or simply as a strategy to maintain healthy relations.[40]

As a theory of justice, the net of restorative justice cannot be so broadly cast without losing sight of its concern for justice. Justice is actually concerned with wrongs – that is, with more than general dysfunction and not as simply an aspiration for the "good." So while the restorative justice tent is bigger than some suggest, it is not without walls. This is not to say, however, that there is no connection between restorative justice (its goals and aspirations) and this broader interest in fostering and maintaining relationships and in living well in relationship with others. In fact, relational theory is helpful in explaining this connection. The intuition that seems to drive those who seek to broaden the meaning of restorative justice is a correct one. They recognize that the relational view that underlies restorative justice has broader significance for our lives – to how we structure our social and political interactions, institutions, and systems. However, once one recognizes that restorative justice is a relational theory of justice, it becomes clear that restorative justice is not the bigger tent that they seek – rather they should look to relational theory.[41] Indeed, as the chapters in this volume demonstrate, relational theory has implications for many of our ideas, values, principles, and thus for our laws and policies and the institutions and systems through which they are applied and realized. The experience of restorative justice can provide a poignant example of our connectedness and of the implications of failing to recognize, and take as central, relationality in the structure of our social, political, legal, and even personal relationships. However, this chapter does not claim that restorative justice is the answer but, rather, that from it we can gain the broader insight that we are relational and that this must shape the understanding of how, and the processes through which, people live, work, and play together.

Notes

The author wishes to acknowledge the support of the Nova Scotia Restorative Justice Community University Research Alliance (funded by the Social Science and Humanities Research Council of Canada). Thanks are owed to the other authors in this volume for their helpful comments and in particular to Christine Koggel and Jocelyn Downie for their insightful and detailed comments. Thanks are also owed to Audrey Barrett for her research assistance and to Blake Brown for his always keen editorial eye.

1 John Braithwaite has argued that restorative principles and ideas have been common throughout history in most cultures. John Braithwaite, *Restorative Justice and Responsive Regulation* (New York: Oxford University Press, 2002) at 5. In its contemporary form, restorative justice has been most commonly applied in domestic contexts with regard to youth criminal justice. More recently, restorative justice has been applied in civil justice, regulatory contexts, in school discipline, and to deal with workplace conflicts. Internationally, restorative justice has been applied in attempts to deal with historical and systemic abuses and in peace building. See Jennifer Llewellyn, "Restorative Justice in Transitions and Beyond: The Justice Potential of Truth Telling Mechanisms for Post-Peace Accord Societies" in T. Borer, ed., *Telling The Truths: Truth Telling and Peace Building in Post-Conflict Societies* (Notre Dame, IN: University of Notre Dame Press, 2006) 83; Jennifer Llewellyn, "Truth Commissions and Restorative Justice" in G. Johnstone and D. Van Ness, eds., *Handbook of Restorative Justice* (Devon, UK: Willan Publishers, 2006) 351. It has been endorsed by the United Nations in the Basic Principles on the Use of Restorative Justice Programmes in Criminal Matters. See United Nations Economic and Social Council, Doc. E/CN.15/2002/5/Add.1 and United Nations Office on Drugs and Crime, *Handbook on Restorative Justice Programmes* (Vienna: United Nations, 2006).

2 For a further discussion of the influences upon the development of the restorative justice movement, see Daniel Van Ness and Karen Heetderks Strong, *Restoring Justice* (Cincinnati: Anderson Publishing, 1997).

3 For a comprehensive synthesis of recent empirical research, see Lawrence Sherman and Heather Strang, *Restorative Justice: The Evidence* (London: Smith Institute, 2007).

4 Howard Zehr, *Changing Lenses: A New Focus for Crime and Justice* (Waterloo, ON: Herald Press, 1990).

5 For a selection of my previous work in which this idea is developed, see Jennifer J. Llewellyn, "Bridging the Gap between Truth and Reconciliation: Restorative Justice and the Indian Residential School Truth and Reconciliation Commission" in Marlene Brant-Castellano, Linda Archibald, and Mike DeGagne, eds., *From Truth to Reconciliation: Transforming the Legacy of Residential Schools* (Ottawa: Aboriginal Healing Foundation, 2008); Jennifer J. Llewellyn, "Truth and Reconciliation Commissions: Restorative Justice in Response to Abuse and Violence" in Johnstone and Van Ness, *supra* note 1; Llewellyn, "Restorative Justice,"

supra note 1; Jennifer J. Llewellyn, "Doing Justice in South Africa: Restorative Justice and Reparations" in C. Villa-Vicencio and E. Doxtader, eds., *Repairing the Unforgiveable: Reparations and Reconstruction in South Africa* (Claremont, South Africa: David Philip Publishers/New Africa Books, 2004) 166; Jennifer J. Llewellyn, "Review of *Aftermath: Violence and the Remaking of a Self*" (2003) 15 C.J.W.L. 392; Jennifer J. Llewellyn, "Restorative Justice in *Borde* and *Hamilton* – A Systemic Problem?" (2003) 8 Criminal Reports (6th) 308; Jennifer J. Llewellyn, "Dealing with the Legacy of Native Residential School Abuse: Litigation, ADR, and Restorative Justice" (2002) 52 U.T.L.J. 253; Jennifer J. Llewellyn, "Justice for South Africa: Restorative Justice and the Truth and Reconciliation Commission" in C.M. Koggel, ed., *Moral Issues in Global Perspective* (Peterborough, ON: Broadview Press, 1999) 96; Jennifer J. Llewellyn and Robert Howse, "Institutions for Restorative Justice: The South African Truth and Reconciliation Commission" (1999) 49 U.T.L.J. 355; Jennifer J. Llewellyn and Robert Howse, *Restorative Justice: A Conceptual Framework* (Ottawa: Law Commission of Canada, 1998).

6   See generally the discussion and citations in the introduction to this volume.

7   Here I recognize that "others" includes human and non-human animals and that a relational conception of the self should also focus attention on the connection between selves and the life world they inhabit. However, this is not my focus in this particular chapter. I am primarily concerned here to explore the implications for thinking about and doing justice in the human realm. I do not intend to suggest by this focus that these issues should take priority over a consideration of justice as it relates to non-human animals or the environment. Indeed, although I do not spell this out within the limited scope of this chapter, I think a relational conception of justice has much to say about justice in the context of non-human animals and the environment. In this volume, Maneesha Deckha explores some of these issues that would illuminate such a consideration of justice in these other contexts in the future. See Maneesha Deckha, "Non-Human Animals and Human Health: A Relational Approach to the Use of Animals in Medical Research" in this volume.

8   Llewellyn and Howse, *Restorative Justice, supra* note 5.

9   These assumptions are often rooted in a retributive conception of justice. For a fuller discussion of the relationship between relational (restorative) justice and retributive justice, see Llewellyn, "Restorative Justice in *Borde* and *Hamilton*," *supra* note 5; Llewellyn and Howse, "Institutions for Restorative Justice," *supra* note 5.

10 For a fuller discussion of the relationship between corrective and relational conceptions of justice, see Llewellyn, "Dealing with the Legacy of Native Residential School Abuse," *supra* note 5.

11 Ronald Dworkin, "What Is Equality? Part 3: The Place of Liberty" (1987) 73 Iowa L. Rev. 1 at 10.

12 See, for example, Llewellyn and Howse, *Restorative Justice, supra* note 5 at 30-37.

13 See generally Ernest J. Weinrib, *The Idea of Private Law* (Cambridge, MA: Harvard University Press, 1995).

14 See generally Georg W.F. Hegel, *Elements of the Philosophy of Right*, translated by H.B. Nisbet and edited by Allen Wood (New York: Cambridge University Press, 1991).

15 John Rawls, *A Theory of Justice* (Cambridge, MA: Harvard University Press, 1971) at 511.

16 Ronald Dworkin, *Taking Rights Seriously* (Cambridge, MA: Harvard University Press, 1977) at 180.

17 For an elaboration of the concept of "relational equality," see Christine M. Koggel, "A Relational Approach to Equality: New Developments and Applications" in this volume. See also Christine M. Koggel, *Perspectives on Equality: Constructing a Relational Theory* (New York: Rowman and Littlefield, 1998). In particular, Koggel distinguishes a relational account from formal and substantive approaches in the liberal tradition.

18 Susan Brison offers a view of the self as "both autonomous and socially dependent, vulnerable enough to be undone by violence and yet resilient enough to be reconstructed with the help of empathetic others." Susan J. Brison, "Outliving Oneself: Trauma, Memory and Personal Identity" in Diana Tietjens Meyers, ed., *Feminist Rethink the Self* (Boulder, CO: Westview Press, 1997). See also Susan J. Brison, *Aftermath: Violence and the Remaking of a Self* (Princeton, NJ: Princeton University Press, 2002).

19 Rawls, *supra* note 15; Dworkin, *supra* note 16.

20 Immanuel Kant, *Grundlegung zur Metaphysik der Sitten* (*Groundwork of the Metaphysic of Morals*), translated by H.J. Paton, volume 4 (1785; reprinted New York: Harper and Row, 1964) at 428-35.

21 See Maneesha Deckha, "Non-Human Animals and Human Health: A Relational Approach to the Use of Animals in Medical Research" in this volume, as the author takes up this point in the context of testing on non-human animals.

22 See, for example, Rawls, *supra* note 15.

23 For a consideration of the implications of relational theory for our conception of rights and rights protection, see Jennifer Nedelsky, "Reconceiving Rights as Relationship" (1993) 1 Rev. Const. Stud. 1.

24 While some liberal accounts use the formulation of respect and concern without moving substantially from the notion of respect described earlier, others see it as requiring some positive actions to support others. See, for example, Barbara Herman, "Mutual Aid and Respect for Persons" (1984) 94 Ethics 577. However, such accounts do not challenge the fundamental assumptions of liberal individualism and generally ground concern for others in some version of self-interest.

25 See discussion in the introduction to this volume.

26 Kent Roach, "A Dialogue about Principle and a Principled Dialogue: Justice Iacobucci's Substantive Approach to Dialogue" (2007) 57 U.T.L.J. 449.

27 If there is a relevant distinction, it is one of scope. Some harms have a farther-reaching effect upon relationships than others. It may be that criminal laws are more likely to touch upon wrongful behaviour with these wider implications, but this is not always the case as is clear from the overlap between the two areas of law with respect to certain conduct. The example of the civil suits in relation to the abuses of residential schools is a case in point.

28 For an example of the role of social dialogue in the realization of social equality, see Jennifer Nedelsky and Craig Scott, "Constitutional Dialogue" in Joel Bakan and David Schneiderman, eds., *Social Justice and the Constitution: Perspectives on a Social Union for Canada* (Ottawa: Carleton University Press, 1992) 59.

29 Jürgen Habermas' work on discourse and democracy might provide some important insights for restorative justice in this respect. See generally Jürgen Habermas, *Between Facts and Norms: Contributions to a Discourse Theory of Law and Democracy*, translated by William Rehg (Cambridge, MA: MIT Press, 1998); Jürgen Habermas, *The Theory of Communicative Action, Volume 1: Reason and the Rationalization of Society; Volume 2: Lifeworld and System: A Critique of Functionalist Reason*, translated by Thomas McCarthy (Boston: Beacon Press, 1984). For a consideration of these issues, see Audrey Barrett, "The Works of Jürgen Habermas: A Tool for Further Understanding the Theory and Practice of Restorative Justice" (LL.M. thesis, Schulich School of Law, Dalhousie University).

30 See, for example, Llewellyn, "Restorative Justice," *supra* note 1; Llewellyn, "Restorative Justice in *Borde* and *Hamilton*," *supra* note 5; Jennifer Llewellyn, "Building, Strengthening and Transforming Communities: Exploring the Possibilities for Restorative Justice in Jamaica" (2002) 27 West Indian L.J. 77; Llewellyn, "Dealing with the Legacy of Native Residential School Abuse," *supra* note 5; Llewellyn, "Justice for South Africa," *supra* note 5.

31 Michael L. Hadley, ed., *The Spiritual Roots of Restorative Justice* (Albany, NY: State University of New York Press, 2001).

32 To give a few examples, relational insights are to be found in science (quantum physics), social science (relational sociology, anthropology, and pyschological attachment theory), medicine, and so on.

33 Zehr, *supra* note 4.

34 For a general discussion of the distinction between cameras and the human eye, see Alex MacLeod, " ⊙ ≠ 📷 (The Eye Is Not a Camera)" at http://www.iconoclastic.net/lezards/looknsee/worthit.html.

35 For an example of this debate, see Ruth Morris, *A Practical Path to Transformative Justice* (Toronto: Rittenhouse, 1994).

36 I have considered the application of restorative justice in these contexts elsewhere, see Llewellyn, "Restorative Justice" *supra* note 1 and "From Truth to Reconciliation"; "Truth and Reconciliation Commissions" and "Justice for South Africa" *supra* note 5.

37   See, for example, Amy Gutmann, "Communitarian Critics of Liberalism" (1985) 14 Philosophy and Public Affairs 308 at 309. See also Elizabeth Frazer and Nicola Lacey, *The Politics of Community: A Feminist Critique of the Liberal-Communitarian Debate* (Toronto: University of Toronto Press, 1993) at c. 5.

38   Jennifer Nedelsky refers to the idea of "nested" relationships. See Jennifer Nedelsky, "The Reciprocal Relation of Judgment and Autonomy: Walking in Another's Shoes and Which Shoes to Walk In" in this volume and *Law, Autonomy and the Relational Self* (Oxford: Oxford University Press, 2012).

39   This term is sometimes employed to denote the application of restorative processes outside the justice realm entirely, for example, in the education context.

40   For a discussion of this approach to restorative justice, see Gerry Johnstone and Daniel W. Van Ness, "The Meaning of Restorative Justice" in Gerry Johnstone and Daniel Van Ness, eds., *Handbook of Restorative Justice* (Portland, OR: Willan Publishing, 2007) 3 at 5.

41   For this reason, the use of the term restorative practice or practices to refer to the use of such an approach outside of the criminal justice or justice realms is potentially problematic. It suggests a focus on the practice or process elements of restorative justice apart from the underlying relational theory. Just as some have approached restorative justice as little more than alternative practice, and thereby missed the different conception of justice at work, the term restorative practices might invite attention to the process without a consideration of the relational theory in which they are rooted. Although I would not advocate an extension of the term restorative justice, a reference to a restorative or relational approach would, I suggest, more accurately capture the significance and potential of such processes.

5
The Self *in Situ*: A Relational Account of Personal Identity

Françoise Baylis

In the early 1980s, Gregory David Roberts, now an international best-selling author and then a convicted armed robber, escaped from an Australian prison to India. In India, on the run from international authorities, he lamented his loneliness and his loss of identity, both of which he attributed directly to lost connections: "I'd lost my family, the friends of my youth, my country and its culture – all the things that had defined me, and given me identity."[1] In India, he made two very close friends – friends that he trusted, friends that he loved. Both of these friends died in discrete traumatic circumstances. Following these untimely deaths, Roberts not only perceived himself as alone but as adrift. Again, he reflects on his loss of identity:

> I'd lost Prabaker and Abdullah, my closest friends, in the same week, and with them I'd lost the mark on the psychic map that says *You Are Here*. Personality and personal identity are in some ways like co-ordinates on the street map drawn by our intersecting relationships. We know who we are and we define what we are by references to the people we love and our reasons for loving them.[2]

With these few words, Roberts captures an important intuition about personhood and personal identity. Persons are interdependent beings, and so it is that a person's identity (including her traits, desires, beliefs, values, emotions, intentions, memories, actions, and experiences) is informed by her personal relationships – relationships characterized by varying degrees and kinds of intimacy and interdependence. This is not all that defines personal identity, however. No less important are the public interactions (social, cultural, and political) that help structure a person's account of herself and her place in the world – her past, her present, and her future.

In this chapter, I propose an account of personal identity that is thoroughly relational and that makes transparent the ways in which persons are constituted in and through their personal relationships, public interactions, and ancestry. Specifically, I develop an account of relational personal identity as a dynamic, socially, culturally, politically, and historically situated communicative activity (based in narrative and performance) that is informed by the interests, perspectives, and creative intentions of close and distant others.

As a prelude to this discussion, I provide background information on: (1) some of my earlier musings on identity; (2) the work of feminist theorists on relational autonomy and relational personhood; and (3) recent scholarship on the narrative construction of personal identity. Strands of these discussions are then woven together into a relational account of personal identity in which "equilibrium" is crucial for identity constitution. In closing, I illustrate the implications of the relational dynamic that I describe in addressing one facet of the question: "Who is Barack Obama?"

Prelude

Early Musings on Identity

The relational account of personal identity that I develop in this chapter is rooted in my earlier work in bioethics, where, in addressing such diverse topics as genetic ancestry tracing, face transplantation, and brain manipulation, I began to explore the idea of identity as a collection of stories constructed and maintained over time – through a series of actions, interactions, reactions, and transactions – by a self in relation with intimate and distant others. According to this view, my identity is neither in my body (*viz.*, the somatic or biological account of personal identity) nor in my brain (*viz.*, the psychological account of personal identity) but, rather, in the negotiated spaces between my biology and psychology and that of others. These others include those who are a part of my familial, social, cultural, and political clusters of meaning and belonging, those who know me from a distance, and still others, near strangers, who do not know me.

This view of identity as changeable and contingent coheres with the perspective offered by Stephen Maturin in Patrick O'Brian's *Master and Commander*:

> The identity I am thinking of is something that hovers between a man and the rest of the world: a mid-point between his view of himself and theirs of him – for each, of course, affects the other continually. A reciprocal fluxion, sir. There is nothing absolute about this identity of mine.[3]

This description of identity as "reciprocal fluxion" captures both the idea that identity is always changing as well as the idea that these changes occur at the intersection of what a person claims about herself and what others claim about her. On this view, identity is a balance between self-ascription and ascription by others.

My first attempt at explaining personal identity in relational terms is an autobiographical article on genes and genetic ancestry tracing in which I argue that racial identity cannot be reduced to genetic identity.[4] Racial identity is not in our genes (our cells, our bodies) but, rather, in the world in which we live and in the stories about race and ethnicity that we are able to construct and maintain through complex social interactions involving an iterative cycle of "self"-perception, "self"-projection, "other"-perception, and "other"-reaction. To be clear on this point, while the wording here makes the process seem linear and fixed, what I have in mind is a cyclical process, with periods of doubling back and periods of skipping forward linking the present to the past and to the future, making integration possible over time.[5]

In this autobiographical article, I share how my "identity as a black person was (and is) carefully constructed for and by me ... [through] stories that are 'acquired, refined, revised, displaced and replaced'[6] over time through introspection and continued lived experience."[7] I explain that my identity is a dynamic interpersonal construct that I fashion in both intimate and public spaces between myself and others as I negotiate my place in the world. I also explore how my identity is encumbered by my past (a history both remembered and learned) that both shapes and directs my life (through a process of reflection and observation) for better or for worse. The lyrics to "Who I Am" by Jessica Andrews capture some of what I mean:

I am Rosemary's granddaughter
The spitting image of my father
And when the day is done
My momma's still my biggest fan

Sometimes I'm clueless and I'm clumsy
But I've got friends that love me
And they know just where I stand
It's all a part of me
And that's who I am

I'm a saint and I'm a sinner
I'm a loser, I'm a winner
I'm steady and unstable
I'm young but I am able.[8]

Further, the idea that identity is a dynamic interpersonal social construct formed by social relations, roles, and practices is consonant with the views of Lawrence Thomas, who observes that

we are constituted through others ... the way in which we conceive of ourselves, at least in part, owes much to how others conceive [of] us, and this
is necessarily so. The way in which we think of ourselves is inextricably tied
to the way in which others think of us.[9]

In later writings on facial transplantation, I revisit the idea that "identity
formation is an ongoing process of self-construction influenced by personal
attributes, life experiences, introspection, and the storying of one's life."[10] I
suggest that "[o]ur intimate and distant interactions influence how we act
and interact in the world, which in turn influences how others see and
interact with us, which in turn influences how we see ourselves."[11] In these
articles, there is particular attention to the fact that persons are not only
socially, culturally, politically, and historically constituted selves but are also
embodied selves.

As Carolyn McLeod and I argue elsewhere, with reference to the bodily
experiences of women,

the body is constitutive of the self insofar as our experience of, and comfort
with, our bodies, as well as our and others' perceptions of our bodies, shape
us (both actually and figuratively). To say that the body is constitutive of
the self ... is to recognize how the body influences who we are and how we
can be in the world. For example, women live in a world in which the idealized woman's body is not even anatomically possible. This fact of the world
informs our and others' perceptions of our actual bodies, which in turn
shape how we see ourselves and how we act, as well as how others see and
act towards us.[12]

Sex and gender, like race, mark the body in visible and intimate ways that,
as Linda Alcoff writes, affect "our relations in the world, which in turn affects our interior life, that is, our lived experience or subjectivity. If social
identities such as race and gender are fundamental in this way to one's
experiences, then it only makes sense to say that they are fundamental to
the self."[13] In brief, personal identities are shaped over a lifetime in relation
to close and distant others, all of whom live lives that are constrained by
socio-cultural and socio-political assumptions, expectations, norms, and
institutions, as well as ancestral connections.

Relational Personhood
The concept of personhood that figures most prominently in contemporary
Western ethical and political theory is that of the independent, rational, self-
aware, self-reliant, self-interested individual thoroughly (if not obsessively)
engaged in the autonomous pursuit of his interests.[14] Although familiar,

this traditional liberal account of personhood is deeply flawed. As Susan Sherwin reminds us,

> no one is fully independent ... the view of individuals as isolated social units is not only false but impoverished: much of who we are and what we value is rooted in our relationships and affinities with others ... all persons are, to a significant degree, socially constructed ... their identities, values, concepts, and perceptions are, in large measure, products of their social environment.[15]

In a similar vein, Margaret Urban Walker notes that the dominant account of personhood "conceals, distorts, or devalues the human reality of individuals who achieve identity and meaning from the cultures, traditions, communities, and roles in which they are embedded."[16]

For most feminists, persons are not independent, purely rational, separate, and self-interested beings. Rather, persons are relational beings shaped by the personal, social, cultural, political, historical, and other contexts into which they are born and raised. Following Annette Baier, persons are really "*second* persons": "essentially successors, heirs to other persons who formed and cared for them."[17] According to this view, individuals are socialized into personhood, and so it is that their autonomy is a product of social relations. This understanding of selves as socially constituted is of pivotal importance in contemporary feminist relational theory, which aims to recognize the social nature of persons and to highlight our relations of mutual vulnerability and interdependence.[18] Feminists also understand that persons are shaped within contexts and circumstances where identity categories such as age, race, ethnicity, gender, class, sexual orientation, and ability are used to privilege or to oppress. Depending upon which stereotypical assumptions are made with reference to any of these identifiable groups or communities and where one is situated relative to these assumptions, the possibilities for who one can be (or become) expand or contract. Thomas writes about these constrained lives in terms of privileged and diminished social categories, where diminished social category persons "are constituted in both masterfully subtle ways and in ever so explicit ways, so as not to see themselves as full and equal members of society ... [In sharp contrast, in] a fully just world, all would be constituted through others so as to be full and equal members of society."[19]

Narrative Construction and Identity

In reflecting on the ways in which fictional narratives overlap with inner and outer storytelling about actual lives lived, Barbara Hardy observes that

> we dream in narrative, day-dream in narrative, remember, anticipate, hope, despair, believe, doubt, plan, revise, criticize, construct, gossip, learn, hate and love by narrative. In order really to live, we make up stories about ourselves and others, about the personal as well as the social past and future.[20]

This understanding of the central place of narrative in lived experience informs recent scholarship on narrative identity.[21] In *The Constitution of Selves*, Marya Schechtman critiques the traditional philosophical literature on personal identity and the problem of re-identification in order to focus instead on issues of identity that are familiar to us from life, psychology, and literature. In these realms, the pivotal identity question is not "what makes a person at time t_2 the same person as a person at time t_1?" but, rather, "what actions, experiences, beliefs, values, desires, character traits and so on (hereafter abbreviated as "characteristics") make a person who she is."[22] In exploring this latter question, which Schechtman dubs the "characterization question," Schechtman argues that "a person creates his identity by forming an autobiographical narrative – a story of his life."[23] Accordingly,

> individuals constitute themselves as persons by coming to think of themselves as persisting subjects who have had experience in the past and will continue to have experience in the future, taking certain experiences as theirs ... A person's identity ... is constituted by the content of her self-narrative, and the traits, actions, and experiences included in it are, by virtue of that inclusion, hers.[24]

On this view, the authoritative answer to the question "What makes a person who she is?" is to be found in the person's self-narrative.

According to Schechtman "self-constitution must be part of a viable account of identity."[25] However, not any concept of self will do: "[O]ne needs a self-concept that is basically in synch with the view of one held by others."[26] In other words, for a self-narrative to be identity-constituting, it must cohere with an "objective" account of the person's life, as would be told by another. More precisely, for a self-narrative to be identity-constituting, it must be capable of local articulation and it must cohere with reality. In regard to the articulation constraint, Schechtman insists that "the narrator should be able to explain why he does what he does, believes what he believes, and feels what he feels."[27] To be clear, Schechtman does not intend that a person should be able to narrate her whole life in a self-conscious way, but she must be able to narrate parts of it.[28] She may not be able to explain her *implicit* self-narrative (her underlying psychological organization), but she must be able to render her *explicit* self-narrative intelligible. As for the reality constraint, Schechtman insists that the self-narrative must cohere with basic

observational facts about humans and their environment and with inter-
pretative facts about the meaning and implications of the observational
facts.

Hilde Lindemann Nelson offers a slightly different account of narrative
identity – one that stresses the importance of social recognition and explores
the role of first and third person narratives in defining identity. Nelson
basically agrees with Schechtman's narrative, self-constitution view of identity but insists that personal identity is only partly constituted by the self:

> If a person's identity "is constituted by the content of her self-narrative"
> and that content comprises those features of our lives and ourselves that we
> care about, there is also an extent to which our identities are constituted by
> the content of *other* people's narratives – the features of our lives and our-
> selves that *they* care most about ... A personal identity thus requires social
> recognition. Identities are not simply a matter of how we experience our
> own lives, but also of how others see and understand us.
>
> Who we can be is often a matter of who others take us to be. Many practical
> identities require more than one person for their construction and mainten-
> ance. Your identity as a competent adult crucially depends on others' [sic]
> recognizing you as such. Your identity as a white person hinges on the ac-
> knowledgment of others that you are indeed white. And your identity as a
> wife is thrown into devastating confusion if your husband decides he no
> longer wants to be married to you. In all these instances and many more, a
> key component of identity is the people around you, who must recognize
> that the identity is properly yours.[29]

In this quotation, Nelson echoes, in part, Alasdair MacIntyre who, in writing
about the narrative concept of selfhood, insists that "I am what I may justifiably be taken by others to be."[30]

According to Nelson, "personal identities consist of a connective tissue"
of overlapping stories from first and third person perspectives.[31] In response
to the question "What makes a person who she is?" Nelson explains that
there are the stories told from the first person perspective that emphasize
the actions, experiences, and characteristics that the person cares about as
well as the roles, relationships, and values to which the person is committed.
In addition to these stories, there are the stories told from the third person
perspective where the things about the person that matter most to others
are front and centre. Often these stories overlap, but on occasion they may
conflict. When they do conflict, the challenge is in knowing which stories
to count. On the "no trump" theory espoused by Nelson, a person's own
stories about who she is do not automatically take precedence over other
people's stories about her. Rather, when there is "a disagreement about which

of two contending narratives should be regarded as identity-constituting, the three credibility criteria [strong explanatory force, correlation to action, and heft] can work together to provide the standards for assessing which is the better story."[32]

A self-narrative has a strong explanatory force when it, above other possible narratives, *best* explains some personal characteristic: "Identity-constituting stories are those that don't just take the evidence into account – they're the ones that fit the evidence best."[33] A second feature of an identity-constituting narrative is that it strongly correlates with a person's actions (which may or may not cohere with a person's expressed beliefs or intentions). And, finally, there is the criterion of heft, which speaks to the weight, the importance, and the care that one attaches to a salient feature in one's narrative. Using these three credibility criteria to assess the merits of two (or more) contending narratives, Nelson maintains that it should be possible to identify the authoritative narrative. If more than one story is acceptable according to the credibility criteria, then the first person narrative prevails.

Nelson's credibility constraint contrasts markedly with Schechtman's reality constraint. For Schechtman, "one needs a self-concept that is basically in synch with the view of one held by others."[34] For Nelson, it is wrong to test a person's self-narrative against a narrative that others would tell since this alternative narrative could be seriously "mistaken, bigoted or hostile."[35] A person may be ignorant, mistaken, self-deceived, or mendacious with respect to her self-narrative, but this could also be the case with third person narratives. As such, there is no principled reason to privilege the perspective of others (even a multitude of others) in deciding whether a narrative is identity constituting – what matters is credibility. With respect to this criterion, at times a person's self-narrative should be taken as authoritative and at other times other people's stories about the person should be taken as authoritative.

Others who believe that self-narratives are co-authored include Paul Ricoeur and MacIntyre. According to Ricoeur, at the very least, others co-author our narrative insofar as they contribute stories from the time of our birth (or perhaps even conception) until such a time as our memories are no longer clouded by early infancy.[36] These stories are selectively incorporated into our self-narrative so that we can answer pivotal questions about who we are. On this view, one is not, and can never be, the sole author of one's narrative. And for MacIntyre, "we are never more (and sometimes less) than the co-authors of our own narratives. Only in fantasy do we live what story we please. In life ... we are always under certain constraints."[37] As Catriona Mackenzie reminds us, "[w]e are always already caught up in relations with others, even prior to birth, and we acquire identities and agency within a community of agents and are constrained by complex networks of social norms, institutions, practices, conventions, expectations, and attitudes."[38] Through these relations, we experience the perceptions, actions, and reactions of others that give rise to interactions and transactions in discrete social, cultural, and political settings.

Taken together, the strands from (1) applied ethics, (2) feminist theory, and (3) narrative construction of personal identity can be woven into a novel perspective on relational personal identity.

A Relational Account of Personal Identity

If one takes seriously the claim that the desires, beliefs, values, emotions, intentions, memories, actions, and experiences that make up a person's self-narrative are shaped by self and others – in particular, socio-cultural and socio-political contexts – it follows that we are constituted in and through personal relationships and public interactions. Indeed, it could not be otherwise. This view is grounded in recent feminist scholarship on relational theory, which helps us to understand selfhood as a dynamic process that emerges over time within networks of relations of mutual recognition. As Sherwin writes,

> relational selves are inherently social beings that are significantly shaped and modified within a web of interconnected (and sometimes conflicting) relationships. Individuals engage in the activities that are constitutive of identity and autonomy (e.g., defining, questioning, revising, and pursuing projects) within a configuration of relationships, both interpersonal and political.[39]

In parallel, recent scholarship on narrative identity helps us to understand how the lives of persons are narrative in form and how these personal narratives enjoy a certain kind of continuity insofar as one's sense of self can be explained longitudinally. Together, these insights undergird the belief that identities are created by relational beings mutually engaged in the never-ending project of constituting themselves in and through personal relationships and public interactions in order to answer such personal questions as: Who am I? Where am I from? Where have I been? Where am I going? What do I care about? What do I stand for? Who do I want to be? Who am I becoming? Indeed, it is through our (more or less conscious) interpretations of our values, memories, actions, experiences, and so on as well as the (more or less conscious) interpretations of these same characteristics by others that we come to embody answers to these pivotal questions, thereby instantiating our place in the world as we continually strive for balance between how we see and understand ourselves and how others see and understand us. Accordingly, personal traits, memories, and lived experiences are salient, incidental, or trivial (and, for this reason, do or do not occupy a prominent place in our self-narrative), depending upon our perceptions, reflections, and performances as well as the perceptions, reflections, and performances of others.[40]

This understanding of relational identity as an amalgam of self-ascription and ascription by others differs markedly from the narrative self-constitution view of identity where personhood and personal identity "rely crucially on an individual's inner life and her attitude toward her actions and experiences."[41] According to Schechtman, persons play an active role in defining their identities, and, as such, persons can properly be described as projects of self-creation. In sharp contrast, with relational identity, personhood and personal identity rely crucially not only on an individual's inner life and attitudes toward her traits, desires, beliefs, and so on but also on the attitudes of others to the same range of characteristics. Family members, friends, colleagues, community or tribal members, acquaintances, and even strangers play an active role in shaping the self-narratives of others not only by contributing to, but also by endorsing, questioning, and, in some cases, actively contesting, another's self-narrative. With relational identity, persons are (and can only be) dynamic complex co-creations informed by the perspectives and creative intentions of others.

To be fair, the narrative self-constitution view of identity espoused by Schechtman does not ignore the importance of context or the role that others play in defining a person's identity, but this influence appears to be understood in rather static terms. For example, Schechtman emphasizes the "general ways in which the past can condition the present ... [insofar as our pasts] give us a 'script' – a sense of self, an idea of who we are and what kind of story we are living."[42]

> The well-nurtured child grows up to view herself as a person who will have a good life, and this affects how she acts, what she expects, and how she experiences the world. The person who is raised to view himself as a loser, however, will have a quite different experience of even the same sorts of episodes.[43]

Persons help define the identities of others well beyond their early formative years, however. As Nelson writes, in many ways, a person's identity is also informed by her present relations (and perhaps even anticipated future relations):

> Much of who we can be depends contingently on other people: on the families we happen to be born into, whether we are orphaned at an early age, the social groups we find ourselves a part of, the reckless driver who left us paralyzed, the kind and quality of education we receive, the voters

who elected us. These people determine the set of possible identities that are open to us.[44]

Nelson's understanding of the role that others play in defining who we are approximates that which is central to my understanding of relational identity, but a critical difference remains. While Nelson understands that personal identity crucially depends on the recognition and acknowledgment of others, she nonetheless imagines that this can play out in the construction of two (or more) competing stories, one of which might be found to be more credible than the other(s). As noted earlier, however, with relational identity, persons are (and can only be) dynamic complex co-creations constituted and maintained through iterative and cyclical as well as public and private performances. For this dynamic self-narrative to be identity-constituting, there must be "equilibrium."

The Equilibrium Constraint

Along with others, I believe that self-narratives are much more than subjective self-understandings. As I have argued elsewhere, it is "[s]ocial intersubjective relations and, in particular, networks of relations of mutual recognition [that] allow the self to emerge and over time help to stabilize the self."[45] In this chapter, I argue that only self-narratives capable of equilibrium are identity defining, which is not to deny the dynamic context in which identities are (and continue to be) projected, assigned, endorsed, challenged, and changed.

Equilibrium – the balance between how a person sees and understands herself and how others see and understand her – requires minimal uptake by others of the projected (that is, preferred or performed) self-narrative. The preferred self-narrative is the story of who the person wants to be. The performed self-narrative is the story of who the person can be, given the ways in which her life is constrained by self and others. In living one's life, one projects a preferred or performed self-narrative or, more likely, some combination thereof. The projected self-narrative may be more or less under the conscious control of the protagonist, and it may be more or less well "read" (that is, perceived) by others. In turn, the perceived narrative necessarily affects the shape and content of the lives that people want to lead, or have to lead, which is what makes for the fluid (iterative and cyclical) process of identity formation.

A self-narrative (preferred, performed, or some combination thereof) that is projected by one and perceived by others can be dismissed, resisted, tolerated, actively endorsed, or actively contested in whole or in part. When a self-narrative (or significant part thereof) is actively disputed or challenged by (some) others, an individual can respond in one or more ways, all of which aim to satisfy the equilibrium constraint. For example, in search of affirmation, the individual might try to project his preferred or performed self-narrative more successfully. Alternatively, he might try to minimally (or radically) revise the self-narrative that he projects, taking into account the perceptions, actions, and reactions of others. A third option would be for him to shift his self-understanding in deference to others, in which case he might acknowledge that others can accurately perceive his performed self-narrative but cannot effectively perceive his preferred self-narrative. A fourth option would be to actively refute the perceptions of others that do not accord with the projected self-narrative by explaining away any and all discrepancies as interpretive errors on the part of others. A further option, which is available to some, would be to change one's community of belonging in favour of a community likely to be more accepting or tolerant of the projected self-narrative. The following scenarios serve to illustrate the point.

Consider the case of Professor Dougherty. She is an unmarried woman in her early fifties who has dedicated her life to the academy. She teaches bioethics to undergraduate and graduate students at an Ivy League school. She has many (albeit short) publications, and she is a frequent guest lecturer at national and international medical and scientific meetings. She wants to be seen as a brilliant philosopher – a real "catch." This is the preferred self-narrative that Dougherty attempts to project. If others perceive Dougherty in this way, then they will endorse (and thereby give meaning to) her story, and (at least for a time) her identity-constituting narrative will be that of the successful, much sought after woman philosopher. However, if this is not how others see and understand her, then they will not provide her with the socio-signals that she needs to instantiate her preferred identity and achieve some level of equilibrium.

Imagine, for example, that the only uncontested characteristic in Dougherty's preferred self-narrative is the claim to be a woman, which for some might be reason enough to disqualify her as a serious philosopher. Further, imagine that while Dougherty has a doctoral degree in philosophy, it is widely believed that her work in bioethics hardly counts as philosophy. In these and other ways, many may actively challenge Dougherty's preferred self-narrative as erroneous and some may even go so far as to present her with an alternative self-narrative – Dougherty as a dowdy spinster, an affirmative action hire whose contributions to the literature are numerous but of marginal importance. From yet another perspective, perhaps others perceive and endorse Dougherty's projected self-narrative of a high achiever with a successful academic career. Behind this projected self-narrative, however, there might be a woman plagued with self-doubt who imagines herself a fraud and fears the day when "the jig is up."

In light of these plausible scenarios, how might one answer the question: "Who is Professor Dougherty?" If Dougherty comes to see and understand herself through the eyes of others, she may (consciously or unconsciously) change how she presents herself to the world in an effort to better reveal to others who she "wants to be" (that is, her preferred self-narrative) and/ or who she "can be" given the constraints under which she lives (that is, her performed self-narrative). If she nevertheless fails to garner support/ endorsement for the self-narrative she projects, then her self-narrative or her community of belonging may need to shift in incremental (or dramatic) ways for her to restore equilibrium by achieving minimal uptake of her self-narrative by others. For example, with the first scenario, the fact that Dougherty is able to keep an academic job might be sufficient minimal uptake of her self-narrative. However, if Dougherty needs further uptake of additional features of her story to effectively balance how she sees and understands herself and how others see and understand her, then either her projected self-narrative or her community of belonging will have to change. If the modified self-narrative is endorsed by others, then Dougherty could find some new level of equilibrium. In the alternative, if the modified self-narrative is considered suspect, then an iterative process involving further revisions might be necessary to restore equilibrium. Then again, Dougherty might achieve equilibrium by happily dismissing any discordance between who she believes herself to be and how others perceive her, as error on the part of others.

With the equilibrium constraint, unlike the reality constraint (advocated by Schechtman), there is neither care nor concern with what others "objectively" believe to be true, except insofar as others' perceptions are invitations to practise one's narrative and performance skills. Further, with the equilibrium constraint, unlike the credibility constraint (advocated by Nelson), there need be no effort to identify the "better" of two or more competing stories. Again, at most, there is an invitation to revise one's projected self-narrative or one's community of belonging to achieve a certain balance through minimal uptake of one's projected narrative. In answer to the question "Who is Professor Dougherty?" then, she is the woman at the intersection of who she says she is and who others will minimally let her be. Her identity is a balance between self-ascription and ascription by others as she (consciously or unconsciously) engages in the never-ending project of tailoring her identity in response to her experiences as well as her perceptions of her world and her place in it. The messages she receives from the world around her shape her options in positive or negative ways.

Consider next the story of Mr. Reilly. As told by David DeGrazia, Mr. Reilly is a man with extreme psychosis whose self-narrative is realistic insofar as it includes accurate biographical information about his family members, his schooling, and his age. However, Mr. Reilly's self-narrative also includes beliefs that do not cohere with what we know about the world. Specifically, Mr. Reilly "believes that his thoughts are controlled by the CIA through the Internet, that most people he sees on the street are spies, that animals are somehow secret agents, and that everything we see in the sky is an optical illusion deliberately created by some international agency."[46] As a result of the discordance between Mr. Reilly's self-narrative and the facts about the world, there is reason, according to DeGrazia, to question the idea that first person narratives should be authoritative. DeGrazia suggests retaining the first person perspective on identity but qualifying its objects. In answer to the identity question "Who is Mr. Reilly?" DeGrazia describes him as "someone who, for example, is X years old, has such-and-such family, and went to these schools ... [and] who *deeply believes* that."[47] In this way, DeGrazia attempts to resolve the discordance between first and third person narratives.

If Mr. Reilly is unaware of the discordance between how he sees and understands himself and how others see and understand him, then he likely will not object to this slightly amended account of who he is. If he is aware of the discordance, however, he may not readily accept the assigned self-narrative, preferring instead the story of a man who is under constant surveillance by CIA agents who use tracking dogs to follow him. It would be normal for anyone under such circumstances to have certain thoughts that might seem paranoid (including the belief that animals are among the secret agents and that everything in the sky is an optical illusion).

In reflecting upon Reilly's identity claim, Schechtman might argue that Reilly is delusional and that just as the person with delusions of being Napoleon cannot sustain this false identity, neither can Reilly. According to Schechtman, "[t]he claim to be Napoleon will, with pressure, fall apart" because when challenged to defend the identity claim, the individual will have to deny too many "clear and obvious facts about the world."[48] Reasoning along similar lines, Schechtman could argue that Reilly's claim to be under the control of the CIA "will, with pressure, fall apart" when he and others are presented with "clear and obvious facts about the world." Similarly, were Nelson to reflect on the Reilly case, she might conclude that the first person narrative is not credible and so would not be authoritative. In her view, the "better story" likely would be the one in which Reilly suffers from delusions that explain his incredible (that is, unbelievable) story. By comparison, with my view of relational identity, all self-narratives (not only those that admit of delusions) are at risk of falling apart if others withhold their (most minimal) endorsement. They need not collapse, however, provided there is an opportunity to shift one's narrative or community of belonging sufficiently for there to be the prospect of achieving some measure of equilibrium.

To recapitulate, for Schechtman, an identity-constituting narrative must satisfy the articulation and reality constraints. Most importantly, it must cohere with what others "objectively" believe to be true about the person. For Nelson, an identity-constituting narrative must satisfy the credibility constraint, and it must be a credible narrative authoritatively narrated by oneself in concert with others or, on occasion, by others in opposition to oneself. For myself, an identity-constituting narrative – a narrative that informs my actions, my memories, my experiences, and so on – must be capable of satisfying the equilibrium constraint – that is, it must be capable of achieving at least temporary (even if very fragile) stability.

To be clear, the equilibrium constraint does not posit "stability" as the end game of identity formation. To do so would be to contradict the claim that personal identity is a dynamic interpersonal communicative activity based on narrative and performance. Rather, equilibrium is a desired and desirable, temporary and temporizing, state of being that allows the self to take notice of her place in the world and through introspection and continued lived experience to refine or (radically) revise how she acts/performs in relations with others. A core feature of relational identity is its dynamic nature, and it is important not to mistake a period of equilibrium as an instantiation of a false belief about finding one's true self. There is no true self, only a dynamic socially, culturally, and politically constituted self that is historically situated and that at any one point in time can be more or less stable. Indeed, it is only in interaction with others and through their instantiation of, or resistance to, a storied and projected self that a person can experience either affirmation or disruption, both of which are relevant to the project of stabilizing one's self-narrative in an effort to achieve a period of equilibrium.

Here, it is important to insist on the fact that all self-narratives are always more or less stable. The nature of the equilibrium varies depending upon the complexity of the self-narrative, how many of the narrative details are subject to multiple interpretations, and the social, cultural, political, historical, and other context(s) in which the self-narrative is projected. For example, a seemingly robust and stable self-narrative in one socio-political context may become a very fragile and unstable self-narrative in another (for example, actively contested by powerful others and so in need of constant revision). In addition, it is expected that over a lifetime, there will be interludes of disequilibrium, the frequency and intensity of which will vary depending upon: (1) the person's skill in projecting who she is to herself as she lives her life and (more or less consciously) reflects on the actions and reactions that inform her interactions and transactions with others; and (2) the socio-cultural and socio-political context in which her actions, reactions, interactions, and transactions occur and are responded to.

Of note, from a moral perspective, an identity-constituting narrative is not, in and of itself, a good thing – much depends on the extent to which the identity is asserted or assigned. This is because equilibrium can be empowering or damaging depending upon whether it is the result of autonomy or oppression.[49] When a person is able to fashion and project an identity-constituting narrative that she values (hopefully a self-narrative that fosters her talents and dreams) and is able to motivate appropriate uptake of the self-narrative she embraces, there may be evidence of autonomy (as opposed to mere agency).[50] Autonomy is manifest when an individual actively contributes to authoring her life in a manner that is consistent with her broader interests, values, and commitments. How she lives in the world and succeeds in having others endorse or instantiate her self-projection is of pivotal importance.[51] In addition, it matters for autonomy that an individual be able to decide which stories provided by others are to be incorporated into her self-narrative and whether to defend or revise her self-narrative in response to questioning, contesting, and possibly even refashioning of her identity by others.

On the other hand, when a person is unable to contribute effectively to a satisfying self-narrative and finds herself forced to live within constraints set by others who have fixed ideas about who she is and who she can be, there may be evidence of oppression. Oppression is manifest when an individual in certain contexts and circumstances is forced to live for periods of time within the confines of another's ideas about what makes for an appropriate self-narrative. An individual can be constrained by stories that are not of her own making but, rather, have been decreed, construed, and constructed by others who limit (in overt, covert, or insidious ways) who she can be, by actively and/or structurally restricting the range of narratives that can be appropriated and successfully enacted. Walker describes these others as persons having "a disproportionate hand in writing stories for [others] ... that are limiting, cruel, oppressive or alienating."[52] Consider, for example, the scope of possible identity-constituting narratives for women living in a patriarchal society. Or imagine the scope of possible identity-constituting narratives for blacks of different complexions (including those who are phenotypically indistinguishable from whites), all of whom live in a racially segregated city. Being a member of a diminished social category – for example, being female and at risk of sexism, or black and at risk of racism – undeniably affects equilibrium.[53] One's position in society, in turn, affects who one can be.

In sum, on my account of relational personal identity, "equilibrium" is crucial for identity constitution. A self requires minimal uptake by others. This uptake may be granted or withheld based upon judgments about "reality," "coherence," "unity," "consistency," "credibility," "plausibility," or the like, but what crucially matters given that we are constituted through our personal and public relations is the prospect of "equilibrium." We now turn our attention to the provocative question: "Who is Barack Obama?"

Who Is Barack Obama?

Accurate answers to this question abound. He is a man named after his father Barack Obama, who in his youth went by the name of Barry. He is a lawyer who practised as a civil rights attorney. He is an accomplished orator. He is a somewhat aloof figure. He is the husband of Michelle Obama and the father of Malia and Sasha Obama. He is the forty-fourth president of the United States of America. Ah ... yes ... but what of the question that both fascinates and troubles many Americans, namely "Is Barack Obama the first black or the first bi-racial President of the United States of America?"

Obama is the son of a black man from Africa and a white woman from America. In Obama's words, his father "was black as pitch, my mother white as milk."[54] For some, these facts alone are reason enough to affirm that Obama is bi-racial. Obama, however, is sure that he is black. Indeed, he describes his 1995 autobiography *Dreams from My Father* as "a personal, interior journey – a boy's search for his father, and through that search a workable meaning for his life as a black American."[55] More recently, and with considerable rhetorical force, Obama remarked in a Public Broadcasting Service interview: "If I'm outside your building trying to catch a cab, they're not saying, 'Oh, there's a mixed race guy.'"[56] And, on the 2010 census form, which includes a question about race, Obama self-identified as "Black, African Am., or Negro."[57]

Obama's lived experience further instantiates his preferred self-narrative as a black man, a narrative endorsed by a range of others: "Obama is married to a black woman. He goes to a black church. He's worked with poor people on the South Side of Chicago, and still lives there."[58] Moving from the personal to the political, on the "one drop rule" introduced in the United States in the early twentieth century and still influential today, a person with any black ancestry is black. Moreover, until 2000, when the Census Bureau revised its forms, no person in the United States could legally self-identify as bi-racial. Until then, Obama's legal race category was "Black or African American."

Setting aside these facts, there are many others who insist that Obama is not black. Some make this claim on technical grounds: "Sen. Barack Obama is the son of a black man from Kenya and a white woman from Kansas. So why is he 'black'? He is, to be accurate, biracial, black and white."[59] Others raise a slightly different point with a particular focus on authenticity. For example, in a *New York Daily News* column entitled "What Obama Isn't: Black Like Me on Race," Stanley Crouch makes the point that "Obama's mother is of white U.S. stock. His father is a black Kenyan. Other than color, Obama did not – does not – share a heritage with the majority of black Americans, who are descendants of plantation slaves."[60] Insisting further on this point, Debra Dickerson writes: "'Black,' in our political and social reality, means those descended from West African slaves."[61] In her view, "[v]oluntary immigrants of African descent (even those descended from West Indian slaves) are ... 'black' as a matter of skin color and DNA, but ... [they are not] politically and culturally black, as we use the term."[62] The fact is that neither Obama nor his ancestors experienced slavery or segregation. Obama readily recognizes this fact – his life experience is "not representative of the black American experience ... [he does not] come from an underprivileged background."[63]

Others who insist that Obama cannot claim a black identity appear to have political motivations. For example, during the 2008 presidential elections, some insisted that while Obama may have experienced some racial stereotyping he had not lived the typical life of a black American.[64] Obama did not grow up in the inner city or in a black neighbourhood. Still others contested Obama's black identity in an attempt to undermine any advantage he might have with black voters. As reported by Joseph Curl in the *Washington Times*, "[i]ndependent presidential candidate Ralph Nader said last month that Mr. Obama calls himself black to appeal to 'white guilt' over slavery and the rampant racial discrimination that reigned in America from its birth until just 50 years ago."[65]

Apparent racism is yet another reason why some question Obama's black identity: "Though it is rarely said openly the white parent is often seen as a stain of inauthenticity on the black identity by both blacks and whites."[66] From another perspective, some appear to believe that Obama cannot be black because he is not like the other (bad) blacks. Most famously, Joe Biden (prior to being named as Obama's running mate) described Obama as the first "mainstream African-American who is articulate and bright and clean and a nice-looking guy."[67] By implication, this statement was widely taken to mean "that the black people who are regularly seen by whites – or at least those who aspire to the highest office in the land – are none of these things."[68]

A striking feature of the public debate on Obama's racial identity is the way in which the debate "appears to be predicated on one or more essentialist conceptions of racial identity."[69] While Obama claims the identity of a black man (notwithstanding the facts about his genetic heritage), others insist that this claimed identity does not cohere with the social identity of those who "legitimately" belong in the category of a "black man." Obama's lived experience does not overlap with the experience of the vast majority of black men in the United States whose lives are steeped in oppression, racism, and poverty. Ironically, both Obama and his critics eschew a realist approach to identity and instead understand identity as a social construct informed by historical, psychological, and cultural facts and values. Yet, in the person of Obama, there is resistance on the part of some to the personal identity claim that Obama makes, as if being black in the United States is (and could only be) one kind of thing.

In the face of such controversy surrounding Obama's identity, what, if anything, might we learn from the accounts of narrative identity canvassed in this chapter? In brief, for Schechtman, Obama is black because he says he is, and there are no legitimate grounds on which to contest his claim. With the narrative self-constitution view of identity, individuals are projects of self-creation. Persons play an active role in defining themselves, and the only constraint on their self-creation is that they satisfy the articulation and reality constraints on identity-constituting narratives. In this regard, it is important to note that Obama is able to articulate his identity as a black man and, moreover, that this identity coheres very nicely with basic observational and interpretive facts. In the real world, at the present time in the United States whatever you look like is what you will be taken as unless you fight to be recognized as something else.[70] Obama is phenotypically black and so is his progeny. In the United States, no more is required to be assigned, or to claim, a black identity. Thus, for Schechtman, according to whom a person's self-narrative is authoritative as long as it is "basically in synch with the view of one held by others," Obama is black given that this is the identity that he claims.[71] Interestingly, if Obama self-identified as bi-racial, then this alternative identity could also be readily endorsed by Schechtman because, in different but no less important ways, this identity could also satisfy the articulation and reality constraints on identity-constituting narratives.

For Nelson, who recognizes that personal identity crucially depends on the recognition and acknowledgment of others, Obama could be black or bi-racial, depending upon one's interpretation of the three credibility criteria – strong explanatory force, correlation to action, and heft. A black identity has strong explanatory force insofar as it best fits the experiential evidence. As well, a black identity correlates with Obama's actions in, for example, marrying a black woman, living in a black community, and attending a black church. Finally, in regard to the criterion of heft, Obama attaches great personal importance to his black identity. From another perspective, a bi-racial identity has strong explanatory force insofar as it best fits the biological evidence. As well, a bi-racial identity correlates with Obama's actions insofar as he recognizes and values his mixed heritage and treasures his personal relationships with his white mother and his white grandparents – facts that are also relevant to the criterion of heft. Following Nelson, if one of these competing narratives can be shown to be more credible than the other, then it prevails. If both of these narratives are equally credible, then Obama's first person narrative as a black man prevails. To be clear on this point, on Nelson's "no trump" theory, there is not always an authoritative account of personal identity. For many specific purposes, however, the personal perspective is the more significant perspective because it is the one that the self lives with and acts upon.[72]

For myself, Obama is a black bi-racial man, as only this complex identity can adequately capture who he says he is (based on his own interpretation and reconstruction of personal stories) and who others will let him be (as mediated through biological, historical, social, cultural, political, religious, and other contexts).[73] With relational identity, one cannot parse genetic, phenotypical, social, or other such data and authoritatively privilege one type of data over another. As such, while my description of Obama as a black, bi-racial man may seem incongruous, at the present time in the United States (a country still struggling with the adolescent problem of racial identity[74]) I maintain that this identity can be stabilized and that equilibrium can be achieved.[75] Non-Americans see this quite plainly and explain it in terms of the United States' troubled history with slavery. So it is that in the months preceding the 2008 US presidential election, Andrew Sullivan wrote for the *Sunday Times*:

> There is no deeper division in America than race. Slavery is America's original sin. Even after its abolition, America was effectively in large swathes an apartheid society until the 1970s ... *Obama is not just potentially America's first black president. He would be America's first bi-racial president*, in many ways a more integrative event.[76]

To repeat, on my account of relational personal identity, Obama is a black, bi-racial man. His identity is not in his genes, his cells, his body, or his psychology but, rather, in the world in which he lives and in the stories he is able to construct and maintain through complex social interactions involving an iterative cycle of "self"-perception, "self"-projection, "other"-perception, and "other"-reaction, with periods of doubling back, skipping forward, and so on. Both self-ascription and ascription by others are critical factors in the making of his identity.

Conclusion

We are all complex interdependent beings whose identity is co-constructed and maintained through iterative and cyclical private and public actions, reactions, interactions, and transactions. As we live our lives, constrained in ever-changing ways by our social, cultural, and political environments, as well as by our historical circumstances, we communicate in overt and covert ways who we are, and we imagine, hope, and despair that others will come to see and understand us as we see and understand ourselves. When this happens (that is, when there is a congruence between self-ascription and ascription by others), our identity temporarily stabilizes until such time as there is a shift in our identity-constituting self-narrative and we enter a period of disequilibrium, looking once again to restore the balance between how we see and understand ourselves with how others see and understand us. So it is that we are who we say we are and who others will let us be.

Notes
Thanks are owed to Marya Schechtman and Hilde Lindemann for their engaging and encouraging correspondence during the initial phases of this writing project. As well, special thanks are owed to Sue Campbell, Dianne Pothier, and the anonymous reviewers for careful

and helpful comments on the penultimate draft. The time and reflection needed to write this chapter would not have been possible without the generosity of the Brocher Foundation, http://www.brocher.ch, and the amiable work environment created by the staff. In addition, this work is supported by the Canadian Institutes of Health Research, NNF 80045, States of Mind: Emerging Issues in Neuroethics, and the Canada Research Chairs program (2004-11).

1 Gregory David Roberts, *Shantaram* (London: Little Brown, 2004) at 334.
2 *Ibid.* at 632 [emphasis in original].
3 Patrick O'Brian, *Master and Commander* (London: Harper Collins Publishers, 2002). This quote also appears in Hilde Lindemann Nelson, *Damaged Identities, Narrative Repair* (Ithaca, NY: Cornell University Press, 2001).
4 Françoise Baylis, "Black as Me: Narrative Identity" (2003) 3 Developing World Bioethics 142.
5 Jeffrey Blustein, *The Moral Demands of Memory* (New York: Cambridge University Press, 2008).
6 Margaret Urban Walker, *Moral Understandings: A Feminist Study in Ethics* (New York: Routledge, 2007) at 119-20.
7 Baylis, *supra* note 4 at 144-45.
8 Jessica Andrews, *Who I Am* (Nashville: DreamWorks Records, 2001).
9 Laurence M. Thomas, "Moral Deference" in Cynthia Willet, ed., *Theorizing Multiculturalism: A Guide to the Current Debate* (Oxford: Blackwell Publishers, 1998) 359 at 365.
10 Françoise Baylis, "A Face Is Not Just Like a Hand: Pace Barker"(2004) 4 Am. J. Bioethics 30 at 31.
11 Françoise Baylis, "Changing Faces: Ethics, Identity, and Facial Transplantation" in David Benatar, ed., *Cutting to the Core: Exploring the Ethics of Contested Surgeries* (Lanham, MD: Rowman and Littlefield, 2006) 155 at 162.
12 Carolyn McLeod and Françoise Baylis, "Feminists on the Inalienability of Human Embryos" (2006) 21 Hypatia 1 at 5.
13 Linda Martín Alcoff, *Visible Identities: Race, Gender, and the Self* (Oxford: Oxford University Press, 2006) at 92.
14 For an insightful discussion of this concept, see Margaret Urban Walker "Career Selves: Plans, Projects and Plots in 'Whole Life Ethics'" in Walker, *supra* note 6 at 137-59.
15 Susan Sherwin, "A Relational Approach to Autonomy in Health Care" in Feminist Health Care Research Network, Susan Sherwin, coordinator, *The Politics of Women's Health: Exploring Agency and Autonomy* (Philadelphia, PA: Temple University Press, 1998) 19 at 34-35.
16 Margaret Urban Walker, "Getting Out of Line: Alternatives to Life as a Career" in Margaret Urban Waker, ed., *Mother Time: Women, Aging, and Ethics* (Lanham, MD: Rowman and Littlefield, 1999) 97 at 98.
17 Annette Baier, *Postures of the Mind: Essays on Mind and Morals* (Minneapolis, MN: University of Minnesota Press, 1985) at 84-85 [emphasis in original].
18 See Catriona Mackenzie and Natalie Stoljar, *Relational Autonomy: Feminist Perspectives on Autonomy, Agency, and the Social Self* (New York: Oxford University Press, 2000); Diana Tietjens Meyers, *Self, Society, and Personal Choice* (New York: Cornell University Press, 1989); Sherwin, *supra* note 15.
19 Thomas, *supra* note 9 at 365.
20 Barbara Hardy, "Towards a Poetics of Fiction: 3) An Approach through Narrative" (1968) 2:1 Novel 5 at 5.
21 See Catriona Mackenzie and Kim Atkins, eds., *Practical Identity and Narrative Agency* (New York: Routledge, 2008).
22 Marya Schechtman, *The Constitution of Selves* (Ithaca, NY: Cornell University Press, 1996) at 73.
23 *Ibid.* at 93.
24 *Ibid.* at 94.
25 *Ibid.* at 95.
26 *Ibid.*
27 *Ibid.* at 114.

28 *Ibid.* at 105.
29 Nelson, *supra* note 3 at 81-82 [emphasis in original].
30 Alasdair MacIntyre, *After Virtue: A Study of Moral Theory*, 2nd edition (Notre Dame, IN: University of Notre Dame Press, 1984) at 217.
31 Nelson, *supra* note 3 at 72.
32 *Ibid.* at 101.
33 *Ibid.* at 93.
34 Schechtman, *supra* note 22 at 95.
35 Nelson, *supra* note 3 at 92.
36 Paul Ricoeur, *Soi-Même Comme un Autre* (Paris: Éditions du Seuil, 2001) at 190.
37 MacIntyre, *supra* note 30 at 213.
38 Catriona Mackenzie, "Introduction: Practical Identity and Narrative Agency" in Mackenzie and Atkins, *supra* note 21, 1 at 15.
39 Sherwin, *supra* note 15 at 35.
40 See Sue Campbell, "Memory, Reparation, and Relation: Starting in the Right Places" in this volume, for an insightful discussion of persons' involvement in each other's memories.
41 Schechtman, *supra* note 22 at 95.
42 *Ibid.* at 111.
43 *Ibid.* at 111-12.
44 Nelson, *supra* note 3 at 102.
45 Baylis, *supra* note 4 at 144.
46 David DeGrazia, *Human Identity and Bioethics* (Cambridge: Cambridge University Press, 2005) at 85.
47 *Ibid.* at 86.
48 Schechtman, *supra* note 22 at 121 and 122.
49 Equilibrium can also be the result of collective self-deception. I thank Sue Campbell for drawing this to my attention and hope to explore this notion in a subsequent publication.
50 See Susan Sherwin, "Relational Autonomy and Global Threats" in this volume, for a discussion of autonomy and agency.
51 For a discussion of agency and identity, see Christine M. Korsgaard, "Personal Identity and the Unity of Agency: A Kantian Response to Parfit" (1989) 18:2 Philosophy and Public Affairs 101.
52 Walker, *supra* note 6 at 127.
53 Thomas, *supra* note 9.
54 Barack Obama, *Dreams from My Father* (New York: Three Rivers Press, 1995) at 10.
55 *Ibid.* at xvi.
56 Joseph Curl, "Who Decided to Call Obama Black?" *Washington Times* (8 July 2008), http://www.washtimes.com/news/2008/jul/08/who-decided-to-call-obama-a-black-man/?page=2.
57 Sam Roberts and Peter Baker, "Asked to Declare His Race, Obama Checks 'Black,'" *New York Times* (2 April 2010), http://www.nytimes.com/2010/04/03/us/politics/03census.html. There is no specific mixed race or bi-racial category on the census questionnaire. Obama could have checked both black and white. Alternatively, he could have checked "some other race" and included a written explanation.
58 Ta-Nehisi Paul Coates, "Is Obama Black Enough?" *Time* (1 February 2007), http://www.time.com/time/nation/article/0,8599,1584736,00.html.
59 Curl, *supra* note 56.
60 Stanley Crouch, "What Obama Isn't: Black Like Me on Race," *New York Daily News* (2 November 2006), http://www.nydailynews.com/archives/opinions/2006/11/02/2006-11-02_what_obama_isn_t__black_like.html.
61 Debra J. Dickerson, "Colorblind," *Salon* (22 January 2007), http://www.salon.com/news/opinion/feature/2007/01/22/obama.
62 *Ibid.* From my perspective, this view is very parochial and does not accord with my own experience living in the United States. Further, it is worth noting that in many countries outside of the United States the word "black" is used to refer to persons on the basis of skin colour and perhaps DNA, and the use of this descriptor has nothing to do with involuntary

immigration into slavery. This is also the case in some non-English-speaking countries such as France where the word "black" will be used instead of "*noir*." Americans do not own the word "black," even while they may own the word "African American," a term that does not apply to all blacks.

63 Obama, *supra* note 54 at xvi.
64 Crouch, *supra* note 60.
65 Curl, *supra* note 56.
66 Shelby Steele, *A Bound Man: Why We Are Excited about Obama and Why He Can't Win* (New York: Free Press, 2008) at 28, cited by Curl, *ibid.*
67 Coates, *supra* note 58.
68 *Ibid.*
69 I owe this wording to one of the anonymous reviewers.
70 Baylis, *supra* note 4.
71 Schechtman, *supra* note 22 at 95.
72 I thank Hilde Lindemann (previously Hilde Lindemann Nelson) for clarification on this point.
73 Baylis, *supra* note 4.
74 I owe this particular insight to Nikki Quist, a black woman born in the United Kingdom, now living in France, who spent several years in the United States and who perceives herself as lucky to have escaped a country where she would have to be confronted with questions of race on a regular basis.
75 To be clear, it is not the case that in the United States any dual racial identity can be stabilized. It has been suggested that if Obama can legitimately claim to be black because he has a black parent, then he can also legitimately claim to be white because he has a white parent (Curl, *supra* note 56). While this suggestion appears sensible in the abstract, things are not so straightforward in the United States where the dual identity of white and bi-racial is only available to those who can pass as white and who, until recently, would have had an interest in denying a bi-racial identity. In any case, the option of claiming to be white and bi-racial is not an option available to Obama because of his complexion. Moreover, even if Obama were light-skinned, claiming a white identity would not be an option for him because of the public life that he leads. If he were able to "pass" as white and claimed to be white, he very likely would be found "guilty" of denying his identity.
76 Andrew Sullivan, "Barack Obama: The Winner," *Sunday Times* (8 June 2008), http://www.timesonline.co.uk/tol/news/world/us_and_americas/us_elections/article4085815.ece [emphasis added].

6
Memory, Reparation, and Relation: Starting in the Right Places
Sue Campbell

> *For Native peoples, the discussion about reparations is not an intellectual exercise. It is a discussion of how the past, present, and future are conjoined and interdependent.*
>
> – *Rebecca Tsosie, from a display at the Museum of Civilization*

One important recent strand in the complex cross-disciplinary discussion of memory is the role of remembering in facilitating or thwarting justice in political contexts characterized by historic harms.[1] How can sharing the memory of harm and wrongdoing across pasts that are linked by (and in some sense) common and toxic history aid reparative projects, and what forms should this sharing take? Since reparative initiatives typically take place between different cultural groups and are meant to help establish or re-establish relations of mutual equality, trust, or respect,[2] Rebecca Tsosie has argued that reparative frameworks must be intercultural.[3] Writing from a Native-American perspective, she is particularly concerned that work from within the "moral universe of Western liberal thought" continues to misrepresent Native perspectives on the integrated nature of the assault to Indigenous cultures, identities, and sovereignty that has characterized Native-Settler relations.[4] Hence, it misrepresents what could count as reconciliation from these perspectives, specifically the enactment of respect for sovereign cultures.[5] Given the inherently relational setting of reparative justice contexts,[6] theorists from Euro-Western traditions must exercise vigilance in maintaining that our predilection for abstract discussions of justice does not simply repeat and reinforce the cultural imperialism that is an integral part of the harm done to Indigenous groups.[7]

In a spirit of vigilance, the present reflection on the importance of relational theorizing about memory to projects of reparative justice seeks to exemplify the centrality of concrete contextual analysis to relational theorizing.[8] My context is the current attempt between Indigenous and non-Indigenous peoples in the Settler society now known as Canada to make progress in renewing relations damaged by colonialist practices of forced assimilation and attempted cultural genocide. In undertaking this renewal, we act toward ideals of well-being that are central to the concerns of this volume. I thus follow Jennifer Llewellyn in understanding the initiatives of reparative or restorative justice. I use these terms interchangeably – not on a model of material compensation for harm even though such compensation may be involved in specific initiatives. Rather, I understand reparative justice as being committed to "taking the fact of relationship and connection as central to the work of justice," which "aims at realizing the conditions of relationship required for well-being and flourishing."[9]

To highlight one instance of the genocidal practices that have been at issue between Indigenous and non-Indigenous Canadians, the Canadian government, in collaboration with the Catholic, Anglican, United, and Presbyterian churches, has operated a system of Indian Residential Schools for well over 100 years, removing Native children from their communities in order to re-socialize and assimilate them into the economic and cultural order of the colonial state. The architects of this system intended this re-education to eradicate the Indigenous cultures whose practices resisted European notions of progress, destroying the relational networks that helped to sustain Indigenous identities, both personal and communal.[10] In 2006, after years of activism and advocacy by the survivors of Residential Schooling, the Assembly of First Nations, and groups of allies, the court-ordered *Indian Residential Schools Settlement Agreement* was endorsed "by the Survivors' legal representatives, churches, and the federal government."[11] The comprehensive settlement agreement includes a five-year Truth and Reconciliation Commission,[12] which is

> mandated to promote education and awareness about the Indian Residential School system and its legacy, as well as provide former students, their families and communities an opportunity to share their Indian Residential School experiences in a safe and culturally-appropriate environment.[13]

Explicitly adopting an intercultural framework, the mandate directs the commission to recognize "the significance of Aboriginal oral and legal traditions in it activities."[14] I shall argue that, as non-Indigenous Canadians, our respect for these traditions requires that we reflect on the importance of sharing memory in the dynamics of group identity formation.

While all political projects of nation building and destroying are infused with attempts to shape and control the significance of the past in order to legitimate and serve a future vision, assimilationist policies implicate the politics of memory in deep and complex ways. Gail Guthrie Valaskakis writes that "assimilation involves repressing old identities by, in part, taking on new social memories."[15] We need detailed analyses of the specific ways in which these processes of obliging others to take on new social memories have been instigated and enacted as well as of the ramifications of these processes for present reparative action that once again involves memory sharing across groups. Critical to such analyses is a fundamental recognition of the deeply relational nature of individual and group identity formation – what I will often call the co-constitution or "co-implication of identities."[16] Attention to memory is important to this recognition, and this chapter seeks to encourage it in a number of distinct but interrelated ways.

I first examine an increased willingness among Western theorists to regard remembering as itself a relational capacity interwoven with identity formation. Second, I situate relational remembering within a general, fluid, relational model of group identity formation found in the work of Valaskakis, Iris Marion Young, and Constance MacIntosh – a model both illuminating and illuminated by the process of Residential Schooling. Remembering is often a key dynamic in the co-implication of group identities. I attend to show the assimilationist agenda of Residential Schooling depended on positioning people as different kinds of rememberers and on privileging certain conceptions of memory in order to control how memory could be shared and with whom. I thus highlight how memory interactions worked to structure the colonizing relations we now seek to repair.

Third, in attending to relational identity constitution, I illustrate that such contextual theorizing can also provide critical insight into the limitations of some recent Western theoretical approaches to memory, justice, and reparative action. While Western theorists would agree that how we negotiate the meaning of the past is critical to political relations, they tend to think of memory as further unifying a group whose relative internal homogeneity and whose independence from other groups is, in fact, already assumed and marked in the invocation of collective memory. Since they lack an adequately relational account of identity, there is no place to consider how practices and conceptions of remembering both enter into the relational co-constitution of identities and might be used to help reform or renew them.

The failure to understand how group identities can be shaped through relations of power that control the sociability of memory would, I contend, make it difficult for these theories to support the intercultural mandate of the Truth and Reconciliation Commission for the Indian Residential Schools and to support its goals of fostering truth, reconciliation, and healing.[17] Indigenous writers speak and write very differently about memory, and I have used their reflections to frame the critical investigation of this chapter.[18] I conclude by suggesting some possible reparative roles for sharing memory in the work of the Truth and Reconciliation Commission if we can show the kind of respect for the relational dimensions of memory prominent in the work of many Indigenous thinkers.

Relational Remembering

The last decade has witnessed the rapid emergence of memory studies as an interdiscipline in the Western academy, drawing theorists from the empirical and cognitive sciences into conversation with those from the humanities, arts, social sciences, and law. The possibility of collaboration among those who have traditionally treated memory as the individual's capacity to recall or re-experience one's personal past and those who have focused on the social processes and institutional structures that embody collective visions of the past has been made possible by more sophisticated analyses of socially situated rememberers. Theorists now recognize that recollection, as the core human capacity through which we learn by experience, is a multi-variant set of practices with cognitive, affective, interpersonal, and political dimensions, engaged in by social and historically embedded agents in particular contexts – material and spatial as well as social – and for a variety of overlapping purposes.[19]

There have been two important insights at the heart of this more dynamic approach to remembering. The first I will assume, and the second I will explore. First, theorists have moved away from an ideal of the memory archive as the storage of unchanging representations impressed at the time of experience. We remember selectively and interpretively in response to the demands of the present and future.[20] Second, we remember with others and in response to their perceptions of both their pasts and our own. Even the recollection of an intensely personal past is often an interactive undertaking. It is worth sampling this new Western consensus on the sociality of memory to see what it makes, and fails to make, salient. Psychologists Paula Reavey and Steven Brown, surveying the interdisciplinary trauma literature, describe the "shift from considering 'memory' as a faculty ... that produces discrete 'memories' to a concern with 'remembering' as a socially constructed practice ... [one that] transcends a neat opposition between the individual and the social since personal 'memories' may be co-constructed and elaborated by others."[21] Our involvement in each other's memories and our vulnerability to others' influence has instigated an associated focus on remembering as an "ethical act, involving questions of responsibility, accountability, and the negotiation of substantive moral" issues.[22]

Barnier et al., working in an interdisciplinary cognitive science context, write that from a social cognition perspective, remembering is a powerful example of how "we live [our] cognitive lives, and engage in the activities that constitute them, in the company of others."[23] It is with these others that we forge, maintain, and share an accurate view of the past or fail to do so.[24] Reliving and re-appropriating the past in memory is also continuously self-constituting, and our evolving self-conceptions, the shifting lenses through which we re-experience the past, are sensitive to how others affirm, correct, or doubt our interpretations. They also note that we engage in re-membering "to teach and inform others, to develop or maintain intimacy, to elicit or show empathy, and to share mundane or significant stories."[25] While these researchers distinguish the epistemic and relational functions of remembering at the analytic level, there is no clear separation at the level of action. For example, to develop intimacy by sharing an important part of one's past invites relation that will inevitably refract back on one's own self-conception, through conveying knowledge both of the past and of who one is.

To observe that remembering is intimately interwoven with capacities to form relations and relational self-conceptions is unremarkable when we consider that we learn to remember by being shown how to attend to, and then recall, events by others who are, at that same time, socializing us through and into relational affiliations. Psychologists such as Robyn Fivish and Elizabeth Waites describe how early relations with our caregivers regulate the attention that is necessary to memory, both explicitly and through their embodied, affectively laden activities, marking what is salient, supplying the concepts and informing the emotions and perspectives through which we come to remember, and teaching us skills of revivifying the past through co-constructing memory narratives.[26] In learning to remember, we are thus encouraged to form shared perspectives on the significance of actions, places, and events, which, even as children, we may sometimes resist. Other studies stress that learning to remember necessitates that our interpretations, per-spectives, and self-narratives evolve with our need for a usable past and our maturing moral agency. For example, we learn to narratively order and re-order our experience, again as guided by others, through coming to under-stand that the meaning of later events can change the significance of earlier ones.[27] Perhaps an action had unintended consequences that demand its retrospective re-experiencing. I unintentionally hurt someone's feelings and now remember with regret – perhaps when I learn what happened to a friend, a bad experience of my own feels trivial in retrospect.

Maurice Halbwachs notes that in adulthood, as in childhood, we remem-ber from perspectives that are never just ours alone but that reflect the shifting contours of the group identifications that are themselves shaped through sharing memory.[28] While theorists find it notable how early these capacities take shape, the tendency of early childhood studies to focus on shared perspectives and group identifications can submerge the most inter-esting implications of this research. We become mature rememberers through developing capacities to re-experience aspects of our past selectively, as shifting in meaning, and as embedded in dynamic causal and narrative structures as a part of forming and negotiating relations and relational self-conceptions while also contributing to shared or conflicting understandings of the past: "We share a past that we remember in highly individual ways while having together to determine its significance."[29] Remembering thus involves the work of judgment, since this, too, is relationally shaped and negotiated.[30]

In adulthood, practices of sharing memory are often mediated by, and expressed through, the development of more complex intra-psychic structures and our abilities to imaginatively engage with others' subjectivities as they are first personally expressed in narrative or art or witnessed and related by others. For example, John Bond, a member of Australia's Sorry Day committee, discusses the effect that the report *Bringing Them Home* had on non-Aboriginal Australians.[31] He comments that "the gulf between Aboriginal and non-Aboriginal Australians was simply too immense for even their pain to flow across it" and that *Bringing Them Home* often exposed this gulf.[32] He relates the following encounter with the report:

> I thought back to my primary school classroom. I can remember the name of every person in that class except the four Aboriginal boys who sat at the back of the class, never asked a question, stuck with each other in the playground, never played with the rest of us. I looked on them as incredibly dull. When I read *Bringing Them Home*, I began to understand what they had probably endured, and why they acted as they did. And I felt ashamed.[33]

This passage expresses a memory that is shifting in meaning as it is publicly shared. We often relive the significance of our school days through relating stories of students and teachers whose names we will remember all of our lives, and we may do so to make connection with others through the opportunity to share like experiences. For this Australian, brought under the influence of others' pasts as encountered in *Bringing Them Home*, a familiar kind of remembering becomes the occasion for affectively reliving its significance as a forgetting of those who had been found dull and not worth the care or attention that is marked in naming those we remember.[34] The writer re-experiences a problematically remembered past with its vivid sociability as the public commitment to a more accurate grasp of school days structured by ignorance, racism, and neglect as the partial grounds for their sociability. To re-remember with shame is potentially to mobilize a shift in understanding and relational self-identification that opens up new political possibilities.[35] Alexis Shotwell describes white shame as an "uneasy optic," where recognition through the eyes of those subject to racism can reveal to white people (as it does to the earlier writer) our implicit and habituated ways of "knowing how" to be racist – for example, the ways that children learn who is worth befriending – while, at the same time, the hope and desire for more appropriate ways of relating and being in relation to others.[36] As Shotwell explains, "[t]he fact of feeling shame indicates a site of potential re-identification in process."[37] In the case at hand, the process involves remembering as it is brought under the influence of others' pasts.

I also use this example as a preliminary comment on the limitations of Western perspectives where reflection on what I have elsewhere called "relational remembering" is still in its infancy.[38] First, while the earlier example shows that it is important to attend to the ethics of remembering, in the literature this focus has been somewhat disappointingly dominated by concerns about accurate recollection that position sociability primarily as a reason for epistemic anxiety:

> On many dominant views in both philosophy of mind and cognitive psychology, the sharing of memories is only of limited significance. The presence and contribution of other people ... is seen at best, as only one external causal trigger for and influence on the real memory in the individual; or, at worst, as a disrupting or contaminating influence on individual autobiographical memory.[39]

The residual fantasy that uninfluenced memory sets the standard for good remembering obscures both the profound social importance of sharing memory and the complexity of its epistemology.

To introduce a theme to which I shall return, sharing memory is a critical way in which we share time with others. Sharing memory revivifies a past in which others can imaginatively, somatically, and affectively engage.[40] We reanimate our pasts for others through expressive choice of detail, narrative strategy, gesture, emotional tone, and the sharing of objects and place while often explicitly encouraging their participation through inviting association, identification, or imagined response.[41] The past is made present through acts of memory, and this sharing of the time I shall now refer to as the present past enters our relational lives at many levels. Since people are historical beings, we do not come to feel that we know them well until we have shared their pasts. In a daily way, sharing significant or trivial memories with others, as made possible and relevant by our ordinary interactions, is an unconscious and habituated way of finding and testing grounds for common understandings, perspectives, or identifications while making our own historical self-identifications vulnerable to the affective force of others' revivified pasts. Moreover, revivifying the past may be a way of calling people into community. The practice of publicly memorializing at wakes or funerals, for example, brings mourners together as a community that shares the present past – the life or legacy of the person mourned. Sharing memory is such a constant and vital attribute of being in relation to others that it is the failure of its possibility that often requires our critical scrutiny.

With respect to epistemic concerns, although most memories are reasonably assessable or challengeable for their fidelity to what happened (some are simply obviously accurate), the example of re-remembering through the complex affective/epistemic/relational optic of shame shows that accurate recall is "neither simple nor singular."[42] As a separation of the epistemic and relational dimensions of memory is an artifact of analysis, so our faithfulness to the past is often a complicated aspiration where accuracy implicates the ethical values of integrity, responsibility, and attentiveness as we together try to understand not only what happened but its significance for how we go on.[43]

A second limitation to the present approaches, which is implicit in the focus on mutuality in psychological studies and more evident when memory theorists confront historic harm directly (see the discussion later in this chapter), is that Western theorists pay little attention to the dynamics of intergroup memory. I include in this group most philosophers, psychologists, and interdisciplinary memory theorists. As my discussion illustrates, there is a limited body of sophisticated reflection on memory as a relationally supported self- and group-constituting process in families. However, to get a reasonable rendering both of the nature of our socialized capacities and of how their expression in turn configures relationships, we must consider how such capacities are developed, exercised, supported, or undermined within the wider sets of social, political, and economic relations in which we find ourselves located.[44] We need to understand the shifting nature of identifications that can occur through sharing memory, not only through actually sharing it but also through structuring the possibilities of its sociality. The next section situates relational remembering within a more general account of group identity formation. I illustrate the importance of remembering in the relational co-implication of identities through the context of Residential Schooling where controlling how memory could be shared and with whom was the cornerstone of a genocidal pedagogy.

Substantial and Relational Approaches to Social Identity
In assessing the contemporary work on identity politics, Iris Marion Young argues that many political writers tend to assume a substantial, rather than a relational, conception of group difference. When we think of groups substantially, each "group is defined by essential attributes that constitute its identity ... Individuals can be said to belong to the group insofar as they have the requisite attributes."[45] Young offers a detailed critique of substantial conceptions. She contends that they typically imply agreement on values or politics that rarely map the reality of group life. Moreover, such conceptions reify the nature of groups and freeze "the experienced fluidity of social relations, by setting up rigid insider-outsider distinctions."[46] Young proposes an alternative relational conception of a social group as a "collection

of individuals, who stand in determinate relations with one another because of the actions and interactions of those both associated with the group and those outside or on the margins of the group"[47]:

> Considered relationally, a social group is a collection of persons differentiated from others by cultural forms, practices, special needs or capacities, structures of power or privilege ... Social groups emerge from the way people interact.[48]

For Young, "[r]elational encounter produces [the] perception[s] of both similarity and difference" through which people are grouped and come to group themselves.[49]

In locating assumptions about shared values and politics as sometimes contributing to a substantial identity model, Young is obviously not accusing other authors of biological essentialism about groups. Rather, I take her to be pointing to the problem that Cressida Heyes labels "methodological essentialism," a politically problematic generalization about a category of people – one fully compatible with a commitment to constructivism about the category – that nevertheless implies that one must have certain properties to be a member.[50] Such generalizations are often rendered striking in anti-oppression theorizing, given our very commitments to diagnose the norms or processes that construct groups in complex hierarchical relations. Methodological essentialism occurs when we generalize about the character of groups at the very moments that we should be more deeply investigating political processes of identity formation and when we can be called politically to account for our failure to do so. For example, Angela Davis intervenes in the second wave feminist critiques of the centrality of women's "unpaid" housework to their oppression and the consequent "wages for housework" campaigns to note that "cleaning women, domestic workers, maids ... know better than anyone else what it means to receive wages for housework."[51] She thus challenges these accounts of "women" as a group that is partly constructed through practices of labour exploitation with erasing the specific exploitative practices and resistant values constituting the positionality and experience of women who were not bourgeois, implicitly excluding them from the analysis of "women." I will return later in this chapter to challenge Western memory theorists with methodological essentialism.[52]

It is not uncommon to illustrate the co-implication of identities by referring to the configurations of Indigenous identities that arose through colonial encounter. Diana Taylor notes of Peru that "the very categories – criollo and Indian – are a product of ... conflict, not its reason for being."[53] Young, herself, notes that "[b]efore the British began to conquer the islands now called New Zealand ... there was no group anyone thought of as Maori."[54] More substantively, Valaskakis, in "Blood Borders: Being Indian and Belonging," offers a powerful and detailed analysis of how a substantial approach to social categories would be wholly inimical to grasping the complexities of contemporary Indigenous identities in Canada and the United States.[55] Noting that the "right to Indian identity has been controlled and curtailed by government policies since the formation" of these countries, Valaskakis details the confusions and complications of colonialist policies involving blood quantum or parentage, complicated by gender, intermarriage, registration, and treaty status, and interacting with the powerful and thorny politics of tribal membership and enrollment that were critical to pronouncements of Native sovereignty.[56] This ongoing relational interaction led to complexities of being Indian in ways that resulted in unstable insider-outsider distinctions and confused and conflicted experiences of identity. As a concrete example of these complexities, Constance MacIntosh discusses the importance of status under Canada's *Indian Act* to the access of health care resources and writes:

> The biological and descent-based criteria of the *Indian Act* sever connections by imposing divisions and separations that are at odds with biological, affinal, and historic relationships. Individuals without status often report being treated as though the fact of not meeting statutory criteria for status signals that they lack something at their core which is possessed by status individuals, that they have lost some sort of authentic connection to indigeneity.[57]

While Valaskakis and MacIntosh describe the "colonial codes that ricochet through time and space to cut across and construct Native identity and tribal affiliation," as obscuring Indigenous "constructions of membership," they also argue that these constructions have persistently re-emerged as Indians "build their own collective subjectivities and social boundaries in a politicized process that expresses not only their resistance, but their cultural continuity."[58]

Valaskakis considers the theoretical momentum toward a relational approach as "an opening to understand colonial experience, nationalist discourse, and identity politics as epistemological and representational knots."[59] While fully alert to the economic politics that fuelled these relational identity constructions – initially "forcible acquisition over land and resources" – she is also interested in how "North Americans' representations of themselves and of Indians are linked in articulation to ways of knowing and experiencing otherness."[60] The rest of this section follows a key thread in these epistemological and representational knots. Groups are often identified through the idea of collective memory as their shared conception of the past. Yet the obvious role of memory in colonial assimilationist policy suggests that this is precisely a place where we need a relational conception of the co-constitution of identities through memory processes or otherwise risk methodological essentialism. My analysis makes use of the idea that representing groups as kinds of rememberers, as those who have certain memory capacities, defects, or virtues is a powerful way of positioning people relationally and politically. For example, in the 1980s and 1990s, in response to historic claims of child sexual abuse, women as a group were represented as having extremely suggestible memory. This representation of defective capacities compromised possibilities for abuse survivors to credibly share their pasts.[61]

Positioning Indigenous peoples as certain kinds of rememberers in order to control the sociality of memory was a damaging epistemological and political representation that responded to their refusal in the 1800s to cede their tribal and national identities and disappear into Canada in exchange for enfranchisement and small individual land grants.[62] In response, as John Milloy writes in his chapter on the "founding vision" of Residential Schools, it was decided that assimilation must take place by other means, by the complete re-socialization of Indian children, so that finally "there is not a single Indian in Canada that has not been absorbed into the body politic, and there is no Indian question, and no Indian Department."[63]

The founding vision, I contend, was one of different kinds of rememberers, one that recognized the importance of sharing both narrative and embodied memory in the dynamics of group identifications and relational self-constitution. Children were, and were understood to be, vulnerable rememberers whose unmaking and remaking, by preventing some relationships while compelling others, could destroy the bonds of intergenerational teaching and learning that sustained Native communities. Hayter Read, who was an official from the Department of Indian Affairs, instructed that "every effort should be directed against anything calculated to keep fresh in the memories of children habits and associations which it is one of the main objects of industrial institutions to obliterate."[64] This intended obliteration of the habits and associations of memory was galvanized, for example, through geographical separation from communities, sometimes for years as children were denied holidays and parents were denied visits; harsh and routine punishment for communicating in the languages that sustained Indigenous world views and helped narratively to constitute Indigenous identities; and the impression of a wholly different temporal rhythm to childhood in order to alter embodied habit. As Milloy explains, "[s]etting the child's cultural clock from the 'savage' seasonal round of hunting and gathering to the hourly and daily precision required by the Industrial order was seen by the Department as an issue of primary consideration."[65] Repressing old identities via new social memories required both retraining children in the embodied practices that would instill European forms of discipline, punctuality, and above all obedience meant for the labouring classes, while schooling children into Christian perspectives through which they were meant to re-remember their families.[66] Anishanaabe Elder and spiritual advisor, Fred Kelly, invites us into a childhood remembering of his mother, who was already unwell:

> In the darkness of the dormitory and alone in bed, I am suddenly overcome by a cold sweat. Although baptized into the Catholic faith, my poor un-suspecting mother still adheres to her traditional spirituality. A boy so loves his mother that he never wants to see her hurt. Yet, in these circumstances she is so precariously close to the door of hell.[67]

This "essentially violent ... onslaught on child and culture" through the severing of intergenerational memory and the imperative to re-remember their communities as heathen and their parents as damned, did not, as in-tended, kill the Indian in the child.[68] As Kelly recalls, "[c]ertainly there was serious and irreversible damage, but no policy could assimilate us."[69] The schooling did create unstable insider-outsiders to both Indigenous and Settler communities, often with confused and conflicted experiences of isolation and belonging. At the same time, it dramatically reshaped the economic, cultural, and relational dynamics of the communities from which children were removed, sometimes generation after generation.[70] While the removal of children from their homes, the forbidding of Indigenous language, and the strict gender segregation that prevented siblings from communicating at school obstructed the sharing of family memory, the pedagogical impera-tives and deliberate isolation of the schools, as well as the trauma and shame of violence and abuse, prevented Indigenous and non-Indigenous children from sharing childhood and school-day memories of similar kinds of experi-ence. These are often the memories that we re-share as adults to foster a kind of generational intimacy. To reframe these points through the insights of Françoise Baylis's account of personal identity, the retraining of memory forecloses on specific possibilities for narrative co-constitution of identities in family and peer relationships.[71]

To illustrate the founding vision of the schools, which was the represen-tational matrix through which Indian identities were to be relationally re-conceived, Milloy comments on a Department of Indian Affairs photograph: "Quewich and his children at the Qu-Appelle Industrial School":

> The ... "influences of Indianism," the father, stooped and wrinkled, already a figure of the past, having reached the limits of evolution, appears to be decaying right in front of the camera, dying off, as was his culture. In sharp contrast, his children, neatly attired in European clothing, the boy's cadet

cap a symbol of citizenship, are ... examples of the future, of the great transformation to be wrought by separation and education in the residential
school.[72]

I have argued elsewhere that such representations also positioned parents
and Elders who had refused to give up their way of life to colonial impera-
tives as kinds of rememberers in order to manipulate the possibility of sharing
memory through a politics or representation.[73] Adults were precisely not
young and vulnerable rememberers: they were not receptive to the savage
experiments on identity intended and prosecuted by the "total institutions"
of the schools.[74] As long as they could teach their children, however, "they
were a hindrance to the civilizing process."[75] In being represented by the
architects of residential schooling as "the old, unimprovable people" – as
those who could not learn and as those who had nothing to teach – adults
were marked, I contend, as those who could not share memory.[76] Department
of Indian Affairs inspector J.R. McCrae wrote: "The circumstances of Indian
existence prevents him from following that course of evolution which has
produced from the barbarian of the past, the civilized man of today."[77] As
his words illustrate, being declared unfit for transformation, parents and
Elders were representationally consigned to the position of the barbarian of
the past, a figure that was already lost to a notion of time as progress toward
the modern industrial age. Anishanaabe legal scholar John Borrows notes
aptly that Indigenous cultures have been located in "once upon a time"
rather than in time.[78] Shown as being lost to an *unrecoverable* past, parents
and Elders were *represented* as those who could not share the present past,
while they were, in fact, prevented from preserving a flexible living heritage
through sharing their language, stories, skills, ceremonies, and traditions
and by living with their children on lands imbued with spirituality and
ancestral presence. In being categorized as barbarian, parents and Elders
were relationally positioned through what Johannes Fabian has described
as "temporal concepts and devices as a political act," specifically through
the denial of *coevalness* understood as "a common, active 'occupation' or
sharing of time."[79] If barred from sharing the present past with their children
or with Settlers, Indigenous parents and Elders could not co-determine its
significance.

Author Lee Maracle, a member of the Sto:loh Nation states: "We are an
oral people: history, law, politics, sociology, the self, and our relationship to
the world are all contained in our memory."[80] It needs finally to be noted
that Western conceptions of memory were, and are complicit in, the powerful representational assault on the performative memory practices of
Indigenous cultures. Performance theorist Diana Taylor writes that "part of
the colonizing project throughout the Americas consisted in discrediting

autochthonous ways of preserving and communicating historical under-standing."[81] That is, colonialist practice did not just attempt to "stamp out," but also to "discredit," embodied and oral memory, typically by recording in writing that these mnemonic practices *could not* preserve the past. As she writes, "if the ancestors of the people called Indians had known writing in early times, then the lives they lived would not have faded from view until now."[82] In other words, Indigenous cultures were lost to an unrecoverable past partly because their ways of remembering could not preserve the past, justifying their representation as "decaying right in front of the [eye of the European] camera" while shifting and twisting the agency of preserving Indigenous culture (now lost rather than living) to colonial historians and their institutions.[83]

Western writings often continue to situate oral memory practices as of the past as a piece with situating oral cultures – cultures such as the Sto:loh in which oral memory practices both were and are central to a sense of cultural integrity – as themselves having passed. For example, Barbara Misztal, in a well-regarded account of theories of social remembering, writes that, "[s]ince memory has traveled from oral expression through print literacy to today's electronic means of communication, we can conclude by saying that memory has its own history."[84] However, while attachment to print does not render us anachronistic – electronic communication has transformed, without obliterating, the idea of text – Misztal misrepresents oral cultures as pre-literate cultures rather than as, for example, the contemporary Sto:loh nation to which Maracle belongs. Although oral cultures begin the story of memory, they become lost to a progress they were allegedly not even able to recognize because, as rememberers, they are incapable of the necessary historical sensibility: "In oral cultures, people *assumed* things were as they had always been, because oral transmission accumulates actual alterations unconsciously."[85]

Non-Indigenous Canadians have rarely participated in activities of sharing memory that would the allow the narratives and embodied practices of First Nations, Inuit, or Métis peoples to have force in re-shaping our experience of pasts that we thus continue to re-live from the colonialist perspective of our forebears. At the same time, as I have so far briefly suggested, Western memory theorists have failed to politicize and historicize the conceptions of memory that are entangled not only with the constitution of Indigenous identities but also with that of Settler identities. In his written attempt to "preserve" Great Lakes Indigenous cultures, physician Edward Walsh writes: "Their History is as mysterious as their fate is severe ... They are gliding from the face of the earth like guilty Ghosts, leaving no memorial, no record that they had ever existed."[86] Museum curators Ruth Phillips and Elizabeth Johnson point out that "[f]or two centuries and more, educated Europeans and Euro-Canadians like Walsh collected and recorded in the belief that they were acting in the noble cause of preserving memory" through the technologies that could do so, showing a collective distortion of character, a self-deceptive confusion of nobility for the arrogance that was consequent on the co-implication of Settler/Indigenous identities.[87]

Although the persistent stereotype of Indigenous peoples as the frozen past has been critically engaged, I believe it needs to be more thoroughly conceptualized within a complex colonialist politics of assimilation/exclusion that depends on controlling the sociability of memory. Eduardo Mendieta has counselled political and legal philosophers to deepen their analyses of racism by looking from institutions such as the law to the dynamics of moral psychology in which they are embedded, since the state maintains racist affect through the control of intimacy. His telling illustration is the continued *de facto* segregation of US schools. He thus focuses on the control of space and place. I hope to have illustrated that there is a significant temporal dimension to possible intimacy – namely our capacity to share the present past with each other – that is also subject to powerful political and ideological moulding.[88]

Methodological Essentialism versus Reparative Remembering

How can non-Indigenous Canadians now take responsibility for the past and act to help de-colonize the relations that are its legacy? One might expect to turn to explicit discussions of memory and justice for a deepened understanding of our task. A number of Western theorists have indeed resisted the current tendency to critique remembering historic harms as an indulgence in a politics of grievance.[89] They have instead argued that since memory is essential to our individual and collective capacities to take responsibility for what we have done, remembering wrongdoing is essential to justice. The accounts that I have referenced in this chapter are theoretically sophisticated, morally serious, and politically sensitive. However, while they recognize the centrality of memory both to identity and to intergroup justice, they have a persistent tendency to elide the relational dynamics of sharing memory in favour of implicating social memory in a substantial logic of group definition. Thus, I challenge them with moments of methodological essentialism inimical to their commitment to reparative justice, and I position sharing memory across groups as potentially critical to intercultural reparative initiatives in Settler societies.[90]

The theories that I discuss are offered as generalized frameworks for considering memory and responsibility for historic harm. They are not committed to close contextual analysis of specific group conflict.[91] The idea of a social group in these theories – whether it is family, community, tribe, or nation – arrives in the discussion of justice and the past as the substrate of social memory, typically named as collective memory. Although memory is offered as an explanation of the group cohesion that these theorists believe is necessary for political agency, that groups are internally homogenous and independent of one another, rather than heterogeneous and interdependent in their development, is assumed in the invocation of collective memory.

For example, James Booth in *Communities of Memory: On Witness, Identity, and Justice* characterizes memory (both habit and narrative) as part of the related boundedness and persistence of a group, "in short ... its identity."[92] The idea of a group enters here:

> Memory collects: it gathers in a past that is mine/ours and that together with future-oriented ... projects map out my/our persistence and distinctness ... It ... sets boundaries, distinguishes one person or community from another ... Autobiographical memory individuates me; group memories define who we are in a world in a way that distinguishes us as a community.[93]

This memory involves "storing the interpretive work of previous generations," building the public institutions of memory and the absorption of memory as habit, as "a tonality of sentiments" that characterize "our life-in-common."[94] Collective memory is wholly insular, an "in-gathering": "the group ... draws its distinctness, its separateness from others by the (manifold) in-gathering of its past. Collective memory as the continuity of life in common does not readily extend beyond the group."[95]

This same undefended homogeneity and insularity to a group characterizes Avishai Margalit's influential *The Ethics of Memory*. Margalit offers a description of natural communities of memory comprised of those who already share "thick relations" – families, communities, and citizenry. For Margalit, as for Booth, how individuals re-experience significant past events is the entrance to a discussion of social memory. Margalit conceives of social memory as shared memory in the sense of an affectively laden representation of a significant communal event that evolves through communication among witnesses: "A shared memory integrates and calibrates the different" and fragmented perspectives of those who remember the episode.[96] Those who have not witnessed the event become involved in remembering it through others' revivifying descriptions and through their access to archives and sanctioned mnemonic sites such as monuments and memorials. A community maintains cohesion through the idea of a shared past, and Margalit refers to shared or collective memory as "cement."[97]

Although memory practices are meant to explain the integrity of the community, the assumption that there is an extremely cohesive community is already assumed in the idea of integrating perspectives into a representation

of the past that allows for a singular description and has a singular significance. The discussion takes for granted that there is a collective perspective
on the past that defines the community in question, though it requires
developed articulation. Even here, the process is mysterious – when Margalit
writes that it is the "shared memory [that] integrates and calibrates" different perspectives, he mystifies the agency involved in social memory since
the explanation simply substitutes a reference to shared memory for the
communal processes that are meant to explain it.

Some theorists are certainly aware that not all group members share a
view of the past. Jeffrey Blustein notes that "the possibility of conflicting
interpretations of the past within a single political community complicates
the process of taking responsibility for past wrongdoing."[98] However, when
we follow out the implication of this insight in his thought, we find that

> [m]emory disputes have to be taken seriously because taking responsibility
> for the past ... depends ... on a more-or-less shared understanding between
> the perpetrators and those who inherit the burden of responsibility on the
> one hand, and the victims and those who represent them on the other.[99]

Conflicting past perspectives become the markers of different groups: perpetrators and victims.

In these discussions of intergroup justice, a group is identified or picked
out via its perspective on the past, and group members are those who share,
or should or will be educated to share, this perspective.[100] Although Booth
and Margalit take collective memory to unify community, a prior assumption of homogeneity underwrites the possibility of the group as the substrate
of such memory. A shared perspective on the past is already inchoate in
Booth's idea of a life in common and in the naturalness of Margalit's communities of memory. Memory itself is personified as an agent releasing
these theorists from confronting the agents and character of actual memory
practices.

These approaches – and here I add Blustein's unmarked assumption that
memory conflict spawns group distinction – imply a level of agreement in
perspective that does not map onto the reality of group life, be it family,
community, or citizenry. Groups subject to aggressive assimilationist strategies will certainly not share a tonality of sensibility from a life in common
or form a natural community of memory. Those who claim Indigenous
identities often belong to geographically fragmented communities and may
be engaged in revitalizing and learning their languages, stories, practices,
and ceremonies in response to the colonialist assault on the possibility of a
life in common. These theories reify the nature of groups and create sharp
insider-outsider distinctions, but, according to theorists such as Valaskakis
and MacIntosh, confused and conflicted experiences of belonging are often

the norm for those who identify as Indigenous in Canada or the United States.[101]

The close inter-definitional relation of group and memory in these theories – social memory as collective memory with an always already-formed group as its substrate – fails to open space for a discussion of memory processes as a key dynamic in the relational formation of group identities. Thus, I challenge these theorists with methodological essentialism. It is their intent to provide frameworks that illuminate our ethical/political responsibilities in the context of historic harms. However, as they describe the circuits of memory as intra rather than intergroup, and as memory practices serve precisely to separate groups from each other rather than to explain their co-constitution, we gain no understanding of assimilation. They thus inadvertently remove an enormous area of historic harm and its effects on communal life from our purview.[102]

I do not deny that practices of sharing of the past often contribute to group identity and group cohesion – we would then again have no account of the harms of assimilation. The embodied practices that enact communal values and are transferred through intergeneration learning are especially significant, and all of these theorists credit a diverse range of memory activities. But those outside or on the margins of the group may also become involved in supporting these values through participation in the activities or in making their pasts and self-identifications vulnerable to the shared experience of others.[103] Thus, it is finally important to signpost the methodological essentialism consequent on an inadequate account of relational identity formation because of the imaginings that it may preclude for renewing and changing relations through sharing memory. The idea of coming together and forming new relationships through sharing memory seems to be prevented by the very function of memory in consolidating extant group identities, and, on the accounts canvassed in this section, the prospects for more diverse communities of memory are indeed dismal. Margalit writes that "the most promising projects of shared memory are those that go through natural communities of memory."[104] Booth writes of our possible responses to occasions when others share family memory:

> [T]hey would be detached, which is not to say unmoved or without impact, but rather removed from the group whose identity is (in part) these memories. This memory defines one community; but outside that framework it is little more than an assemblage of images, stories, names.[105]

Finally, for Blustein, the shared conceptions that characterize the unified groups that have his attention arise from intragroup interaction where "those who belong to the group interact and interrelate in ways that constitute it as a collective body and that are mediated by a conception of community."[106]

These theorists, of course, witness the importance of acknowledging inter-group harm through an accurate and credible understanding of history that would be shared by perpetrator/victim groups. In much writing on repara-tions, social memory stands as representing harm rather than as being often intimately involved in its constitution, and the idea of sharing memory becomes reduced to a shared understanding of history. To return to my context, this reductive approach to sharing memory, which is manifest, for example, in Canadian Prime Minister Stephen Harper's hope that the Truth and Reconciliation Commission will encourage "a relationship based on the knowledge of our shared history," does not respect Aboriginal oral and legal traditions and would fail the intercultural mandate of the commis-sion.[107] To treat sharing experience as another source of historical evidence is to misunderstand the nature of Indigenous memory practices and so to continue to marginalize them.[108]

Cree scholar Winona Wheeler writes that many non-Indigenous historians treat Indigenous oral histories as just another source of "documentary" evidence and do not understand the ways in which a Cree culture "is an oral culture, a listening culture" and that "the Cree are a people to whom understanding and knowledge comes by way of relationships."[109] According to Wheeler, non-Indigenous historians have little patience for the sharing of time that sharing memory in the spirit of learning involves:

> Let's face it, doing oral history the "Indian way" is hard work ... The study of kayâs âcimowina, *stories of long ago,* has taken me moose-hunting and taught me to clean and prepare such fine feast food delicacies as moose-nose and smoked-intestine soup. Traditional copyright teachings come in the wee hours of the morning over cold Tim Horton's coffee in a 4×4 truck heading down the Peace River Highway ... Cree education is based on inter-active and reciprocal relations and all knowledge comes with some degree of personal sacrifice.[110]

According to Richard Morris (Mescalero/Kiowa) and Mary Stuckey, when four Lakota Sioux testified before the 1976 Senate hearings on Wounded Knee by sharing the stories of the massacre in a way that their audience likely found "unnecessary, circular, repetitive, and irrelevant," they were not attempting to give evidence that would settle the historical account:

> Rather the witnesses sought to include every potentially meaningful moment of recollection that could help the living understand how to live. In order to find for themselves an appropriate space in national, collective memory, Indigenous speakers were more interested in opening rather than closing spaces within that memory.[111]

In the 1960s, even when in ill health, Cree Elder John R. McLeod "was unable to turn away from many invitations to speak to non-Indian audiences ... because he sincerely believed in the importance of creating a better understanding between his people and non-Indians."[112] Using a matter-of-fact style of Cree storytelling, he would recount his experiences as a farmer on the Prairies. McLeod "never said what the point of his stories were; he forced the listeners to discover this for themselves":

> [L]isteners were usually staggered to hear, and sometimes almost unwilling to believe, that Indian agents and farming instructors had so completely dominated their Indian charges as recently as the late 1950's by means of sales permits, travel passes, and a variety of other social control mechanisms ... sooner or later have to confess to either him or themselves "I didn't know that."[113]

At that moment, McLeod would know the people there were relating to him, not to the stereotypic figure they had imagined in his place, and only then would he "turn to some of the contemporary issues that meant much to him."[114]

In expressing respect for Aboriginal oral and legal traditions, it is important to follow Young, Valaskakis, and MacIntosh and refuse a substantial notion of Indigenous identities, especially in response to the essentializing tendencies of "North American narratives of dominance" that place "Native people in a time-distanced past that cannot be fully retrieved from the recesses of Indian oral culture."[115] In light of these narratives, it is imperative to recognize "dynamic expressions of culture that emerge, move, and fuse today in response to a changing environment."[116] Contemporary Indigenous revaluings of oral tradition and sharing memory respond to: their devaluing by historians; the discrediting of Indigenous peoples of testifiers; the failure to honour Indigenous ways of preserving and transferring knowledge in North American legal systems; the assault on intergeneration memory and learning by Residential Schools; the still extant stereotypes of a frozen Indigenous past; and the specific nature of the traditions that those of different Indigenous nations engage and the importance of re-appropriating control over the values that ground Indigenous belonging.

Non-Indigenous Canadians can respect this non-essentializing imperative along with the very different and valuable models of sociable memory evident in Indigenous teachings. These teachings express and revitalize rich traditions of public remembering that assume remembering is most naturally an interactive, collaborative, and profoundly ethical activity; that sharing the past is critical to the epistemic and ethical fidelity of memory; that memory plays a fundamental role in making and maintaining relations; and that it is an important way to renew and transform intergroup relations. I want to conclude by offering two suggestions about the reparative role of sharing memory in the context of the Indian Residential School Truth and Reconciliation Commission.

First, the reparative possibilities of the Truth and Reconciliation Commission cannot be adequately enacted through agreement about history for reasons in addition to the continued marginalization of Indigenous memory practices. I have argued that Indigenous/Settler identities have been co-constituted "through temporal concepts and devices as a political act," specifically through the denial of a "common or active 'occupation' ... of time."[117] Pauline Wakeham describes the Settler imaginary as expressing a "taxidermic semiotics" that attempts to "freeze-frame its specimens in an 'allochronic' or 'other time' of suspended pastness."[118] The Indigenous peoples whose territories Canada appropriated and non-Indigenous Canadians might agree that, for example, John Milloy's *A National Crime: The Canadian Government and the Residential School System* is a fairly accurate rendering of some dimensions of our shared history without affecting the force of this destructive semiotics. I have suggested in this chapter that sharing memory – sharing the present past – is a common active "occupation" of time. Insofar as non-Indigenous Canadians participate in this sharing, they can act in a decolonizing spirit to defeat, rather than to re-enforce, this semiotics.

Second, there are potent issues of re-identification at issue in sharing experience. The intent of Residential Schooling was to shift the nature of group identifications so as to extinguish Indianness by controlling how memory was shared across groups. Though not all of our relational self-conceptions shaped through sharing memory are group identificatory, many are, and this fact raises the question of whether sharing memory through the Truth and Reconciliation Commission might transform the group boundaries constituted through colonialism. Given the history of Native/Settler relations, Tsosie is understandably wary of what she terms a reparative strategy of reidentification – she has in mind the call for all Americans to identify themselves "as victims who survived the experience of slavery and of the civil war"[119] – as incompatible with Native sovereignty.[120] However, Valaskakis points out that Indigenous cultural resurgence or "survivance," including reclaiming the heritage of sharing experience, aims to shift power in order to reappropriate the criteria of belonging. The Truth and Reconciliation Commission may fortify this exercise of power in a number of interesting ways, and I conclude, speculatively, by mentioning a few of these.

To aid in renewing and transforming relations, non-Indigenous Canadians might witness and credit the types of Indigenous activism implicit in the work of the Truth and Reconciliation Commission. Through public remembering in this context, Indigenous peoples will act powerfully, pragmatically, and symbolically to reinforce the structure and flow of intergenerational memory that is indeed critical to the flourishing of community and the very process that Residential Schooling sought to disrupt. Mohawk scholar Taiaiake Alfred condemns Canadian Aboriginal policy as insisting "if we are to have a future, it will be one defined by and allowed only at the discretion of the dominant society."[121] The resistance to the Truth and Reconciliation Commission that its supporters anticipate, which is that it does not contest the truth of Indigenous accounts but, rather, their relevance, should be read precisely as resistance to the current Indigenous contending of a colonialist social imaginary that still seeks to control who can share memory in ways that serve the future.[122]

Valaskakis also writes that "in the circulation of Indian narratives ... Native people retell and resist, building the oneness of different First Nations in tribal representations of identity and community ... But the cultural differences of individual Indian nations are also overlaid with a spreading sense of pan-Indianness," itself a consequence of sharing "narratives of pain and empowerment."[123] Thus, stories of the fragmentation of community, the degradation of culture, and the resistance to both may resonate with the experience of Indigenous and non-Indigenous groups who have been targeted by aggressive assimilation potentially encouraging both pan-Indian identifications and more diverse communities of resistance to colonial legacies.

Finally, and despite Tsosie's concerns, Indigenous leaders have invited non-Indigenous Canadians (both those of Settler heritage and newcomers) to share the past in the spirit of a renewed and shared identity. In anticipating the pedagogical function of the Truth and Reconciliation Commission, Elders such as Fred Kelly and Stan McKay remind non-Indigenous Canadians of what we have forgotten: that we are all treaty people. McKay writes that treaties do not have a "best before date" and "they do need to be revisited so that the *spirit* may be kept alive in each generation."[124] Kelly says to the imagined priest who hears his confessions about Residential Schooling: "[L]et me put it more succinctly, Father, you and all Canadians have treaty rights too."[125] Offering the living presence of the treaties as a perspective through which to witness the experience of Residential Schooling opens the possibility of a national level of reidentification that reinforces, rather than undermines, Native sovereignty.

At the moment when we begin to discuss reparations, either in a particular context or at a theoretical level that abstracts from context, we often begin by marking out reparation as a political process that takes place between groups set out and differentiated as perpetrators and victims or as former adversaries.[126] This can be a dangerous moment for the kind of essentialist view of group identities criticized by Young, Valaskakis, Heyes, and others to creep into an account.[127] I have argued through illustration that understanding the intercultural context in which reparation initiatives take place requires analyzing the continued co-implication of identities and that memory can be a powerful node of interaction in this co-implication. Whether the Indian Residential Schools Truth and Reconciliation Commission can make it possible to shift the power and dynamics of relational identification through sharing memory will depend on who controls the imaginings through which the past is revivified and the willing sociality of their engagement.

Notes

This chapter draws on research undertaken for the Indian Residential Schools Truth and Reconciliation Commission. I am especially grateful to Paulette Regan, Seetal Sunga, and Bob Watts for encouraging this research. I am also grateful to the contributers to this volume and especially to Jocelyn Downie, Jennifer Llewellyn, Carolyn McLeod, and Sheila Wildeman for their helpful suggestions on this chapter. I thank Jan Sutherland, as always, for her critical acuity. I am also grateful for the close and accurate readings of this volume by two anonymous referees.

1 Jeffrey Blustein, *The Moral Demands of Memory* (Cambridge: Cambridge University Press, 2008); W. James Booth, *Communities of Memory: On Witness, Identity, and Justice* (Ithaca, NY: Cornell University Press, 2006); Roger I. Simon, *The Touch of the Past: Remembrance, Learning, and Ethic* (New York: Palgrave MacMillan, 2005); Diana Taylor, *The Archive and the Repertoire: Performing Cultural Memory in the Americas* (Durham, NC: Duke University Press, 2003).

2 Pablo De Greiff, "Justice and Reparations" in Pablo De Greiff, ed., *The Handbook of Reparations* (Oxford: Oxford University Press, 2006) 451; Jennifer Llewellyn, "Justice for South Africa: Restorative Justice and the South African Truth and Reconciliation Commission" in Christine M. Koggel, ed., *Moral Issues in Global Perspective: Moral and Political Theory*, 2nd edition (Peterborough, ON: Broadview Press, 2006); Margaret Urban Walker, *Moral Repair: Reconstructing Moral Relations after Wrongdoing* (Cambridge: Cambridge University Press, 2006).

3 Rebecca Tsosie, "Acknowledging the Past to Heal the Future: The Role of Reparations for Native Nations" in Jon Miller and Rahul Kumar, eds., *Reparations: Interdisciplinary Inquiries* (Oxford: Oxford University Press, 2006) 43.

4 *Ibid.* at 55.

5 Tsosie, *ibid.* at 44, writes that even many Western theorists who stress the importance of attending to context still "appear to conceive of reparations under a 'tort model' of compensation," assuming that "Native claims can be parceled out into claims for 'ownership,' for 'equal opportunity,' for 'past wrongdoing' while still factoring in the equitable interests of contemporary citizens, both Native and non-Native" (at 48).

6 Llewellyn, *supra* note 2.

7 For a discussion of cultural imperialism, see Iris Marion Young, *Justice and the Politics of Difference* (Princeton, NJ: Princeton University Press, 1990). I shall refer to theorists from Euro-Western traditions as Western theorists for the remainder of this chapter.

8 Christine Koggel, "Agency and Empowerment: Embodied Realities in a Globalized World" in Sue Campbell, Letitia Meynell, and Susan Sherwin, eds., *Embodiment and Agency* (Philadelphia: Pennsylvania State University Press, 2009) 250.

9 See Jennifer Llewellyn, "Restoring Justice: Thinking Relationally about Justice" in this volume.

10 See Françoise Baylis, "The Self *in Situ*: A Relational Account of Personal Identity" in this volume, for reflection on the importance to our personal and social identities of how we are allowed to be by others..

11 Marlene Brant Castellano, Linda Archibald, and Mike DeGagné, "Introduction" in Marlene Brant Castellano, Linda Archibald, and Mike DeGagné, eds., *From Truth to Reconciliation:*

Transforming the Legacy of Indian Residential Schools (Ottawa: Aboriginal Healing Foundation, 2008) 1 at 3. *Indian Residential Schools Settlement Agreement* (2006), http://www. residentialschoolsettlement.ca/settlement.html.

12 Castellano, Archibald, and DeGagné, *supra* note 11: "The Settlement Agreement provides for a cash payment to Survivors living in 2005 or their estates if deceased, as well as providing an individual assessment process for adjudication of more serious claims of abuse, the creation of memorials, a five-year extension of funding for the Aboriginal Foundation to support community healing initiatives, and the establishment of a Truth and Reconciliation Commission."

13 Indian and Northern Affairs Canada, Federal Representative of Indian Residential Schools, "Highlights" in *Indian Residential Schools Settlement Agreement* (Ottawa: Indian and Northern Affairs Canada, May 2006), http://www.iacobucci.gc.ca/doc-eng.asp?action=h.

14 *Ibid.*, Schedule "N" at 5, http://www.residentialschoolsettlement.ca/SCHEDULE_N.pdf.

15 Gail Guthrie Valaskakis, *Indian Country: Essays on Contemporary Native Culture* (Waterloo, ON: Wilfrid Laurier University Press, 2005) 211 at 216.

16 Chandra Talpade Mohanty, *Feminism without Borders: Decolonizing Theory, Practicing Solidarity* (Durham, NC: Duke University Press, 2003) at 203. Though for me, the terms "co-constitution" and "co-implication" try to get at the same phenomenon, each has a different resonance, and I vary their use in this chapter to capture this fact. "Co-constitution" brings attention to the reality that peoples' identities are reciprocally and dynamically shaped through their relationships. For Mohanty, we must understand "co-implication" in order to comprehend "'difference' as historical" as well as relational, recognizing in particular that we share "certain histories and responsibilities" and that we are relationally implicated in each others' identities through the ideologies that define groups that are typically posed in binary opposition to each other (*ibid.*). The ideologies of concern in this chapter involve the varied representations of groups as kinds of rememberers. See Constance MacIntosh, "Relational Theory, Indigenous Peoples, and Health Law" in this volume, for additional reflection on the importance of historical and intergenerational relationships in considering health law and policy as applied to Indigenous peoples in Canada.

17 The mandate of the commission states: "[T]hrough the Agreement, the Parties have agreed that an historic Truth and Reconciliation Commission will be established to contribute to truth, healing, and reconciliation." Indian and Northern Affairs Canada, *supra* note 13 at 1. While I believe and argue that understanding the importance of sharing memory is critical to the commission's objectives, I do not use the language of healing in this chapter to frame my discussion. It is a language that has been often appropriated by non-Indigenous Canadians with little understanding of its significance for various Indigenous groups or individuals (Roland Chrisjohn and Sherri Young, *The Circle Game: Shadows and Substance in the Indian Residential School Experience in Canada* (Penticton, BC: Theytus Books, 1997)) and at this point in my own research I might well use it inappropriately. See the Aboriginal Healing Foundation (http://www.ahf.ca) for excellent research that represents a diversity of Indigenous perspectives on healing and reconciliation. I am committed to the view that de-colonizing relationships is necessary to any possibility of intergroup healing and reconciliation and that reflection on memory must aid us in this process.

18 I draw on the work of John Borrows, "Listening for a Change: The Courts and Oral Tradition" (2001) 39 Osgoode Hall L.J. 1; Fred Kelly, "Confessions of a Born Again Pagan" in Castellano, Archibald, and DeGagné, *supra* note 11 at 11; Lee Maracle and Sandra Laronde, *My Home as I Remember* (Toronto: National Heritage Books, 2000); Stan McKay, "Expanding the Dialogue on Truth and Reconciliation: In a Good Way" in Castellano, Archibald, and DeGagné, *supra* note 11 at 101; Neal McLeod, *Cree Narrative Memory: From Treaties to Contemporary Times* (Saskatoon, SK: Purich Publishing, 2007); Richard Morris and Mary Stuckey, "Cultured Memories: Power, Memory, and Finalism" (2004) 28:4 Am. Indian Culture & Research Journal 1; Tsosie, *supra* note 3; Valaskakis, *supra* note 15; Winona Wheeler, "Reflections on the Social Relations of Indigenous Oral Histories" in Ute Lischke and David T. McNab, eds., *Walking a Tightrope: Aboriginal People and Their Representations* (Waterloo, ON: Wilfrid Laurier University Press, 2005) 189.

19   Mary Warnock, *Memory* (Cambridge: Cambridge University Press, 1987).
20   Blustein, *supra* note 1; Sue Campbell, *Relational Remembering: Rethinking the Memory Wars* (Lanham, MD: Rowman and Littlefield, 2003); Susan Engel, *Context Is Everything: The Nature of Memory* (New York: W.H. Freeman and Company, 1999); D.L. Schacter, *Searching for Memory: The Brain, the Mind, and the Past* (New York: Harper Collins, 1996); John Sutton, "Remembering" in Philip Robbins and Murat Aydede, eds., *Cambridge Handbook of Situated Cognition* (Cambridge: Cambridge University Press, 2008) 217.
21   Paula Reavey and Steven D. Brown, "Transforming Past Action and Agency in the Present: Time, Social Remembering, and Child Sexual Abuse" (2006) 16:2 Theory and Psychology 179 at 180.
22   *Ibid.*
23   A.J. Barnier et al., "A Conceptual and Empirical Framework for the Social Distribution of Cognition: The Case of Memory" (2008) 9:1-2 Cognitive Systems Research 33 at 35.
24   *Ibid.*
25   *Ibid.*
26   Robyn Fivish, "Constructing Narrative, Emotion and Self in Parent-Child Conversations about the Past" in Ulric Neisser and Robyn Fivish, eds., *The Remembering Self: Construction and Accuracy in Self-Narrative* (Cambridge: Cambridge University Press, 1994) 136; Elizabeth A. Waites, *Memory Quest: Trauma and the Search for a Personal History* (New York: W.W. Norton, 1997).
27   Christoph Hoerl and Theresa McCormack, "Joint Reminiscing as Joint Attention to the Past" in Naomi Eilan et al., eds., *Joint Attention, Communication, and Other Minds* (Oxford: Oxford University Press, 2005) 260 at 270.
28   Maurice Halbwachs, *On Collective Memory*, translated by Louis Coser (Chicago: University of Chicago Press, 1992).
29   Sue Campbell, "Our Faithfulness to the Past: Reconstructing Memory Value" (2006) 19:3 Philosophical Psychology 361 at 374.
30   See Jennifer Nedelsky, "The Reciprocal Relation of Judgment and Autonomy: Walking in Another's Shoes and Which Shoes to Walk In" in this volume.
31   The full name of the report is *Bringing Them Home: Report of the National Inquiry into the Separation of Aboriginal and Torres Strait Islander Children from Their Families* (Sydney, Australia: Equal Rights and Equal Opportunity Commission, 1997), http://www.hreoc.gov.au/social_justice/bth_report/report/index.html.
32   John Bond, "Reconciliation: A Non-Indigenous Australian Perspective" in Castellano, Archibald, and DeGagné, *supra* note 11 at 271.
33   *Ibid.*
34   Avishai Margalit, *The Ethics of Memory* (Cambridge, MA: Harvard University Press, 2002).
35   This potential is often not realized. See Sara Ahmed, *The Cultural Politics of Emotion* (New York: Routledge, 2004) for an insightful analysis of the continued exclusory dimensions of national expressions of shame as expressed through Sorry Book entries.
36   Alexis Shotwell, *Implicit Understanding and Political Transformation* (Ph.D. dissertation, University of California, Santa Cruz, 2006) [unpublished].
37   *Ibid.*
38   Campbell, *supra* note 20.
39   Barnier et al., *supra* note 23 at 35.
40   Margalit, *supra* note 34; David Middleton and Steven D. Brown, *The Social Psychology of Experience: Studies in Remembering and Forgetting* (London: Sage Publications, 2005); Taylor, *supra* note 1.
41   Middleton and Brown, *supra* note 40.
42   Barnier et al., *supra* note 23 at 35.
43   I have argued at length elsewhere that the relational and re-constructive aspects to memory, and the consequence that the meaning of remembering an event may shift as our contexts and concerns change or as our values evolve, in no way diminishes the importance of accuracy or truth in the assessment of memory claims. In fact, we need to understand the reconstructive and relational dimensions of memory to properly assess its complex epistemology. For example, because how we remember the past shapes how we go on both as

individuals and as communities, whether or not we remember the past faithfully will depend not only on whether we have the facts right but also on whether we have given them appropriate significance. Though the ways the past is valued will always be contestible, some ways of valuing can be characterized as more accurate than others. See Campbell, *supra* note 20; Campbell, *supra* note 29; Sue Campbell, "Inside the Frame of the Past: Memory, Diversity, and Solidarity" in Sue Campbell, Letitia Meynell, and Susan Sherwin, eds., *Embodiment and Agency* (Philadelphia: Pennsylvania State University Press, 2009) 211, for discussion as well as Blustein, *supra* note 1.

44 Christine Koggel, *Perspectives on Equality: Constructing a Relational Theory* (Lanham, MD: Rowman and Littlefield, 1998); Susan Sherwin, "A Relational Approach to Autonomy in Health Care" in Feminist Health Care Ethics Research Network, Susan Sherwin, coordinator, *The Politics of Women's Health: Exploring Agency and Autonomy* (Philadelphia: Temple University Press, 1998) 19.

45 Iris Marion Young, *Inclusion and Democracy* (Oxford: Oxford University Press, 2002) at 87.

46 *Ibid.* at 88.

47 *Ibid.* at 89

48 *Ibid.* at 90.

49 *Ibid.*

50 Cressida Heyes, *Line Drawings: Defining Women through Feminist Practice* (Ithaca, NY: Cornell University Press, 2000).

51 Angela Davis, *Women, Race and Class* (London: Vintage, 1983) at 237.

52 It is precisely this kind of essentialism that a contextual analysis focusing on relations of power (including the power of the theorist to make generalization) can render more challengeable. See Mohanty, *supra* note 16, for essays that drive home this point. See also Koggel, *supra* note 8. Since the charge of methodological essentialism is a challenge to generalizing practices, one possible response is to try to defend the validity or importance of generalization in a particular theoretical or political context, as, for example, when theorists defend the political necessity of a provisional identity politics (see, for example, bell hooks, *Yearning* (Boston: Southend Press, 1990)). Such defences are themselves open to challenge but show the theorist's willingness to engage with the theoretical and political complexities of group identity formation, including her own potential complicity as a theorist. See Constance MacIntosh, "Relational Theory, Indigenous Peoples, and Health Law" in this volume, for a self-conscious engagement with generalizing in the context of discussing Indigenous identities. I thank Carolyn McLeod for asking me to respond to the challenge that generalizations about the characteristics of a group are appropriate in some contexts.

53 Taylor, *supra* note 1 at 195. Like Young, Taylor is very critical of the extent to which "these antagonistic positions have been polarized and cemented into the social imaginary." She notes that "this way of thinking of lineage and tradition would certainly insist on keeping the various circuits of memory and transmission separate" (*ibid.*). I am indebted to her work in thinking through the importance of sharing memory across, and in spite of, this cemented social imaginary.

54 Young, *supra* note 45 at 90.

55 Valaskakis, *supra* note 15.

56 *Ibid.* at 212.

57 See Constance MacIntosh, "Relational Theory, Indigenous Peoples, and Health Laws and Politics" in this volume. *Indian Act*, R.S.C. 1985, c. I-5.

58 Valaskakis, *supra* note 15 at 212 and 217. MacIntosh discusses some of the penalties as well as promises of engaging in these politicized processes in the context of access to health benefits. See Françoise Baylis, "The Self *in Situ*: A Relational Account of Personal Identity" in this volume, for an account of the complexities of black identity and belonging that I take to be similar in spirit to this discussion of Indigenous identities. Baylis' discussion marks a very different set of historical, political, and relational complexities and has a sharper focus on the relational constitution of individual or personal identities.

59 *Ibid.* at 213.

60 *Ibid.*

61 Campbell, *supra* note 20.

62 John Milloy, *A National Crime: The Canadian Government and the Residential School System, 1879-1986* (Winnipeg, MB: University of Manitoba Press, 1999).

63 *Ibid.* at 46, quoting Duncan Campbell Scott, Superintendent of Indian Education, in a 1920 speech to a Parliamentary Committee in Ottawa.

64 *Ibid.* at 43.

65 *Ibid.* at 36.

66 See Paul Connerton, *How Societies Remember* (New York: Cambridge University Press, 1993), for an account of social memory as embodied acts of transfer where the proper performance of a practice instantiates, and so conserves and facilitates, the intergenerational transfer of cultural values.

67 Kelly, *supra* note 18 at 15.

68 Milloy, *supra* note 62 at 42.

69 Kelly, *supra* note 18 at 24.

70 Celia Haig-Brown, *Resistance and Renewal: Surviving the Indian Residential School* (Vancouver: Tillacum Library, 1989).

71 Baylis, *supra* note 10.

72 Milloy, *supra* note 62 at 28.

73 Sue Campbell, "Remembering for the Future: Memory as a Lens on the Indian Residential Schools Truth and Reconciliation Commission" (Discussion paper prepared for the Indian Residential Schools Truth and Reconciliation Commission, 2008).

74 Erving Goffman, "On the Characteristics of Total Institutions" in Erving Goffman, *Asylums: Essays on the Social Situation of Mental Patients and Other Inmates* (New York: Doubleday Anchor, 1961) 1.

75 Milloy, *supra* note 62 at 26.

76 *Ibid.* This infamous description is by Reverand E.F Wilson, founder of the Shingwauk Residential School.

77 *Ibid.* at 27.

78 John Borrows, *Recovering Canada: The Resurgence of Indigenous Law* (Toronto: University of Toronto Press, 2002) at 60.

79 Johannes Fabian, *Time and the Other: How Anthropology Makes Its Object* (New York: Columbia University Press, 2002) at xl and 31.

80 Lee Maracle, "Preface" in Maracle and Laronde, *supra* note 18 at i.

81 Taylor, *supra* note 1 at 34.

82 *Ibid.*, quoting from the sixteenth-century *Huarochiri Manuscript* written down by Friar Francisco de Avila, held in the Biblioteca Nacional in Madrid, Spain.

83 Milloy, *supra* note 62 at 28.

84 Barbara A Misztal, *Theories of Social Remembering* (Philadelphia: Open University Press, 2003) at 25.

85 *Ibid.* at 28 [emphasis added]. For further discussion, see Sue Campbell, "Challenges to Memory in Political Contexts: Recognizing Disrespectful Challenge" (Discussion paper prepared for the Indian Residential Schools Truth and Reconciliation Commission, 2008).

86 As cited in Ruth B. Phillips and Elizabeth Johnson, "Negotiating New Relations: Canadian Museums, First Nations, and Cultural Property" in John Torpey, ed., *Politics and the Past: On Repairing Historical Injustice* (Lanham, MD: Rowman and Littlefield, 2003) 149 at 150.

87 *Ibid.*

88 Eduardo Mendieta, "Racial Justice, Latinos, and the Supreme Court: The Role of Law and Affect in Social Change" in Jorge J.E. Gracia, ed., *Race or Ethnicity? On Black and Latino Identity* (Ithaca, NY: Cornell University Press, 2007) 206.

89 For a recent and influential politics of grievance account, see John Torpey, *Making Whole What Has Been Smashed: On Reparations Politics* (Cambridge, MA: Harvard University Press, 2006).

90 I offer Taylor, *supra* note 1, and Simon, *supra* note 1, as striking exemptions to the tendencies I locate in this section.

91 As indicated by references and examples, however, concern with specific groups and conflicts often implicitly underlies these accounts and in my view restricts their vision. The accounts that I reference all make the Holocaust of the European Jewry central to their understanding

of historic injustice and contemporary responsibility. They pay very little attention to the harms of colonization. This would not be a problem unless they purported to be offering general frameworks for understanding the role of memory in addressing historic harm.

92 Booth, *supra* note 1 at iii.
93 *Ibid.* at 11.
94 *Ibid.* at 21.
95 *Ibid.* at 24-25.
96 Margalit, *supra* note 34 at 51.
97 *Ibid.* at 67.
98 Blustein, *supra* note 1 at 140.
99 *Ibid.*
100 Margalit's, *supra* note 34 at 58, account depends on a mnemonic division of labour. As community members, we are not all responsible for every shared memory, although we are responsible for doing our part to see that they are all preserved.
101 *Bringing Them Home, supra* note 31, is an excellent source of evidence for the difficulties of belonging faced by those whose history includes forced removal from their communities. Although I do not have the space to pursue further illustration here, I thank an anonymous referee for indicating the relevance of this work to the argument of this chapter.
102 While I have no wish to do violence to individual accounts by over-generalizing the source of this fairly static approach to identity, it is worth noting that all analogize social to individual memory, treating the social as an individual writ large and thus implicitly de-socializing individual memory though all would in fact affirm our conception of individuals themselves as socially constituted. In an earlier section of this chapter, I sketched the move to an understanding of memory that credits the extent to which personal memory is shaped through relational memory processes and that moves away from a core understanding of memory as a psychic representation of a singular event impressed at the time of experience. If we become rememberers through sharing and re-experiencing an evolving sense of the meaning of our own pasts in relation to diverse others, analogizing social to individual memory may be the wrong place to start in understanding how memory enters into group constitution.
103 See Campbell, *supra* note 43; Paulette Regan, "An Apology Feast at Hazelton: Indian Residential Schools, Reconciliation, and Making Space for Indigenous Legal Traditions" in Law Commission of Canada, ed., *Indigenous Legal Traditions* (Vancouver: UBC Press, 2007) 40, for developed examples of participation in others' memory practices so as to give weight to different values and resistant social imaginaries.
104 Margalit, *supra* note 34 at 82.
105 Booth, *supra* note 1 at xii.
106 Blustein, *supra* note 1 at 122-23.
107 Stephen Harper, "Prime Minster Offers Full Apology on Behalf of Canadians for Indian Residential Schools" (Speech, 11 June 2008), http://pm.gc.ca/eng/media.asp?id=2149.
108 I thank Jennifer Llewellyn here for recognizing my implicit commitment to this distinction, causing me to recognize and sharpen it. Although in thinking of reparations, some writers would place the Truth and Reconciliation Commission at the stage of acknowledging harm as a preliminary to its redress, the argument of this chapter suggests, in keeping with other writers such as Llewellyn, *supra* note 2; Kelly, *supra* note 18; McKay, *supra* note 18; and Walker, *supra* note 2, that they offer more substantive possibilities for reparative activity.
109 Wheeler, *supra* note 18 at 190.
110 *Ibid.* at 199.
111 Morris and Stuckey, *supra* note 18 at 24.
112 Noel Dyck, "Negotiating the Indian 'Problem'" in David Miller et al., eds., *The First Ones: Readings in Indian/Native Studies* (Piapot Reserve: SIFC Press, 1992) 132 at 135.
113 *Ibid.* at 138.
114 *Ibid.* I have been made familiar with Dyck's account through the writing of John McLeod's grandson, Neal McLeod, *supra* note 18.
115 Valaskakis, *supra* note 15 at 215.
116 *Ibid.*

117 Fabian, *supra* note 79 at xi and 31.
118 Pauline Wakeham, *Taxidemic Signs: Reconstructing Aboriginality* (Minneapolis: University of Minnesota Press, 2008) at 17. By social imaginary, I mean the deep background of concepts and discourses, expectations, and representational schemas that shape (most often implicitly) "the ways people imagine their social existence, how they fit together with others, how things go on between them and their fellows." Charles Taylor, *Modern Social Imaginaries* (Durham, NC: Duke University Press, 2004) at 23.
119 Tsosie, *supra* note 3 at 159.
120 John Ralston Saul's provocative claim that Canada is "a Métis civilization," which is an attempt to encourage acknowledgment of the deep influence of Indigenous nations on the values that Canadians cherish, has recently confronted both Indigenous peoples and non-Indigenous Canadians with similar questions about the politics of reidentification. John Ralston Saul, *A Fair Country: Telling Truths about Canada* (London: Penguin Books, 2008).
121 Taiaiake Alfred, *Wasáse: Indigenous Pathways of Action and Freedom* (Peterborough, ON: Broadview Press, 2005) at 131.
122 Sheila Wildeman has pointed out to me that this point is closely connected to the previous one since witnessing and supporting the flow of intergenerational memory is one way to defeat a taxidermic semiotics.
123 Valaskakis, *supra* note 15 at 215-16.
124 McKay, *supra* note 18 at 113.
125 Kelly, *supra* note 18 at 23.
126 Brian Rice and Anna Snyder, "Reconciliation in the Context of a Settler Society: Healing the Legacy of Colonialism in Canada" in Castellano, Archibald, and DeGagné, *supra* note 11 at 46; Kelly, *supra* note 18 at 22.
127 This despite the fact that reparative contexts should be particularly valuable sites for thinking through the relational nature of identities, as they seek to shift self-identification and social norms through encouraging relational interaction.

7
Taking a Feminist Relational Perspective on Conscience
Carolyn McLeod

One would hope that one's health care professional had a conscience. Indeed, the idea of a health care professional without a conscience is an utterly frightening one. I assume then that conscience is something we value among these professionals (which is not to say that their conscience could not be overvalued).[1] The fact that conscience has value in health care is clear.[2] But why conscience has value in health care is opaque, given, for example, how harmful conscientious refusals by health care professionals can be.[3] Why do we care whether a doctor or nurse, say, has a conscience? What understanding of conscience do we need to be able to explain the value of conscience in health care?

One understanding of conscience dominates bioethical discussion about conscience. For obvious reasons, I call it the dominant view.[4] According to this view, to have a conscience is to be compelled to act in accordance with one's own moral values for the sake of one's "integrity." Here, integrity is understood as inner or psychological unity. Conscience is deemed valuable because it promotes this quality. In the chapter that follows, I describe the dominant view, attempt to show that it is flawed, and sketch a positive alternative to it. In my opinion, conscience often fails to promote inner unity (regardless of the degree of inner unity that we have in mind); acting with a conscience leaves many people broken rather than unified. A better view about the value of conscience is that having a conscience encourages morally responsible agency. My goal is to prove that this alternative explains better what it means to value conscience in health care and the extent to which we ought to value it.

My argument proceeds from a feminist relational perspective. I contend that this perspective allows us to see what it means, and why it is important, for beings like us (that is, relational beings) to have a conscience. From a perspective on moral agency that is relational, social relations not only potentially limit moral agency (that is, the ability to make moral choices and to be held morally responsible), but they also help to create it and to make it recognizable. The skills, identities, and behavioural and emotional dispositions of moral agents are all developed and understood within particular social contexts.[5] People do not come into this world fully formed and able to comprehend one another as moral agents, despite how they seem in much analytic moral philosophy. Rather, the social relations into which they enter (often involuntarily) help to make them who they are, which could be a healthy moral agent, a damaged one, or perhaps not a moral agent at all. The relations that shape them, from a *feminist* relational perspective, include political relations of oppression and privilege, which can seriously damage, but also enlighten, them as moral agents. My aim in this chapter is to show, from this perspective on moral agency, that the dominant view is problematic and that an alternative is in order.

This chapter illustrates that feminist relational theory does not simply highlight the importance of social support for developing capacities such as conscience or autonomy. It also often critiques how these capacities are understood (for example, autonomy as mere independence) and develops new understandings of them (for example, "relational autonomy"). There is as yet no feminist relational critique of how bioethicists interpret conscience. Thus, in the first part of this chapter, I present this critique, while in the second part I give my positive, relational view.

Analyzing the Dominant View

The View in a Nutshell
One reason why conscience is relevant to health care is that conscientious objections occur with some frequency in health care. Sometimes these objections target health care practices or policies that are simply corrupt, although all too frequently they aim at practices that are morally essential.[6] For example, conscientious objections by pharmacists to provide women with emergency contraception have been frequent enough in North America to attract the attention of media, legislators, and some bioethicists.[7] And conscientious objections by physicians to abortion are common enough in many parts of the world to limit access to abortion severely.[8] These sorts of refusals raise a number of moral questions, with perhaps the central question being: "Why ought we to take claims to conscience seriously, as explanations for why someone must do, or not do, a certain thing?" The dominant view says that we ought to take these appeals seriously because a person's "integrity" is at stake (hereafter, read "integrity" as inner unity).[9] Supporters of this view give various reasons for connecting conscience and integrity in this way. Let me summarize the dominant view and then outline some of these reasons.

According to the dominant view, our conscience has a particular focus: the impact on the self of violating our deep moral commitments. These violations would bring about guilt, shame, or self-betrayal that aches so much we would be unable to live with ourselves. Negative moral emotions such as these signal a rupture in the self, between one's actions or thoughts and one's moral values. In other words, they reveal a lack of integrity. To have a conscience is to be internally warned or reminded of this consequence (that is, of psychological disunity) should one do or fail to do a certain thing and to be reluctant simply to live with this consequence rather than try to prevent or remove it.[10] This summary suggests that there are two dimensions to having a conscience on the dominant view: (1) being alert to signs of discord between one's actions or thoughts and one's deep moral commitments; and (2) being inclined to assuage the discord. The "voice" of conscience is this alertness and this inclination – our conscience "speaks" to us when we are attentive and prepared to eliminate inner moral discord.[11]

The unity that a conscience promotes is a moral unity, according to the dominant view. What is at stake is our moral integrity. And among our moral commitments, the ones that are most relevant to conscience are those that contribute to our moral identity (these are our "deep" moral commitments) because our psychological unity critically depends on whether we honour them. Failure to do so calls into question what kind of person we are, which can cause severe psychological rupture.

To get clearer on the relation between conscience and moral unity in the dominant view, having a conscience and being morally unified are not identical, but, rather, the one (conscience) fosters the other (moral unity). Having a conscience also may be necessary for moral unity, but it is not sufficient for it, since on top of having a conscience we also need to have moral standards and reasoning capacities (those that allow us to unify our moral lives) in order to be morally unified. As well, according to the dominant view, the moral unity that conscience promotes is not a unity of predetermined or prescribed moral values but, rather, a unity of whatever moral values we happen to hold. The deep moral commitments of a person with a conscience are subjective rather than objective.[12] Thus, the requirement that this person promote her moral values for the sake of her moral integrity is purely formal.

To summarize the dominant view, it states that conscience functions to keep us in a certain relation to ourselves, one in which we have proper regard for, and actively promote, our moral integrity. According to this view, then, the value of conscience is personal rather than social – having a conscience keeps us in "the proper relation" to ourselves but not to others (at least not directly).[13]

Why think that the dominant view is correct? Advocates of it give a number of reasons of which I will highlight two.[14] One has to do with the "dramatic language" that often accompanies an appeal to conscience.[15] Examples include: "I wouldn't be able to live with myself if I did that"; "I wouldn't be able to sleep at night"; or "I would hate myself." People say such things when they imagine having to violate a commitment that they hold dear and when the violation would make them feel so alienated from themselves, so de-stabilized, that they would not be able to go on (or so they say). The self-betrayal and subsequent loss of self-respect, together with feelings of shame or guilt, would be unbearable to them. Ultimately, they would lose integrity. In short, then, the dramatic language of conscientious objectors supports the contention that conscience protects integrity.

A further point made in favour of the dominant view is that it allows us to explain the difference between appealing to conscience to avoid having to perform an action – call it Y – and voicing one's judgment that Y is morally wrong. If there were no difference between the two, then making the appeal to conscience, after explaining that in one's opinion Y is wrong, would be redundant.[16] However, most of us would not agree that the appeal is redundant (that is, that making it is identical to issuing a moral judgment). And that must be because the appeal to conscience does more than express our judgment that Y is wrong. On the dominant view, it says that our integrity is at stake.

For these reasons, among others, the dominant view is dominant in bioethics.[17] The view is compelling because it makes sense of many of our intuitions about the nature and value of conscience. Nonetheless, I think it is deficient as a conception of conscience.

Before turning to its deficiencies, however, let me explain where, according to the dominant view, the value of conscience lies. Clearly, according to this view, conscience is valuable because it protects moral integrity. Yet why is this integrity important? Advocates of the dominant view give two basic answers. One is that unity or inner peace contributes to our having a good life.[18] The other is that unity and the desire to repair "inner division" are admirable characteristics of persons.[19] This last response comes from Jeffrey Blustein. For him – and for others presumably – it is tempting to say of people who are divided internally that they owe it to themselves to try to become unified.[20] They owe it to themselves not simply because division can be difficult but also because they would not be taking themselves seriously as moral agents if they thought little of acting against their moral principles or of having inconsistent principles. Thus, Blustein suggests that we have a moral duty "to ourselves to lead personally integrated lives."[21] He implies that in matters of inner unity, our self-respect is at stake. On the dominant view, inner unity is valuable for these reasons and having a conscience is valuable because it promotes inner unity.

Conscience and Inner Unity: How Strong Is the Connection?

With respect to inner (moral) unity, the dominant view says two things: (1) that acting with a conscience promotes such unity, and (2) that the value of conscience just is the value of such unity. I will examine both of these claims from a feminist relational perspective. Assuming that people can be more or less unified, my discussion will focus on what degree of moral unity a conscience is meant to foster on the dominant view: is it perfect unity, optimal unity, or merely "serviceable" unity?[22] Advocates of the dominant view do not say.[23] This matter is important, however, when analyzing how the dominant view connects conscience with inner unity. In this section, I argue that conscience often does not function to support inner unity or even serviceable unity, and therefore its function and its value must lie elsewhere. To support these claims, I bring in facts about moral agency that are missing from the dominant view, in particular, the following facts about the impact of oppressive social relations on moral agency: normally, these relations (1) influence what people value and therefore what would make them unified, and (2) shape how much power people have to determine the meaning of what they have done and whether what they have done contributes to their inner unity.[24] As I will demonstrate, a careful consideration of such facts would have forced advocates of the dominant view to think more carefully about the connection between conscience and inner unity.

Some clarity about the nature of inner unity is in order first. What does it mean to have inner unity and, more specifically, inner moral unity? According to Blustein, it means that our "actions and motivations [are in] harmony with our principles."[25] Presumably, our principles (moral attitudes and so on) would also have to be in harmony with one another, for otherwise we would be inconsistent or ambivalent, which are both marks of disunity. Unity is something we achieve through critical reflection or examination, for "[t]he words, deeds, and convictions of an *unexamined* life are unlikely to be sufficiently integrated to constitute a singular life."[26]

Since moral principles, attitudes, and actions can be more or less in harmony with one another, inner unity must come in degrees. I have said that the dominant view is unclear about what degree of inner unity a conscience is meant to foster. Could it be perfect unity?

Perfect Unity

Does our conscience aim to make us perfectly unified so that we experience no ambivalence or inconsistency? Is a good conscience completely clean and easy? Would promoting perfect unity even make our conscience valuable? For the sake of argument, I assume that the answer to these questions is "no," and, to be charitable, I assume that advocates of the dominant view would agree with me. Perfect unity is a fantasy for beings such as us, because not everything that we value or do is available to our consciousness so that we can unify it. Yet even if we were transparent to ourselves, our moral lives would be too complex to admit of a perfect unity. To have such unity – perfect moral unity – there would need to be a clear priority ranking to our moral values, so that if they ever conflicted with one another (for example, being honest conflicting with being compassionate), we would know exactly what to do. Most, if not all, of us lack such a straightforward moral system, however, and many of us, especially those of us who are oppressed, experience moral conflicts all of the time.[27] It follows that even if a state of perfect unity were possible for us, we would rarely be in it. Thus, it is reasonable to assume that the inner unity that conscience promotes is not perfect. Consistently acting with a conscience will not allow us to achieve perfect unity, which is not to say, of course, that it will not allow us to be more unified than we would otherwise be.

Optimal Unity
If by "inner moral unity" advocates of the dominant view do not mean perfect unity, then perhaps they mean optimal unity. Moral unity is optimal if it is as much unity as we can hope for given the complexity of our moral lives. The dominant view would be that conscience promotes optimal moral unity and that the value of conscience is the value of this unity, which itself contributes to a good life and a good character. Optimal inner unity can certainly be valuable. I accept from a feminist perspective that it is valuable, for example, when it allows women and others to resist oppression forcefully. Resisters need to be "as whole as it is possible to be" for their resistance to be as powerful as it can be.[28]

However, I question from a feminist relational perspective whether optimal inner unity is always valuable, and for reasons given below (under "serviceable unity") I question whether conscience always promotes optimal unity. Surely such unity does not always contribute to a good life and a good character. Consider a nurse – call her Betty – who suffers from psychological oppression.[29] Overall, she has low self-worth because she has internalized views about nurses being "intelligent machines" that exist "for the purpose of carrying out [doctor's] orders" and about women being second-class citizens.[30] Nurse Betty could be optimally unified around her low self-worth, in which case as many of her actions and thoughts as possible would be consistent with it. Her sense that she matters less than other people would infect as much of her as possible, precisely because she is optimally unified around this diminished perception of herself. I assume that such unity is not good for her – it does not contribute to her having a good life – and neither is it something that she morally ought to encourage. Instead, she would have a better life and a better character if she were to oppose any internal pressure she feels (that is, from her conscience) to be optimally unified in this way. It follows that optimal inner unity does not always promote a good life and a good character. It is not always valuable, which means that conscience would not always be valuable if it promoted such unity.

Someone might object that the dominant view is consistent with the intuition that not all forms of optimal unity are worth protecting. Presumably, according to this view, optimal inner unity, or inner unity in general, is not sufficient for a good life, which means that some unified lives may not be good.[31] In addition, while moral integrity is a virtue, it is not the only virtue. Advocates of the dominant view might say that it is a bad thing that the inner unity of the subjugated nurse comes at the expense of her self-respect, for example. If they would agree with these points (that is, that someone who is optimally unified could have a bad life and a bad character), then they must insist that optimal inner unity is valuable, other things being equal, rather than valuable absolutely. And they must believe the same thing about conscience, given that the inner unity it promotes may not be valuable.[32]

Thus, advocates of the dominant view can reduce the value of conscience to the value of optimal inner unity only by qualifying the former and saying that it exists not absolutely but only when other things are equal. They would have done so explicitly if they had reflected on how, in a society that oppresses people psychologically, some forms of optimal inner unity are not worth protecting. The kinds of social relations in which people are embedded help to shape how valuable their inner unity is. Inner unity and its value are relationally constituted.

The question remains about whether conscience actually does protect optimal inner unity. We have discussed only how valuable conscience would be if it did so. In the next section, I give reasons for thinking that it does not do so regularly for people who are privileged and for those who are oppressed although not psychologically. My main focus there is on whether the function and value of conscience might lie in it promoting a serviceable amount of unity.

Serviceable Unity
A serviceable moral unity is the minimal amount of unity that one needs to get on with life and be morally responsible. It is essential for moral agency – in particular, for our ability to make moral choices, which we lose if we become wracked with guilt or shame and, as a result, are unable to believe that we are truly committed to anything. I assume that feeling such extreme negative moral emotion is bad even if it reinforces one's oppression. For instance, subjugated Nurse Betty could transgress norms about nurses being strictly obedient, but feel so horrible about it, so lost – as though her life no longer had meaning – that the transgression is not worth it.[33] It would be wrong of us to cheer her on in "misbehaving," as she would put it. Cases

such as hers suggest that serviceable moral unity is valuable and that having a conscience is valuable if it protects this degree of unity.

The idea that conscience functions to preserve serviceable unity also coheres well with the dominant view, in particular, with its emphasis on the dramatic language that can accompany an appeal to conscience (for example, "I wouldn't be able to live with myself"). Such language is well suited to people who wish to protect their moral agency – that is, who wish to be unified to a serviceable degree. Thus, the dominant view could very well be that conscience has value because it promotes serviceable moral unity. The question is whether the dominant view would then be correct. Is it true that conscience functions to preserve the minimal amount of unity needed for moral agency? There are at least two reasons for believing that this claim is false.[34]

Consider first that for our conscience to play this role, our moral agency would actually have to be at stake when we do what our conscience says we ought not to do. In other words, it would have to be true that we would not be able to live with ourselves if we ignored our conscience and committed acts that we thought were morally wrong. Perhaps this claim would be true of some of us, depending on what the relevant acts were. For example, killing people or betraying those whom we love dearly would probably forever make some of us unbearable to ourselves.

The empirical evidence indicates, however, that many of us could live with ourselves quite easily after committing acts that we thought we would never commit. We are more resilient, in other words, than our dramatic claims ("I couldn't look at myself in the mirror") suggest. Putting the best spin on what we have done, or what we have learned because of what we have done, allows us to get along just fine.[35] Psychologist Daniel Gilbert argues that people are generally predisposed to find some goodness in what they have done when what they have done is bad, because they want to believe that their lives are going well.[36] However, to find goodness in what they have done, they may have to downplay what they have done – that is, deny responsibility for it by saying, for example, that they were only following orders. James Childress writes that someone who makes an appeal to conscience "claims that he will not be able to deny that the act is his if he performs it."[37] That may be what this person claims – however, he could very well do the opposite if the only route to mental well-being he has available after committing the act is to take no responsibility for it.

People are limited, of course, in how much they can put a positive spin on their actions ("when our team's defensive tackle is caught wearing brass knuckles ... we find it difficult to overlook or forget such facts").[38] How limited people are in this regard, moreover, can depend considerably on their social position. People who are privileged tend to have more power than others to make their behaviour seem benign or good. Paul Benson makes this point about men compared to women in sexist societies: "Men who reap advantages from [sexist social] arrangements are commonly in a position to justify their conduct by appealing to gendered social norms that grant men special prerogatives ('Lighten up! Surely there is nothing wrong in my just looking, teasing') or by professing their innocent motives ('I didn't mean any harm by it')."[39] By contrast, women often lack the power to say "lighten up" or to convince others, in certain contexts at least, that they "didn't mean any harm by [what they have done]." For example, people would tend not to believe this last statement when a woman utters it after having left her husband and children because she found it impossible to continue to play the traditional feminine roles of wife and mother. Such disbelief stems from the thought that, as a woman, she could not have failed to understand the harm that her departure would cause (whereas a man could do so). She must have willed it to happen or, in other words, must have meant some harm by what she did.

In short, people who are socially powerful can often convince others of their innocence, or deflect blame away from themselves and onto others, when they fail to do what their conscience dictates. With such authority, they can live with themselves quite easily if they ignore their conscience. Although they might say that they are loath to draw on this power, they might use it regardless because of a disposition they have to try to be happy (or simply to maintain their power). Hence, their serviceable inner unity is not obviously at stake when they decide whether to listen to their conscience, and their conscience therefore may not function to preserve their serviceable inner unity.

Perhaps repeated violations of conscience, however, would put the serviceable inner unity of people in power at risk.[40] This possibility is germane to discussions about conscience protection for health care professionals, who will probably receive repeated requests for any service to which they conscientiously object. Imagine a family physician who refers all patients who want abortions to abortion providers. His conscience opposes this action, but his profession requires it. He might be able to spin making a referral positively the first time that he does it, but will he be able to do so for each successive referral? Will the referrals not wear on him over time and leave him full of regret? I suspect that they could do so, although I also believe that the physician could receive enough social support in thinking that he is only following orders or is not really complicit in an immoral act that he could keep his conscience quiet. If no one else seriously questions how he defines his behaviour, then he could easily fail to do so himself.

Consider next that people who lack the power to cast themselves and their actions in a positive light may not be able to live with themselves even if they do listen to their conscience. They put their serviceable inner unity (or at least the degree of unity they currently possess) at risk when they heed their conscience. If this is true, then rather than protect their inner unity, their conscience disrupts it. Think of a woman who charges her male co-workers with sexual harassment in an intensely sexist work environment. She has to hope that someone in power will take her complaint seriously, but what if no one does. Then her male co-workers start harassing her even more, saying that she is just an angry b—. Her female co-workers are too afraid to back her up, thinking that if they do they will lose their jobs and the harassment they face will increase. The woman is left with few support-ers, with constant harassment, and with serious threats to her physical security. Imagine that she cannot quit her job because it is the only job she can get that allows her to care financially for her children.[41] Although she listened to her conscience, she may be less morally unified and may lose serviceable moral unity as a result. She may not be able to persist in believ-ing that, by her own lights, what she has done is morally right. For she may think, correctly perhaps, that all she has done is made herself into a pariah in her community, who has to fear for her own safety. Alternatively, others' negative stories about her behaviour may come to seem reasonable to her (she really is just an angry b—). It would be hard, if not impossible, for her to sustain her own story if everyone else's were different.[42] The final result could be that she becomes full of self-loathing and regret.[43]

This example reveals how much social support and the power to determine the meaning of what one has done (for example, been disloyal as opposed to courageous) can shape people's experience of conscientious refusal. The experience may be one of brokenness rather than unity, even serviceable unity. The dominant view does not obviously account for this fact, which simply cannot be accounted for without appreciating how much people are embedded in social relations that influence how successful their attempts at moral action can be.

Arguably, it is implicit, however, within the dominant view that without some social support for one's conscience, acting with a conscience can undermine one's inner unity. Advocates of this view argue in favour of social support for health care professionals' consciences so that these professionals will not have to choose between stiff inner (personal) sanctions if they act without their conscience and stiff outer (social) sanctions if they act with it. The hidden message here is that acting with a conscience can be devastat-ing if the outer sanctions are too great. Yet, among these sanctions, the authors consider only those that are imposed by legal systems or adminis-trative bodies, not those that exist because of oppressive social norms. By contrast, I hope to have made explicit what the social determinants are of surviving a conscientious action as a health care professional or simply as a person in an oppressive society.

At the same time, however, I believe I have cast doubt on the claim that what a conscience does primarily is promote serviceable unity or any other degree of unity for that matter. If it does not serve this function in a whole range of cases, then its function probably lies elsewhere. Unlike with perfect and optimal unity, I do not doubt that serviceable unity is always valuable. However, I have shown that for some people – particularly those with social power – acting against their conscience would not put their serviceable unity at serious risk, which means that doing the opposite – acting with a conscience – could not be required for inner unity. For other people – that is, those with little social power (or power within an organization) – acting with a conscience can undermine their serviceable unity or at least disrupt, rather than promote, their inner unity as a whole. Taking a feminist relational perspective on conscience has allowed us to see these facts and, in turn, to see that the dominant view is probably false.

An Alternate View

I want to be clear that I do not think the dominant understanding of conscience in bioethics is utterly and completely mistaken. People who act in accordance with their conscience and feel justified in doing so will be optimally unified at least at the time of acting. Having listened to their conscience, the majority of them may also be more unified long term than they would otherwise be. Some of those who face severe social sanctions because of their conscientious action could even be more unified because of this action than they would otherwise be. The objector who is sanctioned with inhumane treatment could still feel as though she did the right thing.

Yet having said that there is some truth to the dominant view, I nonetheless doubt that it is the correct view. I believe that conscience functions primarily not to preserve inner unity but, rather, to encourage people simply to act in accordance with their moral values. I also contend that the value of conscience goes beyond its function, rather than being identical to it, which is the case with the dominant view. Conscience is valuable potentially not only when it urges us to take our moral values seriously but also when it forces us to rethink those values, after perhaps clarifying for us what those values are. For example, if my conscience encouraged me to prepare dinner for my husband every night, simply because he is my husband, then I would have to consider seriously how much I have embraced certain feminist values. The function and value of conscience must come apart in this analysis, for it would be inconsistent to claim that conscience functions to get me to reconsider doing what it simultaneously encourages me to do. However, the value of conscience could lie in this after-effect of conscience (that is, in the urge to rethink what one values). These thoughts about the value of conscience are feminist and relational because they take as their starting point a relational subject living with a conscience in a society that oppresses her. I will use these thoughts to explain what is at stake when we deny the conscience of health care professionals.

Let me first elaborate on my view (the "alternate view") about conscience, starting with the function of conscience and then moving on to its value. My understanding of its function – that conscience encourages us to do what we think we morally ought to do – is relatively uncontroversial. It fits with ideas about conscience that appear in most, if not all, theories of conscience, including the dominant view – that conscience "influences (but rarely, if ever, completely controls) [one's] conduct" and that, at bottom, conscience is "a capacity ... to sense or immediately discern that what [one] has done, is doing, or is about to do (or not do) is wrong, bad, and worthy of disapproval."[44] This second idea tells us that the voice of conscience tends to be negative – normally it pipes up when we deserve blame, not praise. Thus, it encourages us to do what we think we morally ought to do by actively discouraging us from doing the opposite.

Elizabeth Kiss calls our conscience our "inner nag."[45] It nags us into doing what we think we ought to do but are somewhat averse to do. Although a conscience and a nag are not similar in all respects – a nag is often ineffective, while a conscience can be very effective (that is, in getting one to do what one thinks one morally ought to do)[46] – the two do have a lot in common. For example, a nag continually harasses us when we wish just to be left alone, and, similarly, our conscience pesters us when we try to ignore it and do what we please.[47] The voice comes unbidden, especially when we persist in doing or planning to do what we feel is morally wrong.[48] In this way, our conscience differs from our conscious moral judgment: we have more control over whether we make such judgments than we do over whether our conscience affects us. Like in the dominant view, in the alternate view, conscience and moral judgment are not identical. Unlike in the dominant view, however, in the alternate view, conscience and moral judgment can and should influence one another, as we will see.

To sum up, the function of conscience in the alternate view is to encourage us to take our moral values seriously. Consider that if conscience functions in this way, then many feminists will be skeptical of its value. The reason why is that for many people their "inner nag" is sexist, racist, or oppressive in other ways. As a result of being embedded in oppressive social relations, many of us are internally compelled to act in ways that are oppressive to others or to ourselves. We are motivated to exercise "agency" but not necessarily "autonomy," as Susan Sherwin would put it.[49] For example, many women feel internal pressure to participate in their own oppression by conforming to patriarchal norms of being a good woman or a good wife (one who makes her husband's dinner). Presumably, the capacity that women have to discern that they are not acting "properly" in these roles is conscience. Why, really, would feminists value such a capacity?[50]

I actually think there are two reasons why feminists should value conscience: (1) the voice of it will not always be simply a voice of internalized oppression, for sometimes it will reflect what the agent genuinely endorses or judges to be correct; and (2) even when conscience is a voice of oppression it can have a positive effect, as illustrated earlier with my example of making my husband's dinner.[51] Conscience can alert us to the fact that we have internalized oppressive values that may be unconsciously influencing our behaviour. In my example of being a wife/cook, my conscience works on me through the threat of false guilt or false shame – that is, guilt or shame that does not reflect what I have endorsed or would endorse.[52] The relevant values are in this sense alien to me, although they are not entirely alien to me for they find some expression in me. My conscience allows me to see just how much these values are a part of me, and it causes me to reflect on how I have been relating to my spouse because of them. Say that I have been making his dinner repeatedly but then want a break from it. Taking a break is not as easy as I thought it would be, however, because my conscience starts to nag me about preparing dinner. I say to myself: "But why should I feel guilty about not making dinner? Do I really believe that I ought to be making his dinner, because I'm his wife? Maybe deep down, I do accept that (which is troubling to say the least)? I should reject these attitudes and resist getting into patterns of 'wifely' behaviour, rather than allow them to develop." Notice the positive role that conscience plays in this story. By making me aware of values that influence my behaviour, negatively in my opinion, it helps me to take responsibility for myself and for how I am structuring my intimate relationships with others.[53] Thus, conscience can help us, especially those of us who are psychologically oppressed, to retool ourselves morally and to develop more authentic moral selves, ones informed by our own moral judgments.[54]

Presumably, retooling myself morally will involve retooling my conscience so that I acquire a conscience that threatens me with genuine guilt or shame rather than with the false variety and with guilt or shame that does not reinforce my oppression. We retool our conscience when judgments about what we morally ought to value sink in, changing what we do value, which in turn changes what our conscience warns us about. Here, our moral judgment influences our conscience, but our conscience also influences our moral judgment because it gets the retooling process going.

While the alternate view of conscience emphasizes the importance of people reflecting on the judgments that inform their conscience, the dominant view says relatively little in this regard. Granted, the dominant view is not as extreme as some religious views that instruct us to tune in to our conscience and put our lives in conformity with it, without questioning what it says.[55] Advocates of the dominant view do accept that at times we might, or indeed should, scrutinize the demands of our conscience.[56] However, they do not associate the value of conscience with its ability to inspire attempts at taking responsibility for what we value.

The process of retooling our conscience to make it more authentic has important relational elements to it. We need social relations that give us a vision of the world that is a positive alternative to whatever vision we have internalized – that can create or confirm a suspicion in us that what we have learned is false.[57] For example, I learned that as a woman I ought to nurture men and children in the ways of a fairly traditional wife and mother. While I rebelled to some extent, I did not feel confident in my rebellion until I went to university and started taking courses in feminist philosophy. While this experience did not rid me of oppressive influences – when I met my spouse, I still wanted to nurture him as my mother did my father – it marked the beginning of my "moral makeover," so to speak. The makeover continues with help from my spouse, who, like me, resists the "gendering of our relationship" (his phrase). If he did not take seriously my concerns about occasionally being a dupe to sexist influences from my upbringing, then I would probably not take these concerns as seriously as I do (especially while I am in a relationship with him). I would be less inclined to see the threat of false guilt from my conscience for what it is – a throwback to my childhood – and might think instead that the guilt is genuine because it reflects a personal belief that I ought to make dinner, because I like cooking more than my spouse does (which, if true, would probably be a throwback to the sexist upbringing that we both received). According to relational theory, our relations with others – especially intimate others – help to shape not only who we are but also who we are trying to become. We cannot retool ourselves, or aspects of ourselves such as our conscience, all by ourselves.

To recapitulate, according to the alternate view, the value of conscience lies in its ability to encourage us not simply to do what we think we morally ought to do but also to revise these thoughts when necessary and to reconstitute itself in the process so that it becomes the voice of what we genuinely (that is, authentically) value. This view about conscience is feminist and relational because it rests on a theory of selves as beings who are fully embedded within relationships, some of which are oppressive.

The question remains about why conscience has value insofar as it prompts us to do what we genuinely (but perhaps falsely) believe to be morally right? My answer is reminiscent of the dominant view: a conscience of this sort promotes our moral integrity, although integrity here is understood not as inner unity but, rather, as abiding by one's best judgment (in this case, moral judgment). Elsewhere, I have defended such a view of integrity, according to which integrity differs importantly from inner unity.[58] Honouring our best judgment will not necessarily promote our inner unity, for our best judgment about our situation may be that different values are at stake in it and that they cannot be reconciled with one another. In addition, the process of coming to decide what our best judgment is may cause us to question a lot of what we have previously taken for granted, which will destabilize us at least initially more than it will unify us. Taking responsibility for our moral selves, which is what moral integrity requires, is not identical to preserving our inner moral unity.[59]

Moral integrity – adhering to our best moral judgment – requires social support, but it is also good for society. Its value is social rather than merely personal. While there is arguably personal value in living an authentic moral life, there is social value in people taking their own best moral judgment seriously. Society needs this commitment from people so that genuine debates about moral right and wrong occur, which have value because they help to improve our moral understanding.[60] These ideas suggest that gaining moral knowledge is a social process,[61] and integrity has social value – it involves being in the "proper relation" to others[62] – because it contributes to this process. In my view about conscience, conscience has social value when it encourages people to act with integrity, which it does when it makes them feel genuine guilt or shame – that is, guilt or shame upon failing to respect their best moral judgment.

In accepting the alternate view, we recognize that not everyone's conscience has the same moral value. People who tune into their conscience and abide by it, even when its message is inconsistent with what they endorse or would endorse (for example, if they were free of psychological oppression), have a conscience with little value to it.[63] People who do not defer to the conscience that they simply find themselves with and who try to revise their moral commitments, but who do it poorly – without having good or even decent reasons for making the changes they make – will also have a conscience with little value to it. Among the latter, I count people who retool themselves so that their moral values become more oppressive than they were before (which is possible given the relational character of conscience and the noxious social environments that people can become immersed in later in life). I assume that when asked to give some rational explanation for these changes, these people will "invariably come up short."[64] I would not want to say that their conscience is worthless, for simply having a conscience suggests that they care about doing what is morally right, as they perceive it, which is better than not caring at all (and being a psychopath). Still, their conscience is worth less than it would be if they had values that they could support. The moral judgments that influence their conscience would add little to social debate about the nature of right and wrong.

While more needs to be said about, and in favour of, the alternate view, hopefully it is clear that this view is preferable to the dominant view. It makes sense of intuitions about conscience that I assume many of us share but that the dominant view cannot explain – the fact that the conscience of the subjugated nurse from the first part of this chapter has little value (for the values that inform her conscience are oppressive to her), that the conscience of someone who is completely unreflective morally – who does not do the work that autonomous judgment demands[65] – has little value, that acting with a conscience can have value even when it does not unify us (for the value might be purely social, which could be the case with the woman who resists workplace harassment),[66] and so on. The conception of conscience that informs the discussion about conscience in bioethics should cohere with these intuitions.

The alternate view may be preferable in many respects to the dominant view, but does it provide us with a reasonable answer to the question that began this chapter: why do or ought we to care whether health care professionals have a conscience? The answer it gives us is this: minimally, we value health care professionals having a conscience because we want them to care about morality. We fear a health care professional who lacks a conscience because we believe not that he has no drive toward inner unity (which he may well have) but, rather, that he cares not a whit about being morally responsible. Some health care professionals will care more about being morally responsible than others and will work to retool their conscience when it does not reflect the best moral judgments that they can make. The dynamic conscience of such a professional is worth more than the conscience of a professional who does little work on her conscience, which will then be a stagnant reminder of whatever values she has internalized. This mental work, or lack thereof, should be evident, moreover, from the professional's responses to questions about why he has the conscience that he does or why he needs to refuse conscientiously to provide a certain service. A professional whose conscience is informed by his autonomous judgment should be able to give a decent answer to this question (that is, an answer other than "I simply believe that this is the case").[67]

The alternate view also suggests that it is important for health care professionals to have a conscience that is authentic and promotes their integrity (as I have understood integrity) so that their moral views can influence ethical debates about health care. Their conscience should prompt them to participate when the debates go in directions that they find morally problematic. Moreover, they should have contributions to make that are at least somewhat worthwhile, insofar as their conscience is authentic. This last point speaks in favour of health care professionals receiving some conscience protection, particularly in the context of professional meetings where policy decisions get made. Members who want to express their conscientious opposition to the status quo at these meetings should have every opportunity to do so and should not suffer harm from doing so.

There are lessons to be drawn from this chapter about how, not why, to value conscience in health care. For example, genuine protection for conscience in health care will require that the culture of health care institutions not be hostile toward individual conscience, especially the conscience of health care professionals who have minority views, who are members of marginalized social groups, or who are powerless relative to doctors or administrators. Surely, if there is to be conscience protection in the health care professions, then it ought to exist for all health care professionals.[68]

To conclude, I have argued that conscience has value in health care and that its value ought to be understood using the alternate view, rather than the dominant view. The former insists that the value of conscience comes in degrees and is to some extent determined by the social relations in which the health care professional is embedded. These relations will affect not only whether the professional's conscience garners respect but also what the content of her conscience is and how motivated she is to retool her conscience so that the guilt or shame with which it threatens her is genuine. Most feminists would agree that conscience has little value when it is simply the voice of internalized moral values that are inauthentic. However, conscience need not be this voice. Instead, it could be the voice that gives the agent integrity (again, as I have understood integrity).

This chapter began with reflections on conscientious refusals in health care and, in the end, demonstrated that a moral analysis of these refusals ought to include an exploration into why and when acting with a conscience is valuable. Conscientious refusals in health care are ethically complex. The value of conscience is but one of a number of ethical issues that these actions force us to confront. Starting with this concern about value is appropriate, however, because our conclusions about it could allow us to say that some consciences are not really worth protecting, which would save us the fuss of deciding how to protect them.

Notes

This chapter benefited a lot from a discussion with members of the Relational Theory and Health Law and Policy group. Thanks to Jocelyn Downie and Jennifer Llewellyn for assembling this wonderful team together. I presented versions of this chapter not only to their group but also to audiences at various conferences and lectures. Audience members at the talk I gave for the Program on Values and Society at the University of Washington were particularly helpful. Thanks to the organizer of that event, Sara Goering. Thanks also to Jeremy Bendik-Keymer for sharing his wisdom early on in the writing process. His help was invaluable to me.

1 For example, Jocelyn Downie claims, rightly I think, that the private member's bill in Canada (Bill C-357, *An Act to Amend the Criminal Code (Protection of Conscience Rights in the Health Care Profession)*, 2nd Sess., 39th Parl., 2008 (first reading in the House of Commons, 16 April 2008)) overvalues conscience for people who are anti-abortion. See Jocelyn Downie, "Resistance Is Essential: Relational Responses to Recent Law and Policy Intiatives Involving Reproduction" in this volume.

2 Patients who face conscientious refusals might disagree, however. They might wish that their health care professionals were motivated less by conscience than they actually are or had different consciences altogether. However, these cases do not belie the fact that patients want health care professionals with a conscience – to some degree or of some sort or other – because the alternative is truly frightening.

3 See Carolyn McLeod, "Harm or Mere Inconvenience? Denying Women Emergency Contraception" (2010) 25:1 Hypatia 11. These refusals are not necessarily harmful to patients. Consider a reproductive endocrinologist from my community who refused to consent to an oocyte-vending program at his clinic, threatening to quit if the program got started. Arguably, on balance, his refusal benefited women in our community. See Françoise Baylis and Carolyn McLeod, "The Stem Cell Debate Continues: The Buying and Selling of Eggs for Research" (2007) 33:12 J. Med. Ethics 726, about possible harms to women from oocyte vending.

4 The advocates include Martin Benjamin, Jeffrey Blustein, James Childress, and Mark Wicclair. See Martin Benjamin, "Conscience" in Warren T. Reich, ed., *Encyclopedia of Bioethics*, volume 1, 2nd edition (New York: Macmillan, 1995) at 469; Jeffrey Blustein, "Doing What the Patient Orders: Maintaining Integrity in the Doctor-Patient Relationship" (1993) 7 Bioethics 289; James Childress, "Appeals to Conscience" (1979) 89 Ethics 315; James Childress, "Conscience and Conscientious Actions in the Context of MCOs" (1997) 7 Kennedy Institute of Ethics Journal 403; Mark Wicclair, "Pharmacies, Pharmacists, and Conscientious Objection" (2006) 16:3 Kennedy Institute of Ethics Journal 225; Mark Wicclair, "Conscientious Objection in Medicine" (2000) 14 Bioethics 205.

5 See Catriona Mackenzie and Natalie Stoljar, "Introduction: Autonomy Refigured" in Catriona Mackenzie and Natalie Stoljar, eds., *Relational Autonomy: Feminist Perspectives on Autonomy, Agency, and the Social Self* (New York: Oxford University Press, 2000).

6 See Carolyn McLeod, "Referral in the Wake of Conscientious Objection to Abortion" (2008) 23:4 Hypatia 30.

7 Among the bioethicists are Robert F. Card, "Conscientious Objection and Emergency Contraception" (2007) 7:6 Am. J. Bioethics 8; Wicclair, *supra* note 4; Elizabeth Fenton and Loren Lomasky, "Dispensing with Liberty: Conscientious Refusal and the 'Morning-After Pill'" (2005) 30 J. Med. & Phil. 579; Julie Cantor and Ken Baum, "The Limits of Conscientious Objection: May Pharmacists Refuse to Fill Prescriptions for Emergency Contraception?" (2004) 351:19 New Eng. J. Med. 2008.

8 See Jeremy Laurance, "Abortion Crisis as Doctors Refuse to Perform Surgery," *The Independent* (16 April 2007); Louis-Jacques van Bogaert, "The Limits of Conscientious Objection to Abortion in the Developing World" (2002) 2:2 Developing World of Bioethics 131; Leslie Cannold, "Consequence for Patients of Health Care Professionals' Conscientious Actions: The Ban on Abortions in South Australia" (1994) 20 J. Med. Ethics 80; Jocelyn Downie and Carla Nassar, "Barriers to Access to Abortion though a Legal Lens" (2008) 15 Health L.J. 143.

9 Many feminists have challenged this way of understanding integrity. See, for example, Victoria Davion, "Integrity and Radical Change" in Claudia Card, ed., *Feminist Ethics* (Lawrence, KA: University of Kansas Press, 1991); Margaret Urban Walker, *Moral Understandings: A Feminist Study in Ethics* (New York: Routledge, 1998); Cheshire Calhoun, "Standing for Something" (1995) 92 J. Phil. 235. I do not do so here in any detail since my purpose is to understand conscience not integrity. However, see Carolyn McLeod, "Integrity and Self-Protection" (2004) 35:2 J. Soc. Phil. 216; Carolyn McLeod, "How to Distinguish Autonomy from Integrity" (2005) 35:1 Can. J. Phil. 107.

10 A conscience can operate prospectively – warning us of inner disunity if we behave badly – or retrospectively – highlighting the inner disunity we suffer after having behaved badly.

11 The dominant view says, of course, that we must heed our conscience if we are to have inner unity – that the conscience that promotes inner unity is a good conscience. However, the view also implies that most of us will heed our conscience most of the time because it will threaten us with disunity so severe that we will be unable to get on with our lives. For this reason and for brevity's sake, I sometimes refer to what promotes inner unity on the dominant view as simply "conscience" or "having a conscience."

12 The same is true for a person with relational autonomy. See Susan Sherwin, "Relational Autonomy and Global Threats" in this volume, although she suspects or hopes that among this person's deep subjective commitments will be a commitment to help eliminate global threats, such as climate change.

13 See Calhoun, *supra* note 9 at 252.

14 Other reasons concern how well the dominant view coheres with three aspects of conscience. First, a good conscience is "quiet," "clean," and "easy," while a bad one is "troubled" or "uneasy." Childress, "Appeals to Conscience," *supra* note 4 at 318; James Childress, "Exploring Claims to Conscience" (presentation delivered at the Should Conscience Be Your Guide? Exploring Conscience-based Refusals in Health Care Conference, 20 June 2006) [unpublished]. When we have a good conscience, we are at peace; we are right with ourselves. In other words, we feel whole. Second, conscience imposes sanctions on our own behaviour and not on the behaviour of others. It makes no sense to claim: "My conscience says ... *you* ought to do this or ought not to have done that." Gilbert Ryle, "Conscience and Moral Convictions" (1940) 7 Analysis 31 at 31, cited in Benjamin, *supra* note 4 at 470. The focus on what "I" do, or do not do, suggests a concern for me – for my self, and perhaps for my integrity – rather than simply a concern for what is morally right. Last, the voice of conscience is often negative. It usually tells us what we ought not to do as opposed to what we ought to do. This description fits with the dominant view that the voice of conscience threatens us (that is, with disunity).

15 See Childress, "Appeals to Conscience," *supra* note 4 at 404; Benjamin, *supra* note 4 at 470.

16 Blustein, *supra* note 4 at 294.

17 And for similar reasons, it has been dominant in modern thinking about conscience. See Jeremy Bendik-Keymer, *Conscience and Humanity* (Ph.D. dissertation, Department of Philosophy, University of Chicago, 2002) [unpublished].

18 See Blustein, *supra* note 4; Benjamin, *supra* note 4 at 470.

19 Blustein, *supra* note 4 at 297.

20 *Ibid.*

21 *Ibid.*

22 The idea of a serviceable amount of unity comes from Margaret Walker. While discussing integrity, she writes that "more coherence, consistency, or continuity is not necessarily better ... We need only so much as will serve." Walker, *supra* note 9 at 115.

23 Among advocates of the dominant view, Martin Benjamin is the only one who qualifies a statement about how much inner unity a conscience promotes. He says that having a conscience allows us to be "*reasonably* unified or integrated." Benjamin, *supra* note 4 at 470 [emphasis added]. However, he does not explain what he means by "reasonable." Is perfect unity reasonable? Is reasonable here a synonym for optimal?

24 They are missing, in fact, from most accounts of moral agency in moral philosophy or in philosophical moral psychology. See Sandra Lee Bartky, "On Psychological Oppression" in Sandra Lee Bartky, *Femininity and Domination: Studies in the Phenomenology of Oppression* (New York: Routledge, 1990) 22 at 95-96.

25 Blustein, *supra* note 4; see also Benjamin, *supra* note 4 at 470.

26 Benjamin, *supra* note 4 [emphasis added].

27 See Marilyn Frye, *The Politics of Reality: Essays in Feminist Theory* (Freedom, CA: Crossing Press, 1983).

28 Aurora Levins Morales, *Medicine Stories: History, Culture and the Politics of Integrity* (Cambridge, MA: South End Press, 1998) at 20.

29 See Bartky, *supra* note 24.

30 Martin Benjamin and Joy Curtis, *Ethics in Nursing*, 3rd edition (New York: Oxford University Press, 1992) at 22.

31 For example, we would hardly say of someone who is optimally unified around an abusive and racist character that his life was good, morally or otherwise. Thanks to an anonymous reviewer for alerting me to this objection.

32 I am not sure that advocates of the dominant view could stomach this conclusion, which implies that having a conscience could be worthless. Like many of us, they would probably say that the statement, "she has a conscience," *does* rather than *could* connote moral praise. They would probably also accept that someone without a conscience is frightening, which implies that having a conscience is always worth something.

33 This scenario is consistent with the feminist claim that some women need to undergo radical change in order to free themselves of psychological oppression. See Davion, *supra*

note 9. The scenario simply suggests that the change cannot happen so quickly or in such a way that it undermines women's agency.

34 And here is a third reason: our conscience can cajole us to honour commitments that are simply not deep enough to shake us to our moral core. I disagree with the dominant view that our conscience encourages us to adhere only to moral commitments that are deep (that is, identity conferring). To illustrate, my conscience could warn me that I will feel guilty if I tell a white lie, even though the relevant moral commitment ("Don't tell white lies") does not inform my moral identity.

35 See Daniel Gilbert, *Stumbling on Happiness* (New York: Knopf, 2006) at c. 8.

36 No one (that is, who is psychologically healthy) wants their life to go badly or to believe that is the case, which is at least partly why people tend to adapt quickly to negative changes in their environment (*ibid.* at 162).

37 Childress, "Appeals to Conscience," *supra* note 4 at 324.

38 Gilbert, *supra* note 35 at 168.

39 Paul Benson, "Feeling Crazy: Self-Worth and the Social Character of Responsibility" in Catriona Mackenzie and Natalie Stoljar, eds., *Relational Autonomy: Feminist Perspectives on Autonomy, Agency, and the Social Self* (Oxford: Oxford University Press, 2000) 72 at 72.

40 Thanks to Sara Goering for raising this important objection.

41 This is what happened to Lois Jensen, who launched the first sexual harassment case in the United States (*Jensen v. Eveleth Taconite Co.*, 139 F.R.D. 657 (D. Minn. 1991)). The film *North Country* (Beverly Hills, CA: Warner Home Video, 2006) is based on her story. Jensen won her case and so was redeemed in the end. Nonetheless, there must be cases such as hers of sexual harassment that do not turn out so well and in which women's lives are ruined because of how others reacted to their complaints.

42 See Françoise Baylis, "The Self *in Situ*: A Relational Account of Personal Identity" in this volume.

43 This theme of people who listen to their conscience but then seriously regret it is common among whistleblowers. C. Fred Alford explains that many whistleblowers wish they had never taken the stand they did because it cost them too much and had no effect on the organization they worked for. C. Fred Alford, *Whistleblowers: Broken Lives and Organizational Power* (Ithaca, NY: Cornell University Press, 2001) at 34. Many of his examples involve people who were not marginalized until they became whistleblowers. For a recent discussion of "[w]hat happens when whistleblowers are also members of an oppressed group," see Peggy DesAutels, "Resisting Organizational Power" in Lisa Tessman, ed., *Feminist Ethics and Social and Political Philosophy: Theorizing the Non-Ideal* (Dordrecht: Springer, 2009) 224.

44 Thomas E. Hill, Jr., "Four Conceptions of Conscience" in Ian Shapiro and Robert Adams, eds., *Integrity and Conscience*, volume 40 (New York: New York University Press, 1998) 13 at 14.

45 Elizabeth Kiss, "Conscience and Moral Psychology: Reflections on Thomas Hill's 'Four Conceptions of Conscience'" in Shapiro and Adams, *supra* note 44, 69.

46 This point comes from Jennifer Nedelsky (group discussion).

47 Unlike in the dominant view, conscience in the alternate view rarely threatens us with complete psychic dissolution. A nag is not so menacing. Our conscience lacks this quality in general because often it encourages us to adhere to moral commitments that are not deep. See note 34 in this chapter.

48 Hill, *supra* note 44.

49 See Sherwin, *supra* note 12.

50 Like the dominant view, the alternate view assumes that the norms that guide our conscience can be unjust. Our conscience is not the voice of moral truth, as it is according to a popular religious conception of conscience. For we have no good reason to believe that all of us have a capacity within us to discern that what we have done, or are about to do, is *in fact* morally wrong.

51 With respect to judgment, which is mentioned in the first point, see Jennifer Nedelsky, "The Reciprocal Relation of Judgment and Autonomy: Walking in Another's Shoes and Which Shoes to Walk In" in this volume.

52 See Gabrielle Taylor, *Pride, Shame, and Guilt: Emotions of Self-Assessment* (New York: Oxford University Press, 1987).

53 See Claudia Card, *The Unnatural Lottery: Character and Moral Luck* (Philadelphia: Temple University Press, 1996).

54 The phrase "retool ourselves morally" comes from Sheila Wildeman (group discussion).

55 This point comes from Jennifer Nedelsky (group discussion).

56 Childress says that we need to do so when we experience a "crisis of conscience" – that is, when our conscience gives us multiple demands that conflict. Childress, "Appeals to Conscience," *supra* note 4 at 320. Blustein says that we could, although need not necessarily, do so after having violated a conscience that gave us one clear demand. We might reconsider the adequacy of the demand in light of what motivated us to ignore it ("sympathies, longings, fears, anxieties, etc." (at 296)).

57 In other words, we need to become immersed in a new and supportive "judging community." See Nedelsky, *supra* note 51.

58 See McLeod, "Integrity and Self-Protection," *supra* note 9; McLeod, "How to Distinguish," *supra* note 9.

59 Recall that Blustein argues that inner unity is valuable because it reveals a desire on the part of moral agents to take themselves seriously as moral agents. One lacks this desire if one thinks little of acting against one's moral principles or of having inconsistent principles. However, I question whether having inner unity is the same as having the earlier desire. One could achieve inner unity (of an optimal sort) by adhering to whatever moral commitments one happens to hold so long as they are consistent. But someone who takes himself seriously as a moral agent would be critical of moral commitments he just happens to hold.

60 See McLeod, "How to Distinguish," *supra* note 9 at 126; see also Calhoun, *supra* note 9; John Stuart Mill, *'On Liberty' and Other Writings,* edited by Stefan Collini (Cambridge: Cambridge University Press, 1989).

61 See Calhoun, *supra* note 9; Walker, *supra* note 9.

62 Calhoun, *supra* note 9 at 252.

63 Some people who behave this way will be like Harry Frankfurt's "wanton" in not caring what desires or values move them to act. Harry Frankfurt, "Freedom of the Will and the Concept of a Person" in Harry Frankfurt, *The Importance of What We Care About* (Cambridge: Cambridge University Press, 1988) 11.

64 McLeod, "Integrity and Self-Protection," *supra* note 9 at 228; see also Adrian Piper, "Higher-Order Discrimination" in Owen Flanagan and Amélie Oksenberg Rorty, eds., *Identity, Character, and Morality: Essays in Moral Psychology* (Cambridge, MA: MIT Press, 1990) 285; Kwame Anthony Appiah, "Racisms" in D.T. Goldberg, ed., *Anatomy of Racism* (Minneapolis: University of Minnesota Press, 1990) 3.

65 See Nedelsky, *supra* note 51.

66 It might not be the case for her, however. As Nedelsky pointed out to me, this woman might come to value what she did after becoming immersed in a relational context that acknowledges sexual harassment to be a crime.

67 This point speaks in favour of having conscientious objectors in health care explain their objections to their employers or professional organizations rather than allowing them to object without explanation. Some conscience clauses in the United States include such a condition (see Brian A. Dykes, "Proposed Rights of Conscience Legislation: Expanding to Include Pharmacists and Other Health Care Providers" (2001-2) 36 Ga. L. Rev. 565), which is something that Jocelyn Downie, *supra* note 1, would applaud. A conscience clause is a statute or regulation that protects the ability of health care professionals to decline to participate in health services that violate their conscience. See Lynn D. Wardle, "Protecting the Rights of Conscience of Health Care Providers" (1993) 14:2 J. Legal Med. 177 at 178. Downie recommends that Canadian health care professionals who make appeals to conscience be required to show that they are genuine, which I think involves them saying why they hold the relevant values (and, to be clear, does not involve them proving that these values are correct).

68 Of course, there ought to be protection for patient conscience as well, which not all creators of conscience clauses recognize. See Downie, *supra* note 1.

Part 2
Health Law and Policy

8
Relational Theory and Resource Allocation in Health Care: Accounting for Difference
Dianne Pothier

What is the measure of the adequacy of a health care system in terms of what is publicly funded? The premise of this chapter is that it is inadequate to approach this question by referring to some version of a generic patient or by identifying what are considered to be the typical needs of those accessing the health care system. Instead, I take the view that the starting point should be a widely diverse population seeking to access health care. Relational theory helps in so situating this analysis. I am not an expert in either health care or health care funding. I will not attempt to unravel the intricacies and complexities of resource allocation decision making in health care that even those who are experts describe as non-transparent.[1] Instead, I want to explore some conceptual underpinnings that relational theory helps to uncover. I want to use relational theory to help in conceptualizing how the collective responds to claims invoking health care needs.[2] More specifically, I want to use relational theory to assess how the collective responds to atypical claims.

Canada has had a national system of publicly funded health care for over four decades. This system represents a political decision to assume collective responsibility in delivering health care. However, that does not mean unlimited resources to do so. The state must make choices about what is and is not funded. The purpose of this chapter is to offer some reflections on the basis on which these choices are made.

Medicare pre-dates the *Canadian Charter of Rights and Freedoms* and was not implemented as a matter of constitutional imperative.[3] Nor does the advent of the *Charter* now make state-funded health care constitutionally required.[4] However, given that the state has chosen to provide medicare, there are some constitutional dictates about how it is implemented in order to conform to the *Charter*.[5] Most notably, the Supreme Court of Canada's decision in *Eldridge v. British Columbia*[6] determined that the absence of state-funded sign language interpretation for deaf patients obtaining hospital or physician services was a denial of substantive equality pursuant to section 15(1) of the *Charter,* which could not be saved by section 1.[7] Where sign language interpretation is required for effective communication with health care providers, a lack of state funding amounts to discrimination on the basis of disability since hearing patients can engage in effective communication with state-funded health care providers without further state assistance. *Eldridge* thus has an impact on resource allocation with respect to access to health care in an overall sense, but it did not engage the question of what specific health conditions are covered by medicare.

For my purposes, given the political decision to adopt state-funded health care, particular heath care services[8] potentially fall into three categories relative to funding: (1) services for which there is an overarching legal requirement to fund (resting on constitutionally based discrimination claims under section 15 of the *Charter* or statutory claims based on human rights legislation); (2) services for which there is currently statutory/regulatory requirement to fund, but which can be unfunded based on political considerations; and (3) services that are currently unfunded, with only political arguments available to challenge the lack of funding. Apart from state funding, medical services range from those for which there are constitutional constraints on limiting access (for example, abortion),[9] those considered to be appropriate for therapeutic reasons (for example, appendectomies), those considered acceptable for non-therapeutic reasons (for example, cosmetic surgery), and those that are considered unethical for a heath care provider to deliver (for example, amputation of healthy limbs).[10] My focus in this chapter is on resource allocation in terms of what specific services are funded by medicare. However, I will be very selective in my analysis, choosing illustrative examples. By selecting atypical claims, I am endeavouring to highlight the diversity of health claims that are sought to be funded.

The federal *Canada Health Act* sets out five criteria underpinning federal cost-sharing of provincial/territorial health care schemes: (1) public administration; (2) comprehensiveness; (3) universality; (4) portability; and (5) accessibility.[11] The criteria of universality and comprehensiveness determine what health care services are publicly funded.[12] Universality within the meaning of the *Canada Health Act* is limited to formal equality – that the same services are available to all. If the only thing that medicare covered was tonsillectomies, the principle of universality would be satisfied as long as everyone was covered for tonsillectomies. Universality alone does not generate a broad coverage of health services. The breadth of coverage is ultimately determined by the principle of comprehensiveness. It is only in unpacking the principle of comprehensiveness that we can assess the heath care system's capacity and willingness to respond to differential need.

In the discussion that follows, I will focus on two examples of differential need – claims related to gender identity and to disability (and will explain why I do not consider the former to be subsumed within the latter). With respect to the example of gender identity, the analysis involves the state's determination of medical necessity. In regard to the example of disability, the discussion examines how demonstrated medical need may be insufficient to require state funding. I have chosen the contexts of gender identity and disability because they involve health issues that most (potential) patients will never face. I want to inquire into how the collective responds to claims that are not personally relevant to most of its members.

How is differential need connected to relational theory? Differential need is reflective of different types of individuals having differing kinds of interdependence with those around them. Both differential need and relational theory are premised on the determination of needs, not in the abstract but, rather, in the context of social relations. As Jennifer Llewellyn explains,

> [i]n place of the liberal individualist vision of the self, relational theorists offer a relational account of the self that takes connection over separation as essential to the constitution and maintenance of the self. Connection and relationship with others is seen as essential to understanding the self and to its making and remaking. Relational theory thus suggests a different starting point from which to understand the world. It compels us to take the fact of relationship, of connectedness, as our starting assumption. As such, relationality must inform the ideas, principles and conceptions that shape our interactions and social life. [note omitted][13]

The flip side of this insight is that assumptions of collective responsibility need to take into account different kinds of relationships with and within the collective.

In a biomedical model, which by definition is focused on the individual, one can expect that patients are viewed as atomistic beings needing to be fixed.[14] A relational theory perspective, in contrast, would ask the medical necessity/requirement question in the context of how patients function in the world around them. In many contexts, the answer would still be the same and for not dissimilar reasons. If someone breaks a leg, the biomedical model says the medically necessary intervention is to fix the broken leg. A relational model concerned with the person's ability to get around will also say that the medically necessary intervention is to fix the broken leg. However, where the medical issue is less typical, the model employed may significantly affect the analysis.

A relational model goes beyond social determinants of health. By itself, a social determinants model would see the individual as a passive recipient. A relational model, in contrast, in emphasizing connections, sees the self as an active participant in relations with others. In a biomedical model, the patient's consent is required for medical interventions, but the patient is generally viewed as being a recipient of medical care premised on what is assumed to be an "objective" assessment. In contrast, a relational theory approach views the patient in a dynamic interaction, not only with health care providers but also with society at large. As will be discussed in this chapter, "objective" assessments are open to question when acknowledging the importance of perspective. Relational identity, autonomy, and judgment are important conceptual underpinnings in evaluating medical questions.

Medically Necessary/Medically Required under the *Canada Health Act*

The structure of the *Canada Health Act*, and of the provincial and territorial health care systems following its dictates, creates a sharp divide between hospital/physician services (characterized as core services) and other services. The principle of comprehensiveness demands funding of "medically necessary" hospital services and of "medically required" physician services.[15] In contrast, the inclusion of services provided by others is discretionary on the part of each province/territory – need is not the ultimate determinant. I will return later in the chapter to the significance of this divide between hospitals/ physicians and other health care providers. First, I will explore the meaning of comprehensiveness in the context of hospital and physician services where need is the key determinant. There is no statutory definition of "medically necessary" or "medically required." In practice, such determinations historically have mostly been left to doctors.[16] However, in the current era in which there are serious constraints on the public purse, politicians are increasingly getting involved in decisions about medical necessity.

Gender Reassignment Surgery as a Litmus Test

In Alberta's April 2009 budget, the Stelmach government announced the de-listing of gender reassignment surgery as a medicare-covered service.[17] For many years, Alberta had been covering gender reassignment surgery itself but not the hormonal drug treatment preliminary to the surgery. This split maps onto the distinction between prescription drugs, which is a discretionary service outside of hospital/physician services, and the surgical component, which is dependent on a determination of medical necessity since it is hospital/physician delivered. The budget was thus adopting a revised assessment of medical necessity as applied to gender reassignment surgery, placing gender reassignment on a par with cosmetic surgery.[18] Neither procedure is publicly funded, based on the theory that they are not medically necessary – they simply reflect personal choice. It is telling that the decision to de-list gender reassignment surgery was announced in the budget, whereas other de-listing decisions awaited input from a panel of medical experts.[19] The de-listing of gender reassignment surgery thus appears to involve political considerations more than medical ones. Alberta's budget prompted complaints to the Alberta Human Rights Commission.[20]

In the press coverage of this budget announcement, Premier Ed Stelmach looked very uncomfortable. I would assume his discomfort was not a matter of ambivalence about the decision to de-list. Rather, given the political context of social conservatism in Alberta, I would surmise that he felt unease at having to publicly acknowledge the existence of transgendered persons. The CBC website posted a comment from a viewer referring to those seeking gender reassignment surgery as "degenerates."[21] No Alberta politician has stooped that low, but is this sentiment coming from the support base to which the budget is catering?

Whether gender reassignment surgery should be covered by medicare has been a contentious issue across the country for some time. For example, Ontario had included it, then de-listed it a dozen years ago, then recently re-listed it after a lengthy battle before the Ontario Human Rights Commission.[22] In sharp contrast, Nova Scotia is among those jurisdictions that have never covered gender reassignment surgery. How should the merits of funding gender reassignment surgery be assessed?

In assessing medicare coverage of gender reassignment surgery, my focus is on the surgical treatment of competent adults, with fully informed consent. Very different concerns arise in the context of intersex conditions where parents are making decisions on behalf of infants or young children where the underlying issue is the propriety of treatment of those unable to consent and/or not involved in the decision-making process.[23] Thus, intersex conditions of children do not significantly engage issues of resource allocation. In contrast, the contention about whether medicare covers gender reassignment surgery for adults does directly engage resource allocation. A determination that gender reassignment surgery is medically necessary commits the state to fund it. A decision to the contrary means that the state is not obliged to pay for the surgery. So how do we, as a society committed to publicly funded health care, assess whether gender reassignment surgery is medically necessary? This discussion requires an analysis of what lies behind a decision to undergo gender reassignment surgery. The contrast between a biomedical assessment and a relational theory approach is very instructive.

The Edmonton Social Planning Council posted the following comments on its website in criticism of the Alberta budget:

> Alberta has been covering gender reassignment surgery (GRS) for more than a decade. It is generally agreed upon in the medical community that GRS is the only known cure for gender dysphoria or gender identity disorder, thus making it a required surgery.[24]

I think this biomedical model approach is a very problematic way of looking at the issue of medical necessity of gender reassignment surgery. A relational theory approach, considering relational identity, autonomy, and judgment, offers a very different perspective.

Gender Reassignment Surgery and Relational Identity

Françoise Baylis' discussion of relational identity is very helpful in understanding a decision to undergo gender reassignment surgery:

> On this view, my identity is neither in my body (*viz.* the somatic or biological account of personal identity) nor in my brain (*viz.* the psychological account of personal identity), but in the negotiated spaces between my biology and psychology and that of others. These others include those who are a part of my familial, social, cultural, and political clusters of meaning and belonging, those who know me from a distance, and still others, near strangers, who do not know me ...

> [W]ith relational identity, personhood and personal identity rely crucially not only on an individual's inner life and attitudes toward her traits, desires, beliefs, and so on but also on the attitudes of others to the same range of characteristics. Family members, friends, colleagues, community or tribal members, acquaintances, and even strangers play an active role in shaping the self-narratives of others not only by contributing to, but also by endorsing, questioning, and, in some cases, actively contesting, another's self-narrative. With relational identity, persons are (and can only be) dynamic complex co-creations informed by the perspectives and creative intentions of others.[25]

Someone contemplating gender reassignment surgery typically claims to have been experiencing a profound sense of disconnect between their self-conception of gender identity and the outward physical manifestations of gender that, by and large, determine the perception of others. The relational aspects concern both the issue of what gender categories (and their cultural and biological attributes) society recognizes in the abstract and what gender identity society is prepared to recognize for an individual. Julia Serano, an "out" transsexual, describes her own and others' experiences as "*gender dissonance*" – "the cognitive dissonance that arises from the fact that their *subconscious sex* does not match their physical sex."[26] This disconnect leads ultimately to an identified sex that is different from the one assigned at birth and a goal that others gender them in accordance with their identified sex rather than with their birth sex.[27] This account of "gender dissonance" is understood as being descriptive of gender variance, which is part of human diversity,[28] rather than the pathologizing labels of "gender dysphoria" or "gender identity disorder."[29]

Carl Elliott has commented:

> People undergoing transsexual surgery often say, "I am really a woman trapped in a man's body." That the surgery will let them be who they really are ... Yet we could also just as usefully speak not of authentic and inauthentic selves, or true or false selves, but of the way that the people in question have imagined themselves to be, the direction in which they envisioned the narrative of their lives going.[30]

When individuals are trying to negotiate between first and third person narratives, Baylis identifies equilibrium and stability as the mediating factors.[31] I would suggest that equilibrium or stability is precisely what someone undergoing gender reassignment surgery is seeking. Gender reassignment surgery is part of the process of the self "making and remaking" itself.[32] Relational theory presents a compelling case for state funding of gender reassignment surgery because it is precisely the relationship with the rest of society that, in large part, produces the perceived need. I will elaborate in the next two sections.

At the same time, it would be improper to assume that all transgendered persons ultimately want gender reassignment surgery.[33] Gender reassignment surgery is only one possible means of negotiating between first and third person narratives and only one possible means of securing "gender concordance."[34] Public funding could only facilitate the choice to undergo gender reassignment surgery, but it cannot in any sense impose it.[35] Serano, for example, advocates allowing the option, without specifically promoting or discouraging it.[36]

Gender Reassignment Surgery and Relational Autonomy

Yet there is a further complexity, even assuming we are dealing with adult choice with fully informed consent. Susan Sherwin draws a distinction between agency and autonomy:

> I used the term "agency" to capture the circumstance where a person reasonably chooses an option that is the most attractive or reasonable under the prevailing conditions but is incompatible with the overall interests of the groups to which that person belongs, and, hence, is in some sense incompatible with her own interests. Because the prevailing social conditions make such behaviour reasonable for individuals even as it is disastrous for the groups, we must acknowledge that the choices they make are pragmatically "rational" and so it is appropriate to describe their behaviour as an expression of agency.

I reserved the term "autonomy" to refer to actions that are consistent with a person's broader interests, values and commitments, including the well-being of her group (based on gender, race, class, sexual orientation, age, ethnicity, and so on). To be autonomous, an action must not only reflect a reasonable calculation of the benefits and costs at issue given the existing background conditions, but it must also not work against the promotion of projects and values that are important for the agent (including reducing the impact of oppression on one's group). Often, oppressed people fail to act with full autonomy because the options that are meaningfully available to them do not include a choice that is compatible with their deepest values and needs or because the rewards and punishments for choosing an action that reinforces oppression outweighs the personal benefits of choosing one that would help to undermine oppression. In such cases, increasing autonomy requires making changes to the background conditions, not (only) the agent.[37]

Could Sherwin's analysis be utilized to support a position that gender reassignment surgery should be excluded from state-funded medicare coverage because it does not represent an autonomous choice?

Could it be said that gender reassignment surgery actually contributes to the oppression of transexuals? Perhaps. It might be said that gender reassignment surgery is giving in to pressures to become "normal" in a way that further marginalizes those who challenge the norm of two totally distinct sexes. I am not sure that we know enough about gender identity to really assess this question. In terms of Sherwin's distinction between agency and autonomy in particular cases, I am not convinced we always know where the dividing line lies. Although Sherwin seems to assume that there is an objective means of identifying oppression, I would contend that relational theory needs to factor in the perspective of members of groups who are thought to be oppressed. There needs to be an assessment of the effects of denying choice because it is judged by the state/society not to be autonomous. I will return to this point in the next section of this chapter.

There is certainly enough known about gender identity to at least give one pause about whether gender reassignment surgery furthers autonomy or oppression. Even if gender reassignment surgery produces equilibrium or stability in terms of gender identity, Baylis' analysis of relational identity warns that equilibrium or stability is not necessarily a good thing.[38] The assumption of two discrete sexes is a cultural norm, not a universal truth.[39] In contrast to our Western cultures that "have many social distinctions that depend on there being (only) two sexes,"[40] there are societies that recognize a third sex/gender.[41] However, even the complication of recognizing a third gender is over-simplistic. Although some among the trans population identify as neither male nor female (uni-gender),[42] others identify as bi-gendered, while still others identify exclusively as one gender (either male or female), just not the one they were ascribed at birth.[43] Moreover, the cultural aspect of being transgendered is reflected in comments that the English language does not have the words to accurately describe the transgender experience.[44]

Serano acknowledges that some transexuals are striving to be normal, but she rejects this observation as a general characterization of transexuals. She contends that "the assumption that we transition in order to 'fit in' to the gender binary has virtually no relevance to most transexuals' lives."[45] Given the stigma attached to gender reassignment surgery, Serano concludes that "the idea that a trans person would transition in order 'to conform to hetero-sexist gender norms' is nothing more than an illogical and disrespectful farce."[46] Instead, she explains that "we transition first and foremost for ourselves, to be comfortable in our own bodies."[47] While this may sound like an individual-focused analysis, it is linked to the level of comfort being contributed to via the gendering by others in accordance with the post-transition self-identification. Thus, Serano's insights are ultimately relational. The further implication of this point, however, is that the perspective of the others doing the gendering cannot be ignored. Relational theory recognizes the self as embodied, with perceptions shaped by dominant norms about how bodies should look and how they should be used.[48]

Alice Dreger's historical account of medical treatment of hermaphrodites in Britain and France in the late nineteenth and early twentieth centuries draws the following conclusion: "[T]he aim of a hundred years ago was much the same, [as now] namely, to reduce and ideally eliminate hermaphroditism using every available tool – conceptual, material, social, rhetorical."[49] Medical practice is assumed to be for the good of the patient – as someone with a condition that needs to be fixed if possible.[50] These assumptions are cultur-ally laden:

[I]llness, health, disability and difference all are connected to a culture and a history, in dialogue with other human beings. My self-description is con-nected to your description of me, and our descriptions of one another are connected to the descriptions of others. Thus what counts as an illness or a disability – or on the other hand, as normal biological variation – will itself depend on its culture and historical location.[51]

In contemplating the question of "what makes a person a male or a female or a hermaphrodite," Dreger concludes that "the answer necessarily changes with time, with place, with technology, and with the many serious implica-tions – theoretical, practical, scientific, and political – of any given answer."[52] Moreover, as medicine has developed increasing surgical capacities to treat intersex/transgender conditions, such persons, according to Dreger, have been made "less and less visible in the world outside hospitals and clinics and medical journals."[53] Medicalizing transexual conditions can contribute to further marginalization. Even if those undergoing gender reassignment surgery are not trying to conform to binary gender norms, an assumption of such conformity may well be, at least in some respects, the overall (socially constructed) effect.

There is thus reason for caution in embracing state funding for gender reassignment surgery. However, even if we could assume that, in some larger sense, gender reassignment surgery contributes to oppression, I do not see how the dominant majority is in a position to tell a tiny minority that the state will not fund gender reassignment surgery for their own good.[54] The stark reality is that, individually and collectively, we are (at least in this juncture of our history) powerless to change the dominant mode of gender relations that produces the pressure for gender reassignment surgery. We cannot postpone decisions about funding gender reassignment surgery until history reassesses the dualism of gender identity. There is currently demand for gender reassignment surgery that the state must decide whether to fund. Although there is some danger that state funding of gender reassignment surgery conveys the message that the transgendered are expected to conform to dominant norms, I think there is greater danger that a decision not to fund it conveys the message that the dominant majority just does not care about the well-being of transexuals. Gender reassignment surgery is such a radical procedure that it would be very rare that anyone would undertake it lightly. And current protocols insist on a long period of preparation that precludes rash decisions.[55] The financial incentive of state funding alone is unlikely to be decisive. On the other hand, since gender reassignment surgery is very expensive on an individual basis, most people could not afford it if they had to pay for it themselves, such that the absence of state funding would be a decisive factor. For those who have come to the conclusion that gender reassignment surgery is what they need to resolve and stabilize their sense of disconnect between first and third person narratives, the surgery becomes a matter of medical necessity. To refuse state funding on the basis that their's is not an autonomous choice would be to force them unwillingly into a role of, and a particular manner of, challenging dominant norms, which cannot be what true autonomy requires.[56]

Gender Reassignment Surgery and Relational Judgment

Each of these considerations engages issues of judgment. How are the people responsible for determining medicare coverage supposed to decide? If the decisions are made on the basis of assumptions of a typical patient, gender reassignment surgery will drop off the table very quickly. For most (that is, the dominant majority whose subconscious sex matches their physical sex), gender reassignment surgery is not remotely on the radar screen of something they would ever contemplate. However, this fact does not make gender reassignment surgery a simple matter of personal choice disconnected from medical necessity. A relational theory of judgment requires taking into account the perspectives of others. As Jennifer Nedelsky explains,

> [t]he language of judgment ... offers ... a conception of judgment as a distinct human faculty that is subjective, but which is not therefore something merely arbitrary. Genuine judgment makes claims of validity – at least for others in the community of judgment. [note omitted] ...
>
> When we form our judgment in the process of imagining trying to persuade others, it is the perspectives of real others that is involved ...
>
> What matters here is ... the ... objective of seeing the link between the perspectives of others and judgment that is autonomous, that can transcend the inevitable limitations of one person's experience, interests and inclinations.[57]

Does the Alberta budget process show any signs of taking into account the perspective of the transgendered? In a very limited sense it does. In agreeing to fund those who have started the process of hormonal drug treatment, the Alberta government is acknowledging their reasonable expectations of state funding – that is, the unfairness of changing the rules mid-stream.[58] Yet, it is an acknowledgment only of an individualized pecuniary interest. It ignores the larger picture of the significance of gender reassignment surgery to the transgendered. More precisely, it ignores the relational significance of gender reassignment surgery, as affecting almost every aspect of life. And there is not the remotest indication that the Alberta government is trying to challenge dominant norms about only two discrete sexes. Rather, it is trying to reinforce them by ignoring the complexities of gender identity. I would guess that the perspective of the transgendered is so far removed from the world view of those creating the budget that it never entered the decision-making process. For a relational theory of judgment, taking into account the perspective of others is the most fundamental challenge:

> The way we take their perspective into account should be shaped both by the kind of judgment that we think was entailed in it as well as by our own humility about our capacity to understand standpoints that are very different from our own and consciousness of the asymmetries of power that may interfere.[59]

Serano argues that those whose subconscious sex matches their physical sex "have the luxury of intellectualizing away subconscious sex."[60] In assessing queer/trans activism, she concludes:

> Rather than focusing on "shattering the gender binary," I believe we should turn our attention instead to challenging all forms of *gender entitlement,*

the privileging of one's own perceptions, interpretations, and evaluations of other people's genders over the way those people understand
themselves.[61]

The Alberta budget process, in reaching the decision to de-list gender reassignment surgery from medicare, shows no signs of seriously trying to understand
the perspective derived from the lived experience of transsexuals. And it is a
process that denies to the transgendered any "voice or power to contribute
to debates, discussion, or decision making about the policies that affect
them."[62]

The Alberta budget process is best characterized as being judgmental rather
than an exercise in proper judgment:

One is not really standing in a relation of equality and respect when one is
being judgmental. Of course, that is not an admonition to abandon the
responsibility for judgment. It is a recognition that one cannot exercise
judgment well when one is being judgmental.[63]

I earlier noted that the effect of the 2009 Alberta budget was to place gender
reassignment surgery on a par with cosmetic surgery, treating both as matters of personal choice that are not funded by medicare. Cosmetic surgery
can be identified as procedures producing changes to appearance only and
is generally unfunded by Canadian medicare. The exceptional circumstances in which what would otherwise be characterized as unfunded
cosmetic surgery arise only when the condition is deemed to be disfiguring.[64] In this context, the potential harmful psychological effects are determined to go beyond the normal effects of mere preference and to meet
the threshold of medical necessity, resulting in medicare funding. The
precise dividing line between what is and is not disfiguring may be difficult
to draw, but the conceptual distinction is important. Can the earlier analysis
of gender reassignment surgery be distinguished from unfunded cosmetic
surgery? Sherwin uses cosmetic surgery as a classic example of agency but
not of autonomy:

I cited examples such as the frequent use of cosmetic surgery and reproductive technology by women. When women are primarily valued in terms of
physical appearance or reproductive capacity (as they are in most societies),
each woman is encouraged to choose these kinds of medical interventions
to promote her own security (and that of her dependents) by increasing her
personal worth through such practices. In doing so, each woman contributes
to the further normalization of the practice in question and thereby puts
pressure on other women to participate in these sorts of activities. In such
ways, each woman ends up reinforcing the problematic social pattern of

improperly judging the worth of women by their instrumental value. Of course, there are many reasons why a woman might choose to engage in such activities other than mere compliance with oppressive norms. Indeed, the many ways in which women find their personal lives enriched by acting in accordance with these sorts of norms (even while actively opposing gender oppression) are constitutive of modern gender oppression. The difficulty is that as long as women are valued instrumentally for their "feminine" attributes, they are not equal members of society. So, while women, as individuals, are likely to find rewards when they choose to act in accordance with these oppressive norms and to risk punishment and personal loss if they choose to resist them, each act of compliance also reinforces the norms and further entrenches women's oppression.[65]

It is easy to agree with Sherwin that the overall impact of cosmetic surgery contributes to the oppression of women. State policy should thus discourage it, on the theory that the effect of not facilitating cosmetic surgery does not impose a recognizable burden on those whose appearance is left unaltered. In this context, state funding of cosmetic surgery is inappropriate. Indeed, I am unaware of any serious contention that cosmetic surgery ought to be covered by medicare. However, cosmetic surgery that alters appearance is of an entirely different order compared to gender reassignment surgery that matches gender identity. Although individuals care about their appearance in myriad ways, it is accepted to be a matter of individual choice. People do not expect the state to pay for cosmetic surgery anymore than they expect the state to pay for clothes, jewelry, or make-up used to enhance one's body image.[66] Our culture contemplates infinite varieties of body images even if it privileges some types over others. Societal pressure to "fix" one's nose, "lift" one's face, or enlarge one's breasts may be quite real in producing a sense that one's body does not conform to the image one desires, but it is still a matter of personal preference that does not affect one's state of health. It is different in kind compared to the "gender dissonance" experienced by someone whose self-image is actually contradicted by their physical self.[67] It is this difference in kind that makes the case for state funding of gender reassignment surgery but not of cosmetic surgery.

Gender Reassignment Surgery and the Prospects of a Legal Challenge to the Refusal to Fund

Thus far, I think I have made the necessary political argument, based on relational theory, to justify state funding for gender reassignment surgery. Does this analysis lay a foundation for a successful *legal* challenge to the refusal of public funding for gender reassignment surgery? It certainly features the power imbalance that is central to a relational theory of equality.[68] A discrimination challenge based on either human rights legislation or section 15 of the *Charter* warrants consideration. The earlier-cited comments of the Edmonton Social Planning Council might suggest that the appropriate ground of discrimination is disability.[69] A biomedical model would analyze gender reassignment surgery as a response to disability by treating "gender dysphoria" or "gender identity disorder" as defects to be fixed.[70] The difference between these pathologizing labels and Serano's description of "gender dissonance" is instructive.[71] The assumption that birth sex and gender expression are expected to match is a societal norm that is not reflective of actual gender variance.[72] Key transgender activists reject the disability label.[73]

I have argued elsewhere that medical conditions should not be equated with disability.[74] Medical conditions do not need to be characterized as disability to be covered by medicare. Disability should not become an all-encompassing category including all physical and mental differences. If such an approach were taken to its logical extreme, sex and race could be subsumed within disability, which would make the disability category meaningless. Yet I do not reject disability as a category. I have a vision impairment that I have no trouble labelling as a disability. Due to Albinism, I have a substantial number of cones in my eyes that do not work. Since birth, I have been borderline legally blind, defined as 20/200 vision in the better eye. A biomedical model would not move beyond that description. A relational model goes further to acknowledge the implications of the poor eyesight on daily living and to interrogate how those implications depend on the ways in which society is organized around assumptions of good eyesight. However, there is no cultural component in the starting premise that my eyes do not see what most eyes see. In contrast, as set out earlier, there is a cultural component in characterizing transgender as anomalous. Analyzing transgender as disability has the implication of creating "artificial hierarchies" of gender identity that are as inappropriate as hierarchies of sex or race.[75]

There is another context where I think it is dangerous to conflate disability and sexuality. I would not classify infertility as a disability. Refusing to classify infertility as a disability does not preclude medicare coverage for infertility treatment, and, indeed, some types of infertility treatment are routinely covered by medicare across the country. However, not all infertility treatment is covered. In *Cameron v. Nova Scotia (Attorney General)*, the Nova Scotia Court of Appeal held that refusal to fund certain kinds of infertility treatment was a *prima facie* breach of section 15 of the *Charter*, as disability discrimination, but that the funding refusal was justified under section 1 of the *Charter*.[76] The Nova Scotia situation challenged in *Cameron* was such that some infertility treatments were funded, but not the (particularly expensive) treatments that the claimants wanted funded. In commenting on this decision, Diana Majury and Daphne Gilbert have argued that infertility is not a disability.[77] I concur. I would distinguish infertility treatment from cosmetic surgery on the basis that infertility does involve a medically recognized impairment that a medical system can be expected to address. Furthermore, if selective funding of infertility treatment were done in a way that was more favourable to men than women (or vice versa), it could amount to sex discrimination.[78] But selective funding of infertility treatment cannot be challenged as disability discrimination if infertility is not a disability. Majury and Gilbert, in challenging infertility as a disability, comment that "[w]e expect the only context in which an infertile individual or couple might self-identify as disabled is as a way to frame their claim for funding for infertility."[79] Moreover, infertility does not affect anything other than the ability to conceive. It does not affect activities of day-to-day living as, for example, does my vision impairment. Disability as a ground of discrimination should be tied to exclusionary effects.[80] Infertility does not so qualify.

Leaving aside the possibility of sex discrimination, I see the extent of coverage of infertility treatment as hinging on a political argument, not a legal one.[81] Where infertility can be "fixed" by medical intervention at a relatively modest cost and with a good chance of success, one could expect medicare coverage, as was the case in the situation in *Cameron*. However, as a political calculation, the exclusion of funding for expensive infertility treatments with dubious chances of success lies within the realm of expected health care policy that should not be vulnerable to legal challenge.[82] Although relational theory should recognize societal responsibility in support of parenting, it should not privilege the biological means of becoming a parent.[83] Categorizing infertility as a disability would have that effect. As with gender identity, artificial hierarchies must be avoided.

Thus, I take as a starting point that neither gender identity nor infertility falls under the rubric of disability. However, the alternative basis of sex discrimination is within the scope of this chapter in regard to gender reassignment surgery. I would concur with the policy of the Ontario Human Rights Commission that gender identity is properly seen as an element of sex.[84] Yet to argue that it is a case of sex discrimination potentially runs into the argument about comparator groups encountered in *Auton v. British Columbia*, which involved a claim on behalf of autistic children for provincial funding of a particular form of treatment:

> [T]he comparator group should mirror the characteristics of the claimant or claimant group relevant to the benefit or advantage sought, except for the personal characteristic related to the enumerated or analogous ground raised as the basis for the discrimination ... As discussed, the appropriate comparator in this case is a member of a non-disabled group or a person suffering a disability other than a mental disability that requests or receives funding for non-core therapy important to present and future health, but which is emergent and only recently becoming recognized as medically required. On the evidence adduced here, differential treatment either directly

or by effect is not established. There was no evidence of how the Province had responded to requests for new therapies or treatments by non-disabled or otherwise disabled people.[85]

This type of comparator group analysis has been criticized for only allowing for formal equality.[86] It may be possible to distinguish gender reassignment surgery from *Auton*, based on an argument that gender reassignment surgery is both core[87] and past emergent.[88] Nonetheless, the fact that gender reassignment surgery is quite unique makes it vulnerable to an argument that no on else is denied funding for anything like gender reassignment surgery. If comparisons are made at such a micro level, in looking for direct parallels in the mirror, identifying substantive inequality through the failure to respond to differential need becomes impossible.[89] The Supreme Court of Canada seems to have acknowledged the validity of such a critique in *Kapp v. Canada*.[90] More recently, although not suggesting the *Auton* was wrongly decided, the Supreme Court of Canada expressly abandoned the mirror approach to comparators in *Withler v. Canada (Attorney General)*.[91] *Withler* should faciliate the argument that failure to fund gender reassignment surgery amounts to discrimination through its direction to search for disadvantage rather than sameness.[92]

If the claimant group is the only group with need for a particular benefit, a formal equality analysis cannot find inequality because, by definition, no one else gets the benefit that no one else needs. The Court in *Eldridge* saw beyond such a formal equality analysis in relation to sign language interpretation that only the deaf needed.[93] It was no answer in *Eldridge* to say that no one got funding for sign language interpretation. Similarly, it should be no answer that no one gets funding for gender reassignment surgery. Substantive equality requires recognition that particular groups of claimants have unique needs. The comparator group analysis must be at a higher level of generality to show that different groups with different needs have their needs met. A relational theory approach should have no trouble identifying the refusal to fund gender reassignment surgery as discriminatory for failing to respond to fundamental medical needs, as medicare generally promises.

Beyond Hospital/Doctor Services in Canada's Health Care Funding

As noted earlier, Canada's current structure of medicare funding gives primacy to services provided by hospitals and doctors. Under federal cost sharing, any such medically necessary/required services are required to be funded, whereas the funding of services by other health care providers is a matter of provincial/territorial discretion. Thus, beyond hospitals and doctors, medical need is not the determining factor. Even a compelling argument of medical necessity does not require state funding. This divide between hospitals/doctors and other health care providers has been described as being irrational.[94] Political moves to reach beyond this divide have been slow in producing results.[95] Constitutional challenges, described in the remainder of this chapter, have been ultimately unsuccessful to date.

Although arbitrariness (parallel to irrationality) has been recognized as a principle of fundamental justice within the meaning of section 7 of the *Charter*, one cannot invoke section 7 without engaging the life, liberty, or security of the person element.[96] And since section 7 is, generally at least, not the source of positive government obligations,[97] section 7 cannot be used to compel state funding of health care.[98] Accordingly, section 7 is not a means of enforcing state funding of medical need outside doctors and hospitals. Who is implicated by the absence of an obligation to fund medical need outside the context of doctors and hospitals? The fact that prescription drugs administered outside hospitals generally fall into this category has a widespread impact, including hormone therapy for the transgendered.[99] More generally, the question is who is more likely to claim medically necessary services outside doctors and hospitals? The connection to this chapter's focus on differential need lies in the contention that this impact falls disproportionately on certain types of persons. I have been involved in litigation, in *Auton*, arguing that the disabled are so implicated.

Auton attempted to use section 15 of the *Charter* to challenge the primacy of hospital/physician services. The Supreme Court of Canada's comparator group analysis set out earlier was a secondary consideration. The Court's primary reason for rejecting the claim was that there was no "benefit of the law" within the meaning of section 15:

> The legislative scheme in the case at bar ... does not have as its purpose the meeting of all medical needs. As discussed, its only promise is to provide full funding for core services, defined as physician-delivered services. Beyond this, the provinces may, within their discretion, offer specified non-core services. It is, by its very terms, a partial health plan. It follows that exclusion of particular non-core services cannot, without more, be viewed as an adverse distinction based on an enumerated ground. Rather, it is an anticipated feature of the legislative scheme. It follows that one cannot infer from the fact of exclusion of ABA/IBI therapy for autistic children from non-core benefits that this amounts to discrimination. There is no discrimination by effect ...
>
> I conclude that the benefit claimed, no matter how it is viewed, is not a benefit provided by law. This is sufficient to end the inquiry.[100]

This is a very odd conclusion. A claim of unconstitutionality based on under-inclusion is met by the answer that it is not included. Previously, section 15 had been identified as the primary vehicle for claims of under-inclusiveness.[101] *Vriend v. Alberta* was a classic example of a successful claim of under-inclusiveness: Alberta's human rights legislation was held unconstitutional for its failure to include sexual orientation as a ground of discrimination.[102] Is *Auton* reconcilable with *Vriend*?

The only way I can see of reconciling them is through an examination of the role of grounds. In *Vriend*, the exclusion of coverage was clearly based on sexual orientation. The omission in the statute reflected a conscious decision to exclude sexual orientation. In *Auton*, in contrast, the link between autism as a disability and the core/non-core services distinction was less obvious. I was counsel for the Women's Legal Education and Action Fund/DisAbled Women's Network (LEAF/DAWN) as an intervenor in *Auton*. We argued that the hospital/physician versus other health care providers divide was not just randomly arbitrary but that, in overall and ultimate effect, it privileged the health needs of the able-bodied over the disabled. We relied on William Lahey to underscore that point:

> [T]he legal compartmentalization of our health care system obscures the nature of the premises and assumptions on which we implicitly rely when we make choices about (for example) funding for treatments that are outside the scope of medicare. These include a premise that medicine is generally superior to other responses to illness, suffering and disability, that curing is more important than caring (as well as prevention), that dealing with the episodic illness of the healthy is more important than dealing with chronic illness and disability, and that physical health takes priority over other dimensions of health, including mental health. Seen in this broader light, the *Auton* case is a manifestation of a decision-making dynamic that cuts across the Canadian health care system.[103]

Although the Supreme Court of Canada never actually said so, it implicitly rejected the factual basis of the claim that the divide between hospital/physician and other health care providers amounts to adverse effects discrimination on the basis of disability.

I am nonetheless convinced that the factual basis for this argument is accurate and that the services offered by doctors and hospitals are skewed in favour of the typical health needs of the able-bodied. This is where relational theory is relevant. Services provided by hospitals and doctors are significantly unresponsive to the needs of the disabled, who have different kinds of interdependence with others. To function in a relational world, persons with particular kinds of disabilities may need prostheses, assistive devices, attendant care, and so on – none of which counts as a core service provided by hospitals or doctors.

The primacy of doctors and hospitals under the *Canada Health Act* is premised on the notion that the primary role of medicine is prevention and cure. However, most disabilities are not capable of being cured (at least at the current stage of medical development). Typically, the most physicians can offer is management of the condition. Even health care providers beyond doctors and hospitals may not meet the needs of the disabled. Where the issue is the ability to function in a world designed for the able-bodied, health itself may be the wrong lens. The availability of, and capacity to produce, large-print documents do far more to meet my needs as an Albino than anything ever done by any doctor or other health care provider. The boundary lines between health care, social services, and education budgets, for example, also reflect an able-bodied perspective. Relational theory demands that such differences be taken into account in determining the collective responsibility assumed by state policy.

In taking differential need into account, care must still be taken in defining that differential need. In *Auton*, the LEAF/DAWN intervention argued that there had been a section 15 breach in the failure of the BC government to provide services for autistic children, but we made a point of not endorsing the Lovaas applied behavioural analysis (ABA) therapy claimed by the applicant parents. This LEAF/DAWN stance was because of concerns that Lovaas itself raises equality problems. Michelle Dawson, who had intervenor status in *Auton* in her individual capacity as an autistic person, went even further. She was, and is still adamantly, opposed to Lovaas as being oppressive to autistic persons. As a result, she is largely laudatory of the Supreme Court of Canada's decision in *Auton* and is alarmed at the increasing funding of ABA treatment in spite of the constitutional loss in the Supreme Court of Canada.[104] Although I disagree with Dawson about the legal analysis in the Supreme Court of Canada, her perspective on Lovaas merits attention. Relational theory emphasizes the importance of the relationship between the self and others, and it needs to be careful about conflating children with their parents. Especially where dealing with disabled children of non-disabled parents, care needs to be taken that the disabled perspective not get buried. In terms of a relational theory of judgment, when the state is deciding what to fund, it is important not to decide based on what is easy for the parents as opposed to what is good for the children. However, as with the treatment of intersex conditions of infants and small children, this goes well beyond the resource allocation issues addressed in this chapter.

Conclusion

A publicly funded health care system must determine what is, and is not, funded by the state. Even an assumption of medical need as the basic starting point leaves much to be determined. Relational theory helps to focus on the implications of differential need and to reveal that those who are marginalized in society are in particular danger of having their needs go unmet. This chapter uses illustrative examples to make this point. The Canadian health care system does take medical necessity as the starting point where doctors and hospital services are involved, but without great clarity as to what medical necessity actually entails. A diverse population means that there can be no generic definition of medical need. Different conditions and circumstances produce differential need. Relational theory offers a robust framework for responding to differential need. Concepts of relational identity, autonomy, and judgment enable an appreciation of how relationships shape the collective responsibility in providing public health care. Legal analysis requires a capacity to generalize beyond unique needs to be responsive to differential need. In this chapter, I have used the question of funding of gender reassignment surgery as a litmus test of how an atypical claim from a marginalized group should be assessed in a relational theory framework. I further argued, in this context, that gender identity is properly seen as an element of sex, not a matter of disability. Outside doctors and hospitals, medical need is not the key determinant of state funding in Canada. Relational theory, in focusing on differential need, looks to the differential impact of the primacy of doctors and hospitals. It is my contention that the doctors and hospitals are, in general, less responsive to the needs of the disabled than they are to needs of the able-bodied. Accordingly, the needs of the disabled are disproportionately unmet. Thus, both in the determination of whether medical need is established and whether medical need is determinative, the responsiveness of our medicare system is uneven and, hence, unequal. Relational theory, in highlighting different relationships with and within the collective, helps in moving beyond a formal, to a substantive, understanding of equality.

Notes

1 William Lahey, "The Legal Framework of Canada's Health Care System" in Jocelyn Downie et al., eds., *Dental Law in Canada* (Markham, ON: LexisNexis, 2004) 29; Colleen Flood and Michael Zimmerman, "Judicious Choices: Health Care Resource Decisions and the Supreme Court of Canada" in Jocelyn Downie and Elaine Gibson, eds., *Health Law at the Supreme Court of Canada* (Toronto: Irwin Law, 2007) 25.

2 See Jennifer Llewellyn, "A Healthy Conception of Rights? Thinking Relationally about Rights in a Health Care Context" in Downie and Gibson, *supra* note 1, 57.

3 *Canadian Charter of Rights and Freedoms*, Part I of the *Constitution Act, 1982*, being Schedule B to the *Canada Act, 1982* (U.K.) 1982, c. 11 [*Charter*].

4 *Chaoulli v. Quebec*, [2005] 1 S.C.R. 791 at para. 104 [*Chaoulli*].

5 *Ibid.*

6 *Eldridge v. British Columbia*, [1997] 3 S.C.R. 624 [*Eldridge*].

7 Section 15(1) of the *Charter* reads as follows:

15.(1) Every individual is equal before and under the law and has the right to the equal protection and equal benefit of the law without discrimination and, in particular, without discrimination based on race, national or ethnic origin, colour, religion, sex, age or mental or physical disability.

Section 1 of the *Charter* reads as follows:

1. The *Canadian Charter of Rights and Freedoms* guarantees the rights and freedoms set out in it subject only to such reasonable limits prescribed by law as can be demonstrably justified in a free and democratic society.

8   I am using the description "services" as shorthand to cover both goods and services, in the absence of a generic term including both, since our medicare system is more apt to fund services.

9   *R. v. Morgentaler*, [1988] 1 S.C.R. 30.

10   Those who desire amputation of healthy limbs self-describe as "wannabes." Most health care providers will refuse to perform such amputations on ethical grounds. For an argument that it should be considered ethical to perform an amputation for a wannabe, see Tim Bayne and Neil Levy, *Amputees By Choice: Body Identity Integrity Disorder and the Ethics of Amputation* (Oxford: Blackwell Publishing, 2005). Given the prevailing refusal to amputate, issues of resource allocation do not arise. Accordingly, I will not pursue the phenomenon of wannabes in this chapter.

11   *Canada Health Act*, R.S.C. 1985, c. C-6, s. 7.

12   Lahey, *supra* note 1 at 59.

13   See Jennifer Llewellyn, "Restorative Justice: Thinking Relationally about Justice" in this volume.

14   Marcia Rioux and Fraser Valentine, "Does Theory Matter? Exploring the Nexus between Disability, Human Rights, and Public Policy" in Dianne Pothier and Richard Devlin, eds., *Critical Disability Theory: Essays in Philosophy, Politics, Policy, and Law* (Vancouver: UBC Press, 2006) 41. Rioux and Valentine contrast models based on individual pathology (such as a biomedical approach) with those based on social pathology. They summarize the latter as follows: "Rather, they assume that the disability is a consequence of the social structure and that the social determinants of disability can be identified and addressed. The pathology is that there is something wrong with the society that needs to be fixed, rather than that there is something wrong with the individual that needs fixing" (at 51). There is significant contention about the notion and meaning of social construction. See for example, Ian Hacking, *The Social Construction of What?* (Cambridge, MA: Harvard University Press, 1999). For my purposes, it is not necessary to engage these issues.

15   *Canada Health Act*, *supra* note 11 at s. 2.

16   Lahey, *supra* note 1; Flood and Zimmerman, *supra* note 1.

17   "Alberta to De-List More Health Care Services," CBC News, http://www.cbc.ca/canada/edmonton/story/2009/04/15/edm-delisting-alberta.html. The budget also announced the de-listing of chiropractic services, which are among the discretionary category, since not provided by doctors or hospitals.

18   The province has agreed to cover those already in the process of gender reassignment surgery as well as those undergoing hormonal drug therapy in anticipation of an application and approval of gender reassignment surgery. However, for the future, those not yet in hormonal drug therapy will have to pay their own way, as much as $80,000 for gender reassignment surgery. *Ibid*.

19   *Ibid*.

20   Trish Audette, "Sex-Change Surgery List Doubles," *Edmonton Journal* (15 April 2009).

21   "Alberta to De-List More Health Care Services," *supra* note 17. It is revealing that CBC thought this comment worthy of inclusion on its website.

22   Audette, *supra* note 20.

23   Joel Frader et al., "Health Care Professional and Intersex Conditions" (2004) 158 Archives of Pediatrics and Adolescent Medicine 426.

24   Edmonton Social Planning Council, "Cutting Coverage for Gender Reassignment Surgery a Terrible Mistake," Edmonton Social Planning Council, http://www.edmontonsocialplanning.ca.

25 See Françoise Baylis, "The Self *in Situ*: A Relational Account of Personal Identity" in this volume.
26 Julia Serano, *Whipping Girl: A Transexual Woman on Sexism and the Scapegoating of Femininity* (Berkeley, CA: Seal Press, 2007) at 27 [emphasis in original].
27 *Ibid.* at 302-3.
28 *Ibid.* at 156. See also Leslie Feinberg, *Trans Liberation: Beyond Pink and Blue* (Boston: Beacon Press, 1998) at 5, 20, 53, and 118.
29 Serano, *supra* note 26 at 160.
30 Carl Elliott, *Bioethics, Culture and Identity: A Philosophical Disease* (New York: Routledge, 1999) at 30. While Elliott sees the description of "a woman trapped in a man's body" as generating support for the trans person, Serano sees it as "mocking" and "dumbing down," ignoring intricacies and nuances. Serano, *supra* note 26 at 215.
31 See Baylis, *supra* note 25.
32 See Llewellyn, *supra* note 13.
33 Feinberg, *supra* note 28 at 20.
34 Serano, *supra* note 26 at 87, 31, and 118.
35 It is certainly improper to promote gender reassignment surgery as a means of suppressing homosexuality.
36 Serano, *supra* note 26 at 158 and 160.
37 See Susan Sherwin, "Relational Autonomy and Global Threats" in this volume.
38 See Baylis, *supra* note 25.
39 Elaine Craig, "Trans-Phobia and the Relational Production of Gender" (2007) 18 Hastings Women's L.J. 137.
40 Alice Dreger, *Hermaphrodites and the Medical Invention of Sex* (Cambridge, MA: Harvard University Press, 1998) at 8.
41 Elliott, *supra* note 30 at 35-36. See also Carl Elliott, "Why Can't We Go on As Three" (1998) 28(3) Hastings Center Rep. 36.
42 Feinberg, *supra* note 28 at 19.
43 Serano, *supra* note 26 at 211.
44 *Ibid.* at 80 and 200; Feinberg, *supra* note 28 at 27.
45 Serano, *supra* note 26 at 153.
46 *Ibid.* at 154.
47 *Ibid.* at 189. Serano does not limit "transition" to those who have undergone gender reassignment surgery. She includes all those who live as a sex different from that ascribed at birth.
48 See Baylis, *supra* note 25. See also Craig, *supra* note 39 at 139-40.
49 Dreger, *supra* note 40 at 197.
50 *Ibid.*
51 Elliott, *supra* note 30 at 48.
52 Dreger, *supra* note 40 at 9.
53 *Ibid.* at 11.
54 In other contexts, I have cautioned against trusting the state to determine what is for the good of marginalized groups. See Dianne Pothier, "But It's for Your Own Good" in Margot Young et al., eds., *Poverty: Rights, Social Citizenship, and Legal Activism* (Vancouver: UBC Press, 2007) 40.
55 It is beyond the scope of this chapter to assess these protocols. For a critique, arguing that they are too restrictive, see Serano, *supra* note 26 at 115-60.
56 Although directed to very different contexts of global threats, Sherwin's current work acknowledges the limitations on individual actions in a strategy of dismantling oppression. *Ibid.* at 25-30, citing in particular Iris Marion Young, "Responsibility and Global Justice: A Social Connection Model" (2006) Soc. Phil. & Pol'y 102.
57 See Jennifer Nedelsky, "The Reciprocal Relation of Judgment and Autonomy: Walking in Another's Shoes and Which Shoes to Walk In" in this volume.
58 Audette, *supra* note 20.
59 See Nedelsky, *supra* note 57.
60 Serano, *supra* note 26 at 155.

61 *Ibid.* at 359 [emphasis in original].
62 See Christine M. Koggel, "A Relational Approach to Equality: New Developments and Applications" in this volume.
63 See Nedelsky, *supra* note 57.
64 For example, port wine stains (birthmarks) on the face. In British Columbia, the RCMP have adopted a policy of paying for tattoo removal of gang-related tattoos in order to assist people in extricating themselves from gangs. "Ex-Gangsters Offered Free Tattoo Removal, CBC News, http://www.cbc.ca/canada/british-columbia/story/2009/08/18/bc-gangster-tattoo-removal.html. It is worth noting that this funding is coming from the administration of justice budget rather than the health care budget, so disfigurement is not the criterion for funding.
65 See Susan Sherwin, "Relational Autonomy and Global Threats" in this volume. I will discuss infertility treatment later in this chapter.
66 The coverage, by private medical insurance, of prosthetic bras for women who have had a mastectomy would fall into the disfigurement category.
67 Serano, *supra* note 26 at 27.
68 See Koggel, *supra* note 62.
69 Edmonton Social Planning Council, *supra* note 24.
70 I.A. Hughes et al., "Consensus Statement on Management of Intersex Disorders" (2006) 91 Archives of Disease in Childhood 554, proposes the generic term: "disorders of sex development."
71 Serano, *supra* note 26 at 27.
72 Feinberg, *supra* note 28 at 20, 29, and 69.
73 Gary Bowen, in *ibid.* at 63; Serano, *supra* note 26 at 160.
74 Dianne Pothier, "*Martin* and *Laseur*: Workers' Compensation under *Charter* Scrutiny" (2004) 11 C.L.E.L.J. 329 at 340-41.
75 Serano, *supra* note 26 at 13. Serano reiterates this point about the inappropriateness of hierarchies, in conjunction with her earlier noted emphasis on "challenging all forms of *gender entitlement*" (at 359) [emphasis in original].
76 *Cameron v. Nova Scotia (Attorney General)* (1999), 177 D.L.R. (4th) 611 (N.S. C.A.), application for leave to appeal dismissed, S.C.C. Bulletin 2000, p. 1271, motion for reconsideration dismissed with costs, S.C.C. Bulletin 2001, p. 2029.
77 Diana Majury and Daphne Gilbert, "Infertility and the Parameters of Discrimination Discourse" in Pothier and Devlin, *supra* note 14, 285.
78 Pursuing that possibility would require a sophisticated substantive equality analysis to take account of the impact of biological difference. This question goes well beyond the scope of this chapter.
79 Majury and Gilbert, *supra* note 77 at 296.
80 Pothier, *supra* note 74 at 341. See also *Granovsky v. Canada (Minister of Employment and Immigration)*, [2000] 1 S.C.R. 703 at para. 39; *Quebec (Commission des droits de la personne et des droits de la jeunesse) v. Montréal (City)*, [2000] 1 S.C.R. 665 at para. 82.
81 Quebec's recent moves to provide extensive medicare coverage of *in vitro* fertilization are based on political calculations, not legal imperatives; "Quebec to Fund In Vitro Fertility Treatments," CBC News, http://www.cbc.ca/health/story/2010/03/11/mtl-quebec-in-vitro-funding.html.
82 Moreover, where infertility treatment is taken to extreme lengths, I agree with Sherwin, *supra* note 65, that it is oppressive to women to put such a high value on reproductive capacity.
83 The Supreme Court of Canada does so in *Reference re Employment Insurance Act (Can), ss 22 and 23*, [2005] 2 S.C.R. 669.
84 Ontario Human Rights Commission, "Policy on Discrimination and Harassment Because of Gender Identity," Human Rights in Ontario, http://www.ohrc.on.ca/en/issues/gender_identity. The Northwest Territories is the only jurisdiction in Canada that currently includes "gender identity" as a separate prohibited ground of discrimination. *Human Rights Act*, S.N.W.T. 2002, c. 18, s. 5. At the federal level, third reading in the House of Commons was given on 9 February 2011 to Bill C-389, a private member's bill introduced by NDP Member

of Parliament Bill Siksay, which would add "gender identity" and "gender expression" as grounds in the *Canadian Human Rights Act*, R.S.C. 1985, c. H-6. The bill was given first reading in the Senate on 10 February 2011, but died on the order paper when the 40th Parliament was dissolved on 26 March 2011, setting the stage for the general election on 2 May 2011. At the close of the second reading debate in the House of Commons (*Hansard,* 8 June 2010), in response to arguments that the bill was unnecessary given rulings by several human rights tribunals that "gender identity" was subsumed within "sex," Siksay said: "A right that has to be explained is not a particularly effective right." During third reading debate (*Hansard*, 7 February 2011), Siksay added: "It is important for absolute clarity. Transpeople should not have to think their way into protection using other categories originally intended to cover other groups in our society ... It is also important that a group that is marginalized in our society and that suffers significant discrimination and prejudice actually see themselves in the law, and that those who would discriminate against them know, beyond a shadow of a doubt, that their actions are not acceptable."

85 *Auton v. British Columbia*, [2004] 3 S.C.R. 657 at paras. 53 and 58 [*Auton*].
86 Dianne Pothier, "Equality as a Comparative Concept: Mirror, Mirror on the Wall, What's the Fairest of Them All?" (2006) 33 Sup. Ct. L. Rev. (2d) 135; Llewellyn, *supra* note 2; Daphne Gilbert and Diana Majury, "Critical Comparisons: The Supreme Court of Canada Dooms Section 15" (2006) 24 Windsor Y.B. Access Just. 111.
87 Recall that "core" in the Canadian health care system refers to services delivered by doctors or hospitals, which covers gender reassignment surgery but not the treatment at issue in *Auton*.
88 There are several decades of experience with gender reassignment surgery, judged to be effective in resolving gender dissonance.
89 *Auton, supra* note 85.
90 *Kapp v. Canada*, [2008] 2 S.C.R. 483 at para. 22.
91 *Withler v. Canada (Attorney General)*, 2011 SCC 12 [*Withler*].
92 *Ibid.* at para. 57.
93 *Eldridge, supra* note 6.
94 Flood and Zimmerman, *supra* note 1 at 29.
95 *Ibid.*
96 *Chaouilli, supra* note 4 at para. 104. Section 7 of the *Charter* reads as follows: "7. Everyone has the right to life, liberty, and security of the person and the right not to be deprived thereof except in accordance with the principles of fundamental justice."
97 *Gosselin v. Quebec*, [2002] 4 S.C.R. 429.
98 *Chaoulli, supra* note 4, succeeded as a claim challenging the prohibition against private insurance. See Llewellyn, *supra* note 2, for a relational theory critique of this decision.
99 Hormone therapy can be either preliminary to gender reassignment surgery or can be the ultimate medical intervention sought for those not wanting gender reassignment surgery.
100 *Auton, supra* note 85 at paras. 43 and 47.
101 *Dunmore v. Ontario*, [2001] 3 S.C.R. 1016.
102 *Vriend v. Alberta*, [1998] 1 S.C.R. 193.
103 Lahey, *supra* note 1 at 79-80.
104 Michelle Dawson, "An Autistic Victory: The True Meaning of the Auton Decision," No Autistics Allowed, http://www.sentex.net/~nexus23/naa_vic.html.

9

Resistance Is Essential: Relational Responses to Recent Law and Policy Initiatives Involving Reproduction

Jocelyn Downie

With the famous striking down of the restrictions on access to abortion set out in the *Criminal Code*,[1] and the rejection of an attempt to involuntarily confine a drug-addicted pregnant woman to protect her fetus,[2] one might be tempted to think that all is well in Canada with respect to state intervention in the lives of pregnant women. However, one would be sorely mistaken to do so. Despite the important victories at the Supreme Court of Canada in the 1980s and 1990s, there remain significant areas within which legislators and policy makers use, are trying to use, or might try to use the power of the state to coercively intervene in the lives of pregnant women.[3]

There are, of course, many points along the human reproduction timeline that are sites for the state to have an impact on the lives of women (for good or for ill). Before pregnancy, we see issues relating to the regulation of new reproductive technologies, surrogacy, and contraception. Can women sell their eggs? How many eggs may be implanted into a woman during in vitro fertilization? Can a surrogacy contract be binding? Can pharmacists refuse to distribute Plan B (an emergency contraceptive)? Can a mother authorize the sterilization of her incompetent daughter? Can a judge make the insertion of an implantable contraceptive a condition of parole? During pregnancy, we see issues relating to prenatal screening and testing of women, prenatal diagnosis of fetuses, abortion, and the involuntary treatment or confinement of women. Can a province implement a system of mandatory HIV testing of pregnant women? Can a woman access prenatal diagnostic services for the purposes of sex selection? Must the state pay for abortion services in free-standing clinics? Can the state hold a woman against her will for the duration of her pregnancy to keep her from abusing drugs? Following delivery, but still in relation to events that occurred leading up to or during pregnancy, we see issues relating to custody, tort, or criminal liability for harms suffered while in utero. Can a woman have her children removed from her care and custody upon delivery on the grounds that she was abusing drugs and alcohol while pregnant? Can a woman be found liable for damages if she failed to take folic acid supplements during pregnancy and her baby was born with a neural tube defect? Law and policy provide answers to many of these questions (again, for good or for ill).

Given space constraints, I must obviously limit the scope of this chapter. From the set of issues arising in relation to pregnancy, I therefore focus on just two issues: the current exclusion of abortion services from the *Interprovincial Reciprocal Billing Agreement* and a recent federal bill on conscientious objection by health care providers. I focus on issues during pregnancy since it is at this point that the balancing of interests of the fetus and the pregnant woman is most explicit and problematic and where relational theory might shed the most light and also where it might be most misunderstood or misused. I focus on these two specific issues during pregnancy since they tend to receive less attention than other issues and yet are very significant for pregnant women. They are also illustrative of the ways in which significant barriers to access to abortion continue to be erected even in the absence of a prohibition or restriction on abortion through the *Criminal Code*. In addition, they also provide an illuminating crucible within which to test the applicability and utility of a relational approach (specifically, relational conceptions of judgment, justice, and conscience as discussed in chapters 2, 4, and 7 of this volume).

The Current Exclusion of Abortion Services from the *Interprovincial Reciprocal Billing Agreement*

Under the *Canada Health Act*, in order to get cash contributions from the federal government for its health budget, a province or territory's health insurance plan must satisfy five criteria: public administration; comprehensiveness; universality; portability; and accessibility.[4] With respect to comprehensiveness, the *Canada Health Act* states:

> In order to satisfy the criterion respecting comprehensiveness, the health care insurance plan of a province must insure all insured health services provided by hospitals, medical practitioners or dentists, and where the law of the province so permits, similar or additional services rendered by other health care practitioners.[5]

Abortion services are insured health services in all provinces and territories in Canada (with some variability in regard to, for example, whether they are funded in hospitals only or also in clinics and whether referrals are required).[6] With respect to portability, the *Canada Health Act* establishes that provinces and territories must provide coverage for insured health services provided to their current residents while they are travelling elsewhere in Canada and to their former residents for a period of up to three months following relocation.[7]

In order to facilitate the meeting of these portability requirements in the face of a mobile population, the Interprovincial Health Insurance Agreements Coordinating Committee (IHIACC) was formed, and the *Interprovincial Reciprocal Billing Agreement (IRBA)* was established.[8] The *IRBA* allows for "reciprocal processing of out-of-jurisdiction medical claims" and thus when an individual from another province is provided with insured services, the other province (rather than the individual) will be presented with the bill for the services.[9] In 1988, the IHIACC issued a list of services excluded under the *IRBA*. This list was modified in 1989 and 1991 and now consists of the following services:

- Surgery for alteration of appearance (cosmetic surgery).
- Sex-reassignment surgery.
- Surgery for reversal of sterilization.
- *Therapeutic abortions.* [emphasis added]
- Routine periodic health examinations including routine eye examinations.
- In vitro fertilization, artificial insemination.
- Acupuncture, acupressure, transcutaneous electro-nerve stimulation (TENS), moxibustion, bio-feedback, hypnotherapy.
- Services to persons covered by other agencies: RCMP, Armed Forces, Workers' Compensation Board, Department of Veterans Affairs, Correctional Services of Canada (federal penitentiaries).
- Services requested by a third party.
- Team conference(s).
- Procedures still in the experimental/developmental phase.
- Genetic screening and other genetic investigations, including DNA probes.
- Lithotripsy for gall bladder stones.
- The treatment of port-wine stains on other than the face or neck, regardless of the modality of treatment.
- Anaesthetic services and surgical assistant services associated with all of the foregoing.[10]

As a result of the exclusion of abortion from the *IRBA*, some provinces have signed bilateral reciprocal billing agreements for some or all of the costs associated with abortions with some other provinces or, in some cases, directly with health care institutions. There is enormous variability and, as a result, considerable confusion in the coverage. Is the agreement with the other province or with specific institutions within the province? Is the coverage for hospital services or for hospital and physician services? Is the coverage for hospital abortions only or also for abortions in free-standing clinics? Is the agreement for reciprocal billing or must the woman pay up front and then be reimbursed? Is prior approval from the government required for there to be coverage? Is post hoc approval required from the government for there to be coverage? If abortion were not excluded from the *IRBA*, much of this confusion would not exist.

In addition, as a result of the exclusion of abortion from the *IRBA*, some women face either a delay or an absolute bar in accessing abortion. Without interprovincial billing, a woman with three children who lives thirty miles from a hospital in another province but 700 miles from the nearest hospital providing abortion services in her home province could face far more significant (often insurmountable) hurdles of finding the financial resources (flight and accommodation), child care coverage (one day versus at least one overnight), and privacy protection (with increased distance, the threats to her privacy are increased given the correlative increased time away from work and home). Without interprovincial billing, a twenty-year-old woman who is at university 3,000 miles from home could have to find funds for a flight and accommodation (if she does not want her parents to know) and, given the greater time required, could face a more significant disruption of her ability to meet her work and school responsibilities. A homeless teenager who ran away from an abusive home in one province to live on the streets of another could face an unwanted pregnancy, delivery, and child. Again, if abortion were not excluded from the *IRBA*, these delays and absolute barriers to access caused by the holes in the existing patchwork quilt would not exist.[11]

One could engage in a discussion of this issue from a substantive perspective. Specifically, for example, one could explore whether the decision to exclude abortion from the *IRBA* violates women's autonomy and equality. Such an exploration is hugely important. However, the substantive issue of access to abortion has been addressed elsewhere by others. Of particular note, liberal feminists, social feminists, and relational feminists have all done important work on this topic.[12] In this chapter, therefore, I focus on process since one can also usefully explore the decision to exclude abortion from the *IRBA* from a procedural perspective, and this has yet to be done. In particular, one can usefully look at the process through the lens of Jennifer Llewellyn's relational conception of justice[13] and Jennifer Nedelsky's relational conception of judgment.[14]

According to Llewellyn's relational conception of justice, a legitimate process for decision making about policies affecting rights and interests involves reflection by the decision makers about the harms to individuals or groups resulting from the decision and the implications of the decision for the realization of the conditions that are necessary for the well-being and flourishing (and, ultimately, equality) of all members of society. It also involves the use of social dialogue processes (that is, processes with direct, dialogical, and otherwise meaningful participation by those affected by the decision).

According to Nedelsky's relational conception of judgment, a legitimate process for decision making involves a meaningful taking into account of the perspectives/viewpoints of others (particularly those who would likely reject the decision makers' viewpoints). Specifically, a legitimate process includes openness, attentiveness, receptivity, and humility exemplified by actually talking with those likely to be affected and/or those holding alternative perspectives. In order for there to be a legitimate process, the decision makers should also be conscious of their assumptions and motivations as well as the limitations on their own knowledge and understanding. The decision makers should disclose their decisions and the reasons for their decisions – particularly to those who they can anticipate will reject their decisions. Finally, the decision makers should periodically reappraise their decisions.

Unfortunately, the features required by Nedelsky and Llewellyn's relational conceptions of judgment and justice respectively are not evident in any available information about the IHIACC processes.[15] Consider each feature in turn. First, one can reasonably infer that the committee did not meaningfully take into account the perspectives/viewpoints of others from the fact that it does not appear to have actually talked with women or abortion providers. The decision-making process was (and remains) far from open, attentive, receptive, and humble. The following information was requested from the IHIACC:

- minutes from the IHIACC for the past three years;
- official titles of members for the past three years;
- copies of any written materials used to inform the IHIACC members in making the decision to exclude (and continue to exclude) abortion from the *IRBA*;
- names and titles of individuals who were consulted to inform the IHIACC's members in making the decision to exclude (and continue to exclude) abortion from the *IRBA*;
- written reasons for any decisions with respect to the exclusion of abortion;
- any correspondence from the IHIACC or the chair explaining reasons for any decisions with respect to the exclusion of abortion; and
- annual reports prepared by the IHIACC for the past three years.[16]

Of this requested information (which could reasonably be expected to reveal the taking into account of the perspectives/viewpoints of others), only a copy of a letter from the IHIACC to the National Abortion Federation (in response to a letter from the federation) was provided. Thus, on the basis of the information available through a review of the web and direct requests, the *IRBA* process appears closed, inattentive, and unreceptive to the viewpoints of others.

Second, one can also reasonably infer that the committee was not conscious of the limitations on its own knowledge and understanding that resulted in the committee's reliance on false information in its decision making. For example, the committee appears to have relied on false information about the barriers to access to abortion in Canada and the effects of the decision to exclude abortion from the *IRBA*. False statements that were given as the justification for not reconsidering the exclusion of abortion services include: "All provinces and territories allow for direct billing of abortion services when certain conditions have been met (for example, that the procedure is performed in an accredited hospital). The costs of abortion services will then be reimbursed by the health insurance plan of the home province or territory."[17] If one believed that the exclusion of abortion from the *IRBA* did not interfere with the ability of women to access abortion services, then the exclusion might appear more reasonable. However, the IHIACC's statement is simply not true. Provincial governments have refused direct billing for abortions provided in accredited hospitals in other jurisdictions.[18] This false information could have been corrected if knowledgeable non-members had been consulted. Furthermore, there is no evidence that the IHIACC members themselves had the expertise or experience needed to understand the impact on women (particularly vulnerable women) of the exclusion of abortion services from the *IRBA*.

The IHIACC also stated: "For a health care service to be reciprocally billed, it must be uniformly insured in all provinces and territories. While abortion services are considered to be insured services in all jurisdictions, the requirements for the coverage differ enough that the service has been placed on the list of excluded services."[19] The outlier with respect to abortion services is New Brunswick, which only covers abortion if it "is performed by a specialist in the field of obstetrics and gynaecology in a hospital facility approved by the jurisdiction in which the hospital facility is located and two medical practitioners certify in writing that the abortion was medically required."[20] However, a review of the *Canada Health Act*'s annual reports clearly demonstrates that there is significant variability in coverage for a variety of services where the service is not placed on the list of excluded services. Consider, for example, the following exclusions under the New Brunswick regulations:

- removal of skin lesions, except where the lesions are, or are suspected to be, pre-cancerous;
- surgical assistance for cataract surgery unless such assistance is required because of risk of procedural failure, other than the risk inherent in removing the cataract itself, due to the existence of an illness or other complication;

- electrocardiogram (ECG), where not performed by a specialist in internal medicine or paediatrics;
- bariatric surgery unless the person (i) has a body mass index of 40 or greater, (ii) has obesity-related co-morbid conditions, and (iii) has, under the supervision of a medical practitioner, commenced and failed an exercise and diet program to reduce the person's weight to a more acceptable level.[21]

Much like the abortion restrictions (which create the variability that the IHIACC relies upon), these restrictions (which also create variability) do not appear in other provinces, and yet the removal of skin lesions, cataract surgery, electrocardiograms, and bariatric surgery are not included on the *IRBA*'s exclusion list. Other examples exist in different provinces to make the point that variability alone is not a sufficient explanation for exclusion, and they support the claim that the IHIACC was not sufficiently aware of the limitations on its knowledge and understanding of the relevant facts.

Third, the IHIACC declined to reappraise the decision to exclude abortion when asked to do so by a group representing abortion providers in Canada.[22] In a letter from the chair of the IHIACC in the summer of 2009, the following statement was made: "This item has been discussed twice at IHIACC since September 2007 and, since the policies of individual jurisdictions with regard to coverage of abortion services have not changed, the committee has decided to maintain this service on the list of excluded services."[23] However, while the policies may not have changed, the effects of the policies could have (for example, availability of abortion services for women across Canada) and new arguments might be available with respect to why the decision made previously was wrong even before 2007. At this point, the IHIACC might respond that it can only consider changes to the list when there is policy change and, as there has not been policy change, it cannot consider reopening the list discussion. Indeed, the chair has stated in a letter that "[i]t is important to emphasize that IHIACC is a committee which deals with the administrative aspects of interprovincial billing. As such, decisions taken by this committee are based on broader policy decisions which have been taken by each jurisdiction and IHIACC members cannot make decisions that would run counter to those policies."[24] However, the IHIACC clearly deals with more than the mere administration of policies made elsewhere since the administrative standard's "uniformity of coverage" does not explain what is on the exclusion list and what is not. Furthermore, its terms of reference are not as narrow as suggested in the chair's letter, and the IHIACC's responsibilities include that it:

- establish criteria to determine what services are subject to reciprocal billing

- facilitate efficiency and easy use of health services to all eligible Canadians and
- provide the necessary steps for the delivery of insured health services outside their home province.[25]

There is no evidence of reflection by the IHIACC upon the harms to women resulting from the decision to exclude abortion from the *IRBA* and the implications of the decision for the realization of the conditions necessary for women's well-being and flourishing. There is no evidence that the IHIACC consulted individuals or organizations with the expertise or experience needed to understand the impact on women (particularly vulnerable women) of the exclusion of abortion services from the *IRBA*. Nor is there any evidence that the IHIACC consulted the relevant literature on the availability of abortion services in Canada. All of these activities could have revealed effects on the "efficiency and easy use" of abortion services; change could have occurred post-2007 that could have affected the exclusion decision. It could be argued, therefore, that the IHIACC failed to meet the relational theory requirements with respect to the reappraisal of decisions.

Finally, there is no evidence of any social dialogue processes. The committee meetings have been closed, and the committee does not appear to have invited any individuals or groups affected by the decision to participate in, or even to observe, their discussions, let alone engaged them in meaningful participation. They have also refused to disclose very basic information about their work.[26] Thus, relational conceptions of judgment and justice provide the basis for a rejection of the process used to exclude, and continue to exclude, abortion services from the *IRBA* by the IHIACC. From a relational perspective, it can be concluded that the exclusion should be revisited and the process by which the IHIACC makes decisions with such significant implications for the well-being of women in Canada should be modified so as to include the features listed earlier.

The Proposed Federal Bill on Conscientious Objection by Health Care Providers

On 16 April 2008, Maurice Vellacott (a Reform, then Alliance, and now Conservative member of parliament for Saskatoon-Wanuskewin and former co-chair of the federal Pro-Life Caucus) introduced a private member's bill, Bill C-537, *An Act to Amend the Criminal Code (Protection of Conscience Rights in the Health Care Profession)*. This bill contains the following key sections:

425.2(1) The definitions in this subsection apply in this section ...

"health care practitioner" means any person who may lawfully provide services to others

(a) as a physician, surgeon, dentist, nurse or other skilled health care provider,

(b) as a person engaged in the provision of medical, dental, hospital, clinical, nursing or other health care service, under the direction of a skilled health care provider or a clinic, hospital, accrediting body or government ministry, or

(c) as a teacher, professor, instructor or other person providing teaching services in any field of health care.

"human life" means the human organism at any stage of development, beginning at fertilization or creation.

"tenet" means a religious doctrine that human life is inviolable or an edict of a religion that requires that human life not be deliberately ended or that human life not be subjected to any increased risk of death when the subjection to increased risk is avoidable.

(2) Everyone is guilty of an offence punishable on summary conviction who, being an employer or the agent of an employer,

(a) refuses to employ a health care practitioner ...

because the health care practitioner is, or is believed to be unwilling to take part, directly or in an advisory capacity, in any medical procedure that offends a tenet of the practitioner's religion, or the belief of the practitioner that human life is inviolable.[27]

Similar provisions prohibit health care educational institutions and professional health care associations from excluding individuals from admission, accreditation, ongoing membership, or advancement on the grounds listed in section 425.2(2).

This bill purports to be about "the protection of conscience rights in the health care profession" and, hence, "[t]his enactment protects the right of health care practitioners and other persons to refuse, without fear of reprisal or other discriminatory coercion, to participate in medical procedures that offend a tenet of their religion, or their belief that human life is inviolable."[28] It was, from its inception, unlikely to be passed in Parliament as it was a private member's bill (and they have a very low success rate) and it was being considered in the context of a very vulnerable minority government that recoiled from allowing discussion of such a politically charged issue.[29] However, lest one think that it is therefore not worth the candle to discuss this bill, it is important to note that it sits in a broader policy context of an active debate about physicians' rights to conscientious objection with respect to abortion and widespread support for protecting such rights (especially among physicians and right-to-life activists).[30]

This context is reflected in a recent set of exchanges about the physician's duty to refer for abortion. Sanda Rodgers and I have elsewhere argued that physicians are under a duty to refer and that the Canadian Medical Association's (CMA) policy "does not allow a right of conscientious objection in relation to referrals."[31] However, Jeff Blackmer, the executive director of the CMA's Ethics Office, claims that we have misrepresented the CMA's position. He gives the following advice to physicians on what to do when confronted with a woman seeking a referral: "You should therefore advise the patient that you do not provide abortion services. You should also indicate that because of your moral beliefs, you will not initiate a referral to another physician who is willing to provide this service (unless there is an emergency) ... At the patient's request, you should also indicate alternative sources where she might obtain a referral."[32] Canadian Physicians for Life (CPL), in turn, interpreted Blackmer's statement as being satisfied by the physician responding to the woman as follows: "As you know, you could go to almost any other doctor in this city and it would be their shortest patient visit of the day – they would send you straight to an abortion clinic. So the issue is not what you could do, the issue is how to decide what is best for you and your baby." The CPL wrote to Blackmer and indicated that it intended to interpret the statements he had made in response to our editorial in this way and that it would "assume that this is an acceptable interpretation of your clarification of the CMA policy unless we hear from you to the contrary." Blackmer responded that "previous statements on this matter stand for themselves," and the CPL then thanked Blackmer for "issuing a statement that supports our position of freedom of conscience from participating in abortion, including the referral process [including referrals to referrals]."[33] Bill C-537 sits in this broader, highly receptive, policy context and, given this context, even though it has died, others such as it may well appear at the federal or provincial/territorial level in the future. A new version is actually more likely to appear at the provincial/territorial level than federal level since extreme positions on abortion tend to survive at that level (see, for example, New Brunswick's and Prince Edward Island's positions on funding abortion), and the jurisdiction for this kind of bill is easier to defend at a provincial/territorial level rather than at a federal level since the bill is arguably not criminal law, which is federal jurisdiction, but, rather, labour law, which is provincial/territorial jurisdiction. The bill can therefore reasonably be described as a representative and illustrative (as opposed to easy) target.

I turn now to an analysis of the bill. Again, as with the *IRBA* issue, various non-relational approaches could be used here to great effect. A straight division of powers argument could prove fatal for the bill since it is vulnerable to an argument that it is not criminal law (federal jurisdiction) but, rather, labour law (provincial/territorial jurisdiction).[34] Even on a traditional individualistic conception of conscience, the bill might also fail.[35] However, once again, because it is the road less travelled and because it raises issues that the division of power and traditional individualistic conceptions of conscience ignore or simply do not see, I will approach the analysis first through Carolyn McLeod's relational conception of conscience[36] and then through a relational approach to rights[37] – specifically, relational aspects of conscience (that is, how it is formed in and through relationships) and a relational analysis of the role and limits of conscience (that is, when conscience can and should be protected). I would argue that, on this relational analysis, the bill is not defensible because of two key features and at least five implications of the bill.

First, with respect to features, it must be noted that the bill protects only those "conscience rights" that pertain to beliefs about the inviolability of human life. Furthermore, it places no burdens whatsoever on the person claiming the protection of "conscience rights" with respect to establishing the basis of the accuracy of claims made in regard to the tenets of their religion or the sincerity or authenticity of the conscience claim. Second, with respect to implications, the following statements would be true if the bill were passed:

- it would be illegal for a hospital to refuse to hire a physician who would not be willing to provide an abortion or, indeed, even to provide a woman with information about abortion as a treatment option even where that would be the only option to save her life;
- it would be illegal for an abortion clinic to fire a physician who would refuse to perform abortions. It would be illegal for a Planned Parenthood helpline designed to provide information on how to access abortion services to fire a nurse who refuses to provide information about the option of abortion in the face of an unwanted pregnancy;
- it would be illegal for a pharmacy to refuse to hire a pharmacist who would refuse to dispense Plan B (an emergency contraception that works after fertilization but before implantation) even if that pharmacist would be the only pharmacist on duty for days at a time with no other pharmacist available for many miles; and
- it would be illegal for a dermatology clinic to refuse to hire a physician unwilling to advise a teenage girl about abortion if she were to become pregnant while on Accutane (the most highly teratogenic drug on the market in Canada).[38]

In sum, the bill could make abortion, a legal and medically necessary service, inaccessible to many women. Many women could face having children that they do not wish to have, and some women could suffer severe psychological trauma (for example, a thirteen-year-old girl forced to carry a fetus to term that resulted from a violent gang rape), severe physical harm (for example, from pre-eclampsia or diabetes), and even death (for example, from heart failure, pulmonary conditions, or clotting disorders). Many more women could have an already difficult situation made more difficult (logistically, psychologically, and physically) as they are forced to overcome obstacles (as opposed to absolute barriers) placed in their way by health care providers engaging in conscientious objection.[39]

Through a Relational Conception of Conscience

The first question to ask when evaluating the bill is whether we should protect health care professionals' conscience at all. The answer to this question, on a relational view, is clearly "yes." As noted by McLeod, conscience is something we do and should value in health care professionals because it "encourages morally responsible agency."[40] We want health care professions to care about morality and so we should, *prima facie*, protect their expressions of conscience.

The next question to ask is whether we should protect health care professionals' conscience as it is protected in the bill. The answer to this question is arguably "no." However, this answer must be broken down since the reasons are complex. First, in order to deserve statutory protection by the state, the conduct being protected must actually be conscience-based. In other words, the conduct must be an actual reflection of moral values and not convenience cloaked in a claim of conscience (for example, not wanting to spend the time on the lengthy conversations with a patient that may accompany a request for an abortion or a referral). However, nothing in the bill requires evidence of the existence of a conscience claim, and so it is not clear that the protected conduct in question (for example, refusals in relation to the provision of abortion services) will even be conscience-based. By not requiring anything more than a mere assertion or even just a perception by a third party of a particular belief, the conscience protected by the bill is at best anemic and at worst illusory. Indeed, in the name of conscience, the bill could simply be protecting preferences and prejudices (for example, a preference not to face abortion protesters when going to work).

Second, even if there is an actual conscience claim, according to McLeod, it might not be of sufficient value to deserve protection given that its protection implies harms for others – in order to deserve protection, conscience claims should be authentic, promote the person's moral integrity, and be grounded in a process of relational retooling.[41] Applying these conditions to the bill, we see that it fails. To be deserving of protection, a conscience claim must be authentic. It must be reflective of what one genuinely values.[42] Yet Bill C-537 fails to limit its protection to authentic conscience claims and, therefore, oversteps its justification. Similarly, a conscience claim does not deserve protection if it does not promote moral integrity. Again, however, the bill fails to limit its protection to claims that represent what the health care provider genuinely believes to be morally right and, therefore, again oversteps its justification.[43] Building on the authenticity and integrity requirements, as McLeod argues, the value of conscience is as provocateur of relational moral retooling – the value of conscience is that it "urges us to take our moral values seriously" and "forces us to rethink those values, after perhaps clarifying for us *what* those values are."[44] For those who are not thoroughgoing deontologists, committed to an anti-abortion position regardless of the consequences for any women (for example, even if the woman will die without the abortion), the process of moral retooling must include reflection on empirical claims (that is, about what the consequences actually are, prior to assessing the value or disvalue of the consequences) as well as reflection on what we ought to believe. And so, for those admitting of at least some role for some consequences, an individual claiming the rights protected in the bill must be well informed about the reasons that women seek abortion in Canada, the barriers to access that confront them, and the other social injustices that have structured her choices and capacity for choice. A health care provider claiming conscience protection should be able to answer the question: "Is the conscience claim grounded in a relational retooling or is it premised upon unreflective false beliefs or beliefs that are not actually related to your position on the inviolability of human life (for example, you mistakenly believe access is possible without you or you have not worked through the difficult moral landscape of the concept of participation, such as providing the service, referring to those who will provide the service, referring to those who will refer, and providing information about where to go to get access or help to access the services)?"[45] An egregious example of a false belief behind a conscience claim is the statement from the CPL cited earlier: "As you know, you could go to almost any other doctor in this city and it would their shortest patient visit of the day – they would send you straight to an abortion clinic." This statement is false on many levels. First, women cannot simply go to "any other doctor in this city" as many physicians are not taking new patients. Second, it is not true that "any other doctor in this city" is willing to provide a referral. Third, not all cities have abortion clinics (indeed, it is a very small minority that have service providers of any sort).[46] Where the claim is not well informed, then, it arguably does not deserve protection. This argument would lead us to a bill that would require the claimant to be expressing a belief that is grounded in a process of serious reflection. The current bill has no such requirement.

Third, moving beyond McLeod's arguments in this volume but consistent with her other writing on a relational conception of conscience, I would argue that even those conscience claims that deserve protection do not necessarily deserve protection at all costs – the value of protecting them may sometimes be outweighed by the value of protecting competing conscience claims and the value of avoiding certain harms.[47] This balancing is required under human rights legislation and so will be discussed further in the next section of this chapter.

This bill overvalues some expressions of conscience, and it places the protection of health care professionals' conscience above the protection of the conscience of women for whom access to abortion is an exercise of their conscience. It also places the protection of some health care professionals' conscience above the protection of the conscience of individuals who wish to establish and run organizations that provide abortion services to women (for example, Henry Morgentaler, whose work has been deeply motivated by conscience). There is no justification provided for doing so. Arguably, this represents an overvaluation of the conscience of anti-abortion health care professionals.

The bill also places the protection of conscience as it relates to the issue of the inviolability of human life over conscience since it relates to many other issues of fundamental importance to many individuals. If conscience must be protected, why is it protected only in relation to the ending or threatening of human life? For example, why not also force hospitals to hire: nurses who will refuse to care for gay or lesbian patients; pharmacists who will refuse to dispense birth control pills to unmarried women; physicians who will refuse to provide artificial insemination to mixed race couples; and Jehovah's Witness surgeons who will refuse to use blood transfusions during surgery? Arguably, the bill represents an overvaluation of conscience as it relates to one specific issue (the value of human life). This bill also places the protection of health care professionals' conscience above the very significant harms for women that are associated with delays and barriers that are facilitated by the respect for conscience that it mandates.

There is a final set of harms that arises given the current health care context (that is, a shortage of family physicians and obstetrician/gynaecologists (ob/gyns) willing to provide abortions and referrals for abortions). Quite simply, we do not have the resources to fill positions with individuals who will not be required to perform the functions associated with the position. There is a finite supply of residency slots in ob/gyn and in family medicine. There is a finite supply of positions for ob/gyns and family physicians in many urban centres (for example, nobody can start a new practice or join an existing ob/gyn practice in Halifax, Nova Scotia). If those scarce positions are filled with individuals who are not willing to provide abortions, there is no way to address the shortage of physicians available to provide abortions and referrals and the consequent harms to women resulting from lack of access. If there was an infinite supply of slots and positions, then this argument would not fly. However, there is not such a supply, and so it can be argued that physicians who fill these slots should not be allowed to exercise conscientious objection to the much-needed functions. In these times of shortage, the objection of an anti-abortion physician to participation in abortion (through provision, referral, or advice) should not get the protection of conscience legislation.

The problem of overvaluing health care providers' conscience over the conscience of others, conscience claims about matters other than the value of life, and the other interests of others is particularly acute since, as McLeod notes, conscience clauses should not be allowed to protect only the powerful groups.[48] Yet this bill protects the powerful (in this case, the right-to-life health care practitioners with access to federal parliamentarians) over those with much less power (in particular, women in need of financially, geographically, and temporally accessible abortion services).

Through a Relational Approach to Rights

It is also useful to reflect on Bill C-537 with reference to human rights instruments (most notably, the *Canadian Charter of Rights and Freedoms* and federal/provincial/territorial human rights legislation), especially when conducting the reflection through a relational lens.[49] Bill C-537 might be challenged as sex discrimination under the *Charter*. The first part of the argument, in a very simplified form, would run as follows: one of the effects of the bill is to reduce access to abortion for women; this creates a disadvantage for pregnant women; and discrimination on the basis of pregnancy is discrimination on the basis of sex and so this is a disadvantage on the basis of sex, which is prohibited under the *Charter*. The response from the proponents of the bill might be that the bill seeks to protect conscience rights – rights that are themselves protected under the *Charter*. However, the *Charter* only protects "sincere" beliefs, and the court has a role in assessing sincerity, which is a question of fact to be answered through reference to, for example, the claimant's credibility and consistency of the claim with other current conduct.[50] Bill C-537 does not require sincerity (either a demonstration or a finding of it), and so it cannot claim that its discriminatory impact is justified by the protection of *Charter*-protected conscience rights. Furthermore, *Charter* jurisprudence makes it very clear that rights must be balanced against one another and that expressions of conscience can – indeed, must – be limited at times when the value of the protection of the conscience will be outweighed by the harms resulting from such protection:

> Conduct which would potentially cause harm to or interference with the rights of others would not automatically be protected. The ultimate protection of any particular Charter right must be measured in relation to other rights and with a view to the underlying context in which the apparent conflict arises.[51]

Evidence of the significant potential harms (when described in light of a rich relational analysis of the damaging effects of allowing health care providers to decline to take part in anything related to abortion) that are associated with the sweeping protections provided for in the bill should be sufficient to persuade the courts to find that the bill is inconsistent with the *Charter* and is therefore unconstitutional. A relational approach could illuminate the hardships that respecting the health care providers' conscience will cause. It could provide support for the claim that the bill protects the conscience rights of some at the expense of the conscience and health rights of others and is not a justifiable limit on these rights in a free and democratic society. The bill does not provide for any consideration of the potential hardships imposed, particularly upon women, by requiring respect for conscientious objections by health care providers. Indeed, it exacerbates them. As such, it is inconsistent with the *Charter* and, arguably, should be struck down.

I would also note here that existing human rights legislation already provides protection for some conscience rights and has an established set of case law to assist in the interpretation of when and how conscience rights should be protected and when and how other interests and rights justify the limitation of expressions of conscience. Human rights legislation, with its capacity for reflecting on the rights and interests of all involved and with its attention to "the underlying context in which the apparent conflict arises,"[52] is far superior (from a relational perspective) to Bill C-537, which seeks to provide absolute rights with respect to conscience, with no space for a consideration of the rights and interests of others or attention to the underlying context within which women seek abortions in Canada.

Consider how a human rights legislation argument, informed by relational theory, would run if an employer sought to force a health care provider to provide abortion services (for example, a referral) to women in the community. First, one would ask whether there is an actual conscientious objection grounded in religion or creed (see the previous discussion of McLeod's relational conception of conscience). If not, then the action would fail. If so, then there would be *prima facie* discrimination on the basis of religion or creed, and the next question would be whether the requirement to perform certain functions constitutes a "bona fide occupational requirement." One could definitely argue that the provision of abortion referrals is a bona fide occupational requirement.[53] First, the purpose of requiring the provision is rationally related to the need for the services (clearly, there is a need for health care providers to provide abortion referrals since many women need advice on where to go for abortion services, and, indeed, referrals are required by hospitals or by law in some jurisdictions).[54] Second, the purpose of the requirement is to ensure that services are available to women and not to punish conscientious objectors. Third, undue hardship will be experienced by women if all conscientious-objecting health care providers are allowed to opt out of providing referrals – while it might be possible to allow opting out of the provision of abortions themselves in large centres with multiple abortion providers, access would be too limited (that is, to the point of undue hardship) if health care providers were allowed to opt out of referrals and, in some locations, the abortions themselves (see the previous relationally driven description of the harms of restricted access). The bona fide occupational requirement would be made out, and conscientious objectors would simply have to provide referrals or get another job since the hardships resulting to women from allowing health care providers to opt out of referrals are simply too great.

In closing, and as McLeod notes and *Charter* and human rights legislation and jurisprudence confirm (particularly when seen through a relational lens), it is important that health care practitioners have a conscience and that this conscience is protected. However, these conclusions do not lead us to this bill. They can lead us to ensure that health care practitioners have the freedom to refuse to participate in abortion (directly or indirectly) where the refusal is grounded in robust conscientious reflection and would not impose undue delay or other costs on women seeking abortion and where the refusal is done in a fashion that does not harm the women seeking abortion (for example, insinuating a negative moral judgment). Of course, in many locations in Canada, this would be quite a rare circumstance given the current shortage of family physicians and abortion providers (both physicians and institutions). These conclusions can also lead us to ensure that health care professionals have the freedom to contribute to the social debate about the ethics of abortion.[55] A bill that protected them from being fired or disciplined by their professional associations or being given poor grades in school for participating in debates about abortion (in writing or in person) would be consistent with this conclusion in regard to the value of conscience and the limits on its protection. However, a bill such as C-537, which does not ensure that the conscience claims that it protects are authentic, promote moral integrity, and are grounded in relational retooling, seriously interferes with the exercise of conscience of many others and contributes to significant harms to the health and well-being of women, is not.

Conclusion

In many ways, pregnant women in Canada are fortunate with respect to the nature and level of state impact on their lives. Abortion is not illegal and, indeed, is considered a medically necessary procedure and is largely funded by the government. Courts do not have the power to order the involuntary confinement or treatment of pregnant women. Very strong statements have been made by the Supreme Court of Canada about women's reproductive autonomy (albeit based on a liberal individualist conception of autonomy). However, security in the reproductive realm for women is at best tenuous and at worst absent for many. Abortions are utterly unavailable, or are available but at an extraordinarily high price, for many women. Efforts have been made to use law and policy to decrease the protection of women's interests.[56] Invitations have been issued to interfere more forcefully and frequently in women's lives.[57] We would be wise to marshall our arguments (developed now through a relational lens) to levy them against current interventions and to be prepared to respond when the state attempts to increase the scope and severity of its interventions.

Notes

I would like to thank all of the participants in the project for their engagement with this chapter and, in particular, Jennifer Llewellyn and Dianne Pothier for their insightful comments on the penultimate draft. I would also like to thank Brad Abernethy for his constant generosity with respect to his exceptional editorial skills.

1 *R. v. Morgentaler*, [1988] 1 S.C.R. 30, 44 D.L.R. (4th) 385, striking down section 251 of the *Criminal Code*, R.S.C. 1970, c. C-34.
2 *Winnipeg Child and Family Services (Northwest Area) v. DFG*, [1997] 3 S.C.R. 925, 152 D.L.R. (4th) 193 [*Winnipeg Child and Family Services*].
3 *Tremblay v. Daigle*, [1989] 2 S.C.R. 530, 62 D.L.R. (4th) 634; *R. v. Sullivan*, [1991] 1 S.C.R. 489; *R. v. Morgentaler*, [1993] 3 S.C.R. 463, 107 D.L.R. (4th) 537.
4 *Canada Health Act*, R.S. 1985, c. C-6, s. 7.
5 *Ibid.* at s. 9.
6 *General Regulation – Medical Services Payment Act*, N.B. Reg. 1984-20, 1984, Sch. 2: "The following are deemed not to be entitled services: (a.1) abortion, unless the abortion is performed by a specialist in the field of obstetrics and gynaecology in a hospital facility approved by the jurisdiction in which the hospital facility is located and two medical practitioners certify in writing that the abortion was medically required." *Excluded Services Regulation*, Man. Reg. 46/93, s. 2.28: "The following services are not insured services ... 28. Therapeutic abortion, unless performed by a medical practioner (a) in a hospital in Manitoba other than a private hospital licenced under the *Private Hospitals Act*; (b) in a hospital outside Manitoba that meets the criteria set out in the Hospital Services Insurance and Administration Regulation made under the Act; or (c) in a facility approved by the minister."
7 Section 11(1) In order to satisfy the criterion respecting portability, the health care insurance plan of a province:

   (a) must not impose any minimum period of residence in the province, or waiting period, in excess of three months before residents of the province are eligible for or entitled to insured health services;
   (b) must provide for and be administered and operated so as to provide for the payment of amounts for the cost of insured health services provided to insured persons while temporarily absent from the province on the basis that

      (i) where the insured health services are provided in Canada, payment for health services is at the rate that is approved by the health care insurance plan of the province in which the services are provided, unless the provinces concerned agree to apportion the cost between them in a different manner, or

      ...

   (c) must provide for and be administered and operated so as to provide for the payment, during any minimum period of residence, or any waiting period, imposed by the health care insurance plan of another province, of the cost of insured health services provided to persons who have ceased to be insured persons by reason of having become residents of that other province, on the same basis as though they had not ceased to be residents of the province.

8 *Interprovincial Reciprocal Billing Agreement,* http://secure.cihi.ca/cihiweb/products/RB_report_2007_e.pdf at Appendix F.

9 *Ibid.*

10 Canadian Institute for Health Information, http://secure.cihi.ca [emphasis added]. In 1989, the following were removed from the excluded services list: routine circumcision of newborn; psychoanalysis; and polysomnograms. In 1991, the following services were added: lithotripsy for gall bladder stones and treatment of port-wine stains on other than the face or neck, regardless of the modality of treatment.

11 Of course, many other barriers to access would still exist. See Jocelyn Downie and Carla Nassar, "Barriers to Access to Abortion through a Legal Lens" (2007) 15 Health L.J. 143. However, one very significant barrier to access would be removed.

12 See, for example, Sanda Rodgers, "Abortion Denied: Bearing the Limits of Law" in Colleen M. Flood, ed., *Just Medicare: What's In, What's Out, How We Decide* (Toronto: University of Toronto Press, 2006) 107; Sanda Rodgers, "Misconceptions: Equality and Reproductive Autonomy in the Supreme Court of Canada" in Sheila McIntyre and Sanda Rodgers, eds., *Diminishing Returns: Inequality and the Canadian Charter of Rights and Freedoms* (Toronto: Butterworths, 2006) 271; Canadian Abortion Rights Action League (CARAL), *Protecting Abortion Rights in Canada: A Special Report to Celebrate the Fifteenth Anniversary of the Decriminalization of Abortion* (Ottawa: CARAL, 2003); Susan Sherwin, *No Longer Patient* (Philadelphia: Temple University Press, 1992).

13 See Jennifer Llewellyn, "Restorative Justice: Thinking Relationally about Justice" in this volume. See also Jennifer J. Llewellyn, "Bridging the Gap between Truth and Reconciliation: Restorative Justice and the Indian Residential School Truth and Reconciliation Commission" in M. Brant-Castellano, L. Archibald, M. DeGagne, eds., *From Truth to Reconciliation: Transforming the Legacy of Residential Schools* (Ottawa: Aboriginal Healing Foundation, 2008) 185; Jennifer J. Llewellyn, "Restorative Justice in Transitions and Beyond: The Justice Potential of Truth Telling Mechanisms for Post-Peace Accord Societies" in T. Borer, ed., *Telling The Truths: Truth Telling and Peace Building in Post-Conflict Societies* (Notre Dame, IN: Notre Dame University Press, 2006) 83; Jennifer J. Llewellyn, "Doing Justice in South Africa: Restorative Justice and Reparations" in C. Villa-Vicencio and E. Doxtader, eds., *Repairing the Unforgiveable: Reparations and Reconstruction in South Africa* (Claremont, South Africa: David Philip Publishers/New Africa Books, 2004) 166; Jennifer J. Llewellyn, "Review of *Aftermath: Violence and the Remaking of a Self*" (2003) 15 C.J.W.L. 392; Jennifer J. Llewellyn, "Justice for South Africa: Restorative Justice and the Truth and Reconciliation Commission" in Christine M. Koggel, ed., *Moral Issues in Global Perspective* (Peterborough, ON: Broadview Press, 1999); Jennifer J. Llewellyn and Robert Howse, *Restorative Justice: A Conceptual Framework* (Ottawa: Law Commission of Canada, 1998) at 1-107.

14 See Jennifer Nedelsky, "The Reciprocal Relation of Judgment and Autonomy" in this volume. See also Jennifer Nedelsky "Embodied Diversity: Challenges to Law" (1997) 42 McGill L.J. 91; Jennifer Nedelsky, "Communities of Judgment and Human Rights" (2000) 1 Theor. Inq. L. 245; Jennifer Nedelsky, "Legislative Judgment and the Enlarged Mentality: Taking Religious Perspectives" in Richard Bauman and Tsvi Kahana, eds., *The Least Examined Branch: The Role of Legislatures in the Constitutional State* (Cambridge: Cambridge University Press, 2006) 93; Jennifer Nedelsky, "Law, Judgment, and Relational Autonomy" in Ronald Beiner and Jennifer Nedelsky, eds., *Judgment, Imagination and Politics: Themes from Kant and Arendt* (Lanham, MD: Rowman and Littlefield, 2001) 103.

15 The following assessment of the *Interprovincial Reciprocal Billing Agreement* (*IRBA*) process is based on a review of the following material: descriptions available online about the Interprovincial Health Insurance Agreements Coordinating Committee (IHIACC) (*Canada Health Act,* http://www.hc-sc.gc.ca/hcs-sss/pubs.cha-lcs/2010-cha-lcs-ar-ra/index-eng.php#nb); an appeal against a refusal by the Ministry of Health and Long-Term Care in Ontario for access

to the agendas and minutes of the IHIACC, Order no. PO-2247, Appeal no. PA-030210-2, Ministry of Health and Long-Term Care, 2004; a letter sent by the chair of the IHIACC to Dawn Fowler (Canadian director of the National Abortion Federation) and Joanna Erdman (director of the Health Equity and Law Clinic at the University of Toronto) in response to a letter from them requesting that the IHIACC review the exclusion of abortion from the excluded services list of the IRBA, remove the exclusion, or, if they decided to retain the exclusion, provide reasons for doing so (Letter from Jean Wright, IHIACC Chair to Joanna N. Erdman and Dawn Fowler (17 November 2008)); and a response sent to the author by Jean Wright in response to a request from the author for information on the IHACC process (Letter from Jean Wright to Jocelyn Downie (22 July 2009)).

16 Letter to Jean Wright from Jocelyn Downie (17 April 2009).
17 Letter from Jean Wright to Joanna N. Erdman and Dawn Fowler (17 November 2008).
18 E-mail from Dawn Fowler to Jocelyn Downie (26 February 2009).
19 Letter from Jean Wright to Jocelyn Downie (22 July 2009).
20 Canada, Health Canada, *Canada Health Act Annual Report 2007-2008* (Ottawa: Health Canada, 2008), at 42, Health Canada, http://www.hc-sc.gc.ca/hcs-sss/pubs/cha-;cs/2008-cha-lcs-ar-ra/page1-eng.php#NB [*Canada Health Act Annual Report*]. Note that the New Brunswick regulations are the subject of an ongoing court challenge (only the standing issue was settled in *Morgentaler v. New Brunswick*, 2009 NBCA 26, 306 D.L.R. (4th) 679).
21 *Canada Health Act Annual Report, supra* note 20 at 42-43.
22 Letter from Jean Wright to Joanna N. Erdman and Dawn Fowler (17 November 2008).
23 This was, in effect, reiterated in a Letter from Jean Wright to Jocelyn Downie (22 July 2009).
24 *Ibid.*
25 Canada, *Interprovincial Health Insurance Agreements Coordinating Committee (IHIACC) "Terms of Reference"* (IHIACC, 2005) at 2 [unpublished, on file with the author].
26 Letter to Jean Wright from Jocelyn Downie (17 April 2009).
27 Bill C-537, *An Act to Amend the Criminal Code (Protection of Conscience Rights in the Health Care Profession)*, 2nd Sess, 39th Parl., 2008, c. 452(2).
28 *Ibid.*
29 Indeed, it subsequently died on the order paper when Prime Minister Stephen Harper prorogued Parliament on 30 December 2009.
30 Conscience legislation is also found in the United States (for example, *Consolidated Appropriations Act, 2005*, Pub. L. No. 108-447, Div. F, Title 2 § 508(d), 118 Stat. 2811 at 3163 (2004) [*Weldon Amendment*]; *Public Health Service Act*, 42 U.S.C. § 238n (1995), s. 245.
31 Sanda Rodgers and Jocelyn Downie, "Access to Abortion," Letter (13 February 2007) 176:4 Can. Med. Assoc. J. 494. See also Sanda Rodgers and Jocelyn Downie, "Abortion: Ensuring Access," Guest Editorial (4 July 2006) 175:1 Can. Med. Assoc. J. 9.
32 Jeff Blackmer, "Clarification of the CMA's Position Concerning Induced Abortion," Letter (24 April 2007) 176:9 Can. Med. Assoc. J. 1310. See also Jeff Blackmer, "Clarification of CMA Policy," E-letter (19 February 2007) Can. Med. Assoc. J. http://www.cmaj.ca/cgi/eletters/176/4/494#7430.
33 Canadian Physicians for Life, Vital Signs Newsletter, Spring/Summer 2007, http://www.physiciansforlife.ca.
34 See discussion of Distribution of Powers (especially chapters 18 and 21) in Peter Hogg, *Canadian Constitutional Law* (Toronto: Carswell, 2009).
35 See Carolyn McLeod, "Taking a Feminist Relational Perspective on Conscience" in this volume.
36 *Ibid.* See also Carolyn McLeod, "Harm or Mere Inconvenience? Denying Women Emergency Contraception" (2010) 25:1 Hypatia 11; Carolyn McLeod, "Referral in the Wake of Conscientious Objection to Abortion" (2008) 23:4 Hypatia 30; Carolyn McLeod, "How to Distinguish Autonomy from Integrity" (2005) 35:1 Can. J. Phil. 107; Carolyn McLeod, "Integrity and Self-Protection" (2004) 35:2 J. Soc. Phil. 216.
37 See generally all of the sources in note 13 and, specifically, Jennifer Llewellyn, "A Healthy Conception of Rights: Thinking Relationally about Rights in a Health Care Context" in Jocelyn Downie and Elaine Gibson, eds., *Health Law at the Supreme Court of Canada* (Toronto: Irwin Law, 2007) 57.

38 A teratogenic drug is a drug that causes damage to an embryo or fetus.
39 Downie and Nassar, *supra* note 11.
40 See McLeod, *supra* note 35.
41 *Ibid.*
42 *Ibid.*
43 *Ibid.*
44 *Ibid.*
45 There are interesting parallels here with the relational conception of judgment used as a lens for the discussion of the *IRBA* earlier in this chapter. This highlights the interplay between conscience and judgment as discussed in chapter 7 (Carolyn McLeod, "Taking a Feminist Relational Perspective on Conscience") and chapter 2 (Jennifer Nedelsky, "The Reciprocal Relation of Judgment and Autonomy") in this volume.
46 See CARAL, *supra* note 12.
47 McLeod, *supra* note 35.
48 See *ibid.*
49 *Canadian Charter of Rights and Freedoms*, Part I of the *Constitution Act, 1982*, being Schedule B to the *Canada Act, 1982* (U.K.) 1982, c. 11 [*Charter*].
50 *Syndicat Northcrest v. Amselem*, [2004] 2 S.C.R. 551 at para. 53 [*Amselem*].
51 *Ibid.* at para. 62. See also *R.B. v. Children's Aid Society of Metropolitan Toronto*, [1995] 1 S.C.R. 315; *Trinity Western University v. British Columbia College of Teachers*, [2001] 1 S.C.R. 772; *A.C. v. Manitoba (Child and Family Services)*, [2009] 2 S.C.R. 181.
52 *Amselem, supra* note 50 at para. 62.
53 For a summary of bona fide occupational requirements, see the Honourable Justice Russel W. Zinn, *The Law of Human Rights in Canada: Practice and Procedure* (Aurora, ON: Canada Law Books, 2009) at c. 14; Stacey Reginald Ball, *Canadian Employment Law* (Aurora, ON: Canada Law Books, 2009) at c. 33.
54 See note 6 in this chapter.
55 See McLeod, *supra* note 35.
56 For example, Bill C-484, *An Act to Amend the Criminal Code (Injuring or Causing the Death of an Unborn Child While Committing an Offence)*, 2nd Sess, 39th Parl. 2007 (a fetal homicide bill). This bill died on the order paper when Parliament was dissolved in September 2008.
57 See, for example, the implied invitation issued in Justice John Major's dissent in *Winnipeg Child and Family Services, supra* note 2.

10
Relational Theory and Indigenous Health: Insights for Law Reform and Policy Development
Constance MacIntosh

This chapter considers the potential of relational theory for improving the conceptualization and treatment of Indigenous health matters. Indigenous health is a particularly pressing matter, given that Indigenous peoples have carried a disproportionate burden of ill health for decades in Canada.[1] The chapter specifically considers how relational theory could inform health laws and policies. It illustrates how relational theory provides a conceptual framework that addresses some of the shortcomings of the social determinants approach to health, which is the approach that currently informs much of Indigenous health policy planning. While the social determinants approach is helpful for identifying elements of the context that informs Indigenous health, and identifying inequalities, its utility is weakened by the fact that it tends to take the individual as its subject and focus upon that which can be expressed in statistical form. Relational theory enables a recasting of the social determinants approach, a route for dislodging it from these constraining tenets. It succeeds in this respect because relational theory is grounded, in part, in the recognition of the co-constitutive nature of community and individuals, which has several important consequences.[2] One of these consequences is that relational theory offers an approach to understanding health determinants that resonates better with Indigenous theories of health. Another is that relational theory enables the identification of relational dimensions of inequality, which may be invisible from a traditional social determinants approach but which are essential for understanding what sort of change is necessary to improve the health and well-being of Indigenous peoples.

These propositions are first explored and explained in the second part of this chapter and then illuminated through a series of interrelated case studies in the third part. One case study considers statute-based definitions, which categorize Indigenous peoples as either "Indian" or not "Indian." It illustrates how these categories, which have a deep history in administrative aspects of the colonial assimilation project, are used to determine access and funding rights in contemporary health policy and programming. In practice, these distinctions could produce access and care outcomes that are statistically neutral on a population-based level, as it may be possible for care and services to be obtained through alternate routes. From a traditional social determinants perspective, statistical neutrality renders the impact of a phenomenon invisible. As shown in detail in the case study, this feature of the social determinants approach makes it hard to identify or even articulate the problems that these distinctions do produce and perpetuate for the well-being of Indigenous communities. A relational approach, on the other hand, provides an optic of analysis and a conceptual framework that can articulate the harm and point to remedies. In particular, it enables the identification of how these health policies produce incentives to differentiate between people on grounds that disable respectful collective relations and deny memory. It does so in part by enabling a rubric that is better able to give expression to inter- and cross-generational consequences. Other case studies similarly point to how health policies and programs serve to support and encourage certain conceptualizations of community and inclusion, where the consequences of those conceptualizations are once again difficult to capture or articulate if one only has recourse to a social determinants approach.

Part of the argument that underlies this chapter is that laws and policies that reflect a relationally informed understanding of such values as equality,[3] autonomy,[4] and justice[5] can help remedy health and other inequalities that arise, or are perpetuated, through the structure of institutional and administrative health arrangements and practices. However, several caveats are in order. One is about the nature of law and social change. Another is about the need to exercise caution when making generalizations about Indigenous peoples. First, the mere fact that a law or policy is enacted – whether relationally informed or otherwise – will not remedy all of the health and other inequalities that Indigenous people experience. For example, when laws or policies target the health inequalities of Indigenous peoples, the law or policy is a public expression that the inequalities are unjust and merit collective or societal recognition and redressing.[6] These legally mandated institutional shifts may have considerable positive consequences for how individuals are able to make choices or experience autonomy. However, while "knowledge creates relationships," "relationships come into being when the knowledge does," and law does have normative force in terms of knowledge production. That is, law's reach has its limits.[7] It cannot cause any individual or community to reflect upon the moral consequences of being constituted relationally, to experience a sense of responsibility about how relational co-constitution unfolds,[8] or to otherwise induce shifts in broader societal and interpersonal recognition of what constitutes inequality. To make a blunt analogy, law cannot force a racist to lose their racism. Although law can restrain racist practices in certain prescribed contexts and instances, and thereby discourage oppression, when it comes to interpersonal exchanges it can only encourage the formation of relationships of equality, which, in turn, support the likelihood of individuals and communities coming to mutually flourish.

Second, whenever the situation of Indigenous peoples is discussed, it is essential to ensure that their diversities are not subsumed by inappropriate assumptions of commonalities.[9] Although the health gap between Indigenous peoples and their non-Indigenous neighbours is consistently large, health care structures and issues still vary enormously, regardless of whether one considers their health situation on a national, provincial, regional, or community level.[10] For example, Indigenous peoples in Canada live in (and may seasonally commute between) cities, small towns, rural areas, and reserves, each setting offering distinct, often disparate community supports and social networks. Some receive public health programming from the federal government, some through band council–governed institutions, some from municipal and provincial levels of government.[11] Some experience a fairly direct line of service, while others experience difficulty in convincing any service provider that they fall within its jurisdictional mandate.[12] Some can access primary health care services with general ease, while others have infrequent access or must travel considerable distances. Some individuals have the option of accessing health care facilities that pride themselves on their culturally sensitive character, while other individuals (particularly those persons residing in urban centres) may not.[13] And, of course, Indigenous peoples represent a diversity of cultures and languages and, presumably with these differences, different aspirations, understandings, and expectations about health and what counts as good care.

There is also the much larger political picture to consider. There are a host of diverse political histories for each Indigenous group in regard to treaties, land claim settlements, and relations with local non-Indigenous communities, all of which may affect how various Indigenous people and peoples may understand their engagement with federal and provincial health law and policy. For example, there are ongoing disputes as to whether the federal government is lawfully obliged to provide health benefits and services to (some portion) of the Indigenous population, either due to treaty promises or as a consequence of historically based fiduciary obligations, or alternatively whether any decision by the federal Crown to provide benefits is entirely at the Crown's discretion.[14]

This diversity is accompanied, however, by some commonalities that lend themselves well to a relational analysis and that are important for understanding the unique health situation of Indigenous peoples. One commonality is the fact of being descended from peoples who have been systematically and over a series of generations subjected to distinct treatment under state law and policy.[15] Much of this state law and policy has been directed at undermining and eradicating *all* Indigenous peoples' cultures and sense of belonging to (their own) political communities.[16] This history has resulted in a fairly unique body of generally shared harms and vulnerabilities.[17] One particularly egregious example of such practices is described in Susan Campbell's work in the first part of this volume.[18] Campbell describes the residential school system as having operated to oblige Indigenous children to repress "old identities" and replace them with "new social memories" to enable assimilation. Cast as a systemic assault on memory, Campbell's work provides considerable insight into why these sorts of policies and practices had, and continue to have, consequences for all Indigenous peoples, not only those who attended residential schools. The fact that Indigenous peoples have had their histories and connections with the past systematically assailed through laws and policies is important to bring to any contemporary analysis. Scholars of Indigenous health such as Fred Wein and Charlotte Loppe Reading connect such "historic trauma" with the health status of current and future generations of Indigenous people.[19] Loppe Reading and Wein write that "[t]he collective burden of a repressive colonial system has created conditions of physical, psychological, economic and political disadvantage for Aboriginal peoples."[20] As I have similarly written elsewhere, approaches to the health situation of Indigenous peoples, "which are not informed by a decolonizing ethic that is responsive to factors such as political identity, cultural needs and historic wrongs may in many cases be of limited utility because it will not assuage the underlying conditions of political marginalization, alienation, and poverty."[21] I return to this commonality in the case studies in the third part of this chapter.

Law and policy have also impacted upon the lives of all Indigenous peoples through the legal and institutionalized division of the Indigenous population into various categories, which, in turn, are operationalized to signal different sorts of statuses and associated rights. These categories are deeply contested.[22] They have effectively created a contingent array of historically constituted groups, imposing equally contingent divisions within and across communities. This matter will centrally inform the case study analysis of health policy discussed later in the chapter. Having clarified grounds upon which generalizations must be avoided, as well as having identified several commonalities that are relevant for thinking about the health of Indigenous peoples, I turn now to showing how relational theory articulates with existing approaches to forming or analyzing health policy. This discussion, in turn, sets the stage for the section of the chapter in which I apply a relational lens to various existing Indigenous health policies.

Relational Theory, the Social Determinants Approach to Health, and Indigenous Theories of Health

How does relational theory articulate with the social determinants approach to health, which currently plays a dominant role in formulating health policy in Canada? Perhaps more importantly, how do relational theory and the social determinants of health approach fit with the conceptualizations of health that Indigenous representative bodies seek to have reflected in health policy?[23] For insight on Indigenous theories of health, I turn to the National Aboriginal Health Organization (NAHO), which is designed and controlled by Indigenous people and whose objective is to influence and advocate for the health and well-being of all Indigenous people in Canada.[24] NAHO offers a description of what health can typically be taken to mean for most Indigenous peoples:

> For Indigenous Peoples ... the inter-relationships between the physical, mental, spiritual, and emotional aspects of being are integral to individual and community health. This holistic view ... is often described in relation to non-medical, or social, determinants of health, such as education, housing, economic status, social capital, etc. Relying solely on bio-medical concepts of disease and of health ... is not necessarily an effective system for disease prevention and public health in Aboriginal populations. Culture and ethnicity are among the key determinants of health now being recognized by Health Canada.[25]

Loppie Reading and Wein similarly write that Indigenous ideologies of health can generally be characterized as holistic ones, grounded in the "interrelatedness" of "physical, spiritual, emotional and mental dimensions" and reflective of a "collectivist" approach to perceiving and addressing health.[26] Obviously, some Indigenous people or groups of people may hold a different view, but given the authority of these sources it seems fair to take these descriptions as reflecting a commonly held theory of health.

How does this approach to health, and the factors that must be considered to understand whether a person is healthy, articulate with a relational approach? They fit together. For example, in Susan Sherwin's chapter in this volume, she stresses that from the perspective of relational theory "identities are formed through personal and political (intimate and impersonal) relationships," which are themselves socially, economically, and historically situated.[27] Jennifer Llewellyn's explanation of how relational theory informs justice similarly ties the presence of justice to the existence of certain "dynamics of relationship."[28] There is a clear resonance between the focus upon interrelationships and collectivist perspectives, which is expressed as being central to the Indigenous understanding of health, and the starting point of relationality, which focuses squarely upon complexes of interdependence.

What of the social determinants approach to health? How does it engage the Indigenous theory of health? Health Canada describes the social determinants approach, and how it broadens what informs health policy formation, as follows:

> There is strong evidence indicating that factors outside the health care system significantly affect health. These "determinants of health" include income and social status, social support networks, education, employment and working conditions, physical environments, social environments, biology and genetic endowment, personal health practices and coping skills, health child development, health services, gender and culture.[29]

Thus, Health Canada identifies "culture" as a health determinant. This fact is taken by NAHO in the earlier quote as signalling, to some degree, the formal recognition of the Indigenous conceptual framework for understanding health as being a relevant determinant – one that should play a factor in health policy formation.[30] For reasons that are interwoven into the following text, I question whether the Indigenous theory of health actually does find substantial expression in the social determinants of health approach, as it is usually formulated.[31] I turn now to exploring the social determinants approach, both for its strengths and its weaknesses. My intention is not to dismiss the social determinants approach but, rather, to illustrate how relational theory can bring the social determinants approach more in line with the Indigenous theory of health and thus improve approaches to health policy formation.

The social determinants approach is a very influential one, and Canada is not alone in ascribing merit to this model as a method for understanding the complex factors that are at play when it comes to health. The World Health Organization (WHO) also espouses this approach. The WHO's Commission on Social Determinants of Health provides the following explanation of what social determinants are and how they relate to health as well as adding an explicit emphasis that ties the social determinants approach to identifying inequalities:

> Poor and unequal living conditions are, in their turn, the consequence of deeper structural conditions that together fashion the way societies are organized – poor social policies and programmes, unfair economic arrangements, and bad politics ... Daily living conditions, themselves the result of these structural drivers, together constitute the social determinants of health.[32]

The social determinants approach is thus open-ended, contextual, and responsive to actual networks and, due to its focus upon ferreting out social injustice through health inequities, permits the specific factors (or relevant determinants) to change with the circumstances.[33] Thus, some Indigenous health researchers try to shape the social determinants approach to meet their needs by composing distinct lists of Indigenous health determinants.[34] The social determinant approach also importantly draws connections between matters that may otherwise be considered as distinct phenomena. One can see some resonance here with the Indigenous approach. The value of the connective insights that are made visible through the social determinants approach has also been recognized and taken up by some relational theorists in their work. For example, Catriona Mackenzie and Natalie Stoljar ground the relational concept of the self as "formed within the context of social relationships and shaped by a complex of intersecting social determinants, such as race, class, gender and ethnicity."[35] This extract from Mackenzie and Stoljars' writing illustrates how the social determinants approach and the relational approach can be complementary. Where the social determinants approach brings in matters that take the individual as its focus of inquiry and are reducible to statistics, such as the "race, class, gender and ethnicity" of a person, relationality operationalizes "the context of social relations."[36] That is, it forces an expansion of scope beyond the individual because relations "require other elements to complete them."[37] They can only be understood by pulling in multiple actors.

To elaborate, while the social determinants approach appears to be an encompassing perspective for thinking about many of the "structural drivers" that influence health equity or inequity, when considered in relation to Indigenous peoples it is not clear that it is capable of meaningfully engaging the consequences of the historical and continuing inter- and cross-generational considerations that affect Indigenous health and well-being just by invoking culture as a determinant.[38] These matters are entailed, however, by a relational analysis. The recognition of historical and intergenerational relations and experiences are central to a relational approach, as these relations are co-constitutive on a multiplicity of levels. The challenge of understanding how a social determinants approach actually illuminates the health situation of Indigenous peoples was commented upon by the WHO in its omnibus report on social determinants. The WHO describes the breadth of the needs that must be captured, which it understands to be the following:

> Indigenous Peoples are unique culturally, historically, ecologically, geographically and politically by virtue of their ancestors' original and long-standing nationhood and their use and occupancy of the land. Colonialism has deterritorialized and has imposed social, political, and economic structures upon Indigenous Peoples ... Indigenous Peoples' lives continue to be governed by specific and particular laws and regulations that apply to no other members of civil states.[39]

As a result of these unique factors, the WHO observes that "Indigenous Peoples have distinct status and specific needs relative to others. Indigenous People's unique status must therefore be considered separately from generalized or more universal social exclusion discussions."[40]

Not surprisingly, it is hard to come by the depth and scope that the WHO states is necessary for a social determinants approach to inform health policy for Indigenous peoples, although scholars of Indigenous health are certainly striving to find ways to do so.[41] The content of the chapter on Indigenous peoples in the leading Canadian textbook on the social determinants of health may be considered to be illustrative of what usually happens in practice.[42] Just as Health Canada identifies "culture" as a determinant of health, so too does the chapter's author, Chandrakant Shah, identify "Aboriginal status" as a determinant of health. This determinant was selected to signal "the interaction of culture, public policy, and the mechanisms by which systemic exclusion from participation in Canadian life profoundly affects [Aboriginal] health." In reading the chapter, though, one finds that the chapter itself does little more than apply the usual categories of social determinants data collection to Indigenous peoples and so largely consists of a recitation of statistics and data listed under various headings.[43] The text provides a clear snapshot of living conditions and of quantifiable inequalities, which is indeed important information to convey. However, the interrelationships that NAHO describes as essential for understanding the Indigenous conception of health, the "interchange" that the chapter's author seeks, and the intergenerational historicity that the WHO evokes, fail to be engaged or mobilized within the analysis. As a result, the text makes little ground in illuminating the diachronic connections that so obviously inform the health situation of Indigenous peoples. We can see the outcome – poor health – but not the complexity that produces and perpetuates the outcome.

This is not to belittle the work of these scholars but, rather, to point to the challenge of making the social determinants approach meaningful for informing Indigenous health policy. Indeed, the WHO also struggles to meet its described benchmarks for mobilizing the social determinants approach when it comes to understanding the health situation of Indigenous peoples. A major collaborative and international report that was to represent connections between social determinants and Indigenous health, and which was overseen by the WHO Commission on Social Determinants of Health, was acknowledged by the WHO to be incomplete since "its main focus is on differential health outcomes."[44] That is, despite extensive participation and contributions from Indigenous health experts, policy groups, and Indigenous communities, they only produced the traditional collection of comparative statistics about housing, poverty, education, and so forth that are present in most discussions of social determinants. Once again, although the collection and dissemination of this data is very important, the report

provides little illumination of the more dynamic and situated understanding of Indigenous peoples' situations, which is clearly contemplated as being
necessary by the WHO and NAHO. The social determinants approach,
through its identification of health inequities and underlying structural
drivers, is well equipped to ferret out the fact that social injustice and con-
comitant harm are present in some types of situations. However, it requires
tools and further methodologies to understand why the harm is present and
what may be necessary to remedy these harms. It also misses some of the
harms. As illustrated in the case studies in the third part of this chapter,
relational theory's collectivist premise, and its attentiveness to interrelations,
offers a framework in which the health situation of Indigenous peoples can
be both diachronically and synchronically informed. It can identify phenomena that cannot be captured – much less addressed – from a traditional
social determinants approach. This recognition moves us closer to achieving
the scope of understanding that the WHO strives for through its deployment
of the social determinants approach and enables a practice that resonates
with NAHO's description of the Indigenous understanding of health. As with
Sherwin's critique of moral duties in this volume, which recognizes that
these duties tend to be considered as though they can be understood and
engaged in isolation, there is much that is left out of the analysis if the
dynamic play of interrelations is not acknowledged.[45] The relationally informed decision to take the fact of relationship as the starting point "because
relationship is essential to the making and unmaking of the human self"
can dislodge the limitations flowing from the individualistic and statistic-
driven focus of the social determinants approach.[46]

To summarize, there are two key propositions that have been introduced
here. First, I am not proposing that the social determinants approach ought
to be turned away from in the face of relational theory. Rather, I am proposing that the social determinants approach can be more effectively mobilized
and enriched if modified to take advantage of relational insights. Second,
an approach to the social determinants of health that is informed by relational theory is of particular value for understanding the health situation
of Indigenous peoples. This is because, based upon statements from NAHO
and others, the Indigenous theory of health appears to be a relational one.
These propositions are developed further in the following section, where I
turn to applying these propositions to some case studies.

Exploring Applications: Relationality, *Indian Act* Categories, and Indigenous Health

This section considers what insights are gained by applying relational theory
to some aspects of how health services and programming for Indigenous
persons are currently structured. The analysis ultimately illustrates how
health policy and practices may shape Indigenous peoples' relational know-

ledge and experiences in a way that undermines the realization of individual and community autonomy. In particular, it shows how statute-based statuses – which are taken up into health programming – may impede the development of positive self-definition and autonomous personhood through relationships as well as limit choices to ones that largely perpetuate historic oppression. As a result, health, as understood both from an Indigenous and a relational perspective, becomes a distant goal.

Health Divisions

Although general jurisdiction over health matters is provincial, in some instances the federal government also has authority over health.[47] Section 91(24) of the Canadian Constitution assigns jurisdiction over "Indians and lands reserved to the Indians" to the federal government, which has been taken to mean that the health of "Indians" is a federal matter.[48] As a matter of policy, the federal government only considers persons whose names have been entered on a registry of "Indians" (who are colloquially referred to as "having status" or "being registered") to fall within its health envelope.[49] The terms for being registered are dictated by the federal government in the *Indian Act*, and these terms are arbitrary, complex, and confusing.[50] In most cases, they require an Indigenous person to have a family history where no more than one of either their two parents or four grandparents was *not* registered as an "Indian" (that is, in general, five of the six must have been registered). So to generalize about the legislation, one generation of procreation with non-registered persons is permissible, but two in a row will usually result in children who do not have the right to be registered according to the terms of the legislation. Variations on such a descent-based system have been in place since 1869.[51] It is important to note that under the *Indian Act*, Indian bands are able to take control of their membership list, which has led to some bands choosing to divorce their criteria for band membership from the status criteria. Band membership carries a distinct set of rights, which include the right to live on a First Nations' reserve. To be clear, neither being a member of a band nor living within an Indigenous community is recognized by the federal government as relevant for qualifying for status.

The result is the existence of health inequalities between Indigenous peoples as a result of the considerable differences in the health services and benefits provided by the federal government to those Indigenous peoples it considers to fall under its jurisdiction and those provided to Indigenous persons by provincial governments.[52] Of particular note is the federal policy to provide coverage for health needs that are outside the scope of most provincial health care benefits plans. The awkwardly named Non-Insured Health Benefits program (NIHB) includes coverage for prescription medication, vision care (including glasses), medical transportation, and dental work.

Given the structure of the *Indian Act*'s terms for eligibility for registration, persons within the same communities and households may have different rights when it comes to receiving these health services and benefits, depending upon how their patterns of sexual and biological relationships – with spouses, children, and parents – fits the federal government's criteria. For example, if a registered woman has one parent who is not status, any children that she has with a registered man will be registerable. However, any children she may have with a man who is not registered, or whose status is not revealed, will not be registerable. Although as a matter of federal policy all children born to registered women receive full federal benefits at birth, these benefits are withdrawn from non-registered children when they reach one year of age.[53] And, obviously, no such benefits are offered to the children of Indigenous families where both parents are non-status or Métis, despite often living in considerable numbers in the same or adjacent communities.[54]

This system, thus, has the potential to create troubling inequalities within families and across populations who have historically self-identified as members of the same communities. On its face, these inequalities are about levels of health benefits. From a traditional social determinants perspective – instead of one that draws upon the insights from relationality – this matter may not register as representing inequities because inequities within a social determinants framework are identified through *differential* health outcomes or levels of service. Moreover, it may well be the case that in some instances non-registerable community members, or Indigenous communities made up of "non-status" persons, end up with the same statistical health outcomes, perhaps as a result of services being covered by other means. For example, coverage may arise through provincial social assistance programs, work-related health plans, or the individual or family covering their own costs. If the health outcome of the policy distinction is statistically neutral within the Indigenous community or population, then the health policy would not create a differential health outcome or health inequity and so would not normally be seen as a structural driver of social determinants of health. The policy would therefore simply pass under the radar as a matter that does not register as negatively affecting the health and well-being of Indigenous peoples. Relational insights trouble this conclusion. They do so by adding the historic and intergenerational complexity that the WHO would seek to bring to a social determinants approach.

From a relational perspective, this legislatively informed approach to health delivery would be problematic but not because health services cannot be patched together from other venues to create an equal service environment. Rather, the problem would be due to the fact that the health service situation is built upon an institutional and historic structure that affronts that which ought to be cherished and enabled pursuant to relational conceptions of what is necessary to realize autonomy, equality, and ownership of memory. People do not just live "in the moment" (and the current moment is what the social determinants toolkit is arguably best at telling us about). They also live – and the multiple valances of this phrase are fully intended – through the past and through their past, current, and future relations.

Floundering, Not Flourishing: Inter- and Cross-Generational Disruption

In Llewellyn's chapter in this volume, she describes relational theory as recognizing the "human connection[s] that are necessary to allow human selves to exist and flourish."[55] This flourishing, she writes, "requires relationships marked by equal respect, concern and dignity."[56] The biological and descent-based criteria of the *Indian Act* erode the possibilities of such relationships developing or being sustained, by imposing divisions and separations that are not only at odds with biological, affinal, and historic relationships but also affront the possibilities of community exercises of autonomy (this last point is returned to later in this chapter). Individuals without status often report being treated as though the fact of not meeting statutory criteria for status signals that they lack something at their core that is possessed by status individuals – that they have lost some sort of authentic connection to indigeneity.[57] This perspective – that status means something about who a person can claim themselves to be and expect to be recognized as – is not only held by some non-Indigenous people.[58] Laws of this sort may also be internalized by Indigenous peoples, who, as John Borrows observes, thereby become "recruits ... in the state's troubling boundary patrol" activities of judging who does and does not count as authentically Indigenous.[59] The relational experience of co-constitution with and by others is an oppressive one.

In this volume, Françoise Baylis writes that from a relational perspective "we are who we say we are and who others will let us be," and Sue Campbell shows how certain relationships prevent us from forming certain identities by assaulting our memories and understandings of our relations and collective history.[60] Part of what they evoke, I believe, is that when institutional structures signal that a person is not connected or deserving recognition on the same terms as other community members, the claim to still belong is placed under considerable stress. The understanding of self as belonging may become diminished to a wish for others to recognize oneself as belonging – that is, the experience is of longing, not belonging – a matter that is described in terms of identity stability in Baylis' chapter in this volume. The legislated terms that instantiate an arbitrary distinction are translated through policy into a reified and embodied form whenever a status or non-status person seeks certain health services. At the very least, it is a source of frustration and discomfort between those who are and are not recognized under the legislation. At worst, it enables relational experiences of alienation given that commonalities for belonging and equal treatment are proscribed by a federal administrative agenda, not by Indigenous peoples.

One might suggest that a response to this situation is to adopt procreative strategies. For example, those unregisterable persons who want their children to have status could strategize to procreate with those whose immediate ancestry deems the children of such a union to "count" under the terms of the *Indian Act.* Those with status who require another registered person as a procreative partner to secure the status of their children could have procreative relations accordingly. Although this suggestion may seem flippant, it is put forward with some seriousness and for several reasons. First, as recently observed by the British Columbia Court of Appeal, the very structure of the legislative scheme, and how it is deployed within federal policy practices, has indeed led people to have "made decisions and planned their lives on the basis ... of whether or not they have Indian status."[61] Second, it is put forward because some communities – as entire communities – have responded to these choices by refusing to participate in the status system's approach to recognizing relations and so have effectively opted out of the *Indian Act,* despite the economic hardship that this decision has created for them.[62] Third, these possibilities and consequences are sometimes discussed and considered – often in the form of joking, but joking with an edge – in conversations about sexual or marriage choices.[63] In these circumstances, one's sense of personhood and the sort of relations one can have with others is garnered in relation to (or against) obtaining or sustaining "status."

Sherwin's work on relational autonomy and her distinctions between acting with agency versus possessing autonomy offer insight into why, from the perspective of relational theory, the answer to these inequalities and imposed divisions is not in being more sexually strategic so that the divisions are avoided on an embodied level.[64] In other words, one does not beat the system by playing it. Sherwin writes: "When social conditions are structured to reward individual women for complying with oppressive norms and to punish them for resisting those norms, most women will pragmatically choose compliance. This pragmatic decision is an expression of 'agency.'"[65] Sherwin uses the term autonomy, on the other hand,

> to refer to actions that are consistent with a person's broader interests, values and commitments, including the well-being of her group (based on gender, race, class, sexual orientation, age, ethnicity, and so on). To be autonomous, an action must not only reflect reasonable calculation of the benefits and costs at issue given the existing background conditions; it must also not

work against the promotion of important projects and values (including reducing the impact of oppression on one's group).[66]

On a practical level, it is clearly commensurate with one's interests to secure for one's children this range of health benefits and so to procreate accordingly. And at the group level of Indigenous communities, it is clearly to their collective interest that their children receive these benefits, especially knowing the abysmal statistics regarding the health of Indigenous children.[67] However, the notion of understanding such strategies as expressions of autonomy fades in the face of how such choices fail to stand against group oppression, sliding as they do into acting out – with one's very body and affinal decisions – a legislated definition of relationships worth recognizing – "status." Writing about colonial interference with Indigenous peoples' societies, and drawing upon the double meaning of "intercourse" as signalling both sexual relations as well as political exchanges, John Borrows asserts that "colonial societies continue to meddle with Indigenous intercourse when they prevent the passage of Indigenous citizenship in accordance with Indigenous peoples' natural biological and political processes."[68] The consequences and perpetuation of this meddling through the instantiation of racist legislated distinctions by way of health and other policies is difficult to capture from a traditional social determinants optic, but it is clearly illuminated when the nature of how relationships are being co-constituted is brought into play.

It is not surprising, given that they live with this state-created apparatus of distinctions that is constantly at play, that Indigenous peoples may conduct themselves in relation to this apparatus. In this case, "command coincides with control to continue colonialism's forced confinements."[69] The inherent "injustice and intolerability" of such situations entrenches stressors and divisions that promote

> Indigenous assimilation and extinction because many people are forced or feel compelled to flee colonialism's firm grip. Alternately, many nestle themselves ever more deeply in its grasp by being in a constant reactive mode, setting their identity solely through oppositional politics, which gives colonialism the power to define the scope of their struggle.[70]

Health policy in these instances, though not necessarily producing a differential quantifiable outcome, is deeply harmful because it encourages oppositional connections and creates choices that tend towards perpetuating oppression. In her discussion of relational autonomy, Sherwin highlights the importance of considering what options are available to individuals and communities and what options are absent. What is immediately obvious is that there is no option offered to Indigenous peoples to play a role in the political process of determining the criteria that are at play. They are left to react, despite the deep consequences of such policies for both individuals and communities.

The problematic aspects of how relationships, community, and self are co-constituted here – in a manner that perpetuates colonially inspired administrative distinctions – is augmented by the federal government's funding approach to its health transfer process. This is a joint federal/Aboriginal initiative to transfer administrative responsibilities over community health programming, which has been (or is currently) planned and delivered by federal agencies to First Nation communities (that is, reserve-based communities).[71] So, under this initiative, First Nations can decide upon their own priorities for how to allocate their funding and the method for delivering such pre-existing community health programs as Communicable Disease Control, Treatment Services, Prenatal Nutrition, and Building Healthy. The level of potential empowerment through these programs is considerable (and this point is taken up later in this chapter).

However, there is once again a tension mitigating against enabling the sorts of institutional, community, and personal relationships that encourage respect, autonomy, mutual concern, and equality. This tension arises due to the funding formula. Current federal policy is that as long as the federal government delivers community health programming, program funding is to reflect the actual number of persons who live in a given Indigenous community, regardless of whether they have status.[72] However, if the programming is transferred, the funding structure is revised to reflect the federal government's status system. Funds to be transferred to enable the community to deliver the programs are calibrated against the number of registered "Indians" who live on-reserve at the time the transfer takes place, not the number of persons with band membership or who otherwise live in the community, or who were actually participating in those community health programs while they were under federal control.[73] Once again, the mechanisms for distinction that are described and legitimated under the *Indian Act* are mobilized in the context of health policy. Although program funding is increased pursuant to a standardized cost-indexing formula, no increases are made to reflect changes to the actual costs or to the actual size of the population served nor to respond to the community's own definition of who belongs or who needs to be served by the program for their community to be healthy.

Such a method for assessing funding once again encourages the dividing of communities, of creating a sense of rightful belonging[74] (if one's body "causes" resources to come into the community) or perhaps of practical and social disenfranchisement (if one's body will draw upon, but not "merit," contributions being made to the financial resource base). Recall, as noted earlier, that Indigenous communities have the right to set their own band membership criteria, and some have done so, resulting in persons living in reserve communities who do not have status. A community that links its band membership criteria to eligibility for registration under the *Indian Act* would receive funding that recognizes the existence of its full population, and so it would be, one would expect, reasonably supported to provide its members with community health programming (or at least as well supported as it was before the transfer.) One example of such a community is the Sawridge Band in Alberta. This band has gained some notoriety for its efforts to not only limit band membership to those who would qualify for registration or status but also to a subset of status "Indians" – those who would have also qualified for status under a prior version of the *Indian Act* that was repealed in 1985 because it was blatantly sexually discriminatory. Where belonging is constituted in a sexually discriminatory way, it is necessarily an oppressive sense of community that results – a community that cannot enable relationships of respect and equality. On the other hand, a community that exercises its power to define membership in a way that ignores how the state defines an "Indian" in the *Indian Act* is, effectively, treated by the funding formula as though they have committed a fundamental error. The legitimacy of the connections that a community may understand as unifying its membership are once again structurally denied in so far as they stray from the federal position on what sorts of relationships merit recognition.

The irony of the situation cannot be overstated. As long as the federal government itself continues to provide community health programming, all persons who live within the community receive these services, regardless of their status. It is only when community members seek to define the goals and values of community health for themselves, and to deliver the practices that they believe enable these goals, that the structure of the *Indian Act* induces a tension about rightful belonging. That is, it only arises when a community seeks to assert autonomy as a community. And so we see another instance of where health policy undermines expressions of collective autonomy and so undermines the realization of health, as understood from a relational and Indigenous perspective.

Once again, one could ask whether a community can raise funds elsewhere or perhaps suggest that it is irresponsible for "divided" communities to enter into transfer arrangements unless they already have an alternate funding source in hand so that their community's integrity is not strained. I believe these options may oversimplify the situation. Certainly, community members could rally together on the basis of their mutual (self-)recognition. Indeed, one could argue from a relational perspective that if individuals value equality and practices of mutual respect then they cannot help but do so. The point, though, is that federal law, coupled with federal health policy, may in this instance serve to nurture the formation of relationships that feature divisions and oppositions instead of the features that enable communities to flourish.[75] In addition, one cannot assume that distinctions induced by the *Indian Act* can just be walked away from given how well instantiated they are within the mindset of many Indigenous peoples. Once knowledge of how status would, does, or has played out is there, to draw upon Marilyn Strathern once again, "information about kin is not something that can be selected or rejected as information. Information already bestows identity."[76]

Bonita Lawrence's writing is particularly helpful for understanding this issue. She writes that "[t]o treat the *Indian Act* merely as a set of policies to be repealed, or even as a genocidal scheme in which we can simply choose not to believe, belies how a classificatory system produces ways of thinking – a grammar – that embeds itself in every attempt to change it."[77] Lawrence observes that the *Indian Act*–based shaping of self and community identity are "now so familiar as to almost seem 'natural'" and so is the idea that rights can be legitimately aligned with those legislated identities.[78] The struggle, then, is to counter how the *Indian Act* has constructed, and continues to construct, identity and relationships in a way that detaches them from the collective interests of the community if it is to realize autonomy.[79] These interests pivotally include developing understandings of who belongs, freed from the constraints that reward those who stick to the *Indian Act* and punish those who understand their membership more broadly. Once again, Sherwin's writing adds insight. She comments that "to make a judgment about the degree of autonomy that may be present in a given context, we must examine the types of options on offer and ask questions about how these have arisen and also inquire about options that are not available or accessible."[80] The option on offer is to self-administer a system whose logics reflect historic strategies to enable assimilation through racist and sexist notions of relationship, community, and Aboriginal authenticity.[81] The restriction on autonomy is clear.

Relational Theory and Health Transfer Policy: Toward Mending Disruptions

Although participating in health transfer may have divisive consequences, the research and writing of Michael Chandler and Christopher Lalonde on Indigenous youth suicide suggests an alignment between participation in health transfer and experiences of individual and collective relational autonomy in British Columbia. In their work, they set out to understand why the suicide rate for Indigenous youth in British Colombia was reported to be five to seven times greater than the national average.[82] Their findings point to factors that seem to correlate with Indigenous communities and individuals flourishing and so lend insight to the topic of this chapter.

In a series of two studies, one covering 1987-92[83] and the second spanning 1993-2000,[84] Chandler and Lalonde investigated youth suicides by members of individual bands and tribal council groups. Their first finding, which shook public perception that suicide was a pan-Indigenous issue, was that 90 percent of the suicides occurred in less than 10 percent of the Indigenous communities. Chandler and Lalonde developed a study to try to understand these figures. A bit of background is in order. Chandler and Lalonde's previous work on youth suicide had led them to develop a hypothesis linking suicide with the presence or absence of "key identity-preserving practices."[85] The links between their hypothesis and relational theory become apparent in the following passage:

[T]he successful development and maintenance of an "identity" (any "identity" – including the self-identities of individual persons and the shared cultural identities of whole communities) necessarily requires that there always be in place some workable personal or collective continuity-preserving mechanism capable of vouchsafing necessary claims of persistence in the face of inevitable change. Life (whether personal life or cultural life) is of course temporally vectored and thus always awash in a stream of exceptionless change. Identities are stops in this changing stream and stand as the test of, and the limit for, change. Identities do this by insisting that something ... remains in common, connecting one moment of inevitable transformation to the next. The battles we as individuals and as cultural groups wage against the currents of change – battles that when won allow both persistent persons and persistent peoples to be identified and reidentified as one and the same across time – are however never decisive but form parts of an ongoing project aimed at sustaining a measure of temporal coherence or biographical continuity.[86]

The resonance between this writing and that of Baylis in the first part of this volume on relational identity is striking. Lalond and Chandler further postulate that what keeps people going during those times when "life hardly seems worth living are all those responsibilities owed to a past that we carry with us and all the still optimistic expectations we hold out for the persons we are en route to becoming."[87] Armed with a theory, Lalond and Chandler sought to apply and substantiate it and, in particular, to try to understand what practices, procedures, or institutions functioned within various Indigenous communities to preserve the necessary sense of community and individual continuity and hoped-for prospects that make "living seem better than dying."[88] They gathered data on many of the traditional socio-economic factors that a social determinants approach tells us may be relevant, such as poverty, community location (that is, isolation), housing density, unemployment, and so on but found that nothing arose from this data that distinguished the communities where suicide was common versus those where it was a rarity.[89] Cutting to the chase, some of the measures in which they found significant correlations arising were when communities had a self-government agreement in place, had pursued litigation in which they claimed rights to their traditional lands, and, through a federal devolution policy, had come to exercise some level of autonomy over educational services, health delivery, and child and family services as well as operating cultural facilities.[90] The more of these measures that were present, the lower the rates of youth suicide. That is, thé more evidence of measures that would appear to reflect community exercises of autonomy, the lower the rates of suicide by their youth. These are indeed important insights for revising how social determinants may operate for Indigenous peoples.

Lalonde and Chandler do not suggest any simple causal relationship in their research or that they have mapped the epidemiological causes for when young Indigenous community members will turn, *en masse*, towards suicide.[91] Instead, they posit that in those Aboriginal communities that "have no suicides, there must be sedimented knowledge about how to create a life that is still worth living."[92] A relational reading suggests that their findings and conclusions signal that in some communities a sense of individual and collective ownership of the past and of the future and of the need to tend to how the individual and collective co-constitute is not easily lost. And, obviously, from their findings it would appear that such communities may manifest that knowledge by working as a community to grasp whatever opportunities for greater autonomy may arise – from demanding collective rights recognition through litigation to asserting the ability and capacity to design and deliver health and child services. In this context, having the option of being able to assume a level of autonomy over community health programming may in some respects be more pivotal for community well-being – for fulfilling a sense of meaningfulness on a community and individual level – than immediately having enough money to fully fund the health programming.[93] Gordon Christie's writing on Indigenous identity reflects a similar conclusion:

> Insofar as decisions about how to live their collective lives are manifestations of their assertions of identity, these sorts of decisions are vitally important ... the power to control their destinies as Aboriginal peoples, to maintain control over their self-definition, must be fundamental ... If Aboriginal communities lose the power to control their self-definition they lose themselves – they effectively become "another."[94]

From this perspective, it is not surprising that these assertions by Indigenous communities – that they know who they are and know what they need their health services to do – seem to arise in conjunction with Indigenous youth feeling able to shoulder the responsibilities and burdens that arise from their personal and collective past as well as imagine a future worth living. These are matters that once again are essential to the Indigenous theory of health and that easily find expression and meaning within a relational analysis. Directions for law in general, and for health law and policy regarding Indigenous peoples in particular, emerge here.

Concluding Comments

The case examples in this chapter point to how relational theory offers a platform for thinking about how health laws and policies may support or impede the emergence of relationships of equality and autonomy as well as the enabling of certain forms of identity. As such, it explores how health policies may positively or negatively impact upon how communities understand themselves to be constituted. This chapter has also presented both conceptual, as well as situationally grounded, arguments about the articulation of Indigenous theories of health, the social determinants approach to health policy analysis and formation, and relational theory. It proposes that the social determinants approach, as traditionally formulated, struggles to substantively lend expression to the Indigenous theory of health but that this situation may change when relational insights are drawn upon and mobilized.

In the background, of course, is a core issue, which is how relational practice (and a theory informing it) can fruitfully engage with law and policy formation. That is, how relational theory can be drawn upon such that the normative scope of law can be more responsive to the social and situational plurality of Indigenous peoples and their health situation as well as the historical injustices informing that plurality and its multiple relational praxes. This matter is made all the more tricky because, as Marilyn Strathern has commented, law primarily recognizes individuals as its subject, not relationships.[95] Relational theory thus requires law and policy formation practices to undergo considerable shifts, such that institutional structures and initiatives reflect the fact that individuals are always already relationally engaged.

This chapter applies relational insights to some specific health policy practices in order to illustrate why these practices perpetuate damage to Indigenous peoples on a multiplicity of levels and also to show how the social determinants approach to health policy formation may be unable to identify or articulate the damage in question. In particular, taking relational theory's premise that community and individual autonomy are both desirable and, in fact, inextricably entwined, it demonstrates that health policies must be disentangled from the definitions of community membership in the *Indian Act* in order to enable Indigenous communities to realize autonomy and well-being. Adherence to these definitions shapes institutional structures and funding practices in ways that suppress relationships based upon equality and respect and sustain incentives to discriminate based upon colonial and sexist visions of indigeneity. Such shifts in health policies and initiatives do not guarantee that relationships of equality and respect will develop, but they certainly make it far more likely. This chapter is an initial exploration into a novel set of connections, and it has only scratched the surface of a number of matters, including how to enhance the articulation between the social determinants approach and relational theory as well as the best way to theorize the foundations for health policies that will better serve Indigenous peoples. As such, it should be taken as a starting point for thinking about these issues.

Notes

1 For an overview of the health gap, expressed both in terms of epidemiological as well as social determinants data, see Constance MacIntosh, "Indigenous Peoples and Health Law and Policy: Responsibilities and Obligations" in Jocelyn Downie, Timothy Caulfield, and Colleen Flood, eds., *Canadian Health Law and Policy*, 4th edition (Markham, ON: LexisNexis, 2011) 575 at 581-84.

2 See, for example, Jocelyn Downie and Jennifer Llewellyn's discussion of the practical implications of approaching health law and policy through relational theory's casting of the self. They write: "The concept of the self that dominates contemporary Canadian health law and policy is a liberal individualistic one. It is isolated, independent, socially unencumbered, rational and self-created." Jocelyn Downie and Jennifer Llewellyn, "Relational Theory and Health Law and Policy" (2008) Health L.J. 193 at 196.

3 See Jennifer Nedelsky, "The Reciprocal Relation of Judgment and Autonomy: Walking in Another's Shoes and Which Shoes to Walk In" in this volume.

4 See Sue Sherwin, "Relational Autonomy and Global Threats" in this volume.

5 See Jennifer Llewellyn, "Restorative Justice: Thinking Relationally about Justice" in this volume.

6 See, for example, Madison Power and Ruth Faden, *Social Justice: The Moral Foundations of Public Health and Health Policy* (Toronto: Oxford University Press, 2006) at 89.

7 Marilyn Strathern, *Kinship, Law and the Unexpected: Relatives Are Always a Surprise* (Cambridge: Cambridge University Press, 2005) at 70.

8 See Sherwin, *supra* note 4, for a discussion of how relational autonomy may relate to acknowledging and taking on responsibilities at all levels of society, from individual to institutional.

9 The stereotyping of Indigenous people as culturally uniform and as being "authentic" or having "lost" their culture has been commented upon in jurisprudence and in scholarly writing. See, for example, *Corbiere v. Canada (Min. of Indian and Northern Affairs)*, [1999] 2 S.C.R. 203 [*Corbiere*], on stereotyping that links the "authenticity" of an Indigenous person's aboriginality with whether they live on reserves. For scholarly commentary, see Wendy Cornet, "Aboriginality: Legal Foundations, Past Trends, Future Prospects" in Joseph Magnet and Dwight Dorey, eds., *Aboriginal Rights Litigation* (Markham, ON: LexisNexis Canada, 2003) 121. For an analysis of how stereotypical categories have emerged through evolutionary social theory, and have been perpetuated through contemporary jurisprudence, see Constance MacIntosh, "Judging Culture and Taxing Indians: Tracing the Legal Discourse of 'Indian Mode of Life'" (2009) 47:3 Osgoode Hall L.J. 399.

10 See Constance MacIntosh, "Jurisdictional Roulette: Constitutional and Structural Barriers to Aboriginal Access to Health" in Colleen Flood, ed., *Just Medicare: What's In, What's Out, How We Decide* (Toronto: University of Toronto Press, 2006) 193 at 194-95; Health Canada, First Nations and Inuit Health Branch, *A Statistical Profile on the Health of First Nations in Canada* (Ottawa: Health Canada, 2002).

11 See, generally, Constance MacIntosh, "Envisioning the Future of Aboriginal Health under the Health Transfer Process" (2008) Health L.J. (Special Edition) 67.

12 See, for example, Douglas Durst and Mary Bluechart, "Urban Aboriginal Persons with Disabilities: Triple Jeopardy!" (Regina: Social Policy Research Unit, University of Regina, 2001). For a discussion of potential vulnerabilities in accessing service in an on-reserve context, see MacIntosh, *supra* note 11 at 87-90.

13 For example, see Donna Kurtz et al., "Silencing of Voice: An Act of Structural Violence. Urban Aboriginal Women Speak Out about Their Experiences with Health Care" (2008) 4:1 J. Aboriginal Health 53.

14 For example, some read Treaty 6's promise in 1876 to provide a "medicine chest," as part of the compensation for Indigenous signatories ceding rights to 120,000 square miles of land, as creating this obligation. For a discussion of the arguments referred to in this paragraph, see MacIntosh, *supra* note 10 at 198-203; Constance MacIntosh, "Indigenous Peoples and Health Law and Policy: Responsibilities and Obligations" in Downie, Caulfield, and Flood, *supra* note 1.

15 See Sue Campbell, "Memory, Reparation, and Relation: Starting in the Right Places" in this volume.

16 For an analysis of the impact of such laws and policies, see Val Napolean, "Extinction by Number: Colonialism Made Easy" (2001) 16:1 Can. J. Law & Soc. 113.

17 See, for example, Laurence Kirmayer and Gail Valaskakis, "Preface" in Laurence Kirmayer and Gail Valaskakis, eds., *Healing Traditions: The Mental Health of Aboriginal Peoples in Canada* (Vancouver: UBC Press, 2009) xiii at xv; Laurence Kirmayer, Caroline Tait, and Cori Simpson, "The Mental Health of Aboriginal Peoples in Canada: Transformations of Identity and Community" in Kirmayer and Valaskakis, *ibid.,* 3 at 18-19.

18 See Campbell, *supra* note 15.

19 Charlotte Loppie Reading and Fred Wein, *Health Inequalities and Social Determinants of Aboriginal Peoples' Health* (Prince George, BC: National Collaborating Centre for Aboriginal Health, 2009) at 22.

20 *Ibid.* at 21.

21 MacIntosh, "Indigenous Peoples and Health Law and Policy," *supra* note 14.

22 For a discussion of how the Indigenous population has been severed into categories and how these categories fail to engage with how the Indigenous population itself self-differentiates as well as some of the consequences of these categories for health law and policy, see MacIntosh, *supra* note 10.

23 Of course, the understandings of health described later in this chapter do not represent every Indigenous individual. Rather, they reflect the generalizations that have been adopted as representative by national Indigenous health organizations and have led Indigenous health researchers.

24 For information on the National Aboriginal Health Organization (NAHO), see their website, http://www.naho.ca.

25 NAHO, *An Overview of Traditional Knowledge and Medicine and Public Health in Canada* (Ottawa: NAHO, 2008) at 3.

26 Reading and Wein, *supra* note 19 at 3.

27 See Sherwin, *supra* note 4.

28 See Llewellyn, *supra* note 5.

29 Health Canada, *Taking Action on Population Health: A Position Paper for Health Promotions and Programs Branch Staff* (Ottawa: Health Canada, 1998) at 1. See also Dennis Raphael, "Introduction to the Social Determinants of Health" in Dennis Raphael, ed., *Social Determinants of Health* (Toronto: Canadian Scholars Press, 2004) 1 at 1, where social determinants of health were defined as "the economic and social conditions that influence the health of individuals, communities, and jurisdictions as a whole." It is important to note that although the social determinants model, or some version thereof, has dominated policy analysis and recommendations for some time (see, for example, Sholom Glouberman and John Millar, "Evolution of the Determinants of Health, Health Policy, and Health Information Systems in Canada" (2003) 93:3 Am. J. Public Health 388) serious questions have been raised as to whether law and state-supported or directed practices actually adhere to these recommendations and reflect this approach. In fact, this is a key premise behind Raphael's book *Social Determinants of Health* (at xi).

30 Constance MacIntosh, "The Intersection of Aboriginal Public Health with Canadian Law and Policy" in Tracey Bailey, Timothy Caulfield, and Nola Ries, eds., *Public Health Law and Policy in Canada,* 2nd edition (Markham, ON: LexisNexis, 2008) 395 at 399.

31 See, for example, Reading and Wein, *supra* note 19.

32 World Health Organization (WHO), Commission on Social Determinants of Health, *Closing the Gap in a Generation: Health Equity through Action on the Social Determinants of Health* (Geneva: WHO, 2008) at 26.

33 *Ibid.* at 26.

34 See, for example, Gwen Healey and Lynn Meadows, "Tradition and Culture: An Important Determinant of Inuit Women's Health" (2008) 4:1 J. Aboriginal Health 25 at 26.

35 Catriona MacKenzie and Natalie Stoljar, eds., *Relational Autonomy: Feminist Perspectives on Autonomy, Agency, and the Social Self* (New York: Oxford University Press, 2000), as cited in Llewellyn, *supra* note 5.

36 *Ibid.*

37 Marilyn Strathern, *Kinship, Law and the Unexpected: Relatives Are Always a Surprise* (Cambridge: Cambridge University Press, 2005) at 63.

38 WHO, *supra* note 32 at 26.

39 *Ibid.* at 36.

40 *Ibid.*

41 Reading and Wein, *supra* note 19; Healey and Meadows, *supra* note 34.

42 Here I am referring to Raphael, *supra* note 29.

43 Chandrakant Shah, "The Health of Aboriginal Peoples" in Raphael, *supra* note 29, 267 at 279. This text from this chapter is in circulation in another textbook as well, *Public Health and Preventative Medicine in Canada,* 5th edition (Toronto: Elsevier Saunders Canada, 2003) at 163.

44 WHO, *Social Determinants and Indigenous Health: The International Experience and Its Policy Implications,* Report on Specially prepared documents, presentations and discussion at the International Symposium on the Social Determinants of Indigenous Health, Adelaide, 29-30 April 2007 for the Commission on Social Determinants of Health (Geneva: WHO, 2007) at 8.

45 See Sherwin, *supra* note 4.

46 See Llewellyn, *supra* note 5.

47 *Schneider v. The Queen,* [1982] 2 S.C.R. 112. For a discussion of the history of providing health services to Indigenous peoples in Canada, see James Waldra, D. Ann Herring, and T. Kue Young, eds., *Aboriginal Health in Canada: Historical, Cultural and Epidemiological Perspectives,* 2nd edition (Toronto: University of Toronto Press, 2006), especially at 194 ff.

48 *Constitution Act, 1867* (UK), 30 and 31 Vict., c. 3, reprinted in R.S.C. 1985, App. II, No. 5.

49 One exception are Inuit persons, who were determined to be "Indians" for the purposes of section 91(24). *Re: Eskimos,* [1939] S.C.R. 104, [1939] 2 D.L.R. 417.

50 *Indian Act,* R.S.C. 1985, c. I-5, s. 6(1) and (2). The following is a simplified description of the registration legislation. For a recent discussion of how the legislation is discriminatory, see *McIvor v. Canada (Registrar, Indian and Northern Affairs),* [2009] B.C.J. 669 (C.A.), 2009 BCCA 153.

51 See, generally, David Elliot, *Law and Aboriginal Peoples in Canada,* 5th edition (Concord, ON: Captus Press, 2005) at 15-20; Bonita Lawrence, *Real Indians and Others: Mixed-Blood Urban Native Peoples and Indigenous Nationhood* (Lincoln, NE: University of Nebraska Press, 2004) at 7-11. The first statute to create the category of "Indian status," as something that could result in people becoming legally "white," was the 1869 *Act to Encourage the Gradual Civilization of Indian Tribes.*

52 Provincial governments treat their residents uniformly, although they may have topic-specific initiatives that target Indigenous residents, such as an HIV prevention program that has been designed to be culturally sensitive to Indigenous persons.

53 MacIntosh, *supra* note 10 at 206.

54 Kirmayer, Tait, and Simpson, *supra* note 17 at 12.

55 See Llewellyn, *supra* note 5.

56 See *ibid*.

57 For a discussion of how Indigenous mobility practices have been and are used by the law to undermine community and Indigenous political rights, see John Borrows, "Physical Philosophy: Mobility and the Future of Indigenous Rights" in Shin Imai, Kent McNeil, and Ben Richardson, eds., *Indigenous Peoples and the Law: Comparative and Critical Perspectives* (Oxford: Hart Publishing, 2009). For a discussion of how these stereotypes operate upon non-status Indigenous persons who also live in urban areas, see Lawrence, *supra* note 51. For a discussion of the pervasiveness of stereotypes of difference relating to whether an Indigenous person lives on or off a reserve, see *Corbiere, supra* note 9 at paras. 17-20 and 71-72. For a discussion of how stereotypes arising from evolutionary theory continue to inform contemporary jurisprudence, see MacIntosh, *supra* note 9.

58 See, for example, "The Mental Health of Aboriginal Peoples in Canada: Transformations of Identity and Community" in Kirmayer and Valaskakis, *supra* note 9, 3 at 21.

59 Borrows, *supra* note 57 at 409.

60 See Françoise Baylis, "The Self *in Situ*: A Relational Account of Personal Identity" and Sue Campbell, "Memory, Reparation, and Relation: Starting in the Right Places" both in this volume.

61 *McIvor v. Canada (Registrar, Indian and Northern Affairs)*, 2009 BCCA 153 at para. 157.

62 For a discussion of several communities whose members have collectively refused to be registered under the *Indian Act*, see *Lovelace v. Ontario*, [2000] 1 S.C.R. 950.

63 This observation is based upon personal experiences, in both professional and informal settings.

64 See Sherwin, *supra* note 4.

65 *Ibid*.

66 *Ibid*.

67 Compare with Janet Smylie and Paul Adomako, eds., *Indigenous Children's Health Report: Health Assessment in Action* (Toronto: Centre for Research on Inner City Health, 2010).

68 John Borrows, *Physical Philosophy: Freedom, Democracy and Indigenous Peoples* [unpublished manuscript, 2011].

69 Borrows, *supra* note 57 at 409.

70 *Ibid*. at 409.

71 For an analysis of likely outcomes under this program, see MacIntosh, *supra* note 11. For a detailed discussion of the development and evolution of health transfer, as well as an evaluation of it, see Josee Lavoie et al., *The Evaluation of the First Nations and Inuit Health Transfer Policy: Final Report: Volume 2* (Winnipeg, MB: Centre for Aboriginal Health Research, 2005). For a critique of the process, see Dara Culhane Speck, "The Indian Health Transfer Policy: A Step in the Right Direction or Revenge of the Hidden Agenda?" (1989) 5:1 Native Stud. Rev. 187.

72 Note that the funding formula for community health programming is at odds with the federal government's typical approach, which is to only provide funding for status Indians. As noted earlier, bands can control their membership criteria and with membership comes the right to live on reserve land. As a result, persons who do not qualify for status (and so are excluded from federal primary health benefits such as the non-insured health benefits), may be band members (and so receive federal community health benefits).

73 MacIntosh, *supra* note 11 at para. 7.

74 The language of belonging that I draw upon here is heavily influenced through conversations with Brian Noble, regarding his work on Indigenous owning and belonging.

75 See Nedelsky, *supra* note 3.

76 Strathern, *supra* note 37 at 69.

77 Bonita Lawrence, "Gender, Race and the Regulation of Native Identity in Canada and the United States: An Overview" (2003) 18:2 Hypatia 3 at 4.

78 *Ibid*. at 3.

79 The call to find a way to cast off the *Indian Act* is found in a great deal of writing by Indigenous peoples. For an example of relationship-building strategies that may enable an internal reconciliation for Gitxsan people, see Napoleon, *supra* note 16 at 142-43

80 See Sherwin, *supra* note 4.
81 For a deep analysis of this system and how its logics reflect and continue to perpetuate nineteenth-century socio-biological evolutionary theories, see MacIntosh, *supra* note 9.
82 Michael Chandler and Christopher Lalonde, "Cultural Continuity as a Moderator of Suicide Risk among Canada's First Nations" in Kirmayer and Valaskakis, *supra* note 9, 221 at 221.
83 Michael Chandler and Christopher Lalonde, "Cultural Continuity as a Hedge against Suicide among Canada's First Nations" (1998) 35:2 Transcultural Psychiatry 191. For a critique of this earlier study's conclusions as being too simplistic, see James Waldram, D. Ann Herring, and T. Kue Young, *Aboriginal Health in Canada: Historical, Cultural and Epidemiological Perspectives* (Toronto: University of Toronto Press, 1997) at 279-81.
84 Chandler and Lalonde, *supra* note 82.
85 *Ibid.* at 222.
86 *Ibid.* at 222-23.
87 *Ibid.* at 223.
88 *Ibid.* at 228.
89 *Ibid.* at 237.
90 *Ibid.* at 238-40.
91 *Ibid.* at 244.
92 *Ibid.* They observe that this knowledge may not be understood in an "explicit or declarative" form (at 246).
93 Obviously, if financing never comes to meet need, then the community may be left to administer its own misery.
94 Gordon Christie, "Law, Theory and Aboriginal Peoples" (2003) 2 Indigenous L.J. 67 at 98.
95 Strathern, *supra* note 37 at 13. Strathern also notes that some legal systems do recognize relationships as subjects of law.

11
Insight Revisited: Relationality and Psychiatric Treatment Decision-Making Capacity

Sheila Wildeman

In this chapter, I explore the implications of relational theory for a highly charged site of administrative state ordering wherein persons subject to, or under scrutiny in light of criteria for, involuntary psychiatric hospitalization undergo assessment of their capacity to make decisions about the psychiatric treatments prescribed to them. While assessment of capacity to make treatment decisions (which I will call assessment of "treatment capacity") is implicit in the act of obtaining legally valid consent to medical treatment in any setting,[1] the institutional mechanisms that are, or are not, in place for testing and disputing this form of decisional capacity in psychiatric hospital settings merit focused scrutiny.[2] I argue, drawing on a decision of the Supreme Court of Canada issued in 2003, *Starson v. Swayze*, that the time is ripe to advance a relational approach to this contested site of medico-legal activity.[3]

In *Starson*, the Supreme Court of Canada overturned an Ontario tribunal's conclusion that Starson, a forensic psychiatric patient, was incapable of refusing medications prescribed for treatment of bipolar/schizoaffective disorder. By re-reading *Starson* in light of relational theory, I seek to reveal the untapped legal and social significance of two key principles articulated in the majority judgment, namely, (1) that the conditions under which treatment capacity is assessed must be carefully examined to ensure that they do not compromise decisional capacity; and (2) that the subject's resistance to the descriptor "mental illness," and/or to associated attributions of negative value to his/her mental condition, should not lead inevitably to a determination of incapacity.

The significance of these two principles, I suggest, is deepened on attending to two forms of relational inquiry aimed respectively at (1) exposing the conditions that enable or disable autonomy in the exercise of treatment choice (a concern exemplified in the work of Susan Sherwin); and (2) exposing the conditions that enable or disable judgment, including impartial adjudicative judgment (a concern exemplified in the work of Jennifer

Nedelsky). Ultimately, I argue that relational theory assists in the important work of reorienting the project of treatment capacity assessment from implicit reliance on the trope of "insight" – deployed in both law and psychiatry as if to connote a neuro-biologically hardwired ability or inability to see ourselves for what/whom we are or rather to see our mental health status for what it is – to a relational conception of treatment capacity (and also "insight") as a function of complex, ongoing processes of cultural and interpersonal interaction and interpretation.

Background: Treatment Capacity and Involuntary Psychiatric Hospitalization

At common law, all adults are presumed capable of making decisions about medical treatment.[4] In some jurisdictions, this presumption is suspended or overridden without any decision-specific legal inquiry where a person is subject to involuntary psychiatric hospitalization. That is, in such jurisdictions, involuntary treatment is authorized where one is deemed to meet the diagnosis- and risk-based criteria that stand at the threshold of involuntary hospitalization (in Canada, this is the case in British Columbia).[5] Here we may note that the risk criteria conditioning involuntary hospitalization vary among jurisdictions, from the high threshold of "dangerousness to self or others" to the lower threshold of "significant risk of serious mental or physical deterioration."[6] Certain jurisdictions additionally include incapacity to make treatment decisions among the criteria of involuntary hospitalization (in Canada, this is true of Saskatchewan, Nova Scotia, and Newfoundland).[7] In such jurisdictions, assessment of capacity to make treatment decisions is an essential component of the involuntary committal process – carried out, typically, during a defined period of confinement for observation purposes.[8]

In still other jurisdictions, adults meeting involuntary hospitalization criteria based solely on diagnosis and risk, as well as adults involuntarily hospitalized under a *Criminal Code* disposition,[9] are presumed capable of making treatment decisions, subject to rebuttal in light of statutory criteria. Of these jurisdictions, some qualify the respect commanded by the contemporaneous and/or prior capable treatment decisions of involuntary patients by providing a best interests (or otherwise interest-balancing) override that is specific to involuntary patients.[10] Others feature no such override (in Canada, Ontario is alone in this regard). Notably for this chapter, persons in Ontario (where the *Starson* case arose) who are involuntarily committed to a psychiatric hospital retain an uncircumscribed right to refuse treatment, so long as they are not deemed incapable of making the relevant treatment choice.[11] Ontario's requirement of respect for contemporaneous and/or prior capable treatment wishes of involuntary patients reflects a background proportionality assessment whereby the interest in retaining control over treatment decisions (while one is capable of making those decisions) is deemed greater than any competing interest, particularly given the containment of background risks effected by involuntary hospitalization.

This proportionality analysis, which is implicit in Ontario's bifurcation of involuntary hospitalization and treatment capacity status, reflects the special concern expressed at law for the interest in bodily and psychological integrity. Moreover, it reflects concerns about the unique nature of psychiatric interventions (which, in and beyond the psychiatric hospital setting, tend to centre primarily, if not exclusively, on psycho-pharmaceutical interventions) and the heightened vigilance expected of the state where such interventions are in issue. This point is made by the majority in *Starson*. On acknowledging that medical treatment decisions clearly engage the interest in autonomy, the majority approves the following statement of the Ontario Court of Appeal in *Fleming v. Reid*: "Few medical procedures can be more intrusive than the forcible injection of powerful mind-altering drugs which are often accompanied by severe and sometimes irreversible adverse side effects."[12] This statement stands as a reminder of the gravity of forcible application of psychiatric medications, reflecting both the seriousness that attends any authorization of physical violence and the special relevance of the intended effect of these interventions – namely, to markedly alter a person's experience of self and world – in addition to the significance and frequency of adverse side effects.[13]

Starson

Background
Scott Starson was forty-three in the summer of 1998, when charges of uttering threats were laid against him following an altercation at his rented premises in Toronto. After a period of involuntary treatment aimed at rendering him fit to stand trial, he was tried and declared not criminally responsible by reason of mental disorder.[14] The disposition of the Ontario Review Board (the provincial body that supervises persons deemed not criminally responsible under the *Criminal Code*) was that he remain involuntarily in psychiatric hospital, subject to that board's mandatory annual reviews.

At that time, Starson already had an extensive medico-legal history, having been a frequent subject of involuntary hospitalization and treatment since about 1985 in Ontario, New York State, and Florida – interventions typically, as was the case in late 1998, following criminal charges of mischief or uttering threats. Yet unfolding during this same period from the mid-1980s on – that is, concurrent with, or in the interstices of, his tumultuous interactions with the mental health and legal systems – was Starson's other history: his significant (or, as the courts reviewing his case ultimately characterized it, "extraordinary") accomplishments as an advanced seminar participant and published author in the area of theoretical physics, despite his lack of formal training in that field.[15]

The treatments proposed by Starson's psychiatrists included anti-psychotics (initially at least, Haldol), anti-parkinsonians (to reduce the side effects of the anti-psychotic(s)), anti-anxiety medications, and mood stabilizers.[16] Starson refused these treatments. This was followed by a formal assessment of his capacity to make that choice, conducted by his attending psychiatrist under authority of Ontario's *Health Care Consent Act (HCCA)*.[17] This statute, apart from incorporating the common law presumption that all adults are capable of making decisions about medical treatment,[18] provides a two-pronged standard that serves as the basis for rebutting the presumption of capacity, on a decision-specific and time-sensitive basis.[19] The standard is stated as follows:

> A person is capable with respect to a treatment ... if the person is able to understand the information that is relevant to making a decision about the treatment ... and able to appreciate the reasonably foreseeable consequences of a decision or lack of decision.[20]

As would be confirmed by the Supreme Court of Canada in Starson's case, the first prong of this test (the ability to "understand" the relevant information)[21] encompasses basic facilities of cognitive comprehension and memory retention,[22] while the second (the ability to "appreciate" the foreseeable consequences of a decision or lack of decision) involves evaluation of projected risks and benefits in light of one's specific circumstances.[23]

In December 1998, Dr. Swayze declared Starson incapable of making the decision to refuse the prescribed treatments following a series of meetings or attempted meetings in which, on Dr. Swayze's account, Starson refused to engage in or resolutely redirected communication of the requisite sort (Starson, for his part, later impugned the brevity and infrequency of these meetings aimed at assessing his treatment capacity status).[24] Starson appealed this determination to the Consent and Capacity Board (CCB), which is the provincial body authorized to hear challenges to, and to confirm or substitute its opinion for, physicians' declarations of (in)capacity under the *HCCA*.[25]

CCB Hearing

Where a declaration of incapacity is disputed before the CCB, the onus rests on the doctor(s) to establish incapacity on a balance of probabilities. At Starson's hearing, both Dr. Swayze and Starson's initial attending psychiatrist during this latest period of involuntary hospitalization, Dr. Posner, appeared in order to state the case against him.[26] The psychiatrists' testimony was pitched in light of the diagnosis of bipolar disorder applied to Starson over the previous fifteen years, along with the more recently applied diagnosis of schizoaffective disorder.[27] Against this background of formal diagnoses, it was argued that Starson could not recognize his illness or need for treatment.

The doctors' argument rested on two main points: first, that Starson persistently denied that the behaviours precipitating his repeated subjection to forensic and/or civil psychiatric processes – typically, unprovoked threats (as inferred from notes on his hospital chart) – were rooted in mental illness; and, second, that he exhibited an exaggerated sense of intellectual superiority (in clinical terms, grandiosity), which manifested not only as an excessive valuation of his accomplishments in theoretical physics but also in the attitude he took to psychiatry, which he deemed less a science than a "religion" or "pseudo-science."[28] This grandiosity, the doctors argued, rendered Starson unable to enter into a meaningful discussion about his condition or the proposed treatments. It was this last point that the doctors brought out most diligently in their testimony, impugning, in turn, Starson's change of name (from Schutzman to Starson), his adoption of the title of professor, his claims to extraordinary intellectual merit and ongoing academic productivity, and his refusal to acknowledge either the scientific validity of psychiatry or the specific efficacy of psychiatric medications.[29] All of these matters were deemed instantiations of an underlying pathology that prevented Starson from recognizing illness in himself, so rendering him unable to acknowledge his need for treatment. In addition, Dr. Posner pressed the thesis that Starson was unable to appreciate that his condition, left untreated, would likely deteriorate such that not only the euphoric states he had transiently experienced hitherto, but also his basic cognitive capacities, would suffer severe impairment as he became increasingly "lost in a psychotic world."[30]

Starson's testimony was delivered with marked aplomb. In response to the doctors' evidence about the nature of his condition, or, more specifically, the symptoms they viewed as grounding an urgent need for treatment, he advanced the position that the threats he had made in the recent and distant past had been provoked (a claim that the courts would find no adequate evidence to rebut, on the record of this hearing). Putting aside the injury that he acknowledged having done to a nurse's leg in resisting a court-ordered injection – on Starson's account, his attempt to make a "record" of the self-perpetuating effects of a violent system – he was, he suggested, a non-violent person. Indeed, he abhorred violence as contrary to a "scientific" approach to dispute resolution.[31] With respect to the reality-based or delusional nature of his claims that he was accomplishing significant work in theoretical physics – accomplishments, he suggested, that were inspiring efforts "to build a starship" in Switzerland – he maintained that these claims were entirely reality-grounded, although they might exceed the appreciation of his doctors.

Perhaps most importantly, Starson resisted characterizing his condition or thought processes on the model of mental illness. Indeed, much of his testimony reflected what Dr. Swayze described as an "enthusiasm" for his abnormal mental condition or aspects of it.[32] That is, while Starson acknowledged that he had had some mental "problems" – and he expressed specific willingness to continue psychotherapy with Dr. Posner in order to address these problems – he nonetheless regarded his unusual thought processes as valuable and specifically as rendering him uncommonly fit for intellectual innovation.[33]

Starson's testimony about his mental condition culminated in an uncompromising denial of the thesis that psychiatric medications had ever been, or could ever be, any good to him – that is, they offered no benefit for him to "appreciate." There were two bases for this claim. The first went to his past experiences of the side effects of psychiatric (particularly antipsychotic) treatments, which he described as "the most horrible experiences of my life," rendering him unable to work or even "communicate with ... loved ones" (or, as one associate suggested in a letter supporting Starson's position, leaving him like "a struggling-to-think drunk").[34] The other basis upon which he rejected the proposition that the medications might benefit him went to their primary intended effect, which he described as aiming to "slow his thoughts down" in order to make him think more like others. In a phrase that resounded with all three levels of court that would review his case, Starson summed up his position on the likely benefits of medication by stating that to be made "normal" by way of psychiatric medications "would be worse than death for me ... because I have always considered normal to be a term so boring it would be like death."[35]

The CCB confirmed the doctors' opinion of Starson's treatment incapacity. This result turned primarily on the board's acceptance of the doctors' argument that Starson was unable to "acknowledge that he suffered from some type of mental disorder, and that his behaviour is being affected by the disorder." That is, in light of his "near total" denial of illness, Starson was unable (as concluded by the board) to weigh the benefits and risks of treatment or non-treatment.[36] Starson appealed the board's decision to the Ontario Superior Court of Justice.

Judicial Oversight of the CCB Decision
In overturning the decision of the CCB, all three levels of court agreed that the decision was both incorrect in law and unreasonable in its application of the law to the facts. The decision was incorrect in law because the board

had, according to the courts, implicitly sought to advance Starson's best interests rather than focusing exclusively upon the legal criteria for displacing the presumption of capacity. And the decision was unreasonable because the CCB had failed to carefully assess the evidence before it in light of the legal test – in particular, it had failed to properly attend to the evidence advanced by Starson.[37]

The Ontario Court of Appeal focused upon three points of Starson's evidence that the CCB had failed to take into account: (1) his recognition that he had some "mental problems" that may benefit from psychotherapy (which conflicted with the finding that he failed to recognize signs of mental illness in himself); (2) his testimony about the inefficacy or otherwise intolerability of past treatments in his case (which conflicted with the expectation that he evince appreciation of likely treatment benefits); and (3) his rejection of the "primary intended effect" of the proposed treatments (also in conflict with the expectation that he evince appreciation of likely benefits). The Ontario Court of Appeal further brought out, with particular acuity, a dilemma – the dilemma of "insight" – that was identified by Starson at his CCB hearing and characterized by him as a form of "catch-22." Thus, in reviewing the CCB's conclusion that Starson had failed to adequately recognize that he was mentally ill, the Ontario Court of Appeal revisited a key part of Starson's testimony as follows:

> Unquestionably, he has a deep distrust of psychiatry, which he likens to a religion. His reply to the question whether he recognizes he is mentally ill was unresponsive but logical: He answered that the question left him in a "catch 22" situation. If he said "yes," the authorities would say he must be treated for it; if he said "no," the authorities would say he must be treated because he lacks insight into his illness.[38]

Arguably, the function of "insight" that surfaces here – as securing the hegemonic trick whereby it is impossible to escape the necessity of treatment – is in great part what provokes the two principles of capacity assessment advanced by a majority of the Supreme Court of Canada in answer to this case. However, it is important to note, on the way to a relational-theoretical analysis, that the logic of "catch-22" was first deployed at the CCB hearing by Starson's doctor, in describing the no-win situation of prescribing treatment to a treatment-resistant patient.[39]

In a six-to-three judgment, the Supreme Court of Canada dismissed the doctors' appeal.[40] The majority held that the CCB had committed the legal error of substituting its perception of Starson's best interests for a careful consideration of the facts in light of the legal standard. Moreover, it deemed unreasonable both the board's determination that Starson was unable to appreciate the nature of his condition and its determination that he was unable to appreciate the foreseeable benefits of treatment or risks of non-treatment.

On the question of Starson's acknowledgment of his mental condition, the majority of the Court, like the courts below, brought out testimony in which he acknowledged "mental problems" and having "exhibited the symptoms of these labels" that his doctors had assigned him as well as corroborating testimony that indicated that Starson had in the past acknowledged that "his perception of reality differed from others" and was "quite comfortable and enthusiastic" about his unconventional mind.[41] In regard to Starson's appreciating the foreseeable benefits of treatment, the majority concluded, first, that there was no clear evidence that the treatments on offer held any likely benefit for Starson (this in light of his "horrible" past experiences as well as evidence that "in general, only 60 percent of patients treated with neuroleptics respond favourably to new treatment")[42] and, more fundamentally, that the CCB had "entirely misapprehended the respondent's reasons for refusing medication," namely that "the cure proposed by his physicians [w]as more damaging than his disorder."[43] Finally, the majority found "scant evidentiary basis" for the thesis that Starson's condition was likely to deteriorate without treatment. Moreover, there was no evidence that the deterioration thesis was ever put to Starson in order to invite his response. Here, the majority stipulated that inquiry into Starson's "ability" to appreciate the consequences of this decision required some canvassing of whether his "perceived failure in this regard might have simply reflected the psychiatrists' failure to inform him of the potential consequences."[44]

Yet the majority judgment of the Court went further than these pronouncements on Starson's case to articulate two key principles, framed as "two important points about" the statutory standard of capacity under the *HCCA*. What I am calling the first of these goes to the distinction between "actual" satisfaction of the statutory criteria and the "ability" to satisfy those criteria. In prefacing this point, the majority stated that

> [i]n practice, the determination of capacity should begin with an inquiry into the patient's actual appreciation of the parameters of the decision being made: the nature and purpose of the proposed treatment; the foreseeable benefits and risks of treatment; the alternative courses of action available; and the expected consequences of not having the treatment. If a patient shows appreciation of these parameters – regardless of whether he weighs or values the information differently than the attending physician and disagrees with the treatment recommendation – he has the ability to appreciate the decision he makes.[45]

At this point, the majority adds the key observation: "However, a patient's failure to demonstrate actual appreciation does not inexorably lead to a conclusion of incapacity." The passage continues: "The patient's lack of appreciation may derive from causes that do not undermine his ability to appreciate consequences." One example of such causes is offered: namely "the attending physician's failure to adequately inform the patient of the decision's consequences."[46]

This point reflects the majority's determination that in Starson's case, the psychiatrist(s) and/or board failed to direct his attention to the negative consequences that might follow a refusal of treatment and to canvas his response, rather than simply assuming that he would not attend to this information. However, we can see that this passage also asserts a general imperative to look, in all cases, beyond the subject's actual appreciation – his/her instantiation or rather non-instantiation of the ability to apply and weigh the relevant information – to the background conditions that might explain a person's apparent inability to meet the standard.

A further point made by the majority in the passage cited earlier is that assessors should not disqualify (as incapable) the subject's views about the information relevant to a treatment decision simply because the subject "weighs or values the information differently" than the assessor. The point – which I am referring to as the *Starson* majority's second principle of capacity assessment – is stated at an even greater level of specificity:

> A patient *is not required to describe his mental condition as an "illness," or to otherwise characterize the condition in negative terms.* Nor is the patient required to agree with the psychiatrist's opinion regarding the cause of that condition. Nonetheless, if the patient's condition results in him being unable to recognize that he is affected by its manifestations, he will be unable to apply the relevant information to his circumstances, and unable to appreciate the consequences of his decision.[47]

In other words, resistance by the subject of a treatment capacity assessment to a given diagnosis, or, more broadly, to the descriptor "mental illness," is not in itself a sufficient basis for assigning the status of incapacity – absent additional failure to recognize "objectively discernible manifestations" of imputed mental illness.[48]

With this second principle, the majority recognizes the significant epistemic, as well as normative, contestation that surrounds the classification of psychiatric conditions in general and in the specific case. That said, the quoted statement poses new difficulties in its distinction between objectively discernible manifestations of one's "mental condition" and the value that is placed upon, or "interpretation" of, those manifestations. However, what is clear is that under this principle, assessors are to strive to ensure that uncommon – even radically uncommon – interpretations of the causes and significance of abnormal psychological or behavioural phenomena are not, or not necessarily, deemed to be determinative of treatment incapacity. At the same time, the majority stops short of asserting the absolute primacy of the individual's self-knowledge – his necessary standing as his "own best expert" – through the idea that he must be able "to recognize that he is affected by" behaviour or thoughts that others regard as abnormal.

This complex injection of value pluralism into the treatment capacity assessment process may be recognized as a response to Starson's assertion of a catch-22 embedded in that process – which is triggered, he argued, whenever subjects of assessment are asked whether or not they are mentally ill. Indeed, stepping back for a moment, we can see that both principles articulated by the majority in *Starson* stand in tension with the model of "insight" or "lack of insight" underwriting Starson's catch-22. It is important to note at this point the special salience of this concept in the thinking of both psychiatric and legal professionals when engaging with treatment refusal among persons diagnosed with serious mental illness (conventionally defined to include schizophrenia, bipolar disorder, and major depression).[49] The meaning of "insight" is significantly ambiguous in and across these professional domains.[50] One influential account of its usage in contemporary psychiatry suggests three overlapping meanings: "recognition that one has a mental illness, compliance with treatment, and the ability to relabel unusual mental events, such as delusions and hallucinations, as pathological."[51] Where a person diagnosed with a serious mental illness fails to evince one or more of these criteria, a lack of insight tends to be ascribed, on the model of an internal deficit or pathology. The frequency of references to insight or lack of insight in legal processes for overseeing treatment capacity assessment suggests that this model holds a powerful place both in psychiatry and medico-legal decision making.[52]

The two principles from *Starson* canvassed earlier may be regarded as reorienting the assessment of treatment capacity in psychiatric hospital settings from implicit reliance on the model of insight or failed insight to a relational model. That is, these principles, in requiring attentiveness to background conditions potentially interfering with one's ability to meet the legal standard and, moreover, in requiring respectful attentiveness to non-dominant values or interpretations of unusual psychological or psycho-social experience, shift the focus from the individual to relationships – or to an account of both treatment capacity and insight as functions of interpersonal, as well as wider institutional and cultural, relationships or processes of interaction.

Before turning to this alternative approach, I should add that the public reception of *Starson* was, with some notable exceptions, highly critical – to the extent that this decision might be regarded as having done more to close down deliberation on what is required to do justice in the arenas of treatment capacity assessment than to inspire such deliberations. Skeptical commentators from the family-based Schizophrenia Society as well as prominent psychiatrists and academic commentators on mental health law and policy suggested that the majority judgment was unduly remote from the realities of mental illness[53] – or, more strenuously, that the majority had succumbed to the romantic fiction of the "happy psychotic" or "mad genius," drawing on parallels advanced in the media between Starson's case and the life of John Nash, which was recently popularized in the biography (and film) *A Beautiful Mind*.[54] The real-world significance of the decision for Starson, the critics asserted, would be the hollow victory of "rotting with his rights on."[55] Some added that the decision was likely to be of little general consequence for psychiatry or law, beyond reinforcing the importance of vigilance on the part of psychiatrists in gathering and presenting evidence to support a declaration of incapacity.[56]

Adding fuel to the fire, Chief Justice Beverley McLachlin, who had penned a vigorous dissent in *Starson*, publicly reflected on the decision as having pitted autonomy understood as negative freedom (a model that she indicated is prone to characterizing psychiatric medications as illicit intrusions) against autonomy understood as self-determination or rational self-direction (a model that, on this account, is more comfortable admitting the possibility that psychiatric medications may support or restore rationality and so autonomy). While the chief justice's reflections offer this interpretation of the central issues in the case without drawing a clear conclusion about the adequacy of the result (so as not to come across as re-trying the case in the court of public opinion), whether the outcome in *Starson* amounted to a substantive victory or loss even from the vantage of concern for autonomy is, on this retrospective account, arguably something of a no-brainer.[57]

Perhaps most prominent among the skeptical voices featured in media accounts following the Supreme Court of Canada's decision was that of Starson's mother, Jeanne Stevens. Stevens had since 1985 assumed the role of advocating for mental health treatment for her son, as the more humane alternative to jail or jail-like conditions – and as the only chance he had to be (or become) "himself." She decried the Court's decision, arguing that the judges had been duped by her son's "brilliant scientist" act and so had missed what clues the record provided (or what clues she might have provided, had she been involved) about the more disturbing aspects of his disrupted thought processes. "My son thinks he is an immortal space alien, yet the law says he is sane enough to refuse the treatment that will make him sane," she stated. "I've lost my son, and my son has lost his dreams. I think the ruling is insane."[58]

More than a decade after his initial involuntary confinement, Starson remains subject to a custodial disposition within Ontario's forensic psychiatric system. He spent three years in the severely restrictive conditions of the province's maximum-security forensic unit at Penetanguishine as his treatment capacity case wound its way up to the Supreme Court of Canada. Subsequently, on being moved to a less restrictive setting at the Royal Ottawa Hospital, he appeared to make significant progress (in response to what authorities suggested was a policy of non-interference).[59] Yet that led to another move, to the Royal Ottawa facilities in Brockville, Ontario – apparently intended as a first step towards re-integration into the community. In the ensuing months, Starson's psychological and physical health declined markedly. Some trace this decline to Starson's inherent mental problems, his refusal of treatment, and the legal requirement that his refusal be respected. Others invoke instead the many years of intolerable deprivations to which he had by then been institutionally subjected. In any case, in 2005, at an emergency hearing of the CCB, Starson (in a condition of life-imperiling self-starvation and unrepresented by counsel) was again declared incapable of making treatment decisions.[60]

Two years of involuntary treatment later, and in light of improvements in his psychological state as well as his pledge to adhere to scheduled antipsychotic injections (despite continuing to deny that he was mentally ill), Starson was granted the privilege of community residency. However, what would seem to have been an occasion for celebration translated, for Starson, into a period of intense hopelessness and self-enforced isolation in his apartment, followed by a renewed refusal of treatment – and a renewed legal challenge to his treatment incapable status. By September 2008, Starson's health and risk status were again deemed to require involuntary hospitalization.[61] So far, his efforts to have his incapacity and/or involuntary status revoked have been unsuccessful.

Critics of the majority decision in *Starson* argue that Starson's ongoing troubled engagement with Ontario's forensic psychiatric system can be chalked up at least in part to an insensitive judiciary that privileged abstract principles over attentiveness to the realities of mental illness, so withholding appropriate deference to psychiatric expertise. In what follows, I argue, to the contrary, that the point of the Supreme Court of Canada decision is precisely to facilitate a closer engagement of legal decision makers (including doctors acting under statutory authority) with the context or conditions of treatment capacity assessment, which necessarily includes the views, and the social positioning, of those subject to assessment. In this way, the efforts of doctors or other health workers to assess treatment capacity are not disrespected in law so much as appropriately reminded of the requisite respect that must be accorded to those whose legal status is in issue.

Treatment Capacity in Light of Relational Theory

One may be forgiven for assuming that a relational account of treatment capacity assessment in the involuntary psychiatric hospitalization setting will expand upon the points made by *Starson*'s critics, who understand the majority decision to promote a thin and impoverished conception of autonomy (as negative freedom), which is insensitive to the complexities of mental illness as it affects individuals and also relationships. One might expect arguments that legalistic, adversarial processes have impeded the objective of building therapeutic relationships. However, I argue in what follows that relational theory can and should take us elsewhere: that the contribution of relational theory (as articulated in this volume) to this contested area of law and policy rests in its propensity to shift the focus of attention from the internal characteristics of the psychiatric subject to the conditions, including the broad background social and institutional conditions, affecting the ways that the laws on treatment capacity are interpreted and applied.[62] The normative lodestar of this shift in focus is not simply relationships but, rather, reciprocity, which I take to be the ideal of legality that animates *Starson*. I refer to an account of law – and so treatment capacity assessment under law – as a mechanism for securing purposive interaction among state authorities and legal subjects – and, moreover, among differently positioned legal subjects.[63] This idea comports with Jennifer Llewellyn's model of restorative justice as a "normative feedback loop."[64] That is, I suggest that treatment capacity assessment, as a form of state-subject interaction under the aegis of the administrative state, aspires toward a kind of "restorative justice" and so toward inclusive processes of law interpretation and justification wherein the views and interests of some (particularly those whose significant interests are at stake) are not subordinated to the views and interests of others (particularly those charged with assessing treatment capacity at law).

With this model of legality in mind, I ask the question: How might relational theory assist in building upon, or drawing out, the concrete implications of the two principles articulated in *Starson*? More specifically, how might relational theory inform our understanding of the ways in which institutional and wider social conditions may operate to disable (or enable) treatment capacity or its instantiation/demonstration at law? And what can relational theory tell us about the institutional and wider social conditions likely to disable (or enable) assessors' ability to judge capacity in a manner that comports with the value of inclusiveness? In what follows, I look first to the work of Susan Sherwin in order to reflect on the implications of the first principle of capacity assessment described earlier – that the assessment of capacity must take account of background conditions that may explain the subject's inability or apparent inability to meet the legal standard. I then turn to Jennifer Nedelsky's work on judgment in order to develop the second principle – that the subject's failure to agree with a diagnosis, or even to describe his mental condition as an "illness," should not be regarded as determinative of treatment incapacity.

Attending to the Conditions in Which Treatment Capacity Is Assessed: Sherwin on Relational Autonomy

I begin by considering the resources within Sherwin's work for constructing a relational analysis of treatment capacity assessment in the involuntary psychiatric hospitalization setting. Sherwin starts with a concern with power, or with relationships of domination and subordination, as the essential backdrop to the project of revisiting treatment decision making in light of the value of autonomy. From this starting point, she argues that conventional approaches to consent to treatment in law and bioethics mask significant tensions between "free and informed" choice, as defined under these models, and the regulative ideal of autonomy, as reconceived on what she terms a relational approach.[65] While Sherwin's work targets the social and institutional structures through which women's oppression is sustained, and, specifically, the ways that health care, as defined and delivered, contributes to this oppression, the power analysis that she advances lends itself to critiques of other forms of domination/subordination (beyond gender oppression) that are also entrenched within health care and wider social systems.[66]

In positioning her account of treatment choice in light of a conception of autonomy that is sensitive to the dynamics of power and oppression, Sherwin calls into question the descriptive and normative adequacy of the conventional model of the medical consent process. According to this model, neutral information is imparted by the professional to the patient, who, asking questions where necessary, subjects that information to a process of rational-instrumental cognition aimed at maximizing her interests. In contrast, Sherwin foregrounds the interpersonal and systemic dynamics that shape treatment choices and, more broadly, that shape our abilities to express or advance our interest in autonomy through these choices.

Sherwin therefore distinguishes "agency," which she identifies with the minimal rationality relevant to conventional accounts of treatment choice (that is, accounts that do not probe the constraints that institutional and wider systemic conditions may produce), along with the less demanding criterion of "competence," from "autonomy."[67] Here, it is important to note that while autonomy is recognized, on Sherwin's account, as attracting continuing contestation even within feminist and relational literatures, in her work the concept is deployed to reflect an explicitly politicized understanding of what it means (and what it takes) to direct one's life in light of one's considered values and commitments.[68] For instance, on Sherwin's account, instantiation of autonomy requires reflection on the ways that oppressive social structures may inform one's unreflective preferences.[69] Moreover, attainment of the requisite reflective abilities is not, and cannot be, a solo endeavour but, rather, requires social supports, including not only opportunities for reflection but also a range of options beyond those rooted in oppressive assumptions or practices. In sum, Sherwin directs us to attend to the conditions supportive of, as well as destructive of, autonomy (so defined) as these may be identified in the doctor-patient relationship and in the broader institutional and social arrangements within which that relationship is situated – which arrangements may fundamentally inform not only the interpretation and valencing of medical conditions but also the range and quality of treatment options.

Sherwin's work is concerned with the regulative ideal of autonomy, while the present chapter is concerned with the minimal criteria of decisional capacity at law (in Ontario, "understanding" and "appreciation" of relevant information) that govern, in practical terms, whether one retains or loses legal authority to make treatment decisions. It is worth noting that law must be careful not to differentially burden psychiatric subjects – those most likely to be subjected to capacity assessment – with a standard of decisional capacity that approximates Sherwin's autonomy: an ideal that is difficult or impossible to measure, let alone fully achieve. However, Sherwin's account of autonomy is relevant to the laws and practices structuring decisional capacity for at least two reasons. First, I suggest that achievement of decisional capacity status, like the achievement of autonomy on Sherwin's account, is co-constituted by background interpersonal and systemic factors that are typically ignored or minimized in theory and in practice.[70] Sherwin's account offers a useful template for locating and drawing out the significance of these factors. Second, I argue that mental health policy makers and practitioners should, to be adequate to the aspirations of law (in particular, the aspiration of state-subject reciprocity) be oriented not merely toward the evaluation of patients' decisional capacity but also, and more fundamentally – even as a condition of fair evaluation – toward enabling reflection of a sort that would befit the broader regulative ideal that Sherwin describes (for example, reflection on the significance of unusual psychological or psycho-social phenomena and alternative therapeutic options).

Thus, I take from Sherwin the importance of situating specific instances of treatment decision making, and, with this, treatment capacity assessment, within a broader understanding of patterns of oppression or marginalization in health and social systems. That is, a relational approach to the conditions disabling or enabling treatment capacity must explore the connections between the narrow arenas in which treatment capacity is assessed and the wider political and economic conditions that influence those assessments or their outcome. In this vein, we may note the particular convergence of serious mental illness and poverty and, moreover, the propensity for material deprivation, homelessness or insecure housing, and the resulting exposure to physical ill health and/or violence to exacerbate such mental health crises as may erode decisional capacity. Also of relevance is the long-decried shortage and/or inaccessibility of voluntary mental health supports in the community (in particular, supports designed to be responsive to diverse perspectives on treatment and quality of life). Finally, we may note the marked exclusion of those individuals most susceptible to involuntary mental health interventions from processes of policy and law reform that are of significance to them – not only processes intended to feed directly into the assessment of treatment capacity and other practices relevant to involuntary psychiatric hospitalization settings but also those relating to the allocation of wealth and vocational and health care options.[71] All of these restrictions upon equal participation in fundamental social goods affect whether or not one ends up targeted for involuntary hospitalization and, with this, treatment capacity assessment, while also conditioning the resources that one will, or will not, have to draw upon if so targeted – for example, basic material well-being and/or a foundation of past opportunities to reflect upon one's condition and therapeutic options.

The latter point speaks to the specific importance of community-based forums wherein persons facing mental health challenges may deliberate together and with other community members about how unusual psychological or psycho-social experiences may affect one's self-understanding and/or broader interests or goals and the therapeutic options whereby one may overcome, integrate, or otherwise cope with such experiences.[72] Such forums might (although they need not) function to assist in fashioning advance directives and/or crisis directives aimed at indicating one's wishes if capacity is lost, while, in any case, attuning one to one's interests and needs in a way that may build treatment capacity or the capacity to demonstrate that capacity at law.

A further point that is of relevance to the social conditions enabling or disabling treatment capacity status goes to stigma – that is, the pervasive social attitudes whereby mental illness or particularly serious mental illness is associated with dangerousness, incapacity, or both.[73] Stigma is arguably an important determinant of treatment incapacity, insofar as it may shape the ways that treatment capacity is defined and deployed and, moreover, inform the attitudes held by those diagnosed and subject to treatment capacity assessment. This is to take up the thesis that denial of illness – even of "objectively discernible manifestations" of illness – may be explained at least in part as a form of psychological defense mechanism: less an expression of pathology than an effort at self-preservation in the face of "the loss of self-esteem, social stigma and despair that can accompany the diagnosis of a potentially chronic debilitating illness like schizophrenia."[74] That is, stigma is arguably one of the determinants of the denials of illness attributed to "lack of insight" and, with this, treatment incapacity. Therefore, redressing pervasive social biases may be essential to enabling, versus disabling, treatment capacity status on the part of those targeted for assessment in involuntary psychiatric hospital settings and beyond.[75]

Sherwin's approach also urges revisiting the more immediate institutional conditions that may disable treatment capacity status in involuntary psychiatric hospitalization settings. Here, factors that may exacerbate conflict and anxiety must be examined for their potential to impair the reflective and evaluative capacities required to evince the requisite understanding and appreciation. That is, where rough or insensitive treatment precipitates a state of terror and resistance, it is far less likely that the individual so treated will be willing or able to engage in such a conversation about the nature of his condition and options for treatment as might avert formal treatment capacity evaluation or otherwise assist in establishing capacity.[76] Moreover, institutional practices that exacerbate crisis may effect a disabling of treatment capacity not only in the short term but also in the longer term, by instilling ongoing attitudes on the part of the subject that may register as a failure to understand or appreciate relevant information.

On the thesis that respectful relationships conducive to reflection build treatment capacity or the opportunity to demonstrate treatment capacity, while combative, crisis-inducing, or crisis-exacerbating actions toward the subject erode treatment capacity, one might consider mechanisms for diverting persons exhibiting signs of psychiatric crisis from hospital emergency intake environments (or, for that matter, police lock-ups). Such mechanisms may include deployment of mobile crisis units trained to engage with persons in a respectful manner aimed at de-escalating crisis, and/or availability of short-stay venues such as peer-run safe houses.[77] Within hospital, one might identify institutional policies or practices aimed at enhancing the opportunity to develop trust and encourage reflection, including staff training in crisis de-escalation, provision of "quiet rooms" designed to help restore a relative sense of calm to persons in distress, and provision for accompaniment by family members or friends upon admission – this, in addition to refraining from such common crisis-exacerbating practices as forced disrobing (compounded in its adverse effects for those who have been subject to historical sexual abuse), the use of restraints, and forced injection with sedatives or anti-psychotic medications as the first line of defense in crisis.[78] All of these initiatives could have a direct bearing on whether a given individual will meet the minimal criteria of treatment capacity. Such considerations are all the more relevant when treatment capacity is positioned as a criterion of involuntary hospitalization, to be assessed during an initial period of observation. Where coercive practices (forced sedation, seclusion, or re-straints) are applied just prior to a legal assessment of capacity and/or risk, the concerns attracted are particularly grave.

Finally, Sherwin's approach to identifying the conditions enabling or disabling autonomy in the context of treatment choice specifically alerts us to the ways in which the subject's capacity for reflection on her condition and any treatment options is bound up in important respects with her re-lationship with the attending physician. Here, the point made by the major-ity in *Starson* on the importance of physicians' transmitting the relevant information to the subject of treatment capacity assessment prior to that assessment may seem obvious. But there is embedded in this point significant challenges, in that the communication that is required to enable treatment capacity is, on reflection, not just a matter of transmitting objective facts but also of engaging in mutual exploration of the significance of the subject's condition and the prospects for therapeutic intervention. The question is how such a process of mutual exploration or reflection may be initiated or sustained in light of the structural asymmetries of power in the involuntary psychiatric hospitalization setting – that is, where the doctor has the power not only to recommend the patient's release from hospital but also to grant a range of valuable privileges short of liberty (for example, permission to leave a given floor, or to go outside periodically to walk and/or to smoke). Embedded in this question is the further question of how a relationship of mutuality or trust may be initiated or sustained in light of the prospect that the doctor may lack the "ability to appreciate," as Sherwin and Carolyn McLeod put it, the significance of the treatment options for one who stands at a significant remove from her in terms of experience, social position, and mental health status.[79]

I address these challenges further in the discussion that follows, in con-nection with Nedelsky's work on judgment and its application to treatment capacity assessment. However, a final point on enabling the reflective cap-acities, and, with this, the ability to evince treatment capacity, of persons subject to involuntary psychiatric hospitalization goes to the importance of making available institutional spaces apart from the doctor-patient relation-ship for dialogical or deliberative engagement on the significance of unusual or disturbing psychological experiences as well as therapeutic options. I refer to the need to provide opportunities for conversation and so sharing and mutual testing of ideas among persons who are facing, or who have faced, a mental health diagnosis and the prospect of treatment.[80] Such opportunities may be regarded as advancing the subject's interest in autonomy – on Sherwin's account, in significant part a matter of countering dominant norms that marginalize or degrade the perspectives of an historically oppressed group – even as they function to enable the reflective processes that may allay or otherwise defeat suspicions of treatment incapacity.

Enabling the Capacity of Assessors: Nedelsky and the "Enlarged Mentality"

In this final section, I shift my attention from the project of enabling the capacity of those who are subject to capacity assessment to the project of enabling the capacity of assessors to judge. This latter capacity is engaged by the second core principle articulated in *Starson* – namely that failure to agree with a diagnosis, or even to assent to a description of one's condition as a form of "mental illness," should not be determinative of treatment incapacity. I suggest that Nedelsky's work on judgment has important implications for the work of constructing institutional supports aimed at enabling assessors to judge treatment capacity in a way that refrains from imposing the assessor's background values and contestable assumptions or opinions on the subject of assessment. In this respect, I argue that the provision of opportunities to build the capacity for judgment on the part of assessors constitutes an important complement to the earlier-stated concerns that institutional actors not disable treatment capacity by, for example, inappropriate or excessive use of force.

Nedelsky's work on judgment begins with a puzzle – the puzzle of a conception of autonomy wherein we rely on background social conditions and relationships to enable our capacity to reflect upon, and so potentially to critically distance ourselves from, those conditions and relationships.[81] On her account, judgment, properly understood, provides a way of solving, or at least of better understanding, this puzzle. That is, the attentiveness to unanticipated perspectives that forms the core of what it is to judge on Nedelsky's account functions as a means of fostering critical distance from inherited assumptions and forms of social bias. Nedelsky's judgment theory, which she has fashioned in light of Hannah Arendt's fragmentary reflections on judgment, affirms the importance of consulting (or "visiting") other (or "foreign") perspectives – both by exercise of imagination and by actual interlocutory efforts – in making political, adjudicative, and other decisions that are not as such defensible on a representational model of truth. Her specific concern with adjudicative judgment goes to how this form of institutional decision making may be deemed fair, or impartial, and so distinguished from arbitrary power or the imposition of the will or interests of those in authority over the will or interests of those subject to authority. In this way, Nedelsky's judgment theory is closely bound up with questions about whether or how we may salvage an account of law's legitimacy from critiques that law is merely a tool of power. And so it is particularly instructive as an indicator of the theoretical, as well as the practical, bases on which treatment capacity status might be defensibly assessed and assigned in the involuntary psychiatric hospitalization setting.

Nedelsky is clear that while judgment requires a process of consulting others' perspectives it does not amount to entirely deferring to, or submitting to, another's perspective. Nor is it simply an additive process whereby all competing perspectives are integrated into an ultimate decisional theorem securing theoretical consensus. Rather, by taking the views of those who are affected by a prospective decision into account, and, moreover, by formulating and justifying the decision in light of these views (a process that must be understood to inform the substantive result), those who judge – and, in particular, those who judge in the course of making decisions under law – do so in a way that differs both from mere submission to the views of another and from the exercise of arbitrary power.

Nedelsky draws on neurologist Antonio Damasio for the thesis that judgment involves the operation of what Damasio terms "somatic markers."[82] This thesis describes socially conditioned affective responses that register in our brains or habits of mind, at a sub- or semi-conscious level, when we are confronted with situations or states of affairs, and/or decisions to be made in light of those situations or states of affairs. These affective responses, Damasio argues, serve to orient us to the salience of one or another set of facts or imagined consequences. They are as such "gut feelings" – "the starting points of decision making." That is to say that the origin of these gut feelings is not the individual or his or her brain viewed in isolation. Rather, our somatic responses are "the product of experience, education, and culture."[83] Nedelsky's concern is with how these unconscious or semi-conscious starting points of decision may be shaped or reformed to avert the perpetuation of stereotypical or prejudicial reasoning. And this is where we return to the primary thrust of her judgment theory – for Nedelsky argues that exposure to diversity in a respectful context (that is, consideration of a wide array of perspectives) is one way of ensuring that those who must judge are less likely to fall prey to unexamined assumptions lodged in their habits of mind at the pre- or semi-conscious stage.

The thesis of somatic markers and the project of dislodging or reforming them is particularly relevant to my concerns, given the tenacity of the traditional insight model in both psychiatry and law. This model is arguably closely related to the earlier-noted pervasive stereotypes (termed stigma) that link serious mental illness with dangerousness, incapacity, or both. In the absence of institutional efforts to dislodge the strong associations between mental illness (particularly serious mental illness) and failed insight/incapacity, those who exercise authority to assign incapacity status may be impeded in their ability to do so fairly by what Nedelsky represents as affective biases. That is, such biases may block assessors' capacity to take account of the perspectives of those they are charged with assessing – despite their intellectual awareness of the need to avoid bias and even their specific awareness of the prohibition (post-*Starson*) against equating denial of serious mental illness with treatment incapacity. Particularly where diagnosis, denial of illness, and treatment refusal coincide, assessors may start from a point of affective incapacity, whereby they are unable to recognize the subject's reasons "as" reasons and, instead, instinctively relegate them to the status of symptoms. This was just the sort of stereotypical thinking targeted by the majority judgment in *Starson,* when it held that the CCB had erroneously based its opinion on its estimation of Starson's best interests, rather than attending to his testimony and drawing the requisite links between this testimony and the standard of treatment capacity.

Turning to some possible responses to the problem of entrenched biases that obstruct attentiveness to the perspectives or values of those who are subject to capacity assessment, one resource that may be of use is the clinical assessment tool. Such tools – a number have been developed in the past couple of decades – aim at structuring the clinician's judgment such that she must more methodically gather evidence, which must then be considered in light of the relevant jurisdiction's legal standard. Without getting into the relative strengths and weaknesses of competing treatment capacity assessment instruments (which would be essential if such a tool were to be seriously entertained), we may nonetheless bring out the point that, where the instrument involves a list of set questions (for example, oriented to gauging the subject's understanding and appreciation of his condition and the proposed treatment, in addition to such factors as reasoning ability and/or the ability to express a choice),[84] it may be better to structure judgment in this manner so that background assumptions such as those "automatically" or semi-automatically associating denial of illness with lack of insight are offset by methodical attention to competing considerations. That said, it is important to also consider, and take measures to counter, the possibility that the use of a clinical tool may displace the building of a relationship between the assessor and the subject of assessment (for example, where such tools are intended by the maker or user to render the process less time-consuming) and, with this, may discourage case-sensitive judgments.

Moving from the front-line assessment to the tribunal process, we may consider how assumptions rooted in the medical model of mental illness, and such facets of this model as the thesis of "lack of insight," may be reinforced by the binding or coalescing of perspectives among professionals in law and medicine (and, with them, the now professionalized lay members of the tribunal). Tacit assumptions and mutual agreement are potentially expressed in subtle fashion – for example, through body language, comfortable chatting, and other interactions that have the explicit or implicit effect of excluding the subject.[85] Such binding of dominant perspectives against the perspective of one who is disputing a declaration of incapacity may be particularly strongly elicited when the individual concerned exhibits unusual mannerisms or speech (including digressive or tangential testimony) that jar with the conventions of legal proceedings.

The problem is exacerbated when there is no provision for counsel for the patient or when the patient's counsel is ineffective in attending to, or airing, the perspective of his client. In such cases, the likelihood that a tribunal decision will be based in unreflective affective responses, which are untested against alternative perspectives, will be all the greater. Counsel may be significantly underprepared – in part because disputes about treatment capacity are typically required to be disposed of in a compressed time period and in part because of economic exigencies such as caps on legal aid funding. According to some commentators, a further significant factor is counsel's frequent unfamiliarity with, and inattention to, this area of law and to the special demands of this area of practice, including a basic understanding of medical terminology and an awareness of the inappropriateness of paternalistic attitudes toward the client.[86]

To assist in enabling counsel to bring out the perspective of the subject of a capacity hearing (or other matter before the CCB), Legal Aid Ontario has published a set of tips devised by persons with experience in this area.[87] The following excerpt reminds us of the weight of prejudicial assumptions that these tips are designed to counter:

- whenever possible speak to the client before reading the chart or speaking to hospital staff;
- approach clients with an open mind, avoid passing judgment on their decisions;
- incapacity, dangerousness, and mental illness are allegations until proven; and
- do not allow preconceived assumptions to interfere with your relationship with the client – approach this client as you would any other.

To these tips may be added guidelines produced by other agencies in Ontario and elsewhere, intended for use by those responsible for capacity determinations in relation to psychiatrized persons, intellectually disabled persons, and older adults, in an effort to break down stereotypical assumptions that might short-circuit capacity assessment.[88]

Again drawing on Nedelsky's judgment theory, other more direct forms of education may be enlisted to do the work of breaking down biased affective responses and, with this, opening up the perspectives of those charged with assessing capacity to the perspectives of those under assessment. In the settings with which I am concerned, such objectives may be operationalized through programs of medical and/or tribunal education, whereby persons with experience of mental health problems and/or the unusual psychological states associated therewith seek to sensitize decision makers to views or experiences that the latter may not initially be equipped to grasp.[89] Here it is important to note the specific importance of bringing to light the ways that cultural or ethnic differences may compound the difficulty of judging treatment capacity and, moreover, the importance of bringing out how intersecting bases of oppression may inform stereotypical attitudes as well as differential needs that assessors might otherwise overlook.[90] Information sessions focused on alternative forms of therapy may further assist in instilling in medical practitioners and legal decision makers an enhanced ability to appreciate those options and the value that some place upon them. The latter suggestion returns us to the background necessity of supporting treatment capacity – and, moreover, autonomy – through the provision of a range of meaningful treatment options, as well as the imperative that qualitative and quantitative research on therapeutic alternatives be supported so that the nature and efficacy of those alternatives, as experienced by differently located subjects, may be more clearly understood.

Finally, another of Nedelsky's practical proposals made in answer to the problem of the unreflective operation of somatic markers is that of diversifying the bench, or populating the field of legal decision makers in a more diverse fashion, so that those authorized to judge must engage in persuading, and so must seek to anticipate the point of view of, a diverse range of colleagues.[91] In the field of treatment capacity assessment, this proposal might mean ensuring that persons with direct experience of mental health problems are among those who assess or oversee assessments. On the one hand, with the increasing willingness of high-profile public figures, including doctors, lawyers, and judges, to publicly discuss their mental health problems, it may be that the aim of informing decision making with direct experience may be met in part through education to encourage openness and reflection on one's own and others' experiences. Alternatively, as in the case of Nova Scotia, one option is to mandate that membership of the tribunal overseeing involuntary admission and treatment must include persons with experience of mental illness or the mental health system.[92] That said, the challenge of securing meaningful representation is intense, given the diversity of conditions, backgrounds, and perspectives of persons diagnosed with mental illness.

A Relational Account of "Insight"

I wish to raise a last point, intended to deepen the foregoing reflections on the implications of relational theory for the contested field of treatment capacity assessment in the involuntary psychiatric hospitalization setting – here, returning to the troubled concept of "insight." I begin with the thesis noted earlier, whereby denial of illness may be accounted for at least in part as a self-protective coping mechanism that is responsive to stigma and more generally aimed at screening negative information about oneself in favour of a more positive and hopeful self-image. This thesis stands as a non-pathologizing explanatory model for the phenomenon of denial of illness and, moreover, as a model that takes account of the interplay of socio-cultural forces in conditioning individual instances of denial.

However, as we have seen, the majority in *Starson* went further in response to Starson's assertions about his preference for his untreated mind over any sought-after approximation of "normalcy" – and in response (as I have suggested) to his allegation that the treatment capacity assessment process ensnared him in a catch-22. Specifically, the majority stipulated that the assignment of incapacity should not turn upon the subject's willingness to accept the negatively valenced label of "mental illness." With this principle, the majority may be understood to endorse the concept of "neuro-diversity": the idea that the experience of being human, and with this, the mechanisms of the human mind, fall across a wide spectrum and should be respected and accommodated as different, but valuable, manifestations of human being. That said, in retaining a distinction between "objectively discernible manifestations" of one's condition or mental state and the plural ways that these may be interpreted or valued, the majority nonetheless asserts an inter-subjective foundation of fact on which to base the assessment of decisional capacity.

But what sort of foundation is that? I close with a further way of modelling "insight" – again, a concept, or as I first described it, a trope that is pervasively deployed in psychiatry, law, and lay discourse as if to describe the functional neuro-biological bedrock that is the proper referent and determinant of treatment capacity status at law. In this, I draw on developments in cultural psychiatry, medical anthropology, and the philosophy of psychiatry (also critical psychiatry or "post-psychiatry"), revisiting insight in relational terms. A key instance of these developments is a recent paper by Constantin Tranulis, Elaine Corin, and Lawrence Kirmayer, in which the authors argue that insight is best understood to describe not an internal attribute or deficit but, rather, "an active, interactional and negotiated process of making meaning of symptoms and illness" at the intersection of "self-understanding and social positioning."[93] That is, insight – and, we may add (re-injecting law into this model), treatment capacity – is a function of negotiations between doctor and patient, which, in turn, are situated within the wider processes of familial, cultural, and intercultural interaction conditioning the experience of illness and treatment. In developing this thesis, the authors offer the following account of the phenomenon of denial of illness as part of an ongoing interpenetration of "cognitive, social and cultural processes in interpreting illness experience" and, moreover, in shaping prognosis:

As currently defined, schizophrenia is a chronic illness that often has a poor prognosis. It is understandable why many people faced with this diagnosis might want to contest it. In fact, this may reflect a valid critique of the diagnostic construct. A review of treatment for schizophrenia over the last 100 years found that the main predictor of outcome was not treatment modality, but diagnostic criteria: when diagnostic criteria require a long period of psychotic symptoms, the subsequent course tends to be poor ... Hence, it may be that the poor prognosis associated with schizophrenia represents a self-fulfilling prophecy associated with diagnostic criteria that require chronicity, rather than being an intrinsic characteristic of the disorder ... If so, in addition to the psychological phenomenon of the simple reluctance to accept "bad news," from a socio-cultural perspective some patients' reluctance to embrace a diagnosis might be viewed as a manifestation of the discrepancy between the psychiatric knowledge about schizophrenia (that "seeps into popular culture like the dye from a red shirt in hot water") and a more benign appraisal of their subjective experience.[94]

In this passage, the authors advance an account of insight that is fundamentally relational – shifting our understanding of the concept "from one of the transparent viewing of an objective state of affairs to a complex and contested interpretation of experience that may look quite different from the perspectives of clinician and patient."[95]

Here, one may wish to return to *Starson* in order to ask: was there ever a point in the troubled history of Starson's interaction with the mental health system that might have served as an opening for conversation, or specifically such conversation as would feature attentiveness to the interpretive dynamics invoked by Constantin Tranulis, Ellen Corin, and Laurence J. Kirmayer? While hindsight is always a dangerous game, is it possible to conceive of an opening through which not only Starson but also his doctors might have escaped the logic of catch-22? Some suggest that the only such opportunity was closed when law stepped in to mandate respect for Starson's refusal of the medications that, administered earlier, might have rescued him. I have argued that a relational approach to treatment capacity takes us elsewhere. Relational theory foregrounds, while pointing us beyond, relationships of domination in the social constitution (or co-constitution) of the self. Applied to the field of contestation that I have examined herein, a relational approach, cognizant of how the (power-infused) conditions wherein treatment capacity is assessed may influence this assessment as well as the need to enable the capacity of assessors to recognize the subject's reasons "as" reasons, shifts our focus to the possibilities for reciprocity inherent in the mutual construction of insight, capacity, and mental health – indeed, in the mutual construction of autonomy. That is, what a relational approach to health law and policy can do for the status of treatment capacity, as assessed and assigned in involuntary psychiatric hospitalization settings (if not in Starson's case, then perhaps in future cases), is to reopen the question of whether or how this capacity may be enabled and judged in a manner that comports with legality – where legality is itself understood as an interactive-purposive phenomenon aspiring toward reciprocity in the processes whereby the public norms under which we are classed and judged are continually tested and refreshed. Ultimately, it is just such a commitment to reciprocity – and not the hollow victory of negative freedom – that is at the core of the majority decision in *Starson*.

Conclusion

In *Starson*, the majority articulated two principles, namely (1) that the conditions under which treatment capacity is assessed must be examined to ensure that those conditions do not unduly compromise decisional capacity, and (2) that the subject's resistance to the descriptor "mental illness" and/or associated attributions of negative value to his mental condition does not lead inevitably to a determination of incapacity. I have argued that a relational analysis not only urges endorsement of those two principles but also orients us to a set of far-reaching institutional and systemic reforms rooted therein. Attention to relational theory assists in shifting the focus of treatment capacity assessment and attendant disputes from the internal characteristics of the psychiatric subject to the conditions, including the background social conditions and more immediate relationships, that affect how this legal status is interpreted and applied in involuntary psychiatric hospitalization settings. As such, relational theory alerts us to the interconnectedness of the assessment of treatment capacity with ongoing dynamics of power and also aspiration conditioning this field of decision making under law. Ultimately, I suggest, relational theory releases us (or, at least, our reading of *Starson*) from what may have appeared to be a forced choice between negative freedom and psychiatric paternalism. In place of that forced choice, we are presented with the work of mutual exploration of the conceptual and material bases of decisional capacity – and, with this, the possibility of new ways of being capable.

Notes

Thanks to the editors, my fellow contributors to this volume, and Brad Abernethy for his outstanding editorial assistance.

1 Incapacity invalidates consent. See Patricia Peppin, "Informed Consent" in Jocelyn Downie, Timothy Caulfield, and Colleen Flood, eds., *Canadian Health Law and Policy*, 3rd edition (Markham, ON: Butterworths, 2007) 189 at 191.

2 This is not to deny the importance of scrutinizing the legal-institutional mechanisms through which treatment capacity is (or is not) assessed in non-psychiatric hospitals, nursing homes, substance-abuse clinics, and general practitioners' offices. Indeed, to fasten upon the psychiatric hospital setting in inquiring into the laws and conduct structuring treatment incapacity is potentially to reinforce stereotypical assumptions about the peculiar

incapacities of those diagnosed with psychiatric illnesses, while unduly minimizing the importance of the issues raised herein for non-psychiatric settings. However, the distinct medical, legal, and wider social policy underpinnings of disputes about treatment capacity in the psychiatric hospital setting ground a need to address this setting in its particularity. I believe the same can be said about the other settings I mention.

3 *Starson v. Swayze*, 2003 SCC 32, [2003] 1 S.C.R. 722 [*Starson 2003*].

4 See Peppin, *supra* note 1. I am not addressing the important question of how law constructs the treatment capacity of minors. Compare *A.C. v. Manitoba (Director Child and Family Services)*, 2009 SCC 30.

5 *Mental Health Act*, R.S.B.C. 1996, s. 31(1).

6 See Peter J. Carver, "Mental Health Law in Canada" in Downie, Caulfield, and Flood, *supra* note 1, 399 at 408-12. As Carver notes, British Columbia's suspension of the individual's authority to make decisions about treatment absent any inquiry into decisional capacity raises important questions of constitutionality under sections 7 and 15 of the *Canadian Charter of Rights and Freedoms*, Part I of the *Constitution Act*, 1982, being Schedule B of the *Canada Act* 1982 (K), 1982, c 11 [*Charter*].

7 See Carver, *supra* note 6 at 419; *Mental Health Care and Treatment Act*, S.N.L. 2006, s. 17(1). Discussion of the capacity to make decisions about hospital admission is beyond the scope of this chapter. See Peter Bartlett, "The Test of Compulsion in Mental Health Law: Capacity, Therapeutic Benefit and Dangerousness as Possible Criteria" (2003) 11 Med. L. Rev. 326 at 336-44.

8 My reflections on the assessment of treatment capacity in involuntary psychiatric hospitalization settings apply as or more urgently to regimes in which treatment capacity constitutes a condition of involuntary hospitalization as to regimes in which standards for involuntary committal and treatment capacity are bifurcated.

9 *Criminal Code*, R.S.C. 1985, c. C-46, part XXI.

10 See Carver, *supra* note 6 at 419.

11 This matter is not addressed under Ontario's *Mental Health Act*, R.S.O. 1990, c. M-7, and so it falls to the general provisions on consent to treatment in the *Health Care Consent Act*, S.O. 1996, c. 2, Schedule A.

12 *Starson 2003*, *supra* note 3 at para. 75, citing *Fleming v. Reid* (1991), 4 O.R. (3d) 74 (C.A.) at 88 (per Robins J.A.).

13 On the side effects of anti-psychotic and other psychiatric medications, see J.K. Aronson, *Meyler's Side Effects of Psychiatric Drugs* (Amsterdam: Elsevier, 2009).

14 Fitness orders constitute the only basis on which the *Criminal Code*, *supra* note 9, s. 672.58, provides authority for an order of involuntary treatment.

15 One published paper, co-authored with Stanford professor emeritus Pierre Noyes and entitled "Discrete Anti-Gravity," Doc. SLAC-PUB-5429, March 1991, is cited by the courts. *Starson 2003*, *supra* note 3 at para. 65. In the summer of 1998, when the events precipitating his involuntary hospitalization arose, Starson had been attending "daily formal research discussions" centring upon the work of a visiting scientist from Bulgaria. Noted in the decision of Justice Molloy, *Starson v. Swayze* (1999), 22 Admin. L.R. (3d) 211 (Ont. S.C.J.) at para. 29 [*Starson 1999*]. Starson had been invited to these sessions by an associate professor of chemistry at York University (Dr. Geoffrey Hunter) who submitted a letter to the Consent and Capacity Board (CCB) in his support.

16 CCB Hearing Transcript, Doc. TO-98/1320 (24 January 1999) [CCB Hearing Transcript] [on file with author].

17 *Health Care Consent Act*, S.O. 1996, c. 2, Schedule A [*HCCA*].

18 *Ibid.*, s. 4(2).

19 Section 15(1) of the *HCCA*, *ibid.*, states: "A person may be incapable with respect to some treatments and capable with respect to others." Section 15(2) states: "A person may be incapable with respect to a treatment at one time and capable at another."

20 *Ibid.*, s. 4(1).

21 The information that is relevant to a treatment decision under the *HCCA*, *ibid.*, ss. 11(2) and (3), tracks the standard for informed consent at common law – namely information about "the nature of the treatment, the expected benefits of the treatment, the material

risks of the treatment, the material side effects of the treatment, alternative courses of action, and the likely consequences of not having the treatment."

22   *Starson* 2003, *supra* note 3 at para. 78 (per Major J.).

23   *Ibid.* Here it should be noted that, according to the leading empirical studies, there is no necessary correlation between serious mental illness, including schizophrenia, and failure to meet criteria intended to approximate or inform the application of such legal standards as those in Ontario. See Thomas Grisso and Paul S. Appelbaum, "The MacArthur Treatment Competence Study: III. Abilities of Patients to Consent to Psychiatric and Medical Treatment" (1995) 19 Law & Human Behavior 149. In a previous paper, I inadvertently misrepresented this study as having assessed the treatment capacity of involuntarily hospitalized patients (as opposed to psychiatric inpatients *per se*), wrongly inferring involuntary status from the authors' use of the term "hospitalized." See Sheila Wildeman, "Access to Treatment of Serious Mental Illness: Enabling *Treatment* or Enabling *Choice*?" in Colleen Flood, ed., *Just Medicare: What's In, What's Out, How We Decide* (Toronto: University of Toronto Press, 2006) 231.

24   CCB Hearing Transcript, *supra* note 16.

25   *HCCA, supra* note 17, s. 32(4).

26   In one of the more acute manifestations of the tensions between security and therapy in Starson's case, Dr. Posner withdrew as Starson's attending psychiatrist after personally bringing further criminal charges against him (again, charges of uttering threats). He explained that he did this for "clinical reasons" – apparently to ensure that Starson would be subject to the forensic psychiatric system and so to a longer period of involuntary hospitalization than might otherwise be the case. See *Starson* 1999, *supra* note 15 at paras. 4-6.

27   Schizoaffective disorder is defined to include co-incident symptoms of schizophrenia and bipolar disorder. Symptoms associated with schizophrenia include delusions, hallucinations, disorganized speech or grossly disorganized or catatonic behaviour, and negative symptoms such as flat affect or "avolition." Symptoms associated with bipolar disorder include "persistently elevated, expansive, or irritable mood," "inflated self-esteem or grandiosity," "decreased need for sleep," "flight of ideas," "increase in goal-directed activity," and/or "excessive involvement in pleasurable activities that have a high potential for painful consequences." American Psychiatric Association, *Diagnostic and Statistical Manual of Mental Disorders*, 4th edition (Washington, DC: American Psychiatric Association, 2000) at s. 295.70.

28   CCB Hearing Transcript, *supra* note 16.

29   Starson argued that his original surname held emotionally distressing significance for him. He defended his use of the title "professor" by arguing that his fellow travellers in theoretical physics had conferred the title upon him (or at least not objected to his use of it) out of recognition of his achievements. See *Starson* 1999, *supra* note 15 at para. 42.

30   CCB Hearing Transcript, *supra* note 16.

31   *Ibid.* As recognized at the Supreme Court of Canada, none of the criminal charges against Starson involved physical assault: "Professor Starson has never caused physical harm to himself or to others, with the exception of reacting against unwanted forcible medication." *Starson* 2003, *supra* note 3 at para. 66.

32   Cited in *Starson* 2003, *supra* note 3 at para. 94.

33   See *ibid.* at paras. 93-94 and 102.

34   *Ibid.* at para. 102. The CCB panel admitted into evidence eight letters written in support of Starson by friends or associates.

35   *Ibid.* at paras. 99 and 102.

36   CCB Hearing Transcript, *supra* note 16.

37   For instance, according to Justice Molloy of the Ontario Superior Court, there was insufficient evidence to establish that any of the unusual claims attributed to Starson were indicative of delusional ideation (that is, objective manifestations of disorder that he was unable to recognize in himself, as opposed to the accomplishments of an extraordinary individual). *Starson* 1999, *supra* note 15 at para. 61.

38   *Starson v. Swayze* (2001), 201 D.L.R. (4th) 123 at para 9 [*Starson* 2001]. Starson argues, at the relevant part of the CCB record, that if he fails to admit illness he will be deemed to have "no insight into my mental illness," whereupon "I'm going to maybe then [be] found

incompetent in some way and they're going to be forcing to treat me." CCB Hearing Transcript, *supra* note 16.

39 As Dr. Swayze explains it, he felt compelled, at least at the inception of Starson's treatment, to prescribe the "dirty" injectable drug Haldol, at a frankly debilitating dosage, precisely because Starson's resistance was so intense (it would be institutionally impossible to administer an oral anti-psychotic). The resulting cycle of force and resistance is characterized by the board as a kind of "catch-22," with which proposition Dr. Swayze agrees. CCB Hearing Transcript, *supra* note 16.

40 *Starson* 2003, *supra* note 3.

41 *Ibid.* at paras. 93 and 94.

42 *Ibid.* at para. 98.

43 *Ibid.* at para. 102.

44 *Ibid.* at paras. 103-5.

45 *Ibid.* at para. 80. I am reversing the order in which the two imperatives are stated, so as to address first the conditions supportive of treatment capacity and, second, what I regard as the challenge to judgment, or impartial judgment, raised by the imperative of recognizing capacity despite conflicts between the assessor's values or guiding assumptions and those of the subject of assessment.

46 *Ibid.* at para. 81. Earlier (at para. 15), the dissenting opinion draws on the same source that the majority draws upon here – David Weisstub's magisterial *Enquiry on Mental Competency: Final Report* (Toronto: Queen's Printer, 1990) – for the point that patient sedation, as well as failure of the doctor to impart relevant information, are among the practical reasons for distinguishing actual understanding or appreciation from the associated abilities.

47 *Ibid.* at para. 79 [emphasis added].

48 *Ibid.*

49 G. Morris, "Judging Judgment: Assessing the Competence of Mental Patients to Refuse Treatment" (1995) 32 San Diego L. Rev. 343; J. Peay, *Tribunals on Trial: A Study of Decision-Making under the Mental Health Act 1983* (London: Clarendon Press, 1989) at 142-3; Kate Diesfeld, "Insights on 'Insight': The Impact of Extra-Legislative Factors on Decisions to Discharge Detained Patients" in Kate Diesfeld and Ian Freckelton, eds., *Involuntary Detention and Therapeutic Jurisprudence: International Perspectives on Civil Commitment* (Hampshire: Ashgate, 2003) 359.

50 Diesfeld, *supra* note 49. See also Constantin Tranulis, Ellen Corin, and Laurence J. Kirmayer, "Insight and Psychosis: Comparing the Perspectives of Patient, Entourage and Clinician" (2008) 54:3 Int'l J. Soc. Psychiatry 225.

51 Xavier F. Amador and Henry Kronengold, "Understanding and Assessing Insight" in Xavier F. Amador and Anthony S. David, *Insight and Psychosis* (Oxford: Oxford University Press, 2004) 3 at 11; Anthony S. David, "Insight and Psychosis" (1990) 161 Br. J. Psychology 599.

52 See Diesfeld, *supra* note 49; Tranulis, Corin, and Kirmayer, *supra* note 50.

53 "Schizophrenia Society Disappointed with Supreme Court Decision," Schizophrenia Society of Canada News Release (6 June 2003) [on file with author]; David S. Goldbloom, "Psychiatry and the Supreme Court of Canada," Canadian Psychiatric Association Bulletin (August 2003), http://ww1.cpa-apc.org:8080/publications/ archives/Bulletin/2003/august/ editorialEn.asp; John E. Gray, Margaret A. Shone, and Peter F. Liddle, *Canadian Mental Health Law and Policy*, 2nd edition (Toronto: LexisNexis Canada, 2008) at 226-30.

54 S. Nassar, *A Beautiful Mind: The Life of Mathematical Genius and Nobel Laureate John Nash* (New York: Simon and Schuster, 2001).

55 See Goldbloom, *supra* note 53. The phrase "rotting with their rights on" originates in controversies in the 1970s over the stringency of legal protections against psychiatric paternalism. See T. Gutheil and P. Appelbaum, "Rotting with Their Rights On: Constitutional Theory and Clinical Reality in Drug Refusal by Psychiatric Patients" (1979) 7 Bull. Am. Academy Psychiatry & L. 306.

56 S.A. Brooks, R.L. O'Reilly, and J.E. Gray, "Implications for Psychiatrists of the Supreme Court of Canada *Starson v. Swayze* Decision," Canadian Psychiatric Association Bulletin (August 2003), http://ww1.cpa-apc.org:8080/publications/archives/Bulletin/2003/august/brooks. asp at 1-2.

57 Remarks of the Right Honorable Beverley McLachlin, P.C., Chief Justice of Canada, "Medicine and the Law: The Challenges of Mental Illness," (speech given at the University of Alberta and University of Calgary, 17-18 February 2005), http://www.scc-csc.gc.ca/court-cour/ju/spe-dis/bm05-02-17-eng.asp.

58 In K. Makin, "High Court Supports Mentally-Ill Physicist: Man Can Choose to Stay Confined instead of Taking Drugs He Feels Dull His Intellect, Judges Rule," *Globe and Mail* (7 June 2003).

59 *R. v. Starson*, [2004] O.J. No. 941, 184 O.A.C. 338 (C.A.) at para. 15.

60 *Re: Professor S; File KI-05-4875*, [2005] O.C.C.B.D. No. 49 (19 February 2005).

61 This history is recounted in *Starson v. Pearce*, 2009 CanLii 46 (Ont. S.C.J.).

62 I cannot address herein the important question of reforms to existing legal standards – for instance, whether the criterion of "appreciation" is unduly susceptible to deployment so as to disqualify the subject's value-laden risk assessments where these conflict with the values of the assessor. I would suggest, however, that current trends in domestic and international law toward requiring (or interpreting existing laws to require) that all means of supporting decision making be exhausted prior to the assignment of treatment incapacity status are consistent with the relational approach suggested herein. See the recent UN *Convention on the Rights of Persons with Disabilities*, G.A. Res. 61/106, 76th Plen. Mtg., UN Doc. A/Res/61/106 (adopted by consensus at the United Nations on 13 December 2006, in force 3 May 2008). See particularly Article 12 (Legal Capacity). And see the comprehensive report on the implications of Article 12 for Canadian law, prepared for the Law Commission of Ontario and released after the present chapter was written. Michael Bach and Lana Kerzner, "A New Paradigm for Protecting Autonomy and the Right to Legal Capacity," Law Commission of Ontario, October 2010, http://www.lco-cdo.org/disabilities/bach-kerzner.pdf.

63 These are ideas I cannot develop here. I refer to a conception of law's legitimacy as based in state-subject reciprocity, which is promulgated in the mid-twentieth-century reflections of Lon L. Fuller and developed in contemporary legal theory, in particular, administrative law theory. See Willem J. Witteveen and Wibren van der Burg, *Rediscovering Fuller: Essays on Implicit Law and Institutional Design* (Amsterdam: Amsterdam University Press, 1999), especially David Dyzenhaus, "Fuller's Novelty," 78 at 97.

64 See Jennifer Llewellyn, "Restorative Justice: Thinking Relationally about Justice" in this volume.

65 Susan Sherwin, "A Relational Approach to Autonomy in Health Care" in S. Sherwin, ed., *The Politics of Women's Health: Exploring Agency and Autonomy, The Feminist Health Care Ethics Research Network* (Philadelphia: Temple University Press, 1998) 19, cited to E. Boetzkes and W. Waluchow, eds., *Readings in Health Care Ethics* (Peterborough, ON: Broadview Press, 2000) 69.

66 Susan Sherwin, *No Longer Patient* (Philadelphia: Temple University Press, 1992) at 54; Sherwin, *supra* note 65 at 71.

67 Sherwin, *supra* note 65 at 77.

68 See Catriona MacKenzie and Natalie Stoljar, "Introduction: Autonomy Reconfigured" in Catriona MacKenzie and Natalie Stoljar, eds., *Relational Autonomy: Feminist Perspectives on Autonomy, Agency, and the Social Self* (New York: Oxford University Press, 2000) 3.

69 Sherwin, *supra* note 65 at 77.

70 The work of Susan Stefan constitutes an important precedent for a relational approach to treatment capacity, as I am configuring the latter, in demonstrating particular sensitivity to power dynamics in capacity assessment. See Susan Stefan, "Silencing the Different Voice: Competence, Feminist Theory and Law" (1993) 47 U. Miami L. Rev. 763; Susan Stefan, "Race, Competence Testing, and Disability Law: A Review of the MacArthur Competence Research" (1996) 2 Psychology, Pub. Pol'y & L. 31.

71 The links between mental illness, poverty/homelessness, lack of access to voluntary supports, and lack of inclusion in law reform processes are developed in an extensive empirical literature. See Standing Senate Committee on Social Affairs, Science and Technology, *Out of the Shadows at Last: Transforming Mental Health, Mental Illness and Addiction Services in Canada* (Ottawa: Standing Senate Committee on Social Affairs, Science and Technology,

2006), http://www.parl.gc.ca/39/1/parlbus/commbus/senate/com-e/soci-e/rep-e/rep02may06-e.htm.

72 Sherwin and McLeod develop this point with reference to women and addiction recovery. Susan Sherwin and Caroline McLeod, "Relational Autonomy, Self-Trust, and Health Care for Patients Who Are Oppressed" in MacKenzie and Stoljar, *supra* note 68, 259 at 274-75 (discussing an egalitarian model of group therapy involving counsellors as well as affected women). See also Sara Goering, "Postnatal Reproductive Autonomy: Promoting Relational Autonomy and Self-Trust in New Parents" (2009) 23:1 Bioethics 9 at 15: "Even in distinctly oppressive conditions, some people succeed in overcoming significant obstacles to self-trust (derision, devaluing, etc. that others may internalize), often through finding solidarity with others who share their experiences." Consider the UK organization Hearing Voices Network, wherein persons affected by this phenomenon may come together with health care workers and supportive family or friends seeking a way of integrating the experience into a positive self-conception and way of life. Hearing Voices Network, http://www.hearing-voices.org/.

73 Standing Senate Committee on Social Affairs, Science and Technology, *supra* note 71, c. 1.4.

74 Tranulis, Corin and Kirmayer, *supra* note 50.

75 However, see Kimberley White on the need for vigilance to ensure that anti-stigma campaigns do not reproduce moral panic around the need to publicly expose and address mental illness, posed as a looming public health, economic, and citizenship crisis. Kimberley White, "Out of the Shadows and Into the Spotlight: The Politics of (In)visibility and the Implementation of the Mental Health Commission of Canada" in Kimberley White, ed., *Configuring Madness: Representation, Context and Meaning* (Freeland, UK: Inter-Disciplinary Press, 2009) 247.

76 Here it is worth noting the recollections of one of Starson's friends who, after finding him in his apartment behaving in bizarre fashion, called the police ("I don't know why we called the police instead of a hospital ... That's just what we did") and accompanied him in the police cruiser on what appears to have been his first emergency psychiatric admission: "He was saying 'Why are they doing this to me? Why are they putting me in this room? Frank, why are you leaving me here? I don't like this game.' He started thrashing and flailing and trying to run. And they were holding him down. They had him in a headlock and shoulder holds. That was the last I saw of him that time. It was heartbreaking." Interview with Frank Cianciotta, reported in "Fighting for the Right to Refuse Treatment, Part 1," *Ottawa Citizen* (11 June 2005), http://www.canada.com/ottawa/ottawacitizen/news/story.html?id=7cd24be1-efb7-41b6-9511-54e1f8e27524.

77 Susan Stefan identifies a set of structural factors conditioning harmful emergency room responses to persons evincing psychological crisis and suggests some far-reaching reforms in her book *Emergency Department Treatment of the Psychiatric Patient: Policy Issues and Legal Requirements* (Oxford: Oxford University Press, 2006). I draw particularly on the recommendations advanced in Chapter 6. Further inquiry into the policy reforms that might begin to redress the marginalization and mistreatment of persons located at the intersection of the mental health and justice systems would do well to attend closely to the eighty recommendations advanced in the recent *Report of the Fatality Inquiry into the Death of Howard Hyde*, Report pursuant to the *Fatality Investigations Act*, prepared by Nova Scotia Provincial Court Judge Anne S. Derrick (Halifax, NS: 30 November 2010) at 350-83, http://www.courts.ns.ca/hyde_inquiry/hyde_inquiry_report.pdf.

78 Stefan, *supra* note 77 at 131-39.

79 Sherwin and McLeod, *supra* note 72 at 268.

80 See *ibid*.

81 See Jennifer Nedelsky, "The Reciprocal Relation of Judgment and Autonomy: Walking in Another's Shoes and Which Shoes to Walk In" in this volume.

82 Antonio Damasio, *Descartes' Error: Emotion, Reason, and the Human Brain* (New York: Putnam, 1994) at 172-75, cited in Jennifer Nedelsky, "Embodied Diversity and the Challenges to Law" in Ronald Beiner and Jennifer Nedelsky, eds., *Judgment, Imagination, and Politics: Themes from Kant and Arendt* (Lanham, MD: Rowman and Littlefield, 2001) 229 at 237. My interest in the thesis of somatic markers is directed not at the possibility that these might

serve as indicators of minimal decisional capacity but, rather, with Nedelsky, at the potential for this thesis to assist in building good adjudicative (and, more broadly, political) judgment. Thus, I am not suggesting that Damasio's model might constitute a nascent "capacimeter."

83 Nedelsky, *supra* note 82 at 242.
84 These are factors taken into account in the treatment capacity assessment instrument widely considered the "gold standard" in the field: Appelbaum and Grisso's MacCAT-T. See Paul S. Appelbaum and Thomas Grisso, *Assessing Competence to Consent to Treatment: A Guide for Physicians and Other Health Professionals* (New York: Oxford University Press, 1998).
85 Compare Michael Perlin's work on the infiltration of "sanism" into legal processes involving psychiatric patients. Michael Perlin, "On Sanism" (1992) 46 S.M.U. L. Rev. 373; Michael Perlin, "Pretexts and Mental Disability Law: The Case of Competency" (1992-93) 47 U. Miami L. Rev. 625, esp. 669-88. See also Morris, *infra* note 86.
86 Grant Morris, "Let's Do the Time Warp Again: Assessing the Competence of Counsel in Mental Health Conservatorship Proceedings" (2009) 46:2 San Diego L. Rev. 283. Morris states: "[E]mpirical studies of attorney performance in civil commitment proceedings conducted in the 1960s and 1970s ... revealed a consistent failure of attorneys to advocate actively for their mentally disordered clients in those proceedings." He adds: "Although numerous commentators have relied upon those studies to denounce attorney passivity and to urge attorneys to aggressively resist involuntary civil commitment of their clients, inadequate performance by attorneys continues to be the rule today, rather than the exception" (at 284). See also Aaron Dihr, "Relationships of Force: Reflections on Law, Psychiatry and Human Rights" (2008) 25 Windsor Rev. Legal & Soc. Issues 103 at 108-10.
87 Legal Aid Ontario, "Helpful Tips for Lawyers Representing Clients before the Consent and Capacity Board," http://www.legalaid.on.ca/en/info/downloads/CCB_tips.pdf.
88 See, for example, *Guidelines for Conducting Assessments of Capacity* (Ontario Ministry of the Attorney General, Capacity Office, May 2005), http://www.attorneygeneral.jus.gov.on.ca/english/family/pgt/capacity/2005-06/guide-0505.pdf.
89 The Ontario CCB has reportedly made efforts in this regard over the years. Interview with current chair Justice E. Ormston (July 2008).
90 Susan Stefan, "Race, Competence Testing, and Disability Law," *supra* note 70 at 31-44. See also A. Mollow, "When Black Women Start Going on Prozac ... : The Politics of Race, Gender, and Emotional Distress in Meri Nana-Ama Danquah's Willow Weep for Me" in Leonard J. Davis, ed., *The Disability Studies Reader*, 2nd edition (New York: Routledge, 2006) 283.
91 Nedelsky, *supra* note 82 at 242-43.
92 Section 65(2)(c) of Nova Scotia's *Involuntary Psychiatric Treatment Act*, S.N.S. 2005, c. 42, stipulates that lay members of the board (that is, those who are neither doctors nor lawyers) express an interest in mental health issues and preferably are, or have been, consumers of mental health services.
93 Tranulis, Corin and Kirmayer, *supra* note 50 at 226. See also Constantin S. Tranulis, Oliver Freudenreich, and Lawrence Park, "Narrative Insight: Rethinking Insight in Psychosis" (2009) 2:1 Int'l J. Culture & Mental Health 16.
94 Tranulis, Corin and Kirmayer, *supra* note 50 at 229.
95 *Ibid.* at 229-30.

12

Non-Human Animals and Human Health: A Relational Approach to the Use of Animals in Medical Research

Maneesha Deckha

As the authors of the first part of this volume note, feminist relational theory (hereinafter referred to as relational theory) is an ideal theory to re-theorize concepts related to health and otherwise. Its promise lies in the quite simple acknowledgment that human beings are relational and interdependent and that law's stark reliance on individualism and independence fails to capture the centrality of relationships and the importance of our responsibilities to others. Relational theory takes human relationships, personal but also public and political, as its departure point for theorizing questions of how society should be ordered and what rights or other legal recognition should ensue. As its name intimates, relationships are its focus. Identifying oppressive power-laden relationships and using law to foster healthy, sustaining, and fulfilling relationships is a core part of the mandate of relational theory.

In this chapter, I embrace these tenets of relational theory but seek to push them farther than they usually extend. Relational theory is subversive of many of law's formative principles constituting the ideology of liberal legalism that underpins Western common law systems as well as the liberal worldview of human beings. However, relational theory remains firmly situated in a humanist paradigm.[1] Many of the concepts discussed earlier in this volume – identity, conscience, memory, and judgment – are widely viewed as distinctive human attributes.[2] Establishing the humanness of various attributes has not preoccupied relational theory since it, like so many other critical theories, has thus far taken the justice-seeking human subject for granted as the norm. Incorporating non-humans into relational theory is a new endeavour, and one of the purposes of this chapter is to contribute to this mapping. Relational theory itself is a relatively new addition to critical discourse. By bringing non-humans – in particular, non-human animals – into its ambit, it is hoped that its signature insights will be enriched and fortified.

My first aim in this chapter is to show how issues related to species' differences are a natural fit for relational theory. With this connection in place, the second aim is to apply relational theory to the controversial practice of using non-human animals in medical research. By the term "non-human animal," my concern extends to all those non-human beings whose bodies are the sites of research interventions. I do not wish here to draw a distinction between animals that are assigned, comparatively speaking, cultural value (such as non-human primates) and those that are not (such as rats). I also do not exclude insects and those beings we view as non-humans but that science technically does not classify as "animal."[3] I acknowledge that there may be valid reasons to reserve our ethical regard in part or in whole for some non-humans rather than others. While important to the growing field of post-humanist/animal studies, these questions of line drawing (who is included/who is excluded) need to be set aside as they will detract from my central concern, which is to gently push relational theory past the species boundary between humans and non-humans.[4]

In the first part of this chapter, I set out the main principles of ecofeminism to show its points of connection with, as well as its differences from, relational theory. I then discuss how a relational understanding of equality, judgment, and justice, as outlined by Christine Koggel, Jennifer Nedelsky, and Jennifer Llewellyn in this volume, may be applied to animals. In the second part, I test what the implications of relational theory, unconstrained by the human/non-human boundary, might be for the larger questions of human health taken up by this volume. Specifically, I explore the relational ethics of using non-human animals (hereinafter simply "animals") in medical research undertaken for the betterment of human health.[5] I help sketch a post-humanist vision of relational ethics, a vision that moves beyond the speciesism and anthropocentrism of the Western humanist tradition.[6] The third part then uses relational theory to consider a proposal for law reform in the area of animal research that would better reflect the obligations, established in the first and second parts, that we have to include animals under relational theory. Recent international legislative initiatives are examined to help recommend policy for Canada.

Medical research on animals is a particularly important topic to explore not merely because it coheres with the subject matter of this volume. It is one of the human practices involving animals that is most resistant to change, due to the feared detrimental effect on human health that would come with ceasing this research. Even where humans are willing to accept limits or outright prohibitions on uses of animals for recreation, consumption, and clothing purposes, substantive intervention into animal research for medical or human therapeutic purposes is more fiercely resisted.[7] Medical research is viewed as a more laudable and important endeavour to safeguard than these other areas since the use of animals is perceived to be necessary to advance human health.[8] The chapter may be said to address, then, one of the most challenging arenas where human beings encounter animals in

Western societies to see what guidance relational theory offers to sort through the perennial controversy regarding animal experimentation.[9]

Relational Theory and Animals: A "Natural" Fit

Early relational theory provided an important critique of universal theories of justice, interrogating the primacy given to a reductive understanding of the capacity for autonomy and reason and developing a more robust role for interdependence, affect, and emotions in our ethical deliberations. Born from Carol Gilligan's widely influential *In a Different Voice*, this early work focused on the centrality of relationships in moral reasoning due to the interdependence of human beings at every stage of their lives.[10] It aimed for the creation of healthy, positive, nurturing, and loving relationships among us so that we may reach our individual and collective potential and highest sense of well-being.[11] As the discipline evolved, it grew beyond an individual orientation to focus on the social, political, economic, and cultural landscape informing our relationships that bring us into being as gendered, raced, and classed subjects through power-laden social practices. In her contribution to this collection in which she theorizes equality, Christine Koggel elaborates on this orientation:

> A relational approach (1) is contextual in that it allows us to attend to the details of the lives of those affected by various kinds of unequal and oppressive relationships – relationships that are in turn shaped by particular social practices and political contexts; (2) uncovers the governing norms and practices that sustain various inequalities for those who are powerless and disadvantaged; and (3) reveals the importance of the perspectives of those adversely affected by relationships of power as sources for learning about various kinds of inequalities and the structures that sustain them.[12]

As Koggel describes it, relational theory is sensitive to the harmful aspects of all kinds of relationships and focuses on replacing harmful relationships with better ones. When it comes to matters of public policy and legal design, relational theory prompts us to select measures that we believe will foster a society adept at undoing the effects of socially constructed differences and their adverse meanings in hierarchically ordered societies.[13] Important to this designing, as Koggel notes earlier, are the perspectives of those harmed by current relations of power.

Humanist Norms

An invisible parameter of relational theory's project has been its humanist norms. It is a theory that has expressed important concerns about human subjects in its focus on human relationships with other humans, corporations, and governments. The fact that the human subject has informed the work of most critical scholars, relational or not, seems to be more a product of the unquestioned humanism that underscores so much of Western philosophical and liberal thought, even of the feminist kind, in which theorization of the animal-human relationship is scant.[14] As Cary Wolfe has noted, the rich set of literatures that impugn classic Western humanism has not turned toward the question of the animal.[15] As he and others, including feminists working in animal ethics, have further commented, this oversight is curious given that the critiques that this set of literatures have lodged against Western humanism also resonate and overlap with post-humanist critiques that question an anthropocentric order.[16] This point is glimpsed if one considers that a primary target of feminism, post-colonial theory, and cultural studies has been the concept of the Other that seeks to justify various hierarchies among different human groups as well as the problematic exclusionary and essentialist concept of the human that has long operated in the liberal humanist tradition to subordinate and oppress.[17] Even attention to animals and the concept of species given by certain influential theorists – witness Jacques Derrida's concept of carnophallogocentrism and Donna Haraway's concept of the cyborg and the social construction of primatology and humanness – has not stimulated a rush to fill in this post-humanist gap in critical theory.[18]

Connections between Relational Theory and Ecofeminism

This conceptual limit is not necessary, particularly in relational theory. While not adopting the explicit label of "relational" or emphasizing as strenuously the "connection over separation as essential to the constitution and maintenance of the self," another branch of feminist theory, ecofeminism, has developed an approach to relationships of power that is very similar to that of relational theory.[19] Ecofeminism, however, to stress a fundamental difference, transcends the human limit. It is a branch of feminist theory that is devoted to revealing the connections between the oppression of women and the oppression of the non-human world. In Western, anglophone circles, the work of ecofeminists Carol Adams, Josephine Donovan, Greta Gaard, Karen Warren, and others have been emblematic of ecofeminist theorizations of animals in particular.[20] Adams's and Donovan's most recent anthology, *The Feminist Care Tradition in Animal Ethics*, documents the ecofeminist scholarship accumulated in recent decades.[21]

As the title of this collection suggests, a substantial part of ecofeminist philosophy has worked to extend a feminist ethic of care to non-human animals. It is important, however, not to sharply differentiate the connectedness focus of relational theory from the caring focus in ecofeminism. Recall from the chapters in the first part of this volume that relational theory identifies an ethic-of-care praxis as too focused on celebrating personal relations to be an antidote to rationalist liberal hyperindividualism. For relational theory, more systemic issues, such as how power structures the relationships in which we are embedded, need to be examined.[22] As Jennifer Llewellyn and Jocelyn Downie distinguish, relational theory's focus has not been on "particular relationships or types of relationships" but, rather, "on the dynamics or characteristics of relationship that need to be supported and encouraged in order to foster human flourishing."[23] Ecofeminism has always had this latter politicized and systemic focus when utilizing caring terminology and frameworks – the primary difference being incorporating a concern for *animal* flourishing. The concern is not simply to value an ethic of care but, rather, to stimulate feminist sensibility that animals matter morally by highlighting their capacities to emote and relate. As ecofeminist Deborah Slicer articulates, "[t]here is no reason why animals' differences, independence, indifference cannot be grounds for caring, for relationships characterized by such ethically significant attitudes as respect, gratitude, compassion, fellow or sisterly feeling, and wonder."[24] Both the route and implication of this relational insight in the context of animals is to urge review and critique of human power over animals.

With this clarification in hand, we can now consider the places of overlap, noting along the way the points of difference between ecofeminism and relational theory. Again, the comparison is meant to demonstrate relational theory's ability to include animals in its purview.

Wariness of Traditional Rights Discourse

Like relational theorists, ecofeminists offer a critique of traditional rights-based/justice-based theories as too wedded to liberalism's unrealistic vision of the rational, self-interested, independent, and autonomous actor who is viewed as truly free when armed with rights that secure his separation from others and his non-interference with the state.[25] In addition to moving away from a rigidly formulated, abstract, and individualist concept of rights, ecofeminists have also raised awareness of the socially constructed nature of differences of race, gender, ability, and so on that embody human actors.

Appreciation of Difference and Embodiment

Like relational theorists, ecofeminists highlight the concepts of difference and embodiment. Unlike relational theorists, ecofeminists have laboured to unravel the effects of Cartesian dichotomies on humans and animals both in structuring our ideas of difference and in connecting our systems of domination.[26] Taking two of these interconnected dualities – the positioning of the mind over the body and reason over emotion in creating a false picture of individuals – we can see that the harmful effects of these dualisms in the social construction of differences that marginalize certain human groups (racialized individuals, women, individuals with mental disabilities) is also something that extends to animals.

While relational theory has not concentrated its critique on the existence of these dualisms explicitly,[27] it shares with ecofeminist theory the underlying concern about the social construction of difference and how the resulting norms shape, and are shaped by, relationships that generate hierarchically ordered social locations. Unlike liberalism where difference is, at best, tolerated, relational theory and ecofeminism are concerned with the stigmatization and second-class status of different bodies and beings that occupy liberalism's periphery (if they appear at all).[28] In this shared focus, both theories highlight the harm perpetuated by myths about reason (who has it, to what extent, and what it consists of) and associations with the body in justifying the subjugation of different groups. Relational theory, like much feminist theory, has taken up this critique in the case of women. Ecofeminism extends the analysis to animals.

One of the primary cultural narratives told about animals in Western society is that their inferiority lies in their lesser capacity for rational thought.[29] The capacity for reason remains one of the current hegemonic justifications given to distinguish human beings from animals and to substantiate the ethical propriety of a human/non-human species boundary.[30] Although animals were once widely thought to be mere automatons incapable of any feeling – an idea we can trace back to Descartes to facilitate the practice of vivisection, no less – today there is more public acknowledgment that they can experience pain and even emotions.[31] Yet, a perception still persists that an animal's sensibilities and overall existence are merely instinctual.[32] It is humans who are thought to govern themselves through rational thinking and thereby to deserve the elevated moral position society bestows on them.[33]

More to the point, it is the humanized humans (through culture, not genetic engineering), as Wolfe refers to them, who are seen as fully human. These are the individuals whose combination of gender, race, class, sexuality, ability, age, and so on has not marked them historically and culturally to be "defective" reasoners and thus not fully human.[34] Under a species grid, as Wolfe terms it, socially constructed differences work to mark certain humans as "humanized" and others as "animalized." Gender, race, class, and so on also work to humanize the bodies of certain animals and animalize those of others.[35] Ecofeminist efforts align with relational efforts to uncover the norms and practices shaped by Western liberal thinking by which some of us (humans) are seen as more or less human and more or less animalized depending on long-standing cultural stories about rational capacity and embodiment.

In this rehabilitation of difference and embodiment, both theories are aware of how socially constructed differences create cultural Others and seek to neutralize Othering relationships. The difference lies only in their foci. Relational theory has heretofore been immersed in the world of human relationships. Ecofeminist theory seeks to enrich this analysis by including human-animal relationships as well. In terms of the implications of extending the network of relationships further than envisioned by relational theorists thus far, this insight would explain that the "human" identity is itself a social construct that is embedded in hierarchies of difference and embodiment and that humans are themselves shaped and reshaped by their relationships with non-human animals. In understanding our own human identity as a relational one with non-humans, we can expand our understanding of animals and our responsibilities to them.

Attention to Context

In addition to sharing critical views on traditional liberal rights discourse as well as the role of the rational and disembodied actor in Western thought, a third tenet of relational theory exhibited in ecofeminist theory is a desire for localized analyses. Ecofeminists are committed to looking at problems in their historical and cultural context in order to tailor situations to the needs of the beings involved.[36] They espouse the post-colonial and post-structural insight adopted by relational theory that analyses are always already partial and contingent and should continually attend to those voices they may exclude. The two theories are in agreement, then, in their deliberate move away from liberalism's penchant for universal principles and their embrace of localized recommendations and conclusions.

Gender Identity of Its Main Advocates

Finally, in addition to the critique of the rational and disembodied actor, respect for difference, and wariness of traditional articulations of rights and universals, another point of connection between relational theory and ecofeminism is worthy of mention – the fact that the overwhelming majority of animal advocates are women, "continu[ing] a historical trend in western societies of female activism for animals."[37] Notably, the anti-vivisection movement was dominated by women in terms of membership.[38] We can set aside the "why" of this phenomenon – whether women are drawn to animal activism due to gender socialization (their propensity to care about suffering and empathize) or because of a recognition of the similarities between the treatment of women and animals. Neither ecofeminism nor relational theory is invested in cultural feminist premises that women "naturally" care about suffering. Yet, the demographics alone should accentuate the interest of feminists that are new to post-humanist queries on the relevance of such queries to feminist and relational projects. This impulse should be strengthened by the knowledge that a popular criticism of animal protection movements targets its female membership as proof of its irrational claims, decrying women's abilities to understand the complexities of science and progress that require animal experimentation and exploitation generally.[39]

Where do all of these shared areas of concern between relational theory and ecofeminism direct us in how we should set our ethical compasses as relational theorists? In a conversation with a critic who does not value relational theory and does not wish to address relationships of power and hierarchies of difference, one would likely have to use standard logical argumentation to reveal to her the tenuousness of the human uniqueness claim on which her desire to exclude animals relies. However, in a conversation with a relational theorist, the repertoire of critique expands due to the shared critique that relational theorists and ecofeminists have of universal theories, including Othering dynamics and the privileging of the rational and disembodied actor in general.[40] Importantly, arguments emphasizing the sameness of humans and animals need not be advanced to dismantle human uniqueness and morality claims. Ecofeminists will find a like-minded audience in relational theorists who value differences and embodiment. In this regard, ecofeminist critique fits well within the existing tenets of relational theory, making human relationships with animals part of the relational matrix to be scrutinized and redressed. Indeed, the way in which Koggel describes what is unique to "a relational approach to theory and policy" matches many of the aspects discussed earlier for ecofeminism:

> [I]ts attention to detail, its uncovering of norms, its legitimizing of perspectives, its critical analysis of power and of relations of power, and its awareness of what can be achieved in and through embodied engagement with different others who are marginalized and powerless.[41]

Equality, Judgment, Justice, and Animals

We can also arrive at the conclusion that relational theory is easily amenable to animals if we consider what equality, justice, and judgment should mean in a relational approach, although they are not currently presented in this way by relational theorists in this volume or otherwise. Recall that the third main point that Koggel identifies in a relational conception of equality is the importance of attending to, and including, the perspectives of Others. This is not just a call to listen to peripheral voices but, rather, to engage "with different others" at levels that subvert traditional positionings of margin and centre.[42] It prompts a focus to unearth structural relationships that are difficult to see because of the various privileges we may hold.[43] Koggel writes:

> We need to pay attention to relationships of power both within and across borders, to how these relationships are created and sustained by inequalities in wealth and income prevalent in the current economic global order, and to why these inequalities entrench a host of other inequalities.[44]

Koggel argues for greater introspection by those benefitting from global capital relations to see how global capital disparities reproduce inequalities and power differentials. A considerable part of the "wealth and income prevalent in the current economic global order" creating these disparities among persons involves our relationships with nonhuman animals. If a relational understanding of equality means confronting global property rights, as Koggel instructs, then a productive place to extend our critical examinations would be to human-animal relationships. While Koggel may not have intended this meaning, the inequalities between humans and animals could easily qualify as one of the "other inequalities" that econimic capital disparities "entrench."

Jennifer Nedelsky's discussion of judgment also moves us to the same conclusion. After all, when we engage in judgment the decisions we make can often have an impact beyond humans, and it seems only fair, as Koggel stresses, to consider the perspectives of Others who will be impacted through our relationships. As one element in an ecosystem, where we live, what we eat, what we wear, what we otherwise consume in the marketplace, how we transport ourselves, and what we may do for remunerated work all have an impact not only on other human beings locally and globally but also on non-humans.[45] If we work with Nedelsky's relational theorization of judgment, it becomes apparent that good judgment requires taking animals into account even though she does not refer to them. Consider Nedelsky's discussion of the enlargement of the mind that must occur in order for good judgment to take place. This process requires imagining the perspectives of others given their embodied social locations and assessing whether one's own perspective is responsive and persuasive to those others. The views of all others must be considered. Discussing Kant's conception of judgment, Nedelsky writes:

> When we "woo the consent" of others, it is the consent of *all* others, at all times, in all places – and thus necessarily only in the imagination. Judgment is founded in an appeal to common sense, but the common sense is shared among all people by virtue of their having the same basic human faculties (understanding and imagination in particular). This common sense is universal.[46]

Nedelsky herself clearly views judgment as a human faculty, and her directive is to include all human Others in terms of evaluating our own perspective in formulating judgment. It is not clear, however, that her account requires the exclusion of animals from this attempt to "woo the consent" of others. Judgment, as Nedelsky emphasizes, is an imaginative enterprise, and what is important is to consider other perspectives and not whether these perspectives can be articulated in a verbal language that we can understand. Even if the direct perspectives of animals were not to be included and imagined, then at least the perspectives of humans who empathize with animal suffering and are against animal exploitation, and that shape their perspectives accordingly, would have to be included in exercising good judgment. The fact that animal perspectives may be more "different" and even unknowable is not a bar under Nedelsky's attentive and power-attuned conceptualization of how to imagine other perspectives:

> The way we take another's perspective into account should be shaped both by the kind of judgment that we think she exercised, as well as by our own humility about our capacity to understand standpoints that are very different from our own and consciousness of the asymmetries of power that may interfere.[47]

Even if we grant that judgment is a distinct human capacity, exercising judgment as Nedelsky would like us to do in a relational framework requires adverting to the perspectives, at least indirectly, of animals.

Relational theory's compatibility with post-humanism is also illustrated by a relational conception of justice. Llewellyn traces the features of a relational account of justice in her chapter. She seeks to move legal understandings of injustice as wrongdoing toward a more systemic-minded restorative justice. She states: "Justice understood relationally, thus, takes as its aim equality of relationship, not in the sense of sameness but, rather, in the sense of satisfying the basic elements required for well-being and flourishing."[48] Although Llewellyn focuses on humans in her delineation of what a relational conception of justice amounts to, there is nothing inherent to her account that necessitates excluding animals. To the contrary, as with relational accounts of equality and judgment provided by Koggel and Nedelsky, a relational conception of justice would appear to incline toward their inclusion.

The theorists in this volume stress a relational account because we are relational beings inherently connected to others. Our flourishing thus depends on the health of these connections. Animals also are relational beings, inherently connected to others (both human and non-human). Their flourishing thus depends on the health of these connections. If we can accept Llewellyn's articulation that "[t]he concern of a relational theory of justice is ... with connection at what one might call a social level – that is, with the basic elements and conditions of relationship required for peaceful and meaningful coexistence and flourishing," we will need to think about our relationships with animals in creating this coexistence even if we are only concerned with our own flourishing.[49] Yet, we need not stop there. It is possible to extend concern to all relational beings with whom we share the planet. Restorative justice models that seek to privilege human relationships over all others would be hard-pressed to find the justification to do so given the organizing premises of relational theory that are canvassed earlier.

This section of the chapter has articulated the salience of the multiple connections between relational theory and ecofeminism. It has also shown the amenability of relational accounts of equality, judgment, and justice to including animals in order to advance the argument that incorporating species difference can and should be an easy move for relational theory. Having established this notion, I now use a relational framework to assess the issue of the ethics of animal-based medical research.

Relational Theory and Animal-Based Medical Research

Canadian Animal Research Landscape

The controversy over the ethics of using animals in medical research is not new.[50] The impact of restrictive regulation in this area is high. The global use of animal bodies for research purposes is extensive, with over 120 million animals experimented on in medical research laboratories every year.[51] Canada, similar to many countries, does not have any nation-wide legislation governing the use of animals in medical research other than the *Criminal Code*'s general anti-cruelty provisions.[52] Oversight takes the form of a system directed by the Canadian Council on Animal Care (CCAC), which is an organization established in the 1960s in response to political pressure from growing public awareness of the issue of animal suffering in research.[53] The CCAC, similar to many of its international counterparts, issues guidelines focusing on "refinement, reduction and replacement."[54] Institutions may voluntarily comply with these guidelines through setting up internal animal care and use committees to monitor the institution's compliance, which are then, in turn, periodically assessed by the CCAC.[55] Institutions that receive government funding must comply with CCAC standards to retain the funding.[56] Some provinces have mandated that institutions conducting animal research within their jurisdiction also comply with CCAC standards as set out in its policies.[57] The sufficiency of the oversight of both the internal animal care and use committees and the CCAC has been impugned by animal advocates as being pro-research and thus unwilling to centre animals' interests and eliminate "unnecessary" suffering in research.[58] Even those who disagree with this criticism acknowledge the CCAC's science-dominated paradigm that informs these voluntary evaluations. Relational norms can challenge this paradigm.[59]

Relationality, Science, and Animal Research

Many feminists today have criticized the hegemonic assumptions of science for explicit or implicit relational reasons. The reverence that our Western

Enlightenment–informed culture has for science and its totalizing claims to objectivity, impartiality, truth, and progress has stimulated the genre of feminist science studies in which theorists have cast a critical lens on science's normative claims.[60] Part of this critique takes aim at the medical industrial complex for its biological determinism and its masculinist, alienating, and disembodied norms that compartmentalize women's bodies and turn them into objects.[61] The medicalization of "women's conditions" such as pregnancy and childbirth has been a prominent focus in this area of feminist theory.[62] Feminists have also commented on the proclivity of expensive medical research to reflect dominant social interests that favour elite sectors of society.[63]

While medical science has endured sharp feminist criticism on these aspects, the use of animal bodies in medical research has not. This silence continues even though, as discussed earlier, women comprise the overwhelming majority of grassroots campaigners against animal-based medical research, and animals have played a prominent role in the knowledge claims that science has made. These claims include the discursive construction and renewal of the human-animal boundary that legitimizes animal use in research in the first place (that is, scientific "proof" that humans are "special" and "above" other animals) at the same time that science tells us that humans are also animals.[64] These inherited cultural and biological discourses about animals themselves come from the use of animals in research.[65] Unpacking these humanist claims and their gendered, raced, and sexualized registers is an emergent enterprise in feminist theory. As I argued in in the first part of this chapter, relational theory is well placed to engage this critique (and advance ecofeminist/post-humanist perspectives in general).

Perhaps an obvious place to start when thinking about animals under a relational framework is with the human-animal relationships that many humans see most easily – those that they have with their domesticated companion animals. It is fair to say that relational theory would not sanction any animal research that is harmful, intrusive, or otherwise violative of the animals' interests on animals to which humans have personal, loving, and familial relationships. However, this anthropocentric standard only protects those animals who we humanize (through culture, not genetic engineering) and incorporate into our families for companionship/affection purposes.[66] While all animals are legally non-persons and classified as a type of property, culturally their value can vary according to those animals that a particular culture sees as cute, as family, and/or as loyal. Recall, for example, that Wolfe describes this process as the "humanization" of certain animals (think of dogs, cats, whales, primates, and dolphins in current Western cultures) and the corresponding animalization of other animals who do not receive a particularly high cultural value (consider rats, pigs, and snakes in current Western cultures).[67] Humanization inclines an anthropocentric society to protect some animals from the exploitation that their non-humanized counterparts routinely suffer. Yet, even these humanized animals in Western cultures, such as dogs, cats, and chimpanzees, are present in research laboratories – the latter often precisely because of their genetic proximity to human beings.

A relational approach would be concerned about the cultural norms that create positive relationships between some animals and humans and oppressive relationships with others. Thus, due to its focus on power structures, relational theory should be equally concerned with the 120 million animals worldwide used in research annually that most of us never see. To permit research on animals merely because they are not in a web of personal relationships with human beings would be a reductive reading of relational theory's understanding of "relationship" and an untenable position in relational theory in any case. Given that relational theory is concerned with developing and sustaining equal and autonomy-enhancing relationships at a systemic and global level, excluding or marginalizing animals who do not already have these bonds would be contradictory.

In short, because relational theory is concerned about social and cultural power imbalances based on embodied differences, attending to the relationships of power that structure a medical research model to use animal bodies primarily for human benefit should be a natural focus for relational theory. I wish to be clear that by focusing on the embodied dimension of the narratives of difference creating the human/animal cultural boundary, I do not seek to posit a singular criterion of what makes a being matter morally. Instead, the focus is meant to illuminate the arbitrariness of constraining relational critique in general to human bodies and beings and open a discussion of what the implications of the critique are when it starts to confront the oppressive nature of this cultural boundary. In the realm of medical research, this would mean recognizing the violence involved in animal research industries.

The starkness of this position – a cessation of the vast majority of animal-based research – for those committed to relational theory but still also convinced of the importance of continuing medical research to save (human) lives might be alleviated by considering the post-humanist criticisms of the top reasons offered by the medical research community and its advocates as to the legitimacy of medical research in the first place. Again, the debate on animal research for human health purposes is extensive and polarizing.[68] I am unable to cover it in this chapter other than to note the hegemonic assumption that animal research is necessary to safeguard human health.[69] However, legal scholar Gary Francione offers several compelling counter-arguments to this position that collectively point to the conclusion that human health research that relies on animal research is neither necessary nor frequently reliable.[70]

Francione notes that it is impossible to accurately test the claim that animal research has been necessary to advances that have occurred in human health since animals have almost always been used in such research. It thus becomes difficult "to know that procedures or discoveries that are attributed to animal use would have occurred in its absence."[71] Other scientists articulate a related position that animal-based medical research is often ineffective.[72] Second, Francione highlights the biological dissimilarity between humans and animals that makes precarious, uncertain, and unreliable the transferability of any results achieved in animals to humans since "there is no species of animal that has reactions identical to those of humans."[73] A third criticism he offers of the position that animal medical research is necessary concerns alternatives. He notes that society is quick to accept animal research as a response to a public health problem rather than (1) explore the political, social, or cultural reasons that prohibit preventive measures to a particular epidemic or disease or (2) expend resources in developing alternatives. He gives as an example the prominence of animal research rather than preventive safe sex and healthy needle exchange strategies in the fight against AIDS.[74]

As further evidence that animal research should stop, Francione cites the inefficacy of a lot of experiments as well as the possibility that a lot of "necessary" research is related to human health disorders caused by the consumption of animals in the first place.[75] If we ceased consuming animal flesh and other animal products, he argues, then we could reduce our "need" to use animal bodies to research cures to diseases caused by eating them.[76] These reasons are additional to the fact that a wide range of animal medical research is frivolous and has little research impact within scientific communities.[77] Francione concludes that the discourse of animal research proponents "involves arguably plausible but questionable claims of necessity."[78]

For those individuals unconvinced by the cumulative force of these reasons and desirous of maintaining current levels of animal research for human health, a dilemma presents itself: arguments to establish the *dissimilarity* between animals and humans to justify research on animals must be articulated in order to fulfil a purpose that emphasizes their *similarity* to humans. If animals are sufficiently unlike humans in a morally relevant biological way to justify human instrumentalization of animals, post-humanist scholars ask why it would be productive to test on them to learn something about ourselves?[79] Arguably, a biological difference must be significant to be morally relevant and, if so, would make animal bodies a curious proxy for human bodies. Again, note that we have not yet canvassed here the post-humanist arguments regarding the illegitimacy of this type of belief in categorical biological difference or the moral salience of biology. The arguments that Francione raises against animal-based medical research provide considerable pause without questioning the anthropocentric order that generates it.

If we understand post-humanist critique to be motivated by an anti-oppressive orientation toward our interaction with other species, and if relational theory by definition incorporates an aversion for oppressive relationships of all kinds, then the practical recommendation under both post-humanist theory and relational theory would be to stop all medical research on animals (and humans) except in exceptional circumstances.[80] Exceptions could include situations where the research is not intrusive, does not cause pain or suffering, and would be useful to the individual animal's well-being or the well-being of her or his species (but it would not permit a researcher to introduce a pathogen or other harmful agent into an animal's body and then study its effects even if the findings would later benefit animals themselves).[81] The central point here is that a relational approach would not reinforce the human/animal boundary that now orders medical research, in terms of whose body is viewed as a research subject in the absence of consent and whose interests receive priority.

These types of developments are not as unlikely to materialize as they might appear. Other international jurisdictions have adopted research measures that attempt to centre animals. New Zealand, for example, has prohibited human research on non-human hominids except where the research is for the benefit of an individual non-human hominid or for non-human hominids in general.[82] New Zealand's *Animal Welfare Act* is one of the few examples in the world of non-instrumental legislation about animals that goes beyond prohibiting certain types of animal fighting and baiting.[83] Other countries have started to follow New Zealand's lead. Brazil, for example, has endorsed the Great Ape Project and its objective of giving certain first generation rights to primates.[84] In this context, a ban on at least some animal research does not seem so fantastical.

At this juncture, we should note that these types of legislative initiatives represent universal or near universal prohibitions. Slicer and other ecofeminists, however, have argued that a universal rejection of all animal testing would violate a fundamental tenet of relational theory to make ethical judgments in a localized manner.[85] According to her, what is missing from abstract accounts "are historical, social, economic, familial, and other details that seem crucial to an assessment of a situation, a decision, or a character."[86] Slicer notes that more traditional rights-based views of animal ethics articulated by Singer and Regan adopt a consistency-based universalist approach to argue against animal testing in all instances.[87] Slicer prefers a less absolutist path but stops short of outlining when it may be legitimate to do research on animals under a contextualized framework.[88] Instead, she affirms ecofeminist commitments to viewing the challenges that women and non-humans face as interconnected and the need for a feminist analysis of this issue to be responsive to marginalized viewpoints at all times.[89]

While Slicer is generally against animal testing, she expresses ambivalence about outlawing it completely given the discomfort she has with universalist rights-based theories as well as the credit she wishes to give to human relationships that might be put at risk without some, albeit infrequent, animal testing.[90] It is odd, though, that Slicer does not express any ambivalence about the suitability at any point of testing humans without their consent. She seems willing to take an absolutist position on humans.[91] Her position, then, on animal testing seems a curious one given her belief in the interconnectedness of women's and animals' oppression. I do not wish to defend universal claims or a rights-based approach toward animal ethics. Yet, the inconsistency in Slicer's ambivalence may be telling of the latent speciesism that may sustain it. While there may be instances in which animal-based research is valid under an expanded relational framework, it remains important to identify these situations in the least anthropocentric manner possible. In the next part of this chapter, I review another international development in the area of animal research that very recently endorsed a greater ethical regard for animals, and I will discuss the measures that Canada may take to express a more relational/ecofeminist approach to animals in the area of medical testing.

A Modest Proposal for Relational Law Reform

Alternatives to animal testing have been pursued in Europe since the 1980s. In 2009, a ban on animal testing for cosmetic purposes came into effect with a related prohibition on the sale or import within Europe of any cosmetic product tested on animals.[92] While medical testing continues and has been on the rise in recent years,[93] the European Union has endorsed thirty-four alternatives to animal testing for medical research and other purposes.[94] In the spring of 2009, it approved a draft directive that, among other welfarist measures in research, would force scientists to share information regarding all experimental results using animals in order to avoid repetition by other scientists not aware that others have already tried a certain experiment. This regulation is meant to benefit scientists as well as to reduce the number of animals used in experimentation.[95]

Similar legislative momentum is lacking in Canada and the United States.[96] Although Canadian laws relating to animal treatment are overdue for substantive review, the likelihood of even a partial ban on animal research being adopted in Canada in the near future appears remote. Indeed, even where purportedly protective animal legislation does exist, research animals may be excluded. The American *Animal Welfare Act*, for example, only protects 1 percent of all animals used in research by exempting the ubiquitous laboratory rat from its purview.[97] The academic characterization of animal issues as a "frontier of justice" and the attention that animal issues attract generally in the public sphere are promising developments. However, the widespread institutional change required to embark upon a posthumanist social order is not on Canada's legislative radar. Given this absence, it might be more effective to consider recommendations that can be put forth to improve animals' welfare in research for human ends.[98]

Swiss Welfarist Dignity Model
In this regard, a recent initiative to model is the legislation in Switzerland that came into effect in 2008. Since 1992, the Swiss Constitution has recognized the "dignity of creation" – a concept that is intended to recognize the inherent value of all animals, plants, and other non-human living beings.[99] It is a measure that is precisely aimed at undoing the anthropocentric understanding of dignity in European thought.[100] A joint statement prepared by the Swiss Ethics Committee on Non-Human Gene Biotechnology (ECNH) and the Swiss Committee on Animal Experiments (SCAE), which are responsible for concretizing the definition of the dignity of creation, describes this intention:

> Against the concept that humans alone are entitled to dignity and protection, the discussion concerning the dignity of creation stands as a corrective to the immoderate and arbitrary way in which humans treat the rest of Nature. Humans are required to show respect and restraint in the face of nature, due to their own interest in sustainable resources as well as by dint of the inherent value ascribed to a fellow living creature. Living creatures should be respected and protected for their own sake.[101]

The post-humanist consciousness evinced in this statement is remarkable given current government discourse elsewhere and the anthropocentrism that typically anchors dignity as a concept. It would be difficult to find a comparable statement in Canada or in many countries worldwide. With this 1992 recognition, Switzerland clearly distinguished itself among Western countries in terms of post-humanist policy and law reform measures by implementing a regard for animals that goes beyond the standard limited scope of anti-cruelty statutes.[102]

Despite this achievement, it is important to understand that "dignity of creation" is not a rights-creating or other entitlement-creating vehicle for animals. This point is made explicitly clear later in the statement when the authors provide more detail on what the practical dimensions of this standard should mean for the multitude of uses to which humans put animals. As they discuss, it is essentially an evaluation of interests that assesses the "damage to dignity" on four grounds: stress (including "suffering, pain, distress, injury"), intervention in appearance (including also the changes to animals' abilities), humiliation, and excessive instrumentalization.[103] Interests on all sides are identified, weighed, and rated under the principle that:

[t]he more serious any interference in the dignity of animals and the more trivial, or even unnecessary, it is in terms of human interests, the more critically it must be evaluated. Conversely, however, the more negligible an intervention is for the affected animals and the more necessary it is in the interest of other living creatures, the more it must be considered tolerable.[104]

It is notable that the interests that should count on the human side are "health, safety, quality of life, pursuit of knowledge, economic and environmental protection, aesthetics, [and] comfort." Recreation and pleasure are not explicitly mentioned.[105] While attempting to go substantially beyond the scope of standard anti-cruelty statutes, dignity of creation under this definition does not demand the application of a Kantian standard of non-instrumental use to animals. Humans may conduct research on animals where the "evaluation of interests" indicates that the dignity of the animals in question is justifiably violated. Paradoxically, according to the statement, any *justified* violations of dignity must respect the dignity of animals.[106] Under this evaluative scheme, the joint statement recommends outlawing uses of animals that are generally "for leisure or sport, as well as animals produced solely for the purpose of manufacturing luxury goods." The prohibition of "the production of genetically modified domestic animals" is also recommended.[107]

The 2008 legislation builds upon this definition of dignity and applies it to an array of animal uses. As Article 1 of the general statute states, its purpose is to protect the dignity and well-being of animals in their relationships with humans.[108] Article 3 defines "dignity" to largely reflect the recommendations made by the joint statement in concretizing the concept – that is, by evaluating a set of interests to see if dignity is at stake.[109] According to the definition, "[t]he dignity of an animal is respected if violation of its dignity is considered justifiable on the basis of a careful evaluation of interests. However, dignity is violated if the evaluation of interests shows that the animal's interests outweigh the interests of the other parties."

In addition, corollary ordinances give precise directions of what this balance entails with respect to a variety of animals.[110] Through them, Switzerland has articulated specific standards of care that humans must provide. For example, human owners of varying species, including farm animals, will have to take an educational course about their animals' species-typical behaviour, needs, and wishes.[111] Bait-and-release fishing is outlawed, as is the use of live "bait" for fishing.[112] Animals classified as "social animals," such as hamsters, parrots, and budgies, must have a companion from their own species in their living environment.[113] In regard to biomedical research, only research that meets the standard of dignity under the evaluation of interests will be authorized to proceed. The law does not currently contain specific mention of what researchers can and cannot do in terms of specific research practices beyond the aforementioned principles.[114] Details that do exist address the treatment and care of animals used in experiments and the conduct of those experiments.[115]

Again, it bears stressing that this new Swiss law is not based on entitlement in design, it does not speak of rights or relationships, and it does not abandon the language of ownership in describing humans' relationship to their animals. The legislation also does not attempt to disrupt legal relationships of property other than to import obligations on human owners that apply to a wide range of animals, both "humanized" and "animalized." Moreover, it permits medical research as long as the animals' "dignity" is not violated. It thus does not reach the endpoint that I have argued a relational analysis should on the issue of medical research. Nevertheless, anchored by the concept of dignity for animals, greater concern for animals is included in Switzerland's research landscape, including research involving human-animal experimentation. In the absence of the prohibition of animal research, a similar welfarist model could be adopted in Canada to mitigate the completely anthropocentric orientation of current research and the exclusionary dignity claim that animates much of it.

What More Is Required from a Relational Approach?

As advanced as the Swiss legislation is, even a welfarist measure can adopt more provisions to mitigate the power imbalance between research animals, the human researchers, and the human public. While the privileging of human interests over animal interests is a clear relation of power that the Swiss model targets, the legislation does not cover the breadth of the power imbalance under which "research" animals suffer. Relational theory helps to identify these missing elements that standard individual-oriented concepts of "dignity" do not emphasize. First, what is missing from the Swiss legislation is a recognition of the beingness and agency of the research animal, especially the animalized rat whose relationality to humans in Western contexts is frequently denied.[116] As Linda Birke, Metta Bryld, and Nina Lykke and others have noted, the most frequently used research animal is turned into a constitutive element of the laboratory through discourses that objectify and render its beingness absent.[117] Birke, Bryld, and Lykke discuss how rats are "made discursively into part of the laboratory" through their representations as "models," "tools," and "data" and, materially, have "been bred to fit the laboratory, its technologies, and its practices."[118] Animals used in research are typically assigned a passive role as objects to be studied or instinctual creatures whose habits are to be narrativized.[119] In both cases, animals are non-participants in the knowledge making, their experiences represented through human interpretation.[120] The Swiss conceptualization of dignity does not address this depth of representational wrong. A relational

approach can help us understand the epistemic wrong in this passive rendering by reminding us of the centrality of relationships of power in these
purportedly neutral representations as well as the positioning of animals
into the discursive category of research animal in the first place, which then
enables their typically caged laboratory locations.

In addition to generating a more agential representation of "research"
animals, relational theory draws our attention to the relationality of animals
themselves. The "laboratory rat" and other "research" animals have a relational identity, as that term is defined by Françoise Baylis in this volume,
but it is one that is severely deformed. As Baylis discusses, we arrive at our
identity not only through our own private thoughts of who we think we
are (referred to as the first personal perspective) but, crucially, also through
the reactions that others have to who we present ourselves to be (referred
to as the third personal perspective). It is an interactive communicative
process that is far from private but dependent on "who others will let us
be."[121] From the standpoint of the third personal perspective, most of us do
not let research animals enter into this realm of "iterative private and public
actions" to establish their own identity or even to seek to hear how they
may be trying to "communicate to others who [they] are."[122] The idea that
the "lab rat" is a being existing in a power relationship with the researcher,
or that the rat could exist as a being that exists in relationships with other
animals, including humans, does not enter the laboratory discourse.
Deliberately left unnamed to avoid the inklings of a biographical being
emerging, the possibility that the lab rat may have an identity other than a
raw resource is foreclosed.[123]

Attempting to foreground the laboratory rat's first personal perspective
naturally proves more difficult in the face of the more fundamental issue of
how humans can know what animals are thinking and feeling.[124] One can
expect that whatever the laboratory rat's self-understanding is, this understanding is at odds with the third personal perspective of the lab researcher.
However, it is difficult to confidently bridge the gap between human ascrip-
tions of the specific identity of the rat and its self-understanding. Put differently, theoretically, one could treat each laboratory rat as a distinct individual,
possessing an individual identity, but precisely how one is to ascertain what
that identity is remains unresolved. Although the nature of the laboratory
rat's self-understanding is unknown, there remains a need for relational
theory to attend to animals.

A relational critique would lament this evacuation of positive relationality
for lab rats and research animals generally and for their reductive conversion
into one of many objectified research tools. It would help cultivate a sense
of animals as unique and relational beings, in need of positive social structures and institutions to help them navigate the power relationships with

humans that determine their flourishing in research contexts. Focusing on their relationality, a relational approach also encourages humans to consider how our own identities are not simply products of our relationships with other humans but also with animals. An account of "dignity" that addresses these elements in medical research models would create a more sophisticated picture of relationships of power and our embodied locations and privileges within them. Once again, the definition of "dignity" in the Swiss model needs more augmentation to be able to reach the same result that a relational account would facilitate. Incorporating these types of relational critiques of research animals into Canadian law reform may be too ambitious at this point in time, but the importance of this type of understanding to remediate standard welfarist measures is nevertheless important to acknowledge.[125]

Conclusion

Carol Quillen reminds us that John Stuart Mill once suggested that the greater the weight of argumentation against a given position, the more its adherents will be fortified in their view, locating it more and more as a deeply held feeling that no amount of empirical evidence or logic will dislodge.[126] This reference may adequately describe the current state of controversy regarding the moral and legal status of animals that is especially surrounding their use in medical research and illustrate, ironically, the combined workings of emotion and reason that ecofeminist theory helps to illuminate in the formation of our worldviews, our relationships, and our perception of others and ourselves.

Theories such as ecofeminism that take animals seriously are still very much the minority. Yet, relational theory is a promising theoretical tool to tackle oppressive power relations with respect to humans and non-humans alike since many main premises of ecofeminist theory are relational. In seeing humans as interdependent with the non-human world and systems of domination as connected, ecofeminism matches relational theory's shift from traditional rights discourses to an orientation designed to examine and undo relationships of power by looking at the economic, social, and cultural locations of bodies. It shares its disapproval of the rational embodied actor as the ideal political and legal subject and has sought to show how the main justifications for excluding animals from our ethical calculations rest on a tenuously maintained species boundary that depends on the devaluation of difference and embodiment.[127] Both theories also express preferences for localized analyses in order to properly attend to the complexity of relationships.

Given such common goals to value difference and embodiment, empower groups Othered by their differentiated bodies, and dismantle corresponding relations of power, relational theory can also follow these commitments past their implicit species border to consider animals in the same way that ecofeminism has. This conclusion is affirmed by the implications of relational concepts of equality, judgment, and justice. The relational articulations of these core concepts by Koggel, Nedelsky, and Llewellyn can easily accommodate and, indeed, appear to logically entail the inclusion of animal interests in reworking relationships. Relational theory could and should take up post-humanism's focus on human-animal relationships when seeking to ensure equality or good judgment, for example.[128]

With an expanded post-humanist scope, the continued use of animals in medical research is difficult to accept under a relational framework. While leaving open the possibility of some animal-based (and human-based) medical research as ethical in carefully assessed circumstances, a more post-humanist relational theory would disfavour the use of animals in medical research. The relationships that the research enables are oppressive and rely on a reductive and anthropocentric view of human relationships with animals. As a modest step toward recognizing the value and worth of animals, law reform similar to recent European Union and notably Swiss measures should be considered in Canada. Although the Swiss law remains a welfarist measure and is an incomplete relational approach, such laws would signal a respect for animals and their dignity that is unprecedented in Canada. The promotion of human health is indeed a laudable goal, but the reliance on animal bodies to achieve that result is a misguided strategy. Relational theory helps illuminate this misstep and encourages a step in a new direction that conforms more to a relational vision of a broad network of relationships that includes humans and animals.

Notes

I am grateful to Jocelyn Downie and Jennifer Llewellyn for including this contribution in the volume and creating rich opportunities for structured and intellectual engagement through the organization of workshops for this and all of the other chapters. This chapter has benefited from comments received by the editors and other authors in this volume during the workshop process. I am particularly grateful for the dedicated and close reading of the chapter provided by Christine Koggel, Sheila Wildeman, and the editors.

1 See, for example, Carol Quillen's excellent relational critique of liberal humanism and Martha Nussbaum's capabilities approach that depends on it for their reliance on a problematic concept of the "human" and anthropocentric focus. Quillen faults Nussbaum for her "lack of attention ... to the constitution of the human person as selves" that "undermines her capacity to analyze existing mechanisms of differentiation and oppression and thus undermines her emancipatory aims." Carol Quillen, "Feminist Theory, Justice, and the Lure of the Human" (2001) 27:1 Signs 87 at 100.

2 At least one other author in this volume, Jennifer Nedelsky, endorses this claim: "[Kant and Arendt] offer us a conception of judgment as a distinct human faculty that is subjective, but which is not therefore something merely arbitrary." This conception is taken up critically later in the chapter. Jennifer Nedelsky, "The Reciprocal Relation of Judgment and Autonomy: Walking in Another's Shoes and Which Shoes to Walk In" in this volume.

3 Of course, it may be unlikely that insects are used as frequently as other animals since the non-humans that are seen as "closer" to humans are the ones that we test because of this

assumed proximity. Nevertheless, I want to be clear that the relational orientation advanced here should extend to an assessment of all human instrumental use of other beings.

4 To be clear at the outset, this analysis does not intend to draw a new boundary line between all living beings and non-living yet meaningful things but, rather, argues for the logical extension of relational theory to animals.

5 Multiple authors have noted the politics entailed in the choice to use the word "animal." They wonder whether it is reductive of the diversity of animals and still too anchored to the anthropocentric (and masculinist) norm that the signifier "human" commands when compared to alternatives such as "non-human animal," "non-humyn animal," and so on. I share these concerns but follow Carol Adams and Josephine Donovan in their use of it in their recent anthology exploring feminist care traditions with respect to animals. See Josephine Donovan and Carol Adams, "Introduction" in Josephine Donovan and Carol Adams, eds., *The Feminist Care Tradition in Animal Ethics: A Reader* (New York: Columbia University Press, 2007) 1.

6 Post-humanism, of course, is concerned with non-human beings other than non-human animals. My reference to it in this chapter is meant to signal a line of critique that investigates the constructedness of species difference and challenges the normally assumed human/non-human social, cultural, and legal boundary that permeates Western political, ethical, and legal thought.

7 Alasdair Cochrane, "Animal Rights and Animal Experiments: An Interest-Based Approach" (2007) 13:3 Res. Publica 293.

8 Gary Francione, "The Use of Nonhuman Animals in Biomedical Research: Necessity and Justification" (2007) 35:2 J. L. Med. & Ethics 241 at 242.

9 It is important to acknowledge that for most human beings, medical research is not the primary determinant of future health. Nor is individual choice. Rather, as feminists working in health issues globally have stressed, "[w]ith a few notable exceptions, infrastructure development has a far greater impact on health than specific medical intervention." Anne Donchin, "Converging Concerns: Feminist Bioethics, Development Theory and Human Rights" (2003) 29:2 Signs 299 at 319. It is also important to recognize that most medical research involving animals and otherwise is done in Western countries (as is most animal consumption) and in relation to conditions that disproportionately affect Western individuals, again underscoring that the best hope for the improvement of health in less affluent spaces would be attention to preventive strategies highlighting the impact of hierarchical social structures and abusive practices (*ibid.* at 300). Thus, the salience of medical research as a site of post-humanist intervention might be less in less affluent geopolitical spaces.

10 Donovan and Adams, "Introduction," *supra* note 5 at 1, citing Carol Gilligan, *Psychological Theory and Women's Development* (Cambridge, MA: Harvard University Press, 1982).

11 Grace Clement, "The Ethic of Care and the Problem of Wild Animals" in Donovan and Adams, *Feminist Care Tradition, supra* note 5, 301 at 302-3.

12 Christine M. Koggel, "A Relational Approach to Equality: New Developments and Applications," in this volume.

13 Jennifer Nedelsky, "Reconceiving Autonomy: Sources, Thoughts and Possibilities" (1989) 1 Yale J.L. & Feminism 7 at 10-11.

14 Linda Birke, Metta Bryld, and Nina Lykke, "Animal Performances: An Exploration of Intersections between Feminist Science Studies and Studies of Human/Animal Relationships" (2004) 5:2 Feminist Theory 167 at 168.

15 Cary Wolfe, "Introduction" in Cary Wolfe, ed., *Zoontologies: The Question of the Animal* (Minneapolis: Minnesota University Press, 2003) ix at x-xi.

16 *Ibid.* at xii.

17 Dawne McCance, "Anatomy as Speech Act: Vesalius, Descartes, Rembrandt or, The Question of 'the animal' in the Early Modern Anatomy Lesson" in Jodey Castricano, ed., *Animal Subjects: An Ethical Reader in a Posthuman World* (Waterloo, ON: Wilfrid Laurier Press, 2008) 63 at 79; Quillen, *supra* note 1 at 97-98; Kay Peggs, "A Hostile World for Nonhuman Animals: Human Identification and the Oppression of Nonhuman Animals for Human Good" (2009) 43:1 Sociology 85 at 88.

18 Jacques Derrida, "The Animal That Therefore I Am (More to Follow)" (2002) 28 Critical Inquiry 369; Donna Haraway, *Simians, Cyborgs and Women: The Reinvention of Nature* (London: Routledge, 1991); Donna Haraway, *Primate Visions: Gender, Race and Nature in the World of Modern Science* (New York: Routledge, 1988); Donna Haraway, *When Species Meet: Posthumanities* (Minneapolis: Minnesota University Press, 2007).

19 Jennifer Llewellyn, "Restorative Justice: Thinking Relationally about Justice" in this volume.

20 Carol J. Adams, *Neither Man nor Beast: Feminism and the Defense of Animals* (New York: Continuum, 1994); Carol J. Adams, *The Sexual Politics of Meat: A Feminist-Vegetarian Critical Theory* (New York: Continuum, 1990); Carol Adams and Josephine Donovan, eds., *Animals and Women: Feminist Theoretical Explorations* (Durham, NC: Duke University Press, 1995); Josephine Donovan, "Feminism and the Treatment of Animals: From Care to Dialogue" (2006) 31:2 Signs 305; Carol J. Adams and Josephine Donovan, eds., *Beyond Animal Rights: A Feminist Caring Ethic for the Treatment of Animals* (Indianapolis: University of Indiana Press, 1996); Greta Gaard, ed., *Ecofeminism: Women, Animals, Nature* (Philadelphia: Temple University Press, 2003); Val Plumwood, *Environmental Culture: The Ecological Crisis of Reason* (London: Routledge, 2002); Val Plumwood, "Androcentrism and Anthropocentrism: Parallels and Politics" (1996) 1:2 Ethics and the Environment 119; Karen Warren, *Ecofeminist Philosophy: A Western Perspective on What It Is and Why It Matters* (New York: Rowman and Littlefield, 2000). Within Southern ecofeminist scholarship that has acquired global prominence, the works of theorist/activist Vandana Shiva and Bina Agarwal stand out. See Bina Agarwal, "Environmental Management, Equity and Ecofeminism: Debating India's Experience" (1998) 25:4 Journal of Peasant Studies 55; Bina Agarwal, "The Gender and Environment Debate: Lessons from India" (1992) 18:1 Feminist Studies 119; Vandana Shiva, *Earth Democracy: Justice, Sustainability, and Peace* (Boston: South End Press, 2005); Vandana Shiva, *Water Wars: Privatization, Pollution, and Profit* (Boston: South End Press, 2002); Vandana Shiva, *Stolen Harvest: The Hijacking of the Global Food Supply* (Boston: South End Press, 2000).

21 Donovan and Adams, *Feminist Care Tradition, supra* note 5.

22 See the example given of Karen Warren's use of the term: "Care, for Warren, extends not just to other human beings, but to the environment as well. In her definition, care is seen as 'a species activity that includes everything that we do to maintain, continue, and repair our "world" so that we can live in it as well as possible.' Here 'world' is broadly defined to include both human and nonhuman others. Thus, just as we can care about the flourishing of another person, so can we care about the flourishing of the environment." Kelly A. Burns, "Warren's Ecofeminist Ethics and Merleau-Ponty's Body-Subject: Intersections" (2008) 13:2 Ethics & Env't 101 at 106, citing Warren, *supra* note 20 at 140 [citation omitted].

23 Jennifer Llewellyn and Jocelyn Downie, "Introduction" in this volume.

24 Deborah Slicer, "Your Daughter or Your Dog?: A Feminist Assessment of the Animal Research Issue" in Donovan and Adams, *Feminist Care Tradition, supra* note 5, 105 at 110.

25 Clement, *supra* note 11 at 302-3.

26 Donovan, *supra* note 20; Colleen Mack-Canty, "Third-Wave Feminism and the Need to Reweave the Nature-Culture Duality" 16:3 N.W.S.A. J. 154 at 167-73.

27 This is not to say that there are not any relational theorists who are centrally concerned with the stigmatization of emotion through dichotomous thinking. See, for example, Jennifer Nedelsky, "Embodied Diversity and Challenges to Law" (1997) 47:1 McGill L.J. 91.

28 Quillen, *supra* note 1 at 98.

29 Cathryn Bailey, "On the Backs of Animals: The Valorization of Reason in Contemporary Animal Ethics" in Donovan and Adams, *Feminist Care Tradition, supra* note 5, 344 at 346-47. This is not to say, of course, that non-Western cultures and societies are void of hierarchical relations to animals. It is instead to recognize the normalcy in non-Western cultures and religions of conceptualizing of animals as beings – even persons – able to relate socially with humans as equals and even with deities. See Paul Nadasdy, "The Gift in the Animal: The Ontology of Hunting and Human-Animal Sociality" (2007) 34:1 American Ethnologist 25 at 29.

30 Bailey, *supra* note 29.

31 Peggs, *supra* note 17 at 90.

32 Joan Dunayer, *Animal Equality: Language and Liberation* (Derwood, MD: Ryce, 2001).

33 I wish to stress that ecofeminism is not generally motivated by essentialist cultural feminist premises to insist that emotion replace reason as an exalted moral capacity that we should all cultivate. Rather, it agrees with the relational understanding of reason and emotion as a "unified sensibility," working always in tandem with the mind as part of the body. Slicer, *supra* note 24 at 114. Ecofeminism's concern is not to marginalize beings based on their capacity for rational thought, thereby sidestepping the ongoing debates about whether animals exhibit this capacity sufficiently to merit ethical consideration. Ecofeminists, of course, are not arguing that animals cannot reason and that is why a moral compass fixed on its presence is flawed. Rather, they seek to respect difference by rejecting the importance of any singular capacity to justify giving or withholding ethical treatment to any being. See, generally, the sources provided in note 20.

34 Cary Wolfe, "Subject to Sacrifice: Ideology, Psychoanalysis and the Discourse of Species in Jonathan Demme's *The Silence of the Lambs*" in Cary Wolfe, *Animal Rites: American Culture, the Discourse of Species, and Posthumanist Theory* (Chicago: University of Chicago Press, 2003) 97 at 101.

35 *Ibid.* at 101-2.

36 Burns, *supra* note 22.

37 Lyle Munro, "Caring about Blood, Flesh and Pain: Women's Standing in the Animal Protection Movement" (2001) 9:1 Society & Animals 43 at 44; Charles W. Peek et al., "Gender, Gender Ideology and Animal Rights Advocacy" (1996) 10:4 Gender & Society 464; Maria Mika, "Framing the Issue: Religion, Secular Ethics and the Case of Animal Rights Mobilization" (2006) 85:2 Social Forces 915 at 918.

38 Diane L. Beers, *For the Prevention of Cruelty: The History and Legacy of Animal Rights Activism in the United States* (Athens, OH: Ohio University Press, 2006) at 123-24. Interestingly, the most recognized faces of animal ethics movements are often men (consider Peter Singer and Tom Regan), although women are quickly found in leadership positions (consider Ingrid Newkirk) in the contemporary animal ethics movement. Munro, *supra* note 37 at 49-50.

39 Munro, *supra* note 37 at 45.

40 *Ibid.* at 110 and 112.

41 Koggel, *supra* note 12.

42 bell hooks, *Feminist Theory: From Margin to Center* (Boston: South End Press, 1984).

43 Koggel, *supra* note 12.

44 *Ibid.*

45 Paul Maltby, "Fundamentalist Dominion, Postmodern Ecology" (2008) 13:2 Ethics & Env't 119 at 130.

46 Nedelsky, *supra* note 2 [emphasis in original].

47 *Ibid.*

48 Llewellyn, *supra* note 19.

49 *Ibid.*

50 Lisa Houde and Claude Dumas, "Animal Ethical Evaluation: An Observational Study of Canadian IACUCs" (2003) 13:4 Ethics & Behaviour 333 at 334.

51 Peggs, *supra* note 17 at 91.

52 Houde and Dumas, *supra* note 50 at 335. *Criminal Code,* R.S.C. 1985, c. C-46.

53 Houde and Dumas, *supra* note 50 at 336.

54 *Ibid.*

55 *Ibid.*

56 See Canadian Council on Animal Care (CCAC), "Animal Use Oversight," http://www.ccac. ca/en/alternatives/oversight_surveillance.html.

57 See, for example, the *Animal Protection Regulation,* Alta. Reg. 203/2005. Other provinces that have also incorporated the CCAC standards into their animal protection statutes are Manitoba, Ontario, New Brunswick, Nova Scotia, and Prince Edward Island. See CCAC, "Legislation in Canada Related to Experimental Animals," http://www.ccac.ca/en_/ education/niaut/stream/cs-guidelines.html.

58 For a stringent critique of the system, see Charlotte Montgomery, *Blood Relations: Animals, Humans and Politics* (Toronto: Between the Lines, 2000), noting, among other criticisms, that monitoring is rarely unannounced, that the composition of the animal care and use committees reflect pro-research perspectives, and that no publicly funded institution as of yet has lost funding under the system (at 96-101). For a more favourable view, see Houde and Dumas, *supra* note 50. Statistics relating to legislation in the United States reveal that the greatest number of reported violations of the federal *Animal Welfare Act*, 7 U.S.C. 2131, s. 2132(g), are committed by animal internal care and use committees and that 75 percent of these committees have at one point or another violated the statute. See Marc Bekoff, "Increasing Our Compassion Footprint: The Animals' Manifesto" (2008) 43:4 Zygon 771 at 774.

59 Houde and Dumas, *supra* note 50 at 337 and 346-47.

60 Nina Lykke, "Feminist Cultural Studies of Technoscience: Portrait of an Implosion" in Anneke Smelik and Nina Lykke, eds., *Bits of Life: Feminism at the Intersections of Media, Bioscience, and Technology* (Seattle: University of Washington Press, 2008) 3 at 9-10. On the feminist and post-colonial critiques of science, see Sandra Harding, *Science and Social Inequality: Feminist and Postcolonial Issues* (Urbana, IL: University of Illinois Press, 2006); Birke, Bryld, and Lykke, *supra* note 14 at 168.

61 Birke, Bryld, and Lykke, *supra* note 14 at 168.

62 Genea Corea, *The Mother Machine: Reproductive Technologies from Artificial Insemination to Artificial Wombs* (New York: Harper and Row, 1979).

63 Beth Humphries, "From Critical Thought to Emancipatory Action: Contradictory Research Goals" in Carole Truman, Donna M. Mertens, and Beth Humphries, eds., *Research and Inequality* (London: UCL Press, 2000) 179, as discussed in Peggs, *supra* note 17 at 91.

64 Birke, Bryld, and Lykke, *supra* note 14 at 173.

65 *Ibid.*

66 *Ibid.* at 175.

67 Wolfe, *supra* note 34.

68 *Ibid.*; Emma Marris, "Grey Matters" (2006) 444 Nature 808 at 808.

69 Thus, I do not canvass the literature of animal medical research, which opposes animal research on ethical grounds. It is also the case, then, that one need not convince humanists to concede human superiority and an exclusionary dignity claim for humans to understand that animal medical research does not facilitate human health.

70 Francione, *supra* note 8 at 243-44. Francione gives seven reasons in this article. I discuss only what strikes me as the most compelling of those reasons in this chapter.

71 *Ibid.* at 243.

72 Peggs, *supra* note 17 at 92.

73 Francione, *supra* note 8 at 243.

74 *Ibid.*

75 *Ibid.*

76 *Ibid.* at 244.

77 *Ibid.* See also Anne Innis Dagg, "Blame and Shame? How Can We Reduce Unproductive Animal Experimentation?" in Castricano, *supra* note 17, 271 at 274-80.

78 Francione, *supra* note 8 at 244.

79 Marie Fox, "Reconfiguring the Animal/Human Boundary: The Impact of Xeno Technologies" (2005) 26:2 Liverpool L. Rev. 149 at 155, citing Barbara Noske's important and early feminist work in this area.

80 Excluding some animals from this conclusion due to their minimally developed capacities or their lack of certain capacities (reason, sentience, language, and so on) that are commonly thought to justify moral consideration is a challenge for a theory such as relational theory that seeks to be responsive to difference and embodiment. However, the issue of deciding which animals matter and which do not cannot be addressed in this chapter.

81 This exception raises the issue of paternalism and the tricky yet preferable practice of obtaining animal consent before conducting research on the animal even where the purpose is therapeutic for that animal rather than for humans. The conundrum presented is how

to ascertain animal consent given the language barrier between humans and animals and the anthropocentric perspectives that indelibly inform our ways of understanding the signals of consent. See D. Thomas, "Laboratory Animals and the Art of Empathy" (2005) 31:4 J. Medical Ethics 197 at 200-1. While ascertaining this could be ruled out altogether given the spectre of paternalism and inaccuracy that attends an anthropocentric perspective, some have explored the possibility of obtaining animal consent through attentive and empathetic interaction and perception with animals. See, for example, Michael Allen Fox and Lesley McLean, "Animals in Moral Space" in Castricano, *supra* note 17, 145 at 159-70 and 183.

82 Peter Sankoff, "Five Years of the 'New' Animal Welfare Regime: Lessons Learned from New Zealand's Decision to Modernize Its Animal Welfare Legislation" (2005) 11 Animal L. 7. See *Animal Welfare Act* 1999 (N.Z.), 1999.

83 *Animal Welfare Act, supra* note 82.

84 See Gap Project, http://projetogap.org.br/en-US. On the basis of these two milestone developments alone, it may be gleaned that it is the "humanized" animals that are singled out for better protection due to their similarities to humans. This logic of similarity is problematic in the exclusions that it maintains. Yet, in a world where animals are so brutalized, the motivation to effect change through this logic, on the basis that it appeals to the public, is understandable if not ultimately defensible. See Taimie Bryant, "Similarity or Difference as a Basis for Justice: Must Animals Be Like Humans to Be Legally Protected from Humans?" (2007) 70:1 Law & Contemp. Probs. 207.

85 Slicer, *supra* note 24 at 111 and 115.

86 *Ibid.* at 111.

87 *Ibid.*

88 *Ibid.* at 120.

89 *Ibid.* at 112 and 120.

90 *Ibid.* at 120.

91 It is not clear to me from reading Slicer if she would object to treatment consented to by a parent/guardian for a child or by a substitute decision maker for adults unable to consent.

92 Alison Abbott, "The Lowdown on Animal Testing for Cosmetics," *Nature* (11 March 2009), http://www.nature.com/news/2009/090311/full/news.2009.147.html; "Animal Testing Rises," *The Guardian* (8 November 2007), http://www.guardian.co.uk/science/blog/2007/nov/08/animaltestingup.html.

93 *Ibid.*

94 Gilbert Gaul, "In US, Few Alternatives to Testing on Animals," *Washington Post* (12 April 2008), http://www.washingtonpost.com/wp-dyn/content/article/2008/04/11/AR2008041103733.html. Certainly, there are criticisms of the European Union measures for not going far enough to amount to effective change. See, for example, "Great Apes Suffer Setback in Animal Testing Vote" (5 May 2009), Reuters, http://www.reuters.com/article/scienceNews/idUSTRE5443IS20090505.

95 "Catheter and Mouse: Sharing Information on Failed Animal Experiments Would Help Both Scientists and Rats," *The Economist* (7 May 2009), http://www.economist.com/opinion/displaystory.cfm?story_id=13610855.

96 *Ibid.* While the United States lags behind the European Union in developing alternatives, a recent report is encouraging in its science-based recommendation to eliminate animal testing in chemical toxicity testing through *in vitro* research involving human cultures. The report mostly discusses product safety concerns stemming from the use of outdated animal tests that are ill designed for calibrating toxins in many substances. Amazingly, toxicology is the sole life science field where the methodology of testing has remained relatively stagnant for the past fifty to eighty years, "when knowledge of the biology underlying toxic response was primitive." See Daniel Krewski et al., "Toxicity Testing in the Twenty-First Century: Implications for Human Health Risk Assessment" (2009) 29:4 Risk Analysis 474 at 474. These efforts at revolutionizing toxicology tests link with similar efforts in Europe. "Keynote Address: Current State of the Science of Toxicity Testing" (Presented at International Implications of the US National Research Council Report on Toxicity Testing

in the Twenty-First Century: Challenges and Opportunities in Implementation, Ottawa, ON, 29 June 2009). See also US National Research Council (NRC), "Toxicity Testing in the Twenty-First Century: A Vision and a Strategy" (Washington, DC: National Academic Press, 2007). An international working group comprised of ethicists, lawyers, and scientists is studying how to best implement the NRC report. This group includes animal advocates. The first symposium was held in Ottawa on 29-30 June 2009 with subsequent meetings to follow. The vision is for "a not-so-distant future where all routine toxicity testing will be conducted in human cells or cell lines in vitro by evaluating perturbations of cellular responses in a suite of toxicity pathway assays." See Melvin Andersen, "Response and Comment to Keynote Address" (presented at International Implications of the US National Research Council Report on Toxicity Testing in the Twenty-First Century: Challenges and Opportunities in Implementation, Ottawa, ON, 29 June 2009, citing Melvin E. Andersen and Daniel Krewski, "Toxicity Testing in the Twenty-First Century: Bringing the Vision to Life" (2009) 107:2 Toxicological Sciences 324.

97 Bekoff, *supra* note 58 at 774. See *Animal Welfare Act, supra* note 58.
98 A long-standing debate persists in animal ethics regarding the desirability of measures aimed at improving the lives of animals used instrumentally in a variety of human industries such as factory farming, entertainment, and research. It is beyond the scope of this chapter to canvass this debate. For a critique of "welfarist" strategies even when deontological results appear Utopian, see Gary Francione, *Rain without Thunder: The Ideology of the Animal Rights Movement* (Philadelphia: Temple University Press, 1996) and Gary Francione, "Reflections on Animals, Property and the Law and Rain without Thunder" (2007) 70:1 Law & Contemp. Probs. 9. I assume that "welfarist" measures, while not ideal, are productive and consider what they would look like in the research context.
99 Swiss Ethics Committee on Non-Human Gene Biotechnology (ECNH) and the Swiss Committee on Animal Experiments (SCAE), *The Dignity of Animals*, translated by Nicolette Chisholm (Berne, Switzerland: ECNH and SCAE, 2005) at 5.
100 *Ibid.* at 4.
101 *Ibid.*
102 *Ibid.* at 6. For a critique of the inability of anti-cruelty laws to protect animals from all but the most gratuitous or sadistic forms of human exploitation, see Gary Francione, *Animals, Property and the Law* (Philadelphia: University of Pennsylvania Press, 1995).
103 ECNH and SCAE, *supra* note 99 at 6 and 9.
104 *Ibid.* at 8.
105 *Ibid.* at 9.
106 *Ibid.*
107 *Ibid.*
108 *Loi fédérale du 16 décembre 2005 sur la protection des animaux*, No. 455, 16 December 2005, Art. 2; *Ordonnance du 23 avril 2008 sur la protection des animaux*, No. 455.1, 23 April 2008.
109 *Loi fédérale du 16 décembre 2005 sur la protection des animaux, supra* note 108 at Art. 3.
110 *Ordonnance du DFE du 5 september 2008 sur les formations à la détention d'animaux et à la manière de les traiter*, No. 455.109.1, 5 September 2008; *Ordonnance de l'OVF du 27 août 2008 sur la détention des animaux de rente et des animaux domestiques*, No. 455.110.1, 27 August 2008.
111 *Ibid.*
112 *Ordonnance sur la protection des animaux*, No. 455.1, Art. 23.
113 *Ibid.*, Art. 13.
114 *Loi fédérale sur la protection des animaux*, No. 455, Articles 17-19. Whether jurists or researchers will follow the ECNH and SCAE's joint recommendation to prevent genetically modified animals remains an open question.
115 *Ordonnance sur la protection des animaux*, No. 455.1, Arts. 112-41.
116 Birke, Bryld, and Lykke, *supra* note 14.
117 *Ibid.* at 172-74; Fox, *supra* note 79.
118 Birke, Bryld, and Lykke, *supra* note 14 at 172.
119 *Ibid.* at 171.
120 *Ibid.*

121 Françoise Baylis, "The Self *in Situ*: A Relational Account of Personal Identity" in this volume.

122 *Ibid.*

123 Mary T. Phillips, "'Proper Names and the Social Construction of Biography': The Negative Case of Laboratory Animals" (1994) 17:2 Qualitative Sociology 119.

124 John Webster, *Animal Welfare: Limping towards Eden* (Oxford: Blackwell Publishing, 2005) at 2; Lily N. Edwards, "Animal Well-Being and Behavioural Needs on the Farm" in Temple Grandin, ed., *Improving Animal Welfare: A Practical Approach* (Cambridge: Cambridge University Press, 2010) 139; Marc Bekoff, *The Emotional Lives of Animals* (Novato: New World Library, 2007) at 111.

125 A notable connection can be established between the post-humanist vision of relational ethics that I am advocating and Sherwin's work on relational autonomy for public ethics, discussed in the first chapter of this volume. In exploring the relational ethics of using animals for biomedical research, it is useful to acknowledge Sherwin's critique of the ways in which social, economic, and political patterns enable and constrain the taking up of responsibilities with respect to exploitive social practices. Animal research is a multibillion-dollar industry. Government is generally the primary source of funding for research in addition to private-sector organizations such as pharmaceutical companies, educational institutions, and other foundations and agencies. Donna Yarri, *The Ethics of Animal Experimentation* (Oxford: Oxford University Press, 2005). Thus, as Sherwin suggests, in attempting to reform the most perilous structures and practices (such as animal experimentation), it is often necessary to establish reform through collaborative engagement with various sorts of human organizations. Identifying the responsibilities of participants at all levels of social organization is critical to extending beyond the Western humanist tradition.

126 As discussed in Quillen, *supra* note 1 at 97, while discussing the merits of Nussbaum's capabilities approach.

127 Mack-Canty, *supra* note 26 at 173.

128 Slicer, *supra* note 24 at 109.

Contributors

Françoise Baylis is one of the leading philosophers working in bioethics in Canada. She is an elected fellow of both the Royal Society of Canada and the Canadian Academy of Health Sciences. She holds a Canada Research Chair in Philosophy and Bioethics, and is the founder of the NovelTechEthics research team at Dalhousie University. Françoise's research and publications span a wide range of topics including novel technologies, assisted human reproduction, stem cell research, research involving humans, women's health, and feminist ethics. Her work is widely regarded as original and thought provoking. She has a number of applied ethics articles on genetics, race, face transplantation, and interventions in the brain that address issues of identity.

Sue Campbell (1957-2011) was the leading Canadian scholar on relational theory and memory. A professor in the departments of Philosophy and Gender and Women's Studies at Dalhousie University, she pursued research in philosophical psychology, feminist theory, the philosophy of emotions, and the social/political dimensions of memory experience. Among her publications are the highly regarded book *Relational Remembering: Rethinking the Memory Wars* and a co-edited volume, *Embodiment and Agency*. She is deeply missed.

Maneesha Deckha is a professor in the Faculty of Law at the University of Victoria. She has held the Fulbright Visiting Chair in Law and Society at New York University and has been a Visiting Scholar at the Hastings Institute for Bioethics. Her research interests include critical animal studies, intersectionality, feminist analysis of law, law and culture, animal law, and bioethics. Her scholarship often addresses these topics in tandem and has been supported by the Canadian Institutes of Health Research and the Social Sciences and Humanities Research Council.

Jocelyn Downie is a Professor of Law and Medicine at Dalhousie, where she holds a Canada Research Chair in Health Law and Policy, and is an elected fellow of both the Royal Society of Canada and the Canadian Academy of Health Sciences. She was awarded the Abbyann Day Lynch Award in Bioethics by the Royal Society of Canada for her book *Dying Justice: An Argument for the Decriminalization of*

Assisted Suicide and Euthanasia in Canada. She has published numerous books and articles on various topics within health law, including a paper introducing relational theory to health law and policy. Her current research involves the intersection of relational theory and health law and policy.

Christine Koggel is the Harvey Wexler Professor of Philosophy and chair of the Department of Philosophy at Bryn Mawr College, and former director of the Centre on Values and Ethics and the Bower Carty Professor of Ethics and Public Affairs at Carleton University. She is a leader in the development of a relational conception of equality; her publications in this area include *Perspectives on Equality: Constructing a Relational Theory* and many articles. She has also edited or co-edited two of the leading moral issues textbooks, *Moral Issues in Global Perspective* and *Contemporary Moral Issues.* Christine is now also applying relational theory to development ethics and to the global context.

Jennifer Llewellyn is a leading scholar in relational theory and restorative justice, and has written extensively on these topics. She has also researched and published in the area of health law and policy and has argued for the application of a relational theory framework to health law and policy issues. She is an associate professor at the Schulich School of Law at Dalhousie University, and is presently the director (principle investigator) of the SSHRC-funded Nova Scotia Restorative Justice Community University Research Alliance.

Constance MacIntosh is an associate professor of Law at the Schulich School of Law, Dalhousie University, and a leading scholar in the area of aboriginal health law and policy. She has spoken on this topic at several of the National Health Law conferences and has published numerous articles in the field. Formerly the leader of the Policing, Justice and Security Domain of the Atlantic Metropolis Centre of Excellence, she is now the director of the Health Law Institute.

Carolyn McLeod is an associate professor of philosophy and an affiliate member of the Department of Women's Studies and Feminist Research at the University of Western Ontario. She does research and teaches in health care ethics, ethical theory, and feminist theory. Her book *Self-Trust and Reproductive Autonomy* is representative of her research interests in general, covering areas at the intersection of moral theory, reproductive ethics, and feminist theory. Many of her published articles discuss moral dilemmas that occur in reproductive health care and the moral concepts needed to resolve those dilemmas. The practical issues on which she has written include miscarriage, *in vitro* fertilization, embryo and oocyte donation, and contract pregnancy. The concepts she has studied include trust, autonomy, integrity, objectification and commodification.

Jennifer Nedelsky is a professor of law at the University of Toronto and a prominent thinker in relational theory. She developed a groundbreaking relational account of rights, judgment, and autonomy. She has numerous articles in relational theory, feminist theory, theories of judgement, and comparative constitutionalism, and recently completed work on two books, *Law, Autonomy and the Relational Self: A Feminist Revisioning of the Foundations of Law* and *Human Rights and*

Judgment: A Relational Approach. She has been a member of the Board of Directors of the American Society for Legal History, and in 2000 she was awarded the Bora Laskin National Fellowship in Human Rights Research.

Dianne Pothier is a professor in the Schulich School of Law at Dalhousie University and is a leading expert in disability law and policy, Canadian constitutional law, and labour law. She is widely published in these areas and recently co-edited (with Richard Devlin) *Critical Disability Theory: Essays in Philosophy, Politics, Policy, and Law.* She has also been involved in litigating leading equality cases in the areas of disability and women's rights, including appearing as counsel at the Supreme Court of Canada. She was the recipient of the 2005 Frances Fish Women Lawyers' Achievement Award from the Nova Scotia Association of Women and the Law.

Susan Sherwin is a professor emeritus of philosophy at Dalhousie University. She is one of Canada's most prominent philosophers, and her pioneering work on relational autonomy has been foundational to the development of relational theory. She has been awarded the Killam Prize in Humanities and a Lifetime Achievement Award from the Canadian Bioethics Society, and she has been named a Distinguished Women Philosopher by the American Society for Women and Philosophy, selected as a University Research Professor at Dalhousie, and elected to the Royal Society of Canada.

Sheila Wildeman is an assistant professor in the Schulich School of Law at Dalhousie University. Her primary research interests include administrative law doctrine and mental health law. Her recent research has focused upon Canadian laws relating to decision-making capacity, supported decision making and substitute decisions.

Index

relational theory, 267-68, 267-80, 284*n*62; restorative justice, 267; socio-cultural links, 277; standards and criteria, 258, 262, 263; tribunal process, 275, 276, 277. *See also* psychiatric treatment decisions; *Starson v. Swayze*
Treaty 6, 251*n*14
treaty rights, 153
tribal cultures, 21
Tronto, Joan, 21, 71
Truth and Reconciliation Commission, 133, 134, 152-54, 155*n*17
Tsosie, Rebecca, 132, 152, 153, 154*n*5
Turner, Chris, 66

unemployment, 67
uni-gender, 192
United Nations Development Program (UNDP), 63, 64, 69-70, 77
United States *Animal Welfare Act,* 302, 312*n*58
United States Census, 125, 130*n*57
United States National Research Council (NRC), 312*n*81
United States Senate, Wounded Knee hearings, 150-51
University of Toronto, 47

Valaskakis, Gail Guthrie, 133-34, 141, 148, 151, 152, 153-54
Valentine, Fraser, 205*n*14
vegetarianism, 45
Vellacott, Maurice, 216
violence: agency, 31; destructive model of relationships, 93; ethnic, 22; and oppression, 33*n*16; restorative justice movement, 102-3
vision impairment, 198, 199
vivisection, 292, 293
Vriend v. Alberta, 202

Waites, Elizabeth, 136
Wakeham, Pauline, 152
Walker, Margaret Urban, 14, 21, 112-13, 124, 179*n*22
Walsh, Edward, 145, 146
wannabes, 205*n*10

war, 24
Warren, Karen, 290, 310*n*22
Washington Times, 126
Wein, Fred, 233, 234
Weisstub, David, 283*n*46
well-being, 72
Western culture and thought: common law, 256, 258, 281*n*21, 287; concepts of justice, 90-91; Enlightenment and science, 297; historic harm, 132, 146, 158*n*91; 233; humanism, 290, 311*n*33, 311*n*38, 312*n*69; individual rationality, 93-94; liberal justice, 92, 95-98; memory, 134, 138, 139; sexual identity, 192-94
Wheeler, Winona, 150
whistleblowers, 180*n*43
White, Kimberly, 285*n*75
white shame, 137-38
Wildeman, Sheila, 83, 160*n*122, 255-86
Wilson, E.F., 158*n*76
Withler v. Canada (Attorney General), 200
Wolfe, Cary, 290, 292, 298
women: as embodied selves, 112; globalization, 65; health care and oppression, 268; infertility treatments, 207*nn*81-82; oppression, 197, 268; political participation, 68; proper role, 45; societal values, 18, 197, 207*n*82; state intervention in pregnancy, 209-10, 225-26; Third World countries, 68; women's rights and bioethics, 15. *See also* reproductive technology policy
Women's Court of Canada, 49
Women's Legal Education and Action Fund/DisAbled Women's Network (LEAF/DAWN), 202, 203
World Bank, 63, 81, 83-85
World Health Organization (WHO), 235-38, 240
Wounded Knee hearings, 150-51
wrongdoing, 89, 91, 95-98, 107*n*27, 146, 296

Young, Iris Marion, 29-31, 33*n*16, 76, 134, 139-40, 151-54, 157*n*53

Zehr, Howard, 89, 100-101

Andrew S. Thompson
In Defence of Principles: NGOs and Human Rights in Canada (2010)

Aaron Doyle and Dawn Moore (eds.)
Critical Criminology in Canada: New Voices, New Directions (2010)

Joanna R. Quinn
The Politics of Acknowledgement: Truth Commissions in Uganda and Haiti (2010)

Patrick James
Constitutional Politics in Canada after the Charter: Liberalism, Communitarianism, and Systemism (2010)

Louis A. Knafla and Haijo Westra (eds.)
Aboriginal Title and Indigenous Peoples: Canada, Australia, and New Zealand (2010)

Janet Mosher and Joan Brockman (eds.)
Constructing Crime: Contemporary Processes of Criminalization (2010)

Stephen Clarkson and Stepan Wood
A Perilous Imbalance: The Globalization of Canadian Law and Governance (2009)

Amanda Glasbeek
Feminized Justice: The Toronto Women's Court, 1913-34 (2009)

Kimberley Brooks (ed.)
Justice Bertha Wilson: One Woman's Difference (2009)

Wayne V. McIntosh and Cynthia L. Cates
Multi-Party Litigation: The Strategic Context (2009)

Renisa Mawani
Colonial Proximities: Crossracial Encounters and Juridical Truths in British Columbia, 1871-1921 (2009)

James B. Kelly and Christopher P. Manfredi (eds.)
Contested Constitutionalism: Reflections on the Canadian Charter of Rights and Freedoms (2009)

Catherine E. Bell and Robert K. Paterson (eds.)
Protection of First Nations Cultural Heritage: Laws, Policy, and Reform (2008)

Hamar Foster, Benjamin L. Berger, and A.R. Buck (eds.)
The Grand Experiment: Law and Legal Culture in British Settler Societies (2008)

Richard J. Moon (ed.)
Law and Religious Pluralism in Canada (2008)

Catherine E. Bell and Val Napoleon (eds.)
First Nations Cultural Heritage and Law: Case Studies, Voices, and Perspectives (2008)

Douglas C. Harris
Landing Native Fisheries: Indian Reserves and Fishing Rights in British Columbia, 1849-1925 (2008)

Peggy J. Blair
Lament for a First Nation: The Williams Treaties in Southern Ontario (2008)

Lori G. Beaman
Defining Harm: Religious Freedom and the Limits of the Law (2007)

Stephen Tierney (ed.)
Multiculturalism and the Canadian Constitution (2007)

Julie Macfarlane
The New Lawyer: How Settlement Is Transforming the Practice of Law (2007)

Kimberley White
Negotiating Responsibility: Law, Murder, and States of Mind (2007)

Dawn Moore
Criminal Artefacts: Governing Drugs and Users (2007)

Hamar Foster, Heather Raven, and Jeremy Webber (eds.)
Let Right Be Done: Aboriginal Title, the Calder *Case, and the Future of Indigenous Rights* (2007)

Dorothy E. Chunn, Susan B. Boyd, and Hester Lessard (eds.)
Reaction and Resistance: Feminism, Law, and Social Change (2007)

Margot Young, Susan B. Boyd, Gwen Brodsky, and Shelagh Day (eds.)
Poverty: Rights, Social Citizenship, and Legal Activism (2007)

Rosanna L. Langer
Defining Rights and Wrongs: Bureaucracy, Human Rights, and Public Accountability (2007)

C.L. Ostberg and Matthew E. Wetstein
Attitudinal Decision Making in the Supreme Court of Canada (2007)

Chris Clarkson
Domestic Reforms: Political Visions and Family Regulation in British Columbia, 1862-1940 (2007)

Jean McKenzie Leiper
Bar Codes: Women in the Legal Profession (2006)

Gerald Baier
Courts and Federalism: Judicial Doctrine in the United States, Australia, and Canada (2006)

Avigail Eisenberg (ed.)
Diversity and Equality: The Changing Framework of Freedom in Canada (2006)

Randy K. Lippert
Sanctuary, Sovereignty, Sacrifice: Canadian Sanctuary Incidents, Power, and Law (2005)

James B. Kelly
Governing with the Charter: Legislative and Judicial Activism and Framers' Intent (2005)

Dianne Pothier and Richard Devlin (eds.)
Critical Disability Theory: Essays in Philosophy, Politics, Policy, and Law (2005)

Susan G. Drummond
Mapping Marriage Law in Spanish Gitano Communities (2005)

Louis A. Knafla and Jonathan Swainger (eds.)
Laws and Societies in the Canadian Prairie West, 1670-1940 (2005)

Ikechi Mgbeoji
Global Biopiracy: Patents, Plants, and Indigenous Knowledge (2005)

Florian Sauvageau, David Schneiderman, and David Taras,
with Ruth Klinkhammer and Pierre Trudel
The Last Word: Media Coverage of the Supreme Court of Canada (2005)

Gerald Kernerman
Multicultural Nationalism: Civilizing Difference, Constituting Community (2005)

Pamela A. Jordan
Defending Rights in Russia: Lawyers, the State, and Legal Reform in the Post-Soviet Era (2005)

Anna Pratt
Securing Borders: Detention and Deportation in Canada (2005)

Kirsten Johnson Kramar
Unwilling Mothers, Unwanted Babies: Infanticide in Canada (2005)

W.A. Bogart
Good Government? Good Citizens? Courts, Politics, and Markets in a Changing Canada (2005)

Catherine Dauvergne
Humanitarianism, Identity, and Nation: Migration Laws in Canada and Australia (2005)

Michael Lee Ross
First Nations Sacred Sites in Canada's Courts (2005)

Andrew Woolford
Between Justice and Certainty: Treaty Making in British Columbia (2005)

John McLaren, Andrew Buck, and Nancy Wright (eds.)
Despotic Dominion: Property Rights in British Settler Societies (2004)

Georges Campeau
From UI to EI: Waging War on the Welfare State (2004)

Alvin J. Esau
The Courts and the Colonies: The Litigation of Hutterite Church Disputes (2004)

Christopher N. Kendall
Gay Male Pornography: An Issue of Sex Discrimination (2004)

Roy B. Flemming
Tournament of Appeals: Granting Judicial Review in Canada (2004)

Constance Backhouse and Nancy L. Backhouse
The Heiress vs the Establishment: Mrs. Campbell's Campaign for Legal Justice (2004)

Christopher P. Manfredi
Feminist Activism in the Supreme Court: Legal Mobilization and the Women's Legal Education and Action Fund (2004)

Annalise Acorn
Compulsory Compassion: A Critique of Restorative Justice (2004)

Jonathan Swainger and Constance Backhouse (eds.)
People and Place: Historical Influences on Legal Culture (2003)

Jim Phillips and Rosemary Gartner
Murdering Holiness: The Trials of Franz Creffield and George Mitchell (2003)

David R. Boyd
Unnatural Law: Rethinking Canadian Environmental Law and Policy (2003)

Ikechi Mgbeoji
Collective Insecurity: The Liberian Crisis, Unilateralism, and Global Order (2003)

Rebecca Johnson
Taxing Choices: The Intersection of Class, Gender, Parenthood, and the Law (2002)

John McLaren, Robert Menzies, and Dorothy E. Chunn (eds.)
Regulating Lives: Historical Essays on the State, Society, the Individual, and the Law (2002)

Joan Brockman
Gender in the Legal Profession: Fitting or Breaking the Mould (2001)

Printed and bound in Canada by Friesens

Set in Stone by Artegraphica Design Co. Ltd.

Copy Editor: Stacy Belden

Proofreader: Theresa Best

Indexer: Lillian Ashworth

ENVIRONMENTAL BENEFITS STATEMENT

UBC Press saved the following resources by printing the pages of this book on chlorine free paper made with 100% post-consumer waste.

TREES	WATER	ENERGY	SOLID WASTE	GREENHOUSE GASES
7	3,151	3	200	699
FULLY GROWN	GALLONS	MILLION BTUs	POUNDS	POUNDS

Environmental impact estimates were made using the Environmental Paper Network Paper Calculator. For more information visit www.papercalculator.org.